JavaScript Cookbook

JavaScript Cookbook

Shelley Powers

O'REILLY®

Beijing · Cambridge · Farnham · Köln · Sebastopol · Taipei · Tokyo

JavaScript Cookbook
by Shelley Powers

Copyright © 2010 Shelley Powers. All rights reserved.
Printed in the United States of America.

Published by O'Reilly Media, Inc., 1005 Gravenstein Highway North, Sebastopol, CA 95472.

O'Reilly books may be purchased for educational, business, or sales promotional use. Online editions are also available for most titles (*http://my.safaribooksonline.com*). For more information, contact our corporate/institutional sales department: 800-998-9938 or *corporate@oreilly.com*.

Editor: Simon St.Laurent	**Indexer:** Potomac Indexing, LLC
Production Editor: Adam Zaremba	**Cover Designer:** Karen Montgomery
Copyeditor: Colleen Toporek	**Interior Designer:** David Futato
Proofreader: Kiel Van Horn	**Illustrator:** Robert Romano

Printing History:

July 2010:   First Edition.

ISBN: 978-0-596-80613-2

[SB]

1278085236

Table of Contents

Preface

I wrote my first book on JavaScript 15 years ago, and had to scramble just to find enough material to fill a book. With the *JavaScript Cookbook*, I had to choose among hundreds of uses to determine what to include. After all these years of watching JavaScript grow, I am still surprised at how far-reaching the use of JavaScript has become. In my opinion, there is no more useful programming language or development tool. About the only technology with wider use is HTML.

This book is for those who have dabbled with JavaScript and wish to try out new techniques, or increase their grasp of both fundamentals and advanced features of JavaScript. Along the way, I'll demonstrate how to:

- Work with the JavaScript objects, such as `String`, `Array`, `Number`, and `Math`
- Create reusable objects
- Query and create new elements in the Document Object Model (DOM)
- Use the new Selectors API for efficient and targeted querying
- Use JavaScript with new HTML5 technologies, such as the new media elements, video and audio
- Create interactive applications
- Manage your web page space
- Store data in various ways, from the simple to the complex
- Use JavaScript with Scalable Vector Graphics (SVG) and the canvas element
- Work with some of the interesting data structures, like Microformats and RDFa
- Package your library for others to use, as well as use other libraries in your applications
- Ensure your JavaScript applications are accessible through the use of Accessible Rich Internet Applications (ARIA)
- Work in environments other than the typical desktop browser, such as creating mobile phone web applications, or extending Photoshop with new behaviors
- Use and create jQuery plug-ins
- Develop Ajax applications

- Debug your applications using your browser's debugger
- Work with the new HTML5 drag-and-drop
- Communicate using the new HTML5 cross-documentation techniques
- Implement concurrent programming with Web Workers
- Use the File API to access a desktop file directly in client-side JavaScript

It's not a complete encyclopedia of JavaScript use today—no one book can cover all there is to cover. But hopefully, you'll come away with an appreciation of all you can do with JavaScript.

Bon appetit!

Audience, Assumptions, and Approach

Readers of this book should have some exposure to web development, and the use of JavaScript. In addition, the recipe format means I'll be focusing on specific tasks, rather than providing an overall general introduction. I won't cover every last aspect of a JavaScript topic, such as Strings. Instead, I'll focus on the more common tasks, or challenges, associated with the topic.

There will be lots of code, some of it in code snippets, some in full-page applications. The recipes are also cross-referenced, so if I mention a specific topic in one recipe that was covered in another, I'll include this information in the "See Also" section for the recipe. To assist you, I've also created example code for all of the recipes that you can download and work with immediately.

Target Browsers

Throughout the book, I'll mention the target browsers. The majority of example code in this book has been designed for, and tested to work with, the latest releases of the most commonly used browsers:

- Firefox 3.6x on Mac and Windows
- Safari 4.0x on Mac and Windows
- Opera 10.x on Mac and Windows
- Chrome 5.x on Windows
- Internet Explorer 8 on Windows

I didn't have a Linux machine to test for that environment, but, knock on wood, most of the recipes should work in a Linux environment with Firefox. I also didn't have a System 7 for testing the IE9 preview, but most of the applications should work, including those using SVG (a new addition for IE9).

Some of the recipes required a specialized environment, such as a mobile device or emulator, or beta (or alpha) release of the browser. I made a note where an example would not work with the target browsers, or required a specialized environment or browser. In addition, I'm introducing several new technologies and APIs that are only implemented in alpha/beta releases of certain of the browsers. Again, I included a note about browser support.

Many of the examples won't work with IE6. Before I even began the book I decided not to provide support for IE6—including any workaround code. Many major sites no longer support this far too old and too insecure browser, including Amazon, Google, YouTube, and Facebook. In addition, the workarounds necessary for IE6 are so well-known and so well-documented online, that I felt it wasn't necessary to also include coverage in this book.

Most of the examples that work with IE8 will work with IE7, with some exceptions. IE7 doesn't support `getAttribute`/`setAttribute` on the common attributes, such as `style`, `id`, and `class`, and doesn't support `hasAttribute` at all. In addition, IE7 doesn't support either the CSS selectors, or the Selectors API methods, such as `docu ment.querySelectorAll` (covered in Chapter 11).

Where IE7 doesn't work, either I provide IE7-specific workarounds in comments in the example code you can download, or I make a note about nonsupport in the recipe— or both.

Sample Code Conventions

There are many code snippets and full-page examples all throughout the book. Most are based in HTML, but there are some that are based in XHTML, the XML serialization of HTML. In addition, most of the examples are based in HTML5, though I've also used a couple of other HTML versions, especially with the SVG examples:

HTML5

```
<!DOCTYPE html>
```

XHTML5

```
<!DOCTYPE html>
<html xmlns="http://www.w3.org/1999/xhtml">
```

XHTML+SVG

```
<!DOCTYPE html PUBLIC
    "-//W3C//DTD XHTML 1.1 plus MathML 2.0 plus SVG 1.1//EN"
    "http://www.w3.org/2002/04/xhtml-math-svg/xhtml-math-svg.dtd">
```

There's only a couple of differences in the samples based on the HTML version. If the example is X/HTML5, you don't need a `type` attribute for either the `style` or `script` elements. Additionally, in many of the XHTML sample pages, I surround the code with a CDATA section, like the following:

```
<script>
//<![CDATA[
```

```
...

//--><![]]>
</script>
```

The reason for using a CDATA section for the script block in XHTML is that characters such as the angle bracket (< >) and ampersand (&) are meaningful in JavaScript, but they're also meaningful as markup. When an XML parser sees the characters, it wants to interpret them as markup. To prevent this, the CDATA section tells the parser to ignore the section.

I tried to keep all of the style settings and script in the same page to simplify the examples. However, in the real world, you'll want to separate your stylesheet and script into separate files, as much as possible. Doing so keeps your HTML files clean, and makes it easy to change both style and script.

Approach

In the book, I cover basic JavaScript functionality that's been around since the dawn of time, and is still essential for application development. I also include recipes covering some of the newer functionality, including working with the canvas element, trying out the new cross-domain widget communication technique (`postMessage`), working with the new File API and Web Workers, integrating your code with the popular jQuery library—even working with the new HTML video and audio elements (which was a lot of fun). I also introduce some of the newer uses of JavaScript, such as in mobile devices and offline desktop applications, as well as the different forms of data storage, and accessing metadata such as Microformats and RDFa in the web page.

Organization

The book is a relatively esoteric blend of topics, primarily covering those areas where I've seen both interest and growth in the last few years. I also include an introduction to the new ECMAScript 5 and HTML5 innovations.

However, this book does consist of two rather general sections: the first focuses on existing JavaScript functionality and objects; the second focuses more on JavaScript used within environments, such as a browser. If you're relatively new to JavaScript, I recommend working through all of the recipes in the first 10 chapters before tackling the recipes later in the book.

Following is a chapter breakdown of the book:

Chapter 1, *Working with JavaScript Strings*
> Covers some of the more commonly occurring String tasks, such as concatenating strings, trimming white space, breaking strings into tokens, as well as finding substrings within strings.

Chapter 2, *Using Regular Expressions*

Demonstrates the use of regular expressions, as well as working with the JavaScript RegExp object. Recipes include basic how-tos such as swapping words, replacing HTML tags with named entities, validating a Social Security number (and other patterned objects), and globally replacing values.

Chapter 3, *Dates, Time, and Timers*

Describes how to access dates and times, as well as how to format date strings, track elapsed time, find a future date, and using both the new and old ISO 8601 JavaScript functionality. The chapter also introduces JavaScript timers and working with timers and function closures.

Chapter 4, *Working with Numbers and Math*

Includes basic number functionality, such as keeping an incremental counter and including conversions between hexadecimals and decimals, generating random colors, converting strings in tables to numbers, as well as converting between radian and degrees (important when working with canvas or SVG).

Chapter 5, *Working with Arrays and Loops*

Arrays are the thing in this chapter, which provides a look at how to use arrays to create FIFO queues and LIFO stacks, as well as how to sort an array, work with multidimensional arrays, traverse arrays, use the new ECMAScript 5 array functionality to create filtered arrays, and validate array contents. The chapter also covers associative arrays, as well as various ways to traverse arrays.

Chapter 6, *Building Reusability with JavaScript Functions*

The JavaScript Function is the heart and soul of this language, and this chapter focuses on how to create functions, pass values to and from the function, create a recursive function, as well as build a dynamic function. The chapter also includes how to use Memoization and Currying, to enhance application efficiency and performance, as well as how to use an anonymous function in order to wrap global variables.

Chapter 7, *Handling Events*

Covers basic event handling tasks, including capturing events, canceling events, accessing the Event object, as well as working with both mouse and keyboard events. The chapter also covers the new HTML5 drag-and-drop functionality, as well as working with Safari's Orientation Events (for mobile development).

Chapter 8, *Browser Pieces*

This chapter gets into the basic working components all browsers, and many other user agents, share. This includes creating new windows, changing a stylesheet, modifying an image, adding a bread crumb to a web page, bookmarking a dynamic page, as well as preserving the back button in Ajax applications. The chapter also introduces the new HTML5 History functionality for preserving dynamic state.

Chapter 9, *Form Elements and Validation*

This chapter continues the introduction of regular expressions from Chapter 2, but focuses on form elements and validation. The chapter also covers how to enable and disable form elements and hide or display elements, and includes how to modify a selection list, and canceling a form submission.

Chapter 10, *Debugging and Error Handling*

None of us like it, all of us need it: this chapter focuses on error handling in applications, as well as how to use the different debugging tools in the book's target browsers.

Chapter 11, *Accessing Page Elements*

This chapter covers the various ways you can access one or more document elements. Included are discussions on accessing all elements of a certain type, a specific element, or using the newer Selectors API to use CSS-like syntax to find elements. Also included is a discussion of namespace specifics, where appropriate.

Chapter 12, *Creating and Removing Elements and Attributes*

The chapter includes ways to create and add elements to a web document, including adding text, paragraphs, working with table elements, and moving and removing document elements. The chapter also covers how to add and access element attributes, and includes coverage of namespace specifics, where appropriate.

Chapter 13, *Working with Web Page Spaces*

The web page is a canvas on which we create, and this chapter covers how to determine the area of the web page, the size of page elements, their location, as well as how to hide and show page sections. Popular behaviors such as expandos/accordions and page overlays, as well as tabbed pages are included, as is how to create a collapsible sidebar and a hover-based pop-up message.

Chapter 14, *Creating Interactive and Accessible Effects with JavaScript, CSS, and ARIA*

For the longest time, our dynamic web page effects were literally silent to a significant web community—those using screen readers. This chapter introduces the new Web Accessibility Initiative–Accessible Rich Internet Applications (WAI-ARIA) attributes and roles and demonstrates how they can make a web page come alive for all readers, not just those who are sighted. The chapter also covers other very common interactive effects, including providing a flash of color to signal an event, working with pop-up messages, creating Live Regions, and providing accessible effects when validating forms.

Chapter 15, *Creating Media Rich and Interactive Applications*

I am not the most artistic of souls, but I do know how to make JavaScript work with the canvas element and SVG. In this chapter, I provide the basic steps needed in order to work with both of these media, as well as the newer WebGL 3D environment, and the new HTML5 video and audio elements.

Chapter 16, *JavaScript Objects*

Probably one of the most important chapters in the book, this chapter covers the basics of creating JavaScript objects, including how to keep data members private, adding Getters/Setters, using the new ECMAScript 5 object protection functionality, chaining object methods, and using the new `Prototype.bind`.

Chapter 17, *JavaScript Libraries*

All of the book focuses on creating your own JavaScript objects and applications. This chapter introduces us to jQuery, one of the more popular JavaScript framework libraries. It covers common library tasks such as how to package your code into libraries, how to test the libraries, and how to build a jQuery plug-in, as well as how to use your library with other libraries, such as jQuery.

Chapter 18, *Communication*

Most of the chapter is focused on Ajax tasks, including preparing the data for sending, creating an `XMLHttpRequest` object, checking for errors, and processing the results. Also included are how to use a timer for a continuously updated query, how to create a dynamic image pop-up, and how to use JSON-P for cross-domain requests. The chapter introduces the `postMessage` functionality, for communicating between a remotely hosted widget and your own application.

Chapter 19, *Working with Structured Data*

Tasks covered include how to process an XML document returned from an Ajax call, using the new JSON object to parse JSON or *stringify* a JavaScript object. The chapter also includes how to work with Microformats or RDFa in the page.

Chapter 20, *Persistence*

This chapter covers how to create and use an HTTP cookie, of course, and how to store data using the page URL, but also provides recipes for working with the new `sessionStorage` and `localStorage` persistence techniques introduced with HTML5, and an introduction to client-side SQL databases.

Chapter 21, *JavaScript Outside the Box*

This chapter briefly gets into all the various ways that JavaScript can be used now, none of which have anything to do with traditional web page development. Included are discussions on creating mobile and desktop widgets, mobile device application development, creating add-ons and extensions for browsers, as well as how JavaScript can be used with so many of our applications, such as OpenOffice (which I used to write this book) and Photoshop. I also include a discussion of desktop application development, including support for offline applications, and featuring examples of both the Web Workers API, and the File API.

Conventions Used in This Book

The following typographical conventions are used in this book:

Italic

Indicates new terms, URLs, email addresses, filenames, and file extensions.

`Constant width`

Indicates computer code in a broad sense, including commands, arrays, elements, statements, options, switches, variables, attributes, keys, functions, types, classes, namespaces, methods, modules, properties, parameters, values, objects, events, event handlers, XML tags, HTML tags, macros, the contents of files, and the output from commands.

`Constant width bold`

Shows commands or other text that should be typed literally by the user.

`Constant width italic`

Shows text that should be replaced with user-supplied values or by values determined by context.

 This icon signifies a tip, suggestion, or general note.

 This icon indicates a warning or caution.

Websites and pages are mentioned in this book to help you locate online information that might be useful. Normally both the address (URL) and the name (title, heading) of a page are mentioned. Some addresses are relatively complicated, but you can probably locate the pages easier using your favorite search engine to find a page by its name, typically by writing it inside quotation marks. This may also help if the page cannot be found by its address; it may have moved elsewhere, but the name may still work.

Using Code Examples

This book is here to help you get your job done. In general, you may use the code in this book in your programs and documentation. You do not need to contact us for permission unless you're reproducing a significant portion of the code. For example, writing a program that uses several chunks of code from this book does not require permission. Selling or distributing a CD-ROM of examples from O'Reilly books does require permission. Answering a question by citing this book and quoting example code does not require permission. Incorporating a significant amount of example code from this book into your product's documentation does require permission.

We appreciate, but do not require, attribution. An attribution usually includes the title, author, publisher, and ISBN. For example: "*JavaScript Cookbook*, by Shelley Powers. Copyright 2010 Shelley Powers, 9780596806132."

If you feel your use of code examples falls outside fair use or the permission given here, feel free to contact us at *permissions@oreilly.com*.

How to Contact Us

Please address comments and questions concerning this book to the publisher:

O'Reilly Media, Inc.
1005 Gravenstein Highway North
Sebastopol, CA 95472
800-998-9938 (in the United States or Canada)
707-829-0515 (international or local)
707-829-0104 (fax)

We have a web page for this book, where we list errata, examples, and any additional information. You can access this page at:

http://oreilly.com/catalog/9780596806132

To comment or ask technical questions about this book, send email to:

bookquestions@oreilly.com

For more information about our books, conferences, Resource Centers, and the O'Reilly Network, see our website at:

http://oreilly.com

Safari® Books Online

Safari Safari Books Online is an on-demand digital library that lets you easily search over 7,500 technology and creative reference books and videos to find the answers you need quickly.

With a subscription, you can read any page and watch any video from our library online. Read books on your cell phone and mobile devices. Access new titles before they are available for print, and get exclusive access to manuscripts in development and post feedback for the authors. Copy and paste code samples, organize your favorites, download chapters, bookmark key sections, create notes, print out pages, and benefit from tons of other time-saving features.

O'Reilly Media has uploaded this book to the Safari Books Online service. To have full digital access to this book and others on similar topics from O'Reilly and other publishers, sign up for free at *http://my.safaribooksonline.com*.

Acknowledgments

I want to thank Simon St.Laurent, who has been a long-time editor and friend, for all the help and encouragement he's provided, in this book and in my previous books.

I also want to thank those who contributed time and expertise to review the book, and helped me do a better job: Elaine Nelson, Zachary Kessin, Chris Wells, and Sergey Ilinsky. My thanks also to Gez Lemon, who provided thoughtful commentary and help with my ARIA chapter, and Brad Neuberg for his help with SVGWeb in Chapter 15.

I also want to thank my copyeditors, and others in the production staff: Colleen Toporek, Adam Zaremba, Rob Romano, Kiel Van Horn, and Seth Maislin.

My gratitude, also, to those who helped create the specifications, such as HTML5 and ECMAScript 5, the tools, the APIs, the libraries, the browsers, and all the other fun stuff that helps make JavaScript development as exciting today as it was 15 years ago.

CHAPTER 1

Working with JavaScript Strings

1.0 Introduction

JavaScript strings are the most important component of JavaScript, probably used more than any other data type. Though you may get numeric values from web page forms, the values are retrieved as strings, which you then have to convert into numeric values.

Strings are also used as parameters when invoking server-side application calls through Ajax, as well as forming the basic serialization format of every JavaScript object. One of the methods that all JavaScript objects share is `toString`, which returns a string containing the serialized format of the object.

A String Primitive

A JavaScript string can be both a *primitive* data type or an object. As a primitive type, it joins with four other JavaScript primitive types: number, Boolean (true or false), `null` (no value), and `undefined` (unknown). In addition, as a primitive data type, strings are also JavaScript *literals*: a collection that includes numbers (as either floating point or integer), the literal format for arrays, objects, and regular expressions, as well as numbers and Booleans.

 We'll see more about the literal formats for the various JavaScript objects throughout the book.

A string is zero or more characters delimited by quotes, either single quotes:

```
'This is a string'
```

Or double quotes:

```
"This is a string"
```

There is no rule for which type of quote to use. If you're including single quotes within the text, you'll most likely want to use double quotes:

```
"This isn't a number."
```

If you mix up the quote types—begin a string with a single quote and end with a double—you'll receive an application error:

```
var badString = 'This is a bad string"; // oops, error
```

Both quote types are used interchangeably in the book.

A String Object

A string object is called String, appropriately enough, and like all other JavaScript objects has a set of properties that come prebuilt into the object type.

A String object can be instantiated using the JavaScript new operator, to create a new object instance:

```
var city = new String("St. Louis");
```

Once instantiated, any one of the available string properties can be accessed on it, such as in the following code, where the string is lowercased using the String object method toLowerCase:

```
var lcCity = city.toLowerCase(); //  new string is now st. louis
```

If you access the String constructor without using new, you'll create a string literal rather than a String object:

```
var city = String("St. Louis");
```

If you do need to access a String object method on a string literal, you can. What happens is the JavaScript engine creates a String object, wraps it around the string literal, performs the method call, and then discards the String object.

When to use String, as compared to using a string literal, depends on the circumstances. Unless you plan on using the String object properties, you'll want to use string literals wherever possible. However, if you'll be using String methods, then create the string as an object.

See Also

Mozilla has a terrific page that discusses the concept of JavaScript literals and the different types. You can access the page at *https://developer.mozilla.org/en/Core_Java Script_1.5_Guide/Literals*.

1.1 Concatenating Two or More Strings

Problem

You want to merge two or more strings into one.

Solution

Concatenate the strings using the addition (+) operator:

```
var string1 = "This is a ";
var string2 = "test";

var string3 = string1 + string2; // creates a new string with "This is a test"
```

Discussion

The addition operator (+) is typically used to add numbers together:

```
var newValue = 1 + 3; // result is 4
```

In JavaScript, though, the addition operator is *overloaded*, which means it can be used for multiple data types, including strings. When used with strings, the results are *concatenated*, with the strings later in the equation appended to the end of the string result.

You can add two strings:

```
var string3 = string1 + string2;
```

or you can add multiple strings:

```
var string1 = "This";
var string2 = "is";
var string3 = "a";
var string4 = "test";
var stringResult = string1 + " " + string2 + " " +
                   string3 + " " + string4; // result is "This is a test"
```

There is a shortcut to concatenating strings, and that's the JavaScript *shorthand assignment operator* (+=). The following code snippet, which uses this operator:

```
var oldValue = "apples";
oldValue += " and oranges"; // string now has "apples and oranges"
```

is equivalent to:

```
var oldValue = "apples";
oldValue = oldValue + " and oranges";
```

The shorthand assignment operator works with strings by concatenating the string on the right side of the operator to the end of the string on the left.

There is a built-in `String` method that can concatenate multiple strings: `concat`. It takes one or more string parameters, each of which are appended to the end of the string object:

```
var nwStrng = "".concat("This ","is ","a ","string"); // returns "This is a string"
```

The `concat` method can be a simpler way to generate a string from multiple values, such as generating a string from several form fields. However, the use of the addition operator is the more commonly used approach.

1.2 Concatenating a String and Another Data Type

Problem

You want to concatenate a string with another data type, such as a number.

Solution

Use the exact same operators, such as addition (+) and shorthand assignment (+=), you use when concatenating strings:

```
var numValue = 23.45;
var total = "And the total is " + numValue; // string has "And the total is 23.45"
```

Discussion

A different process occurs when adding a string and another data type. In the case of another data type, such as a Boolean or number, the JavaScript engine first converts the other data type's value into a string, and then performs concatenation:

```
// add a boolean to a string
var boolValue = true;
var strngValue = "The value is " + boolValue; // results in "The value is true"

// add a number to a string
var numValue = 3.0;
strngValue = "The value is " + numValue; // results in "The value is 3"
```

The automatic data conversion also applies if you're concatenating a `String` object with a string literal, which is a necessary capability if you're not sure whether the strings you're working with are objects or literals but you still want to create a concatenated string:

```
var strObject = new String("The value is ");
var strngLiteral = "a string";
var strngValue = strObject + strngLiteral; // results in "The value is a string"
```

The resulting string is a string literal, not a `String` object.

1.3 Conditionally Comparing Strings

Problem

You want to compare two strings to see if they're the same.

Solution

Use the *equality* operator (==) within a conditional test:

```
var strName = prompt("What's your name?", "");

if (strName == "Shelley") {
   alert("Your name is Shelley! Good for you!");
} else {
   alert("Your name isn't Shelley. Bummer.");
}
```

Discussion

Two strings can be compared using the equality operator (==). When used within a conditional statement, a block of code is run if the test evaluates to true (the strings are equal):

```
if (strName == "Shelley") {
   alert("Your name is Shelley! Good for you!");
}
```

If the strings are not equal, the first statement following the conditional statement block is processed. If an *if...else* conditional statement is used, the block of code following the else keyword is the one that's processed:

```
if (strName == "Shelley") {
   alert("Your name is Shelley! Good for you!");
} else {
   alert("Your name isn't Shelley. Bummer.");
}
```

There are factors that can influence the success of the string comparison. For instance, strings have *case*, and can consist of uppercase characters, lowercase characters, or a combination of both. Unless case is an issue, you'll most likely want to convert the string to all lowercase or uppercase, using the built-in String methods toLowerCase and toUpperCase, before making the comparison, as shown in the following code:

```
var strName = prompt("What's your name?", "");

if (strName.toUpperCase () == "SHELLEY") {
   alert("Your name is Shelley! Good for you!");
} else {
   alert("Your name isn't Shelley. Bummer.");
}
```

Note that the toUpperCase method (and toLowerCase) do not take any parameters.

In Recipe 1.2, I discussed that data type conversion occurs automatically when concatenating a numeric or Boolean value, or a `String` object to a string. This same type of data type conversion also occurs with the equality operator if one value is a string. In the following, the number 10.00 is converted into the string "10", and then used in the comparison:

```
var numVal = 10.00;
if (numVal == "10") alert ("The value is ten"); succeeds
```

There may be times, though, when you don't want automatic data conversion to occur—when you want the comparison to fail if the values are of different data types. For instance, if one value is a string literal and the other is a `String` object, you might want the comparison to fail because the two variables are of different data types, regardless of their perspective values. In this case, you'll want to use a different equality operator, the *strict equality* operator (===):

```
var  strObject = new  String("Shelley");

var  strLiteral  =  "Shelley";

if (strObject  ==  strLiteral) // this comparison succeeds

...

if (strObject === strLiteral) // fails because of different data types
```

The comparison fails if the two variables being compared are different data types, even though their primitive string values are the same.

Sometimes, you might want to specifically test that two strings are *not* alike, rather than whether they are alike. The operators to use then are the *inequality* operator (!=) and *strict inequality* operator (!==). They work in the same manner as the previous two operators just discussed, but return true when the strings are not alike:

```
var strnOne  =  "one";
var strnTwo  =  "two";
if (strnOne != strnTwo) // true, as they are not the same string value
```

The strict inequality operator returns true if the strings are not the same value or the data type of the two *operands* (values on either side of the operator) is different:

```
var strObject = new String("Shelley");
var strLiteral = "Shelley";
if (strObject !== strLiteral) // succeeds, because data type of operands differs
```

If you're more interested in discovering how two strings may differ, you can use other *comparison operators*, as shown in Table 1-1.

Table 1-1. Comparison operators

Operator	Description	Example
Equality ==	True if operands are the same; otherwise false	`var sVal = "this";` `if (sVal == "this") // true`

Strict equality ===	True if operands are the same, and the same data type; otherwise false	`var sVal = "this";`
		`var sVal2 = new String("this");`
		
		`if (sVal === sVal2) // not true`

Inequality !=	True if operands are not the same; otherwise false	`var sVal = "this";` `if (sVal == "that") // true`

Strict inequality !==	True if operands are not the same, or are not the same data type; otherwise false	`var sVal = "this";`
		`var sVal2 = new String("this");`
		
		`if (sVal !== sVal2) // true`

Greater than >	True if first operand is greater in value than second operand	`var sOne = "cat";`
		`var sTwo = "dog";`
		
		`if (sOne > sTwo) // false`

Greater than or equal >=	True if first operand is greater than or equal to second operand	`var sOne = "Cat";`
		`var sTwo = "cat";`
		
		`if (sOne >= sTwo) // true`

Less than <	True if second operand is greater than first operand	`var sOne = "cat";`
		`var sTwo = "Cat";`
		
		`if (sOne < sTwo) // true`

Less than or equal <=	True if second operand is greater than or equal to first operand	`var sOne = new String("cat");`
		`var sTwo = "cat";`
		
		`if (sOne <= sTwo) // equal, true`

Comparison operators work numerically with numbers, but lexically with strings. For instance, the value "dog" would be lexically greater than "cat", because the letter "d" in "dog" occurs later in the alphabet than the letter "c" in "cat":

```
var sOne = "cat";
var sTwo = "dog"
if (sOne > sTwo // false, because "cat" is lexically less than "dog"
```

If two string literals only vary based on case, the uppercase characters are lexically greater than the lowercase letter:

```
var sOne  = "Cat";
var sTwo  = "cat";
if (sOne >=  sTwo) // true, because 'C' is lexically greater than 'c'
```

There is no *strict greater than* or *strict less than* operators, so it makes no difference if the data type of the operands differs:

```
var sOne = new String("cat");
var sTwo = "cat";
if (sOne <= sTwo) // both equal, so true, as data type doesn't matter
```

Before leaving this recipe, there is another approach you can use to compare strings, but this one has a little kick to it. It's based on the String method, `localeCompare`.

The `localeCompare` method takes one parameter, a string, which is compared against the string value to which it is attached. The method returns a numeric value equal to 0 if the two strings are the same; −1 if the string parameter is lexically greater than the original string; 1 otherwise:

```
var fruit1 = "apple";
var fruit2 = "grape";
var i = fruit1.localeCompare(fruit2); // returns -1
```

For the most part, you'll probably use the comparison operators rather than the `localeCompare` method, but it's always interesting to see more than one approach.

See Also

For more on string-to-number conversion, see Recipe 4.5.

1.4 Finding a Substring in a String

Problem

You want to find out if a substring, a particular series of characters, exists in a string.

Solution

Use the `String` object's built-in `indexOf` method to find the position of the substring, if it exists:

```
var testValue = "This is the Cookbook's test string";
var subsValue = "Cookbook";

var iValue = testValue.indexOf(subsValue); // returns value of 12, index of substring

if (iValue != -1) // succeeds, because substring exists
```

Discussion

The `String indexOf` method returns a number representing the *index*, or position of the first character of the substring, with 0 being the index position of the first character in the string.

To test if the substring doesn't exist, you can compare the returned value to −1, which is the value returned if the substring isn't found:

```
if (iValue != -1) // true if substring found
```

The `indexOf` method takes two parameters: the substring, and an optional second parameter, an index value of where to begin a search:

```
var tstString = "This apple is my apple";
var iValue = tstString.indexOf("apple", 10); // returns 17, index of second substring
```

The `indexOf` method works from left to right, but sometimes you might want to find the index of a substring by searching within the string from right to left. There's another `String` method, `lastIndexOf`, which returns the index position of the last occurrence of a substring within a string:

```
var txtString = "This apple is my apple";
var iValue = tstString.lastIndexOf("apple"); // returns 17,
                                    // index of last occurrence of substring
```

Like `indexOf`, `lastIndexOf` also takes an optional second parameter, which is an index value of where to start the search, counted from the right:

```
"This apple is my apple".lastIndexOf("apple"); // returns value of 17
"This apple is my apple".lastIndexOf("apple",12); // returns value of 5
"This apple is my apple".lastIndexOf("apple", 3); // returns value of -1, not found
```

Notice that the value returned from `lastIndexOf` changes based on the starting position, as counted from the string's right.

 It's odd to see a `String` method called directly on quoted text, but in JavaScript, there's no difference in calling the method on a string literal, directly, or on a string variable.

See Also

The `String` method `search` is used with regular expressions in order to find a specific pattern within a string, and is discussed in Recipe 2.3. The `String` method `replace` can be used to replace a substring found using a regular expression, and is discussed in Recipe 2.4.

1.5 Extracting a Substring from a String

Problem

You have a string with several sentences, one of which has a list of items. The list begins with a colon (:) and ends with a period (.). You want to extract just the list.

Solution

Use the `indexOf` `String` method to locate the colon, and then use it again to find the first period following the colon. With these two locations, extract the string using the `String` substring method:

```
var sentence = "This is one sentence. This is a sentence with a list of items:
cherries, oranges, apples, bananas.";
```

```
var start = sentence.indexOf(":");
var end = sentence.indexOf(".", start+1);

var list = sentence.substring(start+1, end);
```

Discussion

The list is delimited by a beginning colon character and an ending period. The indexOf method is used without the second parameter in the first search, to find the colon. The method is used again, but the colon's position (plus 1) is used to modify the beginning location of the search for the period:

```
var end = sentence.indexOf(".",start+1);
```

If we didn't modify the search for the ending period, we would have ended up with the location of the first sentence's period, rather than the location of the second sentence's period.

Once we have the beginning and ending location for the list, we use the substring method, passing in the two index values representing the beginning and ending positions of the string:

```
var list = sentence.substring(start+1, end);
```

The resulting string in list is:

```
cherries, oranges, apples, bananas
```

We could then use a method, such as String.split to split the list into its individual values:

```
var fruits = list.split(",") ; // array of values
```

There is another string extraction method, substr, but it's based on the index position of the start of the substring, and then passing in the length of the substring as the second parameter. In a real life application, we won't know the length of the sentence.

See Also

See Recipe 1.7 for more on using the String.split method.

1.6 Checking for an Existing, Nonempty String

Problem

You want to check that a variable is defined, is a string, and is not empty.

Solution

Use a combination of the `typeof` operator, the general `valueOf` method (which all Java-Script objects share), and the `String length` property to create a conditional test that ensures a variable is set, is a string, and is not empty:

```
// true if variable exists, is a string, and has a length greater than zero
if(((typeof unknownVariable != "undefined") &&
      (typeof unknownVariable.valueOf() == "string")) &&
    (unknownVariable.length > 0)) {
   ...
}
```

Discussion

Probably the most important built-in property for `String` is `length`. You can use `length` to find out how long the string is, and to test whether the string variable is an *empty string* (zero length) or not:

```
if (strFromFormElement.length == 0) // testing for empty string
```

However, when you're working with strings and aren't sure whether they're set, you can't just check their length, as you'll get an undefined JavaScript error if the variable has never been set. You have to combine the length test with another test for existence, and this brings us to the `typeof` operator.

The JavaScript `typeof` operator returns the type of a variable. The list of possible returned values are:

- `"number"` if variable is a number
- `"string"` if variable is a string
- `"boolean"` if variable is a Boolean
- `"function"` if variable is a function
- `"object"` if variable is null, an array, or another JavaScript object
- `"undefined"` if variable is undefined

The last value is what interests us right now, because a variable that has never been defined has a data type of `undefined`.

When a data type test is combined with a test of string length via a logical AND (`&&`) operator, the only time the entire statement will succeed is if the variable has been defined, *and* it contains a string with a length longer than zero:

```
// succeeds if variable exists, and has length greater than zero
if ((typeof unknownVariable !== "undefined") && (unknownVariable.length > )) {
  ...
}
```

If the first test fails—whether the variable has been defined—the second condition isn't processed, as the entire statement fails. This prevents the error of accessing a property on an undefined variable.

The conditional statement in the last code snippet works, but what happens if the variable is defined, but is not a string? For instance, if the variable is a number? Well, in this case, the condition still fails, because the `length` property is undefined for a number. However, what if the value is a `String` object?

If you're not sure what type the variable is, you can also explicitly test for the `"string"` data type before testing the length:

```
// succeeds if string with length greater than zero
if ((typeof unknownVariable == "string") && (unknownVariable.length > 0)) {
   ...
}
```

If the test succeeds, you know exactly what you have: a string, with a length greater than zero. However, if the variable is a `String` object, not a literal, `typeof` returns a data type of `"object"` not `"string"`. That's why the solution incorporates another JavaScript object method, `valueOf`.

The `valueOf` method is available for all JavaScript objects, and returns the primitive value of whatever the object is: for `Number`, `String`, and `boolean`, their primitive values; for `Function`, the function text, and so on. So if the variable is a `String` object, `valueOf` returns a string literal. If the variable is already a string literal, applying the `valueOf` method to it temporarily wraps it in a `String` object, which means the `valueOf` method will still return a string literal.

Our conditional test then ends up incorporating a test to see if the variable has been set, and if so, whether it is a `String` object or literal using `valueOf`, and, finally, whether the length of the string is greater than zero:

```
// true if variable exists, is a string, and has a length greater than zero
if(((typeof unknownVariable != "undefined") &&
    (typeof unknownVariable.valueOf() == "string")) &&
   (unknownVariable.length > 0)) {
   ...
}
```

Seems like a lot of work, but typically your application won't have to be this extensive when testing a value. Generally you'll only need to test whether a variable has been set, or find the length of a string, in order to ensure it's not an empty string.

1.7 Breaking a Keyword String into Separate Keywords

Problem

You have a string with keywords, separated by commas. You want to break the string into an array of separate keywords, and then print the keywords out with a keyword label.

Solution

Use the `String split` method to split the string on the commas. Loop through the array, printing out the separate values. Example 1-1 shows a complete web page demonstrating this approach. The keywords are provided by the web page reader, via a prompt window, and are then processed and printed out to the web page.

Example 1-1. Demonstrating use of String split to get keyword list

```
<!DOCTYPE html>
<head>
<title>Example 1-1</title>
<meta http-equiv="Content-Type" content="text/html;charset=utf-8" >
<script type="text/javascript">

window.onload = function() {

  // get keyword list
   var keywordList = prompt("Enter keywords, separated by commas","");

  // use split to create array of keywords
  var  arrayList = keywordList.split(",");

  // build result HTML
  var resultString = "";
  for (var i = 0; i < arrayList.length; i++) {
    resultString+="keyword: " + arrayList[i] + "<br />";
  }

  // print out to page
  var  blk = document.getElementById("result");
  blk.innerHTML = resultString;
}

</script>
</head>
<body>
<div id="result">
</div>
</body>
</html>
```

Discussion

The `String` `split` method takes two parameters: a required parameter with the character representing the separator for the split method; the second parameter (optional) is a number representing a count of the number of splits to make. In Example 1-1, the separator is a comma (,), and no second parameter is provided. An example of using the second parameter is the following:

```
var strList = "keyword1,keyword2,keyword3,keyword4";
```

The following `split` method call would generate an array with two entries:

```
var arrayList = strList.split(",",2); // results in two element array
```

Not specifying the second parameter will split on every occurrence of the separator found:

```
var arrayList = strList.split(","); // results in four element array
```

Here's an interesting use of `split`: if you want to split a string on every character, specify the empty string (' ') or ("") as the separator:

```
var arrayList = strList.split("");
```

You can also use a regular expression as the parameter to split, though this can be a little tricky. For instance, to find the same sentence list as returned from the example code in the solution, you could use a couple of regular expressions:

```
var sentence = "This is one sentence. This is a sentence with a list of items:
cherries, oranges, apples, bananas.";
var val = sentence.split(/:/);
alert(val[1].split(/\./)[0]);
```

The regular expression looks for a colon first, which is then used for the first split. The second split uses a regular expression on the resulting value from the first split, to look for the period. The list is then in the first array element of this result.

Tricky, and a little hard to get your head around, but using regular expressions with `split` could be a handy option when nothing else works.

See Also

See Recipe 5.3 for a discussion about creating a string from an array. See Recipe 11.1 about accessing a page element with the document object, and Recipe 12.1 about using the `innerHTML` property. Chapter 2 provides coverage of regular expressions. Recipe 2.6 covers using capturing parentheses and a regular expression to get the same results as the solutions demonstrated in this recipe.

1.8 Inserting Special Characters

Problem

You want to insert a special character, such as a line feed, into a string.

Solution

Use one of the *escape sequences* in the string. For instance, to add the copyright symbol into a block of text to be added to the page (shown in Figure 1-1), use the escape sequence \u00A9:

```
var resultString = "<p>This page \u00A9 Shelley Powers </p>";

// print out to page
 var blk = document.getElementById("result");
 blk.innerHTML = resultString;
```

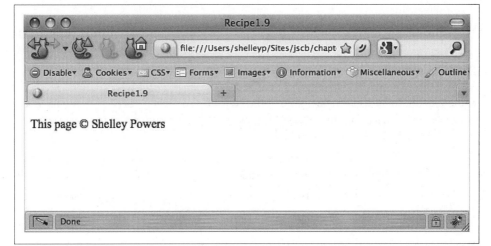

Figure 1-1. Page demonstrating use of escape sequence to create copyright symbol

Discussion

The escape sequences in JavaScript all begin with the *backslash character*, (\). This character lets the application processing the string know that what follows is a sequence of characters that need special handling.

Table 1-2 lists the other escape sequences.

Table 1-2. Escape sequences

Sequence	Character
\'	Single quote
\"	Double quote
\\	Backslash
\b	Backspace
\f	Form feed
\n	Newline
\r	Carriage return
\t	Horizontal tab
\ddd	Octal sequence (3 digits: *ddd*)
\xdd	Hexadecimal sequence (2 digits: *dd*)
\udddd	Unicode sequence (4 hex digits: *dddd*)

The last three escape sequences in Table 1-2 are patterns, where providing different numeric values will result in differing escape sequences. The copyright symbol in the solution is an example of the Unicode sequence.

All of the escape sequences listed in Table 1-2 can also be represented as a Unicode sequence. For instance, the horizontal tab (\t), can also be represented as the Unicode escape sequence, \u0009. Of course, if the user agent disregards the special character, as browsers do with the horizontal tab, the use is moot.

One of the most common uses of escape sequences is to include double or single quotes within strings delimited by the same character:

```
var newString = 'You can\'t use single quotes in a string surrounded by single
quotes';
```

1.9 Processing Individual Lines of a textarea

Problem

You want to be able to process individual lines from a textarea box.

Solution

Use the String split method, combined with the line break escape sequence (\n) to split the contents of the textarea into its separate lines:

```
var txtBox = document.getElementById("inputbox");
var lines = txtBox.value.split("\n");

// print out last line to page
```

```
var blk = document.getElementById("result");
blk.innerHTML = lines[lines.length-1];
```

Discussion

Escape sequences can be used for more than building strings; they can also be used in pattern-matching operations. In the solution, the **textarea** string is split into its separate lines by looking for the escape sequence for the newline character (\n).

This approach is also a way to convert text that may be encoded with escape sequences, such as the newline character, into properly formatted HTML. For instance, to modify the example to output the **textarea** exactly as typed, but as HTML, use the following:

```
// get textarea string and split on new lines
var txtBo x = document.getElementById("test");
var lines = txtBox.value.split("\n");

// generate HTML version of text
var resultString  = "<p>";
for (var i = 0; i < lines.length; i++) {
    resultString += lines[i] + "<br />";
}
resultString += "</p>";

// print out to page
var blk = document.getElementById("result");
blk.innerHTML = resultString;
```

This code snippet converts all line breaks into the HTML **br** element. When added back to the page, the text is printed as it was found in the **textarea**, line breaks and all. This is a popular technique used to echo comments, as they are typed for a live preview, in many blogs.

See Also

Another approach to replacing characters in a string is to use a regular expression with the **String** **replace** method, covered in Recipe 2.5.

1.10 Trimming Whitespace from the Ends of a String

Problem

You want to trim the whitespace around a string that you've accessed from a form element.

Solution

Use the new ECMAScript 5 **String** **trim** method:

```
var txtBox = document.getElementById("test");
var lines = txtBox.value.split("\n");
```

```
var resultString = "";

for (var i = 0; i < lines.length; i++) {
    var strng = lines[i].trim();
    resultString += strng + "-";
}
alert(resultString);
```

Discussion

Prior to the release of ECMAScript 5, you had to use regular expressions and the `String`
`replace` method to trim the unwanted whitespace from around a string. Now, trimming
a string is as simple as calling the `trim` method.

 Firefox already supported a `trim` method, but its use was nonstandard
before ECMAScript 5.

Most, if not all, browsers will eventually support `trim`. Among the target browsers for
this book, the only one that doesn't is IE8. A workaround you can use is outlined below,
which not only allows for the use of `trim`, but a fallback if trim does not exist.

First, at some point before you need to use the `trim` functionality, you must test to see
if `trim` exists as a property of the `String` object. If it doesn't, you'll need to use the
`String prototype` to add a customized `trim` method to the object:

```
if (typeof String.trim == "undefined") {
    String.prototype.trim = function() {
        return this.replace(/(^\s*)|(\s*$)/g, "");
    }
}
```

Once this code is processed, when you call the `trim` method on any string, it will return
a string with whitespace trimmed from both ends (as long as the application is within
page scope). This functionality happens regardless of whether the method is already
built-in by the browser, or added by your hack:

```
var strng = lines[1].trim();
```

 Most of the JavaScript framework libraries, such as jQuery, which I introduce in Chapter 17, have already added the `trim` method.

Other new, related methods from ECMAScript 5 are `trimLeft`, which trims the whitespace on the left side of the string, and `trimRight`, which does the same on the right
side of the string.

See Also

The use of regular expressions is covered in Chapter 2. The use of the JavaScript object `prototype` property is covered in Recipe 16.3.

1.11 Left- or Right-Pad a String

Problem

You need to create a string that's left- or right-padded with a given character.

Solution

Test the length of the string, then generate a padding string consisting of duplications of a given character to either concatenate to the original string (if padding to the right) or attaching to the beginning of the string (if padding to the left). The following left-pads the existing string with the nonbreaking space named character (` `):

```html
<!DOCTYPE html>
<head>
<title>Recipe 1.12</title>
</head>
<body>
<div id="result"></div>
<script>

   var prefLineLength = 20;
   var oldStr = "This is a string";

   var diff = prefLineLength - oldStr.length;
   var filler = ' ';

   for (var i = 0; i < diff; i++) {
      oldStr=filler + oldStr;
   }

  document.getElementById("result").innerHTML=oldStr;

</script>

</body>
```

Discussion

You don't want to pad strings that go into a database, because you want to keep the data in the database as small and efficient as possible. But you might want to pad the value before you display it in the web page.

The characters you use to pad the string are guided by the use. Typically, you'll use spaces. However, if the value is inserted into a web page that disregards multiple spaces, you'll either have to use the named entity ( ) or its numeric equivalent( ) if your content needs to be XHTML-compatible. Or you can just use CSS to format the text positioning. For instance, to right-align the text, create the CSS rule:

```
.rightformatted
{
   text-align: right:
}
```

And then apply the rule when you add the string to the page. You can use the CSS rule as a class name with the innerHTML property:

```
var div = document.getElementById("item");
item.innerHTML="<p>" + strValue + "</p>";
```

or you can use DOM (Document Object Model) Level 2 functionality:

```
var num = 123.55;
var item = document.getElementById("item");

// create text node and paragraph element
var txt = document.createTextNode(num);
var p = document.createElement("p");

// attach text node to paragraph
p.appendChild(txt);
p.setAttribute("class","rightformatted");

// append paragraph to document element
item.appendChild(p);
```

See Also

See Chapters 11 and 12 for more on using the Document Object Model (DOM) to access, create, and remove web page elements and element attributes.

CHAPTER 2

Using Regular Expressions

2.0 Introduction

Regular expressions are search patterns that can be used to find text that matches a given pattern. For instance, in the last chapter, we looked for the substring `Cookbook` within a longer string:

```
var testValue = "This is the Cookbook's test string";
var subsValue = "Cookbook";

var iValue = testValue(subsValue); // returns value of 12, index of substring
```

This code snippet worked because we were looking for an exact match. But what if we wanted a more general search? For instance, we want to search for the words *Cook* and *Book*, in strings such as "Joe's Cooking Book" or "JavaScript Cookbook"?

When we're looking for strings that match a pattern rather than an exact string, we need to use regular expressions. We can try to make do with `String` functions, but in the end, it's actually simpler to use regular expressions, though the syntax and format is a little odd and not necessarily "user friendly."

Recently, I was looking at code that pulled the RGB values from a string, in order to convert the color to its hexadecimal format. We're tempted to just use the `String.split` function, and split on the commas, but then you have to strip out the parentheses and extraneous whitespace. Another consideration is how can we be sure that the values are in octal format? Rather than:

```
rgb (255, 0, 0)
```

we might find:

```
rgb (100%, 0, 0)
```

There's an additional problem: some browsers return a color, such as a background color, as an RGB value, others as a hexadecimal. You need to be able to handle both when building a consistent conversion routine.

In the end, it's a set of regular expressions that enable us to solve what, at first, seems to be a trivial problem, but ends up being much more complicated. In an example from the popular jQuery UI library, regular expressions are used to match color values—a complicated task because the color values can take on many different formats, as this portion of the routine demonstrates:

```
// Look for #a0b1c2
if (result = /#([a-fA-F0-9]{2})([a-fA-F0-9]{2})([a-fA-F0-9]{2})/.exec(color))
    return [parseInt(result[1],16), parseInt(result[2],16), parseInt(result[3],16)];

// Look for #fff
if (result = /#([a-fA-F0-9])([a-fA-F0-9])([a-fA-F0-9])/.exec(color))
    return [parseInt(result[1]+result[1],16), parseInt(result[2]+result[2],16),
parseInt(result[3]+result[3],16)];

// Look for rgba(0, 0, 0, 0) == transparent in Safari 3
if (result = /rgba\(0, 0, 0, 0\)/.exec(color))
    return colors['transparent'];

// Otherwise, we're most likely dealing with a named color
    return colors[$.trim(color).toLowerCase()];
```

Though the regular expressions seem complex, they're really nothing more than a way to describe a pattern. In JavaScript, regular expressions are managed through the RegExp object.

A RegExp Literal

As with String in Chapter 1, RegExp can be both a literal and an object. To create a RegExp literal, you use the following syntax:

```
var re = /regular expression/;
```

The regular expression pattern is contained between opening and closing forward slashes. Note that this pattern is *not* a string: you do not want to use single or double quotes around the pattern, unless the quotes themselves are part of the pattern to match.

Regular expressions are made up of characters, either alone or in combination with special characters, that provide for more complex matching. For instance, the following is a regular expression for a pattern that matches against a string that contains the word Shelley and the word Powers, in that order, and separated by one or more whitespace characters:

```
var re = /Shelley\s+Powers/;
```

The special characters in this example are the backslash character (\), which has two purposes: either it's used with a regular character, to designate that it's a special character; or it's used with a special character, such as the plus sign (+), to designate that the character should be treated literally. In this case, the backslash is used with "s", which transforms the letter s to a special character designating a whitespace character, such as a space, tab, line feed, or form feed. The **\s** special character is followed by the plus sign, **\s+**, which is a signal to match the preceding character (in this example, a whitespace character) one or more times. This regular expression would work with the following:

```
Shelley Powers
```

It would also work with the following:

```
Shelley      Powers
```

It would not work with:

```
ShelleyPowers
```

It doesn't matter how much whitespace is between *Shelley* and *Powers*, because of the use of **\s+**. However, the use of the plus sign does require at least one whitespace character.

Table 2-1 shows the most commonly used special characters in JavaScript applications.

Table 2-1. Regular expression special characters

Character	Matches	Example
^	Matches beginning of input	/^This/ matches "This is..."
$	Matches end of input	/end?/ matches "This is the end"
*	Matches zero or more times	/se*/ matches "seeee" as well as "se"
?	Matches zero or one time	/ap?/ matches "apple" and "and"
+	Matches one or more times	/ap+/ matches "apple" but not "and"
{n}	Matches exactly *n* times	/ap{2}/ matches "apple" but not "apie"
{n,}	Matches *n* or more times	/ap{2,}/ matches all p's in "apple" and "appple" but not "apie"
{n,m}	Matches at least *n*, at most *m* times	/ap{2,4}/ matches four p's in "apppppple"
.	Any character except newline	/a.e/ matches "ape" and "axe"
[...]	Any character within brackets	/a[px]e/ matches "ape" and "axe" but not "ale"
[^...]	Any character but those within brackets	/a[^px]/ matches "ale" but not "axe" or "ape"
\b	Matches on word boundary	/\bno/ matches the first "no" in "nono"
\B	Matches on nonword boundary	/\Bno/ matches the second "no" in "nono"
\d	Digits from 0 to 9	/\d{3}/ matches 123 in "Now in 123"
\D	Any nondigit character	/\D{2,4}/ matches "Now " in "Now in 123"
\w	Matches word character (letters, digits, underscores)	/\w/ matches "j" in javascript
\W	Matches any nonword character (not letters, digits, or underscores)	/\W/ matches "%" in "100%"
\n	Matches a line feed	
\s	A single whitespace character	

Character	Matches	Example
\S	A single character that is not whitespace	
\t	A tab	
(x)	Capturing parentheses	Remembers the matched characters

RegExp As Object

The RegExp is a JavaScript object as well as a literal, so it can also be created using a constructor, as follows:

```
var re = new RegExp("Shelley\s+Powers");
```

When to use which? The RegExp literal is compiled when script is evaluated, so you should use a RegExp literal when you know the expression won't change. A compiled version is more efficient. Use the constructor when the expression changes or is going to be built or provided at runtime.

As with other JavaScript objects, RegExp has several properties and methods, the most common of which are demonstrated throughout this chapter.

 Regular expressions are powerful but can be tricky. This chapter is more an introduction to how regular expressions work in JavaScript than to regular expressions in general. If you want to learn more about regular expressions, I recommend the excellent *Regular Expressions Cookbook (http://oreilly.com/catalog/9780596520694)* by Jan Goyvaerts and Steven Levithan (O'Reilly).

See Also

The jQuery function shown in the first section is a conversion of a jQuery internal function incorporated into a custom jQuery plug-in. jQuery is covered in more detail in Chapter 17, and a jQuery plug-in is covered in Recipe 17.7.

2.1 Testing Whether a Substring Exists

Problem

You want to test whether a string is contained in another string.

Solution

Use a JavaScript regular expression to define a search pattern, and then apply the pattern against the string to be searched, using the RegExp test method. In the following, we want to match with any string that has the two words, *Cook* and *Book*, in that order:

```
var cookbookString = new Array();

cookbookString[0] = "Joe's Cooking Book";
cookbookString[1] = "Sam's Cookbook";
cookbookString[2] = "JavaScript CookBook";
cookbookString[3] = "JavaScript BookCook";

// search pattern
var pattern = /Cook.*Book/;
for (var i = 0; i < cookbookString.length; i++)
  alert(cookbookString[i] + " " + pattern.test(cookbookString[i]));
```

The first and third strings have a positive match, while the second and fourth do not.

Discussion

The `RegExp test` method takes two parameters: the string to test, and an optional modifier. It applies the regular expression against the string and returns true if there's a match, false if there is no match.

In the example, the pattern is the word *Cook* appearing somewhere in the string, and the word *Book* appearing anywhere in the string after *Cook*. There can be any number of characters between the two words, including no characters, as designated in the pattern by the two regular expression characters: the decimal point (.), and the asterisk (*).

The decimal in regular expressions is a special character that matches any character except the newline character. In the example pattern, the decimal is followed by the asterisk, which matches the preceding character zero or more times. Combined, they generate a pattern matching zero or more of any character, except newline.

In the example, the first and third string match, because they both match the pattern of *Cook* and *Book* with anything in between. The fourth does not, because the *Book* comes before *Cook* in the string. The second also doesn't match, because the first letter of *book* is lowercase rather than uppercase, and the matching pattern is case-dependent.

2.2 Testing for Case-Insensitive Substring Matches

Problem

You want to test whether a string is contained in another string, but you don't care about the case of the characters in either string.

Solution

When creating the regular expression, use the ignore case flag (`i`):

```
var cookbookString = new Array();

cookbookString[0] = "Joe's Cooking Book";
```

```
cookbookString[1] = "Sam's Cookbook";
cookbookString[2] = "JavaScript CookBook";
cookbookString[3] = "JavaScript cookbook";

// search pattern
var pattern = /Cook.*Book/i;
for (var i = 0; i < cookbookString.length; i++) {
  alert(cookbookString[i] + " " + pattern.test(cookbookString[i],i));
}
```

All four strings match the pattern.

Discussion

The solution uses a regular expression flag (i) to modify the constraints on the pattern-matching. In this case, the flag removes the constraint that the pattern-matching has to match by case. Using this flag, values of *book* and *Book* would both match.

There are only a few regular expression flags, as shown in Table 2-2. They can be used with RegExp literals:

```
var pattern = /Cook.*Book/i; // the 'i' is the ignore flag
```

They can also be used when creating a RegExp object, via the optional second parameter:

```
var pattern = new RegExp("Cook.*Book","i");
```

Table 2-2. Regular expression flags

Flag	Meaning
g	Global match: matches across an entire string, rather than stopping at first match
i	Ignores case
m	Applies begin and end line special characters (^ and $, respectively) to each line in a multiline string

2.3 Validating a Social Security Number

Problem

You need to validate whether a text string is a valid U.S.-based Social Security number (the identifier the tax people use to find us, here in the States).

Solution

Use the String match method and a regular expression to validate that a string is a Social Security number:

```
var ssn = document.getElementById("pattern").value;
var pattern = /^\d{3}-\d{2}-\d{4}$/;
if (ssn.match(pattern))
  alert("OK");
```

```
else
  alert("Not OK");
```

Discussion

A U.S.-based Social Security number is a combination of nine numbers, typically in a sequence of three numbers, two numbers, and four numbers, with or without dashes in between.

The numbers in a Social Security number can be matched with the digit special character (\d). To look for a set number of digits, you can use the curly brackets surrounding the number of expected digits. In the example, the first three digits are matched with:

```
\d{3}
```

The second two sets of numbers can be defined using the same criteria. Since there's only one dash between the sequences of digits, it can be given without any special character. However, if there's a possibility the string will have a Social Security number without the dashes, you'd want to change the regular expression pattern to:

```
var pattern = /^\d{3}-?\d{2}-?\d{4}$/;
```

The question mark special character (?) matches zero or exactly one of the preceding character—in this case, the dash (-). With this change, the following would match:

```
444-55-3333
```

As would the following:

```
555335555
```

But not the following, which has too many dashes:

```
555---60--4444
```

One other characteristic to check is whether the string consists of the Social Security number, and only the Social Security number. The beginning-of-input special character (^) is used to indicate that the Social Security number begins at the beginning of the string, and the end-of-line special character ($) is used to indicate that the line terminates at the end of the Social Security number.

Since we're only interested in verifying that the string is a validly formatted Social Security number, we're using the String object's match method. We could also have used the RegExp test method, but six of one, half dozen of the other; both approaches are acceptable.

There are other approaches to validating a Social Security number that are more complex, based on the principle that Social Security numbers can be given with spaces instead of dashes. That's why most websites asking for a Social Security number provide three different input fields, in order to eliminate the variations. Regular expressions should not be used in place of good form design.

In addition, there is no way to actually validate that the number given is an actual Social Security number, unless you have more information about the person, and a database with all Social Security numbers. All you're doing with the regular expression is verifying the format of the number.

See Also

One site that provides some of the more complex Social Security number regular expressions, in addition to many other interesting regular expression "recipes," is the Regular Expression Library (*http://regexlib.com/*).

2.4 Finding and Highlighting All Instances of a Pattern

Problem

You want to find all instances of a pattern within a string.

Solution

Use the RegExp exec method and the global flag (g) in a loop to locate all instances of a pattern, such as any word that begins with *t* and ends with *e*, with any number of characters in between:

```
var searchString = "Now is the time and this is the time and that is the time";
var pattern = /t\w*e/g;
var matchArray;

var str = "";
while((matchArray = pattern.exec(searchString)) != null) {
  str+="at " + matchArray.index + " we found " + matchArray[0] + "<br />";
}
document.getElementById("results").innerHTML=str;
```

Discussion

The RegExp exec method executes the regular expression, returning null if a match is not found, or an array of information if a match is found. Included in the returned array is the actual matched value, the index in the string where the match is found, any parenthetical substring matches, and the original string.

index
    The index of the located match

input
    The original input string

[0] *or accessing array directly*
    The matched value

```
[1],...,[n]
```
    Parenthetical substring matches

In the solution, the index where the match was found is printed out in addition to the
matched value.

The solution also uses the global flag (g). This triggers the RegExp object to preserve the
location of each match, and to begin the search after the previously discovered match.
When used in a loop, we can find all instances where the pattern matches the string.
In the solution, the following are printed out:

```
at 7 we found the
at 11 we found time
at 28 we found the
at 32 we found time
at 49 we found the
at 53 we found time
```

Both *time* and *the* match the pattern.

Let's look at the nature of global searching in action. In Example 2-1, a web page is
created with a **textarea** and an input text box for accessing both a search string and a
pattern. The pattern is used to create a RegExp object, which is then applied against the
string. A result string is built, consisting of both the unmatched text and the matched
text, except the matched text is surrounded by a **span** element, with a CSS class used
to highlight the text. The resulting string is then inserted into the page, using the
innerHTML for a div element.

Example 2-1. Using exec and global flag to search and highlight all matches in a text string

```
<!DOCTYPE html>
<html xmlns="http://www.w3.org/1999/xhtml">
<head>
<title>Searching for strings</title>
<style type="text/css">
#searchSubmit
{
    background-color: #ff0;
    width: 200px;
    text-align: center;
    padding: 10px;
    border: 2px inset #ccc;
}
.found
{
    background-color: #ff0;
}
</style>
<script type="text/javascript">
//<![CDATA[

window.onload=function() {
    document.getElementById("searchSubmit").onclick=doSearch;
```

```
}

function doSearch() {
    // get pattern
    var pattern = document.getElementById("pattern").value;
    var re = new RegExp(pattern,"g");

    // get string
    var searchString = document.getElementById("incoming").value;

    var matchArray;
    var resultString = "<pre>";
    var first=0; var last=0;

    // find each match
    while((matchArray = re.exec(searchString)) != null) {
      last = matchArray.index;
      // get all of string up to match, concatenate
      resultString += searchString.substring(first, last);

      // add matched, with class
      resultString += "<span class='found'>" + matchArray[0] + "</span>";
      first = re.lastIndex;
    }

    // finish off string
    resultString += searchString.substring(first,searchString.length);
    resultString += "</pre>";

    // insert into page
    document.getElementById("searchResult").innerHTML = resultString;
}

//--><!]]>
</script>
</head>
<body>
<form id="textsearch">
<textarea id="incoming" cols="150" rows="10">
</textarea>
<p>
Search pattern: <input id="pattern" type="text" /></p>
</form>
<p id="searchSubmit">Search for pattern</p>
<div id="searchResult"></div>
</body>
</html>
```

Figure 2-1 shows the application in action on William Wordsworth's poem, "The Kitten and the Falling Leaves," after a search for the following pattern:

```
lea(f|ve)
```

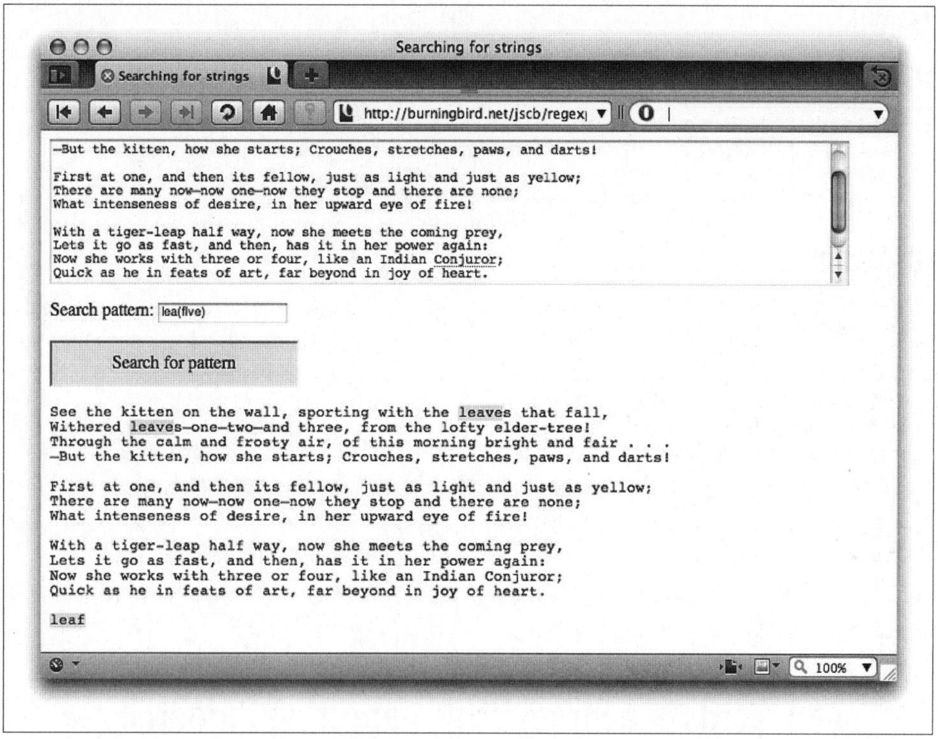

Figure 2-1. Application finding and highlighting all matched strings

The bar (|) is a conditional test, and will match a word based on the value on either side of the bar. So a word like `leaf` matches, as well as a word like `leave`, but not a word like `leap`.

You can access the last index found through the RegExp's `lastIndex` property. The `lastIndex` property is handy if you want to track both the first and last matches.

See Also

Recipe 2.5 describes another way to do a standard find-and-replace behavior, and Recipe 2.6 provides a simpler approach to finding and highlighting text in a string.

2.5 Replacing Patterns with New Strings

Problem

You want to replace all matched substrings with a new substring.

Solution

Use the `String` object's `replace` method, with a regular expression:

```
var searchString = "Now is the time, this is the time";
var re = /t\w{2}e/g;
var replacement = searchString.replace(re, "place");
alert(replacement); // Now is the place, this is the place
```

Discussion

In Example 2-1 in Recipe 2.4, we used the `RegExp` global flag (g) in order to track each occurrence of the regular expression. Each match was highlighted using a `span` element and CSS.

A global search is also handy for a typical find-and-replace behavior. Using the global flag (g) with the regular expression in combination with the `String replace` method will replace all instances of the matched text with the replacement string.

See Also

Recipe 2.6 demonstrates variations of using regular expressions with the `String replace` method.

2.6 Swap Words in a String Using Capturing Parentheses

Problem

You want to accept an input string with first and last name, and swap the names so the last name is first.

Solution

Use capturing parentheses and a regular expression to find and remember the two names in the string, and reverse them:

```
var name = "Abe Lincoln";
var re = /^(\w+)\s(\w+)$/;
var newname = name.replace(re,"$2, $1");
```

Discussion

Capturing parentheses allow us to not only match specific patterns in a string, but to reference the matched substrings at a later time. The matched substrings are referenced numerically, from left to right, as represented by the use of "$1" and "$2" in the `String replace` method.

In the solution, the regular expression matches two words, separated by a space. Capturing parentheses were used with both words, so the first name is accessible using "$1", the last name with "$2".

The captured parentheses aren't the only special characters available with the `String` `replace` method. Table 2-3 shows the other special characters that can be used with regular expressions and `replace`.

Table 2-3. String.replace special patterns

Pattern	Purpose
$$	Allows a literal dollar sign ($) in replacement
$&	Inserts matched substring
$`	Inserts portion of string before match
$'	Inserts portion of string after match
$n	Inserts *n*th captured parenthetical value when using RegExp

The second table entry, which reinserts the matched substring, can be used to provide a simplified version of the Example 2-1 application in Recipe 2.4. That example found and provided markup and CSS to highlight the matched substring. It used a loop to find and replace all entries, but in Example 2-2 we'll use the `String replace` method with the matched substring special pattern (`$&`)

Example 2-2. Using String.replace and special pattern to find and highlight text in a string

```
<!DOCTYPE html>
<html xmlns="http://www.w3.org/1999/xhtml">
<head>
<title>Searching for strings</title>
<style>
#searchSubmit
{
    background-color: #ff0;
    width: 200px;
    text-align: center;
    padding: 10px;
    border: 2px inset #ccc;
}
.found
{
    background-color: #ff0;
}
</style>
<script>
//<![CDATA[

window.onload=function() {
    document.getElementById("searchSubmit").onclick=doSearch;
}
```

```
function doSearch() {
    // get pattern
    var pattern = document.getElementById("pattern").value;
    var re = new RegExp(pattern,"g");

    // get string
    var searchString = document.getElementById("incoming").value;

    // replace
    var resultString = searchString.replace(re,"<span class='found'>$&</span>");

    // insert into page
    document.getElementById("searchResult").innerHTML = resultString;
}

//--><!]]>
</script>
</head>
<body>
<form id="textsearch">
<textarea id="incoming" cols="100" rows="10">
</textarea>
<p>
Search pattern: <input id="pattern" type="text" /></p>
</form>
<p id="searchSubmit">Search for pattern</p>
<div id="searchResult"></div>
</body>
</html>
```

This is a simpler alternative, but as Figure 2-2 shows, this technique doesn't quite preserve all aspects of the original string. The line feeds aren't preserved with Example 2-2, but they are with Example 2-1.

The captured text can also be accessed via the RegExp object when you use the RegExp exec method. Now let's return to the Recipe 2.6 solution code, but this time using the RegExp's exec method:

```
var name = "Shelley Powers";
var re = /^(\w+)\s(\w+)$/;
var result = re.exec(name);
var newname = result[2] + ", " + result[1];
```

This approach is handy if you want to access the capturing parentheses values, but without having to use them within a string replacement. To see another example of using capturing parentheses, Recipe 1.7 demonstrated a couple of ways to access the list of items in the following sentence, using the String split method:

```
var sentence = "This is one sentence. This is a sentence with a list of items:
cherries, oranges, apples, bananas.";
```

Another approach is the following, using capturing parentheses, and the `RegExp exec` method:

```
var re = /:(.*)\./;
var result = re.exec(sentence);
var list = result[1]; // cherries, oranges, apples, bananas
```

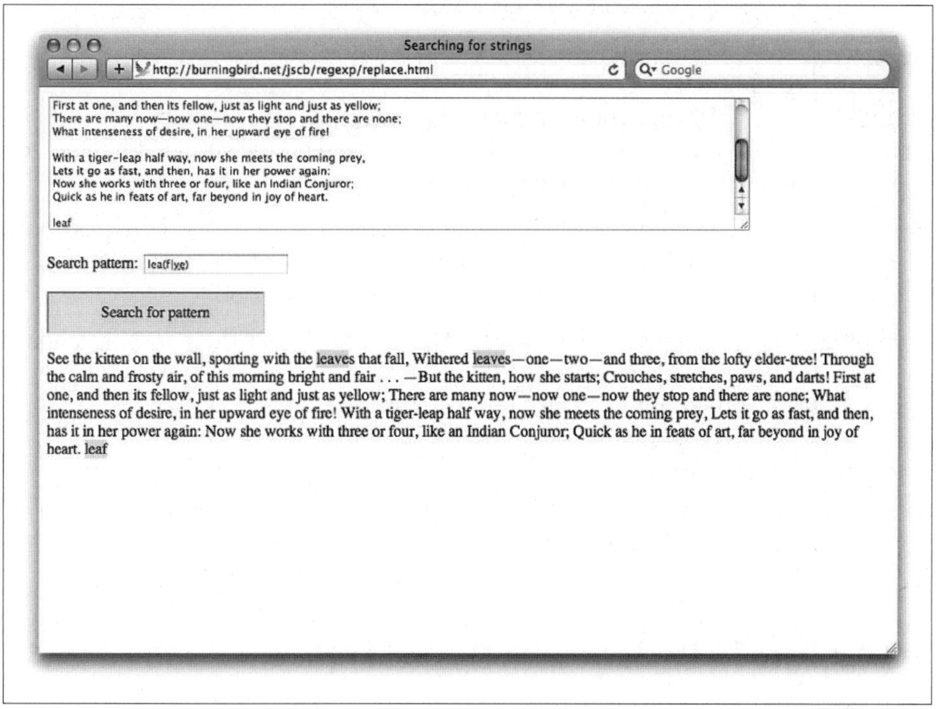

Figure 2-2. Using Example 2-2 to find and highlight text in a string

2.7 Using Regular Expressions to Trim Whitespace

Problem

Before sending a string to the server via an Ajax call, you want to trim whitespace from the beginning and end of the string.

Solution

Prior to the new ECMAScript 5 specification, you could use a regular expression to trim whitespace from the beginning and end of a string:

```
var testString = "   this is the string    ";

// trim white space from the beginning
```

```
testString = testString.replace(/^\s+/,"");

// trim white space from the end
testString = testString.replace(/\s+$/,"");
```

Beginning with ECMAScript 5, the `String` object now has a `trim` method:

```
var testString = "    this is the string    ";
testString = testString.trim(); // white space trimmed
```

Discussion

`String` values retrieved from form elements can sometimes have whitespace before and after the actual form value. You don't usually want to send the string with the extraneous whitespace, so you'll use a regular expression to trim the string.

Beginning with ECMAScript 5, there's now a `String trim` method. However, until ECMAScript 5 has wider use, you'll want to check to see if the `trim` method exists, and if not, use the old regular expression method as a fail-safe method.

In addition, there is no left or right trim in ECMAScript 5, though there are nonstandard versions of these methods in some browsers, such as Firefox. So if you want left- or right-only trim, you'll want to create your own functions:

```
function leftTrim(str) {
    return str.replace(/^\s+/,"");
}
function rightTrim(str) {
    return str.replace(/\s+$/,"");
}
```

2.8 Replace HTML Tags with Named Entities

Problem

You want to paste example markup into a web page, and escape the markup—have the angle brackets print out rather than have the contents parsed.

Solution

Use regular expressions to convert angle brackets (<>) into the named entities < and >:

```
var pieceOfHtml = "<p>This is a <span>paragraph</span></p>";
pieceOfHtml = pieceOfHtml.replace(/</g,"&lt;");
pieceOfHtml = pieceOfHtml.replace(/>/g,"&gt;");
document.getElementById("searchResult").innerHTML = pieceOfHtml;
```

Discussion

It's not unusual to want to paste samples of markup into another web page. The only way to have the text printed out, as is, without having the browser parse it, is to convert all angle brackets into their equivalent *named entities*.

The process is simple with the use of regular expressions, using the regular expression global flag (g) and the `String replace` method, as demonstrated in the solution.

2.9 Searching for Special Characters

Problem

We've searched for numbers and letters, and anything not a number or other character, but one thing we need to search is the special regular expression characters themselves.

Solution

Use the backslash to escape the pattern-matching character:

```
var re = /\\d/;
var pattern = "\\d{4}";
var pattern2 = pattern.replace(re,"\\D");
```

Discussion

In the solution, a regular expression is created that's equivalent to the special character, \d, used to match on any number. The pattern is, itself, escaped, in the string that needs to be searched. The number special character is then replaced with the special character that searches for anything but a number, \D.

Sounds a little convoluted, so I'll demonstrate with a longer application. Example 2-3 shows a small application that first searches for a sequence of four numbers in a string, and replaces them with four asterisks (****). Next, the application will modify the search pattern, by replacing the \d with \D, and then running it against the same string.

Example 2-3. Regular expression matching on regular expression characters

```
<!DOCTYPE html>
<html xmlns="http://www.w3.org/1999/xhtml">
<head>
<title>Replacement Insanity</title>
<script>
//<![CDATA[

window.onload=function() {

  // search for \d
```

```
  var re = /\\d/;
  var pattern = "\\d{4}";
  var str = "I want 1111 to find 3334 certain 5343 things 8484";
  var re2 = new RegExp(pattern,"g");
  var str1 = str.replace(re2,"****");
  alert(str1);
  var pattern2 = pattern.replace(re,"\\D");
  var re3 = new RegExp(pattern2,"g");
  var str2 = str.replace(re3, "****");
  alert(str2);
}
//--><!]]>
</script>
</head>
<body>
<p>content</p>
</body>
</html>
```

Here is the original string:

```
I want 1111 to find 3334 certain 5343 things 8484
```

The first string printed out is the original string with the numbers converted into asterisks:

```
I want **** to find **** certain **** things ****
```

The second string printed out is the same string, but after the characters have been converted into asterisks:

```
****nt 1111******** 3334******** 5343********8484
```

Though this example is short, it demonstrates some of the challenges when you want to search on regular expression characters themselves.

CHAPTER 3

Dates, Time, and Timers

3.0 Introduction

JavaScript's date and time functionality is quite extensive, and more than sufficient for most applications.

The Date object contains a number representing the date and time, rather than a string representation. The numeric value for the Date object is the number of seconds since January 01, 1970 UTC. Leap seconds are ignored.

Strings used to create dates are parsed and converted into this numeric value. Older browsers required that this string be UTC (Coordinated Time Universal or Greenwich Mean Time) format. Beginning with ECMAScript 5, ISO 8601 parsing is supported, which I'll cover later in the chapter.

The Date Object

Dates are managed through the Date object. You can create a date using a variety of techniques (see Recipe 3.1 for a discussion of different approaches), and modify the date using an extensive number of methods.

You can also access every aspect of a date: year, month, day of week, time, and so on, using specialized get and set methods, described in Tables 3-1 and 3-2.

Table 3-1. Date object get methods

Method	Purpose
getDate	Returns day of the month (0–31)
getDay	Returns day of the week (0–6)
getFullYear	Returns 4-digit full year
getHours	Returns local hour (0–23)
getMilliseconds	Returns local milliseconds (0–999)
getMinutes	Returns local minute (0–59)

Method	Purpose
getMonth	Returns local month (0–11)
getSeconds	Returns local second (0–59)
getTime	Returns number of seconds since January 1, 1970 00:00:00 UTC
getTimezoneOffset	Returns time zone from UTC
getUTCDate	Returns day of month in UTC time (0–31) method (Date)
getUTCDay	Returns day of the week in UTC time (0–6)
getUTCFullYear	Returns 4-digit UTC year
getUTCHours	Returns UTC hours (0–23)
getUTCMilliseconds	Returns UTC milliseconds (0–999)
getUTCMinutes	Returns UTC minutes (0–59)
getUTCMonth	Returns UTC month (0–11)
getUTCSeconds	Returns UTC seconds (0–59)

Table 3-2. Date object set methods

Method	Purpose
setDate	Sets the day of month (1–31)
setFullYear	Sets 4-digit full year
setHours	Sets the hour (0–23)
setMilliseconds	Sets the date's milliseconds (0–999)
setMinutes	Sets the date's minutes (0–59)
setMonth	Sets the month (0–11)
setSeconds	Sets the seconds (0–59)
setTime	Sets the date's time as milliseconds since January 1, 1970 00:00:00 UTC
setUTCDate	Sets the date's day of month in UTC
setUTCFullYear	Sets the full year in UTC
setUTCHours	Sets the date's hours in UTC
setUTCMilliseconds	Sets the date's milliseconds in UTC
setUTCMinutes	Sets the date's minutes in UTC
setUTCMonth	Sets the month in UTC
setUTCSeconds	Sets the seconds in UTC

You can also calculate a future date by adding a number of days or weeks to any given date.

JavaScript Timers

JavaScript also provides another way to work with time, through the use of recurring or one-time-only timers. I've always thought these should be a component of the `Date` object, but they're actually `Window` object methods: `setInterval` and `setTimeout`.

The difference between the two is that `setInterval` creates a recurring timer that refires until canceled, while `setTimeout` creates a one-time-only timer. Both take a timer value, in milliseconds, as well as an expression to evaluate when the timer fires.

3.1 Printing Out Today's Date

Problem

You want to print out the current date and time to a web page.

Solution

Create a new `Date` object, without any parameters, and output its value to the web page:

```
var dtElem = document.getElementById("date");
var dt = new Date();
dtElem.innerHTML = "<p>" + dt + "</p>";
```

Discussion

When you construct a new `Date` object, you can pass various parameters to the constructor to create a specific date:

```
var dt = new Date(milliseconds); // milliseconds since 1 January 1970 00:00:00 UTC
var dt2 = new Date(dateString); // string representing a valid date
var dt3 = new Date(year,month,date[,hour,minute,second,millisecond]);
```

If you don't specify the time parameters of a date, as shown in the last example, they're set to zero by default. At a minimum, you must provide the month, day, and year. If you don't provide any form of a date string to the `Date` constructor, the `Date` object is set to the local date and time of the computer used to access the web page.

You can access components of the date using a variety of `Date` methods. You can directly print the entire date, as shown in the solution, and the resulting string will look like the following:

```
Thu Oct 01 2009 20:34:26 GMT-0500 (CST)
```

If you prefer a different format, you can access the individual components of the `Date`, using methods such as `getMonth`, `getFullYear`, `getTime`, `getDate`, and then build the date string:

```
var dt = new Date();
var month = dt.getMonth();
month++;
```

```
var day = dt.getDate();
var yr = dt.getFullYear();
dtElem.innerHTML = "<p>" + month + "/" + day + "/" + yr;
```

The above outputs the following string to the page:

10/1/2009

The month is a zero-based integer, which is why I had to increment the month value in the example to get the actual numeric month value. To get the month name, you'll most likely want to use an array:

```
var months = ['January','February','March','April','May','June','July','August',
'September','October','November','December'];
var month = dt.getMonth();
var monthString = months[month];
```

3.2 Printing Out the UTC Date and Time

Problem

You want to print out the current UTC (universal time) date and time, rather than the local time.

Solution

Use the UTC JavaScript methods in order to access the current date and time as universal time:

```
var dateElement = document.getElementById("date");
var today = new Date();
var utcDate = today.toUTCString();
dateElement.innerHTML = "<p>local datetime: " + today + " UTC datetime: " +
utcDate + "</p>";
```

Discussion

The Date toUTCString method returns the date/time string formatted in universal convention. This not only returns the UTC equivalent of the local datetime, it also returns it the UTC format, which varies just slightly from the datetime for the local time. The printout from the solution would be:

```
local datetime: Thu Oct 08 2009 13:58:35 GMT-0500 (CDT)
UTC datetime: Thu, 08 Oct 2009 18:58:35 GMT
```

There are a couple of differences between the two date printouts. First of all, the time zone designation differs, which we would expect. I'm currently in Central Daylight Time (CDT), which is five hours behind universal time (UTC/GMT). In addition, the day of week in the UTC string is followed by a comma, which doesn't occur with the local time printout.

Rather than the entire date string, you can access the UTC equivalent of the month, day, year, and time using the relevant `Date` methods. Instead of `getMonth`, use `getUTCMonth`, and so on. Using these `getUTC` methods with the local date, you could build a printout string identical to that given with the local time, or to match any other formatting, such as the ISO 8601 standard formatting. There are equivalent methods to set each of these values.

See Also

The `get` methods are detailed in Table 3-1 and the `set` methods are detailed in Table 3-2.

3.3 Printing Out an ISO 8601 Formatted Date

Problem

You need a date string with the date formatted according to the ISO 8601 standard format.

Solution

Construct the `Date`, access the individual elements, and create the ISO 8601 formatted string:

```
var dt = new Date();

// get month and increment
var mnth = dt.getUTCMonth();
mnth++;

var day = dt.getUTCDate();
if (day < 10) day="0" + day;
var yr = dt.getUTCFullYear();

var hrs = dt.getUTCHours();
if (hrs < 10) hrs = "0" + hrs;

var min = dt.getUTCMinutes();
if (min < 10) min = "0" + min;

var secs = dt.getUTCSeconds();
if (secs < 10) secs = "0" + secs;

var newdate = yr + "-" + mnth + "-" + day + "T" + hrs + ":" + min + ":" + secs + "Z";
```

Discussion

The ISO 8601 is an international standard that defines a representation for both dates and times. It's not unusual for applications that provide APIs to require ISO 8601 formatting. It's also not unusual for most dates to and from APIs to be in UTC, rather than local time.

The solution shows one variation of ISO 8601 formatting. Others are the following:

- 2009
- 2009-10
- 2009-10-15
- 2009-10-15T19:20
- 2009-10-15T19:20:20
- 2009-10-15T19:20:20.50

The values are year, month, date, then "T" to represent time, and hours, minutes, seconds, and fractions of sections. The time zone also needs to be indicated. If the date is in UTC, the time zone is represented by the letter "Z", as shown in the solution:

```
2009-10-15T14:42:51Z
```

Otherwise, the time zone is represented as +hh:mm to represent a time zone ahead of UTC, and -hh:mm to represent a time zone behind UTC.

The solution assumes you want to access the current UTC time. If you need to convert a given date into an ISO 8601 formatted UTC date, create the Date using the date string, and then use the UTC get methods to get the date components, as shown in the solution:

```
var dt = "October 15, 2009 15:10:10";
```

Eventually, you won't need this special functionality to print out an ISO 8601 formatted date, because one of the new Date extensions released with ECMAScript 5 is a new method, toISOString:

```
var dt = "October 15, 2009 15:10:10";
alert(dt.toISOString());
```

Currently only a few browsers support this new functionality (Firefox 3.5 and the WebKit nightly). Until there is broader support, you'll still need the functionality outlined in the solution to output the correctly formatted ISO date. However, you can extend the function to check for the existence of toISOString first, and use it if supported.

See Also

A padding function, such as the one described in Recipe 1.10, can be used to pad the numbers. The W3C "Note on Date and Time Formats" describing the ISO 8601 format can be found at *http://www.w3.org/TR/NOTE-datetime*.

3.4 Converting an ISO 8601 Formatted Date to a Format Acceptable to the Date Object

Problem

You need to convert an ISO 8601 formatted date string into values that can be used to create a new Date object.

Solution

Parse the ISO 8601 string into the individual date values, and use it to create a new JavaScript Date object:

```
var dtstr= "2009-10-15T14:42:51Z";

dtstr = dtstr.replace(/\D/g," ");
var dtcomps = dtstr.split(" ");

// modify month between 1 based ISO 8601 and zero based Date
dtcomps[1]--;

var convdt = new
Date(Date.UTC(dtcomps[0],dtcomps[1],dtcomps[2],dtcomps[3],dtcomps[4],dtcomps[5]));
```

Discussion

If you attempt to create a JavaScript Date with an ISO 8601 formatted string, you'll get an invalid date error. Instead, you'll have to convert the string into values that can be used with the JavaScript Date.

The simplest way to parse an ISO 8601 formatted string is to use the String.split method. To facilitate the use of split, all nonnumeric characters are converted to one specific character. In the solution, the nonnumeric characters are converted to a space:

```
dtstr = dtstr.replace(/\D/g, " ");
```

The ISO formatted string would be converted to:

```
2009 10 15 14 42 51
```

ISO months are one-based, in values of 1 through 12. To use the month value in Java-Script Dates, the month needs to be adjusted by subtracting 1:

```
dtcomps[1]--;
```

Finally, the new Date is created. To maintain the UTC setting, the Date object's UTC method is used to create the date in universal time, which is then passed to the Date constructor:

```
var convdt = new
Date(Date.UTC(dtcomps[0],dtcomps[1],dtcomps[2],dtcomps[3],dtcomps[4],dtcomps[5]));
```

The task gets more challenging when you have to account for the different ISO 8601 formats. Example 3-1 shows a JavaScript application that contains a more complex JavaScript function that converts from ISO 8601 to allowable Date values. The first test in the function ensures that the ISO 8601 format can be converted to a JavaScript Date. This means that, at a minimum, the formatted string must have a month, day, and year.

Example 3-1. Converting ISO 8601 formatted dates to JavaScript Dates

```
<!DOCTYPE html>
<html xmlns="http://www.w3.org/1999/xhtml">
<head>
<title>Converting ISO 8601 date</title>
<style type="text/css">
#dateSubmit
{
    background-color: #ff0;
    width: 200px;
    text-align: center;
    border: 1px solid #ccc;
}
</style>
<script type="text/javascript">
//<![CDATA[

window.onload=function() {
   document.getElementById("dateSubmit").onclick=convertDate;
}

function convertDate() {
  var dtstr = document.getElementById("datestring").value;
  var convdate = convertISO8601toDate(dtstr);
  document.getElementById("result").innerHTML=convdate;
}

function convertISO8601toDate(dtstr) {

  // replace anything but numbers by spaces
  dtstr = dtstr.replace(/\D/g," ");

  // trim any hanging white space
  dtstr = dtstr.replace(/\s+$/,"");

  // split on space
  var dtcomps = dtstr.split(" ");

  // not all ISO 8601 dates can convert, as is
  // unless month and date specified, invalid
  if (dtcomps.length < 3) return "invalid date";
  // if time not provided, set to zero
  if (dtcomps.length < 4) {
    dtcomps[3] = 0;
    dtcomps[4] = 0;
    dtcomps[5] = 0;
```

```
    }

    // modify month between 1 based ISO 8601 and zero based Date
    dtcomps[1]--;

    var convdt = new
Date(Date.UTC(dtcomps[0],dtcomps[1],dtcomps[2],dtcomps[3],dtcomps[4],dtcomps[5]));

    return convdt.toUTCString();
}

//--><!]]>
</script>
</head>
<body>
<form>
<p>Datestring in ISO 8601 format: <input type="text" id="datestring" /></p>
</form>
<div id="dateSubmit"><p>Convert Date</p></div>
<div id="result"></div>
</body>
</html>
```

Another test incorporated into Example 3-1 is whether a time is given. If there aren't enough array elements to cover a time, then the hours, minutes, and seconds are set to zero when the UTC date is created.

There are other issues related to dates not covered in the application. For instance, if the ISO 8601 formatted string isn't in UTC time, converting it to UTC can require additional code, both to parse the time zone and to adjust the date to incorporate the time zone. I'll leave that as an individual exercise, though.

Eventually, you won't need this special processing, because ECMAScript 5 includes new support for ISO 8601 dates. This means you'll be able to create a new Date object using an ISO 8601 formatted string. However, only a few browsers (Firefox 3.5 and WebKit-based browsers) currently support the new ISO 8601 formatting, so you'll still need to provide the conversion functionality included in this section for the near future.

3.5 Creating a Specific Date

Problem

You want to create a Date object given a month, day, and year.

Solution

Construct a Date object, passing in the month, day, and year as parameters:

```
var month = 10; // Month 10, in zero based system, is November
var day = 18;
```

```
var year = 1954;
var dt = new Date(year,month,day); // time is set to zero by default
```

Discussion

The month, day, and year are integer values passed into the Date constructor. Because the time values were not given, they're set to zero by default.

In the solution, a November date is wanted, which is typically written out as 11. However, months with the Date object are zero-based, which means that November would be designated, numerically, as 10.

3.6 Scheduling a Future Date

Problem

You want to generate a future date.

Solution

Use a combination of the Date object's get and set methods in order to create a future date. In the following, a new date is created that's 10 days in the future:

```
var futureDate = new Date();
futureDate.setDate(futureDate.getDate() + 10);
```

Discussion

You can use a combination of get and set methods to find either a future or past date. Which methods you use depends on how you want to derive the new date. If you want to add or subtract days, you'll use getDate and setDate; for years, use getFullYear and setFullYear; for hours, use getHours and setHours; and so on.

Here's a list of the paired methods to use, and the incremental amounts:

- getDate and setDate to adjust the date by days
- getFullYear and setFullYear to adjust the date by years
- getHours and setHours to adjust the date and time by hours
- getSeconds and setSeconds to adjust the date and time by seconds
- getMilliseconds and setMilliseconds to adjust the date and time by milliseconds
- getMinutes and setMinutes to adjust the date and time by minutes

You can also use the UTC versions of the same methods.

To derive a date in the past, subtract the unit by the amount of the change:

```
var pastDate = new Date();
pastDate.setFullYears(pastDate.getFullYears() - 18);
```

3.7 Tracking Elapsed Time

Problem

You want to track the elapsed time between events.

Solution

Create a `Date` object when the first event occurs, a new `Date` object when the second event occurs, and subtract the first from the second. The difference is in milliseconds; to convert to seconds, divide by 1,000:

```
var firstDate;
window.onload=startTimer;

function startTimer(){
  firstDate = new Date();
  document.getElementById("date").onclick=doEvent;
}

function doEvent() {
  var secondDate = new Date();
  alert((secondDate - firstDate) / 1000);
}
```

Discussion

Some arithmetic operators can be used with `Date`s, but with interesting results. In the example, one `Date` can be subtracted from another, and the difference between the two is returned as milliseconds. However, if you "add" two dates together, the result is a string with the second `Date` concatenated to the first:

```
Thu Oct 08 2009 20:20:34 GMT-0500 (CST)Thu Oct 08 2009 20:20:31 GMT-0500 (CST)
```

If you divide the `Date` objects, again the `Date`s are converted to their millisecond value, and the result of dividing one by the other is returned. Multiplying two dates will return a very large millisecond result.

 Only the `Date` subtraction operator really makes sense, but it's interesting to see what happens with arithmetic operators and the `Date` object.

3.8 Creating a Timeout

Problem

You want to trigger a timeout based on an event.

Solution

Use the `window.setTimeout` method to create a one-time-only timer:

```
window.onload=function() {
  setTimeout("alert('timeout!')",3000);
}
```

Discussion

The `setTimeout` method takes two parameters: the expression to process, and the time (in milliseconds) when the expression is evaluated. In the solution, the expression is code, contained in a text string, that's processed three seconds after the `setTimeout` function is run.

The first parameter can also be the name of a function:

```
setTimeout(functionName, 2000);
```

In addition, you can create an expression that's a combination of function and parameters by providing the optional parameters after the time:

```
setTimeout(functionName, 2000, param1, param2, ..., paramn);
```

You can cancel a timeout, using the `clearTimeout` method:

```
var timer1 = setTimeout(functionName, 2000);
...
window.clearTimeout(timer1);
```

There's no absolute guarantee that the timer event fires when it is supposed to fire. Timers run on the same execution thread as all other User Interface (UI) events, such as mouse-clicks. All events are queued and blocked, including the timer event, until its turn. So, if you have several events in the queue ahead of the timer, the actual time could differ. Probably not enough to be noticeable to your application users, but a delay can happen.

See Also

John Resig offers an excellent discussion on how timers work, and especially the issues associated with event queues and single threads of execution, at *http://ejohn.org/blog/how-javascript-timers-work/*.

3.9 Creating Recurring Timers

Problem

You need to run the same function several times at regular intervals.

Solution

Use the `Window.setInterval` method to create a recurring timer:

```
var x = 0;
setInterval(moveElement,1000);

function moveElement() {
   x+=10;
   var left = x + "px";
   document.getElementById("redbox").style.left=left;
}
```

Discussion

Dynamic animations in a web page, SVG, or Canvas, are dependent on the `setTime out` and `setInterval` methods. In particular, any flashing, moving, or following type of animation is dependent on a timer calling a method at specified intervals.

The `setInterval` method requires two parameters: the code or function to process, and the delay between timer events. The first parameter can be a function name:

```
setInterval(functionName,3000);
```

The first parameter can also be a function call with parameters in a text string:

```
setInterval ("alert('hello')", 3000);
```

The second parameter is the time, in milliseconds, of the timer delay. Unlike `setTime out`, discussed in Recipe 3.8, the `setInterval` timer will continue to cycle until the JavaScript application (the web page) is unloaded, or until the `clearInterval` method is called:

```
var intervalid = setInterval(functionName, 3000);
...
clearInterval(intervalid);
```

If the first parameter is a function name, you can pass parameters, optionally, following the timer delay:

```
setInterval(functionName, 2000, param1, param2, ..., paramn);
```

Being able to pass parameters to the function is handy if you're creating an animation and generating the parameters dynamically. Unfortunately, passing parameters in this way doesn't work with IE8. However, you can instead use function closures with the timer, as covered in Recipe 3.10.

3.10 Using Function Closures with Timers

Problem

You want to provide a function with a timer, but you want to add the function directly into the timer method call.

Solution

Use an anonymous function as first parameter to the `setInterval` or `setTimeout` method call:

```
var x = 10;
var intervalId=setInterval(function() {
        x+=5;
        var left = x + "px";
        document.getElementById("redbox").style.left=left;}, 100);
```

Discussion

Recipes 3.8 and 3.9 use a function variable as the first parameter to the timer methods. However, you can also use an anonymous function, as demonstrated in the solution. This approach is especially helpful, because rather than have to use a global value that's used in the timer function, you can use a variable local to the scope of the enclosing function.

Example 3-2 demonstrates the use of an anonymous function within a `setInterval` method call. The approach also demonstrates how the use of this function closure allows access to the parent function's local variables within the timer method. In the example, clicking the red box starts the timer, and the box moves. Clicking the box again clears the timer, and the box stops. The position of the box is tracked in the `x` variable, which is within scope for the timer function, since it operates within the scope of the parent function.

Example 3-2. Using an anonymous function within a setInterval timer parameter

```
<!DOCTYPE html>
<head>
<title>interval and anonymous function</title>
<style>
#redbox
{
  position: absolute;
  left: 100px;
  top: 100px;
  width: 200px; height: 200px;
  background-color: red;
}
</style>
<script>
```

```
var intervalId=null;

window.onload=function() {
  document.getElementById("redbox").onclick=stopStartElement;
}
function stopStartElement() {
    if (intervalId == null) {
       var x = 100;
       intervalId=setInterval(function() {
                        x+=5;
                        var left = x + "px";
                        document.getElementById("redbox").style.left=left;}, 100);
    } else {
       clearInterval(intervalId);
       intervalId=null;
    }
}

</script>
</head>
<body>
<div id="redbox"></div>
</body>
```

See Also

See more on functions as parameters and anonymous functions in Chapter 6, especially Recipe 6.5.

CHAPTER 4

Working with Numbers and Math

4.0 Introduction

Numbers and numeric operations in JavaScript are managed by two different JavaScript objects: `Number` and `Math`.

Like the `String` and `RegExp` objects discussed in earlier chapters, numbers can be both a literal value and an object. No surprises there, but the `Math` object is different: it has no constructor, and all properties and methods are accessed directly from the object.

The Number Object and Number Literal

Numbers in JavaScript are floating point, though there may not be a decimal component present. If no decimal is present, they act as if they're integers:

```
var someValue = 10; // treated as integer 10, in base 10
```

Numbers can be defined in the range of -2^{53} to 2^{53}. Most numbers in JavaScript are literal values, assigned as values to variables, and used in various computations:

```
var myNum = 3.18;
var newNum = myNum * someValue;
```

You can also construct a `Number` using a constructor method:

```
var newNum = new Number(23);
```

You can assign a literal number to a variable, but when you access a `Number` method on the variable, a `Number` object is created to wrap the literal value, which is discarded when the method is finished.

The `Number` object's methods provide various display operations, such as providing an exponential notation:

```
var tst = .0004532;
alert(tst.toExponential()); // outputs 4.532e-4
```

In addition, there are several static `Number` properties, which can only be accessed via the `Number` object directly:

```
alert(Number.MAX_VALUE); // outputs 1.7976931348623157e+308
```

There's a special `Number` static property, `NaN`, which is equivalent to the global `NaN`, and stands for *Not a Number*. Anytime you try to use a value in a number operation that can't be parsed as a number, you'll get a `NaN` error:

```
alert(parseInt("3.5")); // outputs 3
alert(parseInt("three point five")); // outputs NaN
```

The Math Object

Unlike the `Number` object, the `Math` object does not have a constructor. All of the object's functionality, its properties and methods, are static. If you try to instantiate a `Math` object:

```
var newMath = new Math();
```

You'll get an error. Rather than create a new `Math` instance, access properties and methods directly on the object instead:

```
var topValue = Math.max(firstValue, secondValue); // returns larger number
```

The `Math` object has a considerable number of properties and methods, including several trigonometric methods. The precision of the methods is at the same level of precision that we would find using a language like C.

Table 4-1 provides a listing of the `Math` properties, and Table 4-2 contains a listing of the `Math` methods.

Table 4-1. Math object static properties

Property	Purpose
E	The number value for e, the base of natural logarithms
LN2	Natural logarithm of 2
LN10	Natural logarithm of 10
LOG2E	Base 2 logarithm of e, and the reciprocal of LN2
LOG10E	Base 10 logarithm of e, and the reciprocal of LN10
PI	The number for π
SQRT1_2	Square root of 1/2, reciprocal of SQRT2
SQRT2	Square root of 2

Table 4-2. Math object static methods

Method	Purpose
abs (x)	Returns absolute value of x; if x is NaN, returns NaN
acos (x)	Returns arc cosine of x; if x is greater than 1 or less than 0, returns NaN
asin (x)	Returns arc sine of x; if x is greater than 1 or less than -1, returns NaN
atan (x)	Returns the arc tangent of x
atan2 (x, y)	Returns the arc tangent of the quotient of x, y
ceil (x)	Returns the smallest integer equal to or greater than x
cos (x)	Returns the cosine of x
exp (x)	Returns E^x where E is the base of natural logarithms
floor (x)	Returns the largest integer equal to or less than x
log (x)	Returns logarithm of x
max $(x1, x2, ..., xn)$	Returns largest of given arguments
min $(x1, x2, ..., xn)$	Returns smallest of given arguments
pow (x,y)	Returns result of raising x to power of y
random $()$	Returns random number greater than or equal to 0, and less than 1
round (x)	Rounds number to closest integer
sin (x)	Returns the sine of x
sqrt (x)	Returns the square root of x

4.1 Keeping an Incremental Counter

Problem

You want to maintain an incremental counter in code.

Solution

Define a number variable, either locally or globally, or as part of an object's properties, and increment the variable's value with each iteration of code:

```
var globalCounter = 0;
function nextTest() {
   globalCounter++;
   ...
}
```

Discussion

The simplest way to increase or decrease a number is using the increment (++) and decrement (--) operators, respectively. They're equivalent to:

```
numValue = numValue + 1; // equivalent to numValue++
numValue = numValue - 1; // equivalent to numValue--
```

Both operators can be used prefix or postfix, which means the operators can be placed before or after the operand. How they're positioned is significant. If the operator is placed before the operand, the operand's value is adjusted first, before the operand is used:

```
var numValue = 1;
var numValue2 = ++numValue; // numValue and numValue2 are both 2
```

If the operator is postfix (placed after the operand), the operand is used first, and then its value is adjusted:

```
var numValue = 1;
var numValue2 = numValue++; // numValue is 2 and numValue2 is 1
```

The point at which the counter is incremented depends on its use. If it's needed in a loop, the value is incremented in the loop:

```
var counter = 0;
while (counter <= 10) {
    ...
    counter++;
}
```

If the counter is needed more globally, it can be declared as a *global variable*, but use with caution. A global variable is one that's declared outside of a function, and isn't redeclared within a function. It can easily conflict with any other global variables that might exist in the application or other libraries you use:

```
var counter = 0;
function someFunction() {
    counter++;
}
```

Another approach is to add the counter as property to an object, persisting as long as the object, and accessible by all object methods.

See Also

Chapter 16 covers how to create JavaScript objects.

4.2 Converting a Decimal to a Hexadecimal Value

Problem

You have a decimal value, and need to find its hexadecimal equivalent.

Solution

Use the `Number` object's `toString` method:

```
var num = 255;
alert(num.toString(16)); // displays ff, which is hexadecimal equivalent for 255
```

Discussion

By default, numbers in JavaScript are base 10, or decimal. However, they can also be created and used in hexadecimal and octal notation. Hexadecimal numbers begin with `0x` (a zero followed by lowercase x), and octal numbers always begin with zero:

```
var octoNumber = 0255; // equivalent to 173 decimal
var hexaNumber = 0xad; // equivalent to 173 decimal
```

Other base numbers can be created using the `Number` object's `toString` method, passing in the base radix, in a range from 2 to 36:

```
var decNum = 55;
var octNum = decNum.toString(8); // value of 67 octal
var hexNum = decNum.toString(16); // value of 37 hexadecimal
var binNum = decNum.toString(2); // value of 110111 binary
```

To complete the octal and hexadecimal presentation, you'll need to concatenate the zero to the octal, and the `0x` to the hexadecimal value.

Although decimals can be converted to any base number (between a range of 2 to 36), only the octal, hexadecimal, and decimal numbers can be manipulated, directly, as numbers.

See Also

The decimal to hexadecimal conversion is used in Recipe 4.4.

4.3 Creating a Random Number Generator

Problem

You need to generate a random number, between 0 and 255.

Solution

Use a combination of JavaScript `Math` methods: `random` to generate a random value between 0 and 1, which is then multiplied by 255, and `floor` to truncate the number.

```
var randomNumber = Math.floor(Math.random() * 255);
```

Discussion

The `random` method generates a random number between 0 and 1. To increase the range, multiply the result by the upper end of the range of values you want. If you need a random number with a higher lower end, such as a number between 5 and 10, multiply the value from `random` by a number equal to the upper range, minus the lower range, minus 1, and then add the lower range to the result:

```
var randomNumber = Math.floor(Math.random() * 6) + 5;
```

The `floor` method rounds down the floating-point value to the nearest integer.

4.4 Randomly Generating Colors

Problem

You need to randomly generate a web color.

Solution

Use the `Math` object to randomly generate each RGB (Red-Green-Blue) value:

```
function randomVal(val) {
  return Math.floor(Math.random() * val);
}

function randomColor() {
   return "rgb(" + randomVal(255) + "," + randomVal(255) + "," +
randomVal(255) + ")";
}
```

Discussion

Web color can be expressed either in hexadecimal notation, or as an RGB value. With the RGB value, each color is represented as a number between 0 and 255. The example demonstrates one technique to generate a color, using one function to randomly generate the number, and a second to return an RGB formatted string.

Older browsers may not support the RGB notation. To use a hexadecimal notation, the `randomColor` function can be altered to:

```
function randomColor() {
   // get red
   var r = randomVal(255).toString(16);
```

```
        if (r.length < 2) r= "0" + r;

        // get green
        var g = randomVal(255).toString(16);
        if (g.length < 2) g= "0" + g;

        // get blue
        var b = randomVal(255).toString(16);
        if (b.length < 2) b= "0" + b;

        return "#" + r + g + b;
    }
```

The hexadecimal notation is used (*#ffffff*), and the generated decimal number is converted to hexadecimal notation, using the `Number` object's `toString` method. Since a decimal value of something like zero converts to a single-digit character and the format needs to be double-digit, the length is tested and modified accordingly.

All the target browsers support both the RGB and hexadecimal notation, except IE7, which only supports hexadecimal.

See Also

See Recipe 4.1 about converting between decimal and hexadecimal notation, and Recipe 4.3 for how to randomly generate numbers.

4.5 Converting Strings in a Table to Numbers

Problem

You want to access values in an HTML table and convert to numbers for processing.

Solution

Access the numbers using the Document Object Model (DOM) API, and use the global function `parseInt` to convert the strings to number values:

```
 var rows = document.getElementById("table1").children[0].rows;
var numArray = new Array();

for (var i = 0; i < rows.length; i++) {
   numArray[numArray.length] = parseInt(rows[i].cells[1].firstChild.data);
}
```

Discussion

The `parseInt` global function has two arguments: a required numeric string, and an optional radix (base). If the radix is not provided, it's assumed to be 10, for decimal.

If the string provided doesn't contain a number, `NaN` is returned. If the string contains a partial number, the parser will convert the number up to the point where a nonnumeric value is reached, and return the result:

```
var numString = "133 hectares";
var numHectares = parseInt(numString); // returns 133
```

If the number is in floating-point format, `parseInt` stops when it reaches the decimal, and returns just the integer part of the number. If the string could contain a floating-point number and you want the result to be a floating-point number, use the `parseFloat` global function, instead:

```
var numString = "1.458 hectares";
var fltNum = parseFloat(numString); // returns 1.458
```

4.6 Summing All Numbers in a Table Column

Problem

You want to traverse all of the values in a table column, convert the values to numbers, and then sum the values.

Solution

Traverse the table column containing numeric values, convert to numbers, and sum the numbers:

```
var sum = 0;

// use querySelector to find all second table cells
var cells = document.querySelectorAll("td:nth-of-type(2)");

for (var i = 0; i < cells.length; i++)
    sum+=parseFloat(cells[i].firstChild.data);
```

Discussion

Both global functions `parseInt` and `parseFloat` convert strings to numbers, but `parseFloat` is more adaptable when it comes to handling numbers in an HTML table. Unless you're absolutely certain all of the numbers will be integers, `parseFloat` can work with both integers and floating-point numbers.

As you traverse the HTML table and convert the table entries to numbers, sum the results. Once you have the sum, you can use it in a database update, print it to the page, or pop up a message box, as the solution demonstrates.

You can also add a sum row to the HTML table. Example 4-1 demonstrates how to convert and sum up numeric values in an HTML table, and then how to insert a table row with this sum, at the end. The code uses `document.querySelectorAll`, which uses a CSS selector, *td + td*. This selector finds all table cells that are preceded by another table cell.

Example 4-1. Converting table values to numbers and summing the results

```
<!DOCTYPE html>
<html xmlns="http://www.w3.org/1999/xhtml">
<head>
<title>Accessing numbers in table</title>

<script type="text/javascript">
//<![CDATA[

window.onload=function() {

    var sum = 0;

    var dataTable = document.getElementById("table1");

    // use querySelector to find all second table cells
    var cells = document.querySelectorAll("td + td");

    for (var i = 0; i < cells.length; i++)
        sum+=parseFloat(cells[i].firstChild.data);

    // now add sum to end of table
    var newRow = document.createElement("tr");

    // first cell
    var firstCell = document.createElement("td");
    var firstCellText = document.createTextNode("Sum:");
    firstCell.appendChild(firstCellText);
    newRow.appendChild(firstCell);

    // second cell with sum
    var secondCell = document.createElement("td");
    var secondCellText = document.createTextNode(sum);
    secondCell.appendChild(secondCellText);
    newRow.appendChild(secondCell);

    // add row to table
    dataTable.appendChild(newRow);

}

//--><!]]>
</script>
</head>
<body>
<table id="table1">
    <tr>
        <td>Washington</td><td>145</td>
    </tr>
    <tr>
        <td>Oregon</td><td>233</td>
```

```
    </tr>
    <tr>
        <td>Missouri</td><td>833</td>
    </tr>
</table>
</body>
</html>
```

Being able to provide a sum or other operation on table data is helpful if you're working with dynamic updates via an Ajax operation, such as accessing rows of data from a database. The Ajax operation may not be able to provide summary data, or you may not want to provide summary data until a web page reader chooses to do so. The users may want to manipulate the table results, and then push a button to perform the summing operation.

Table rows are simple to add, as long as you remember the steps:

1. Create a new table row using `document.createElement("tr")`.

2. Create each table row cell using `document.createElement("td")`.

3. Create each table row cell's data using `document.createTextNode()`, passing in the text of the node (including numbers, which are automatically converted to a string).

4. Append the text node to the table cell.

5. Append the table cell to the table row.

6. Append the table row to the table. Rinse, repeat.

If you perform this operation frequently, you'll most likely want to create functions for these operations, and package them into JavaScript libraries that you can reuse. Also, many of the available JavaScript libraries can do much of this work for you.

See Also

See more on JavaScript libraries in Chapter 17. View more demonstrations of creating web page components in Chapter 12. The `document.querySelectorAll` is one of the new Selectors API methods, and won't work with older browsers. It is not supported in IE7. For new browsers, there may also be restrictions on its use. More examples and discussion of the Selectors API can be found in Recipe 11.4.

4.7 Converting Between Degrees and Radians

Problem

You have an angle in degrees. To use the value in the `Math` object's trigonometric functions, you need to convert the degrees to radians.

Solution

To convert degrees to radians, multiply the value by (`Math.PI` / 180):

```
var radians = degrees * (Math.PI / 180);
```

To convert radians to degrees, multiply the value by (180 / `Math.PI`):

```
var degrees = radians * (180 / Math.PI);
```

Discussion

All `Math` trigonometric methods (`sin`, `cos`, `tin`, `asin`, `acos`, `atan`, and `atan2`), take values in radians, and return radians as a result. Yet it's not unusual for people to provide values in degrees rather than radians, as degrees are the more familiar unit of measure. The functionality provided in the solution provides the conversion between the two units.

4.8 Find the Radius and Center of a Circle to Fit Within a Page Element

Problem

Given the width and height of a page element, you need to find the radius of the largest circle that fits within that page element, and its center point.

Solution

Find the smaller of the width and height; divide this by 2 to find the radius:

```
var circleRadius = Math.min(elementWidth, elementHeight) / 2;
```

Given the page element's width and height, find the center by dividing both by 2:

```
var x = elementWidth / 2;
var y = elementHeight / 2;
```

Discussion

Working with graphics requires us to do things such as finding the center of an element, or finding the radius of the largest circle that will fit into a rectangle (or largest rectangle that can fit in a circle).

Example 4-2 demonstrates both of the solution calculations, modifying an SVG circle contained within an XHTML document so that the circle fits within the `div` element that surrounds it.

Example 4-2. Fitting a SVG circle into a div element

```
<!DOCTYPE html>
<html xmlns="http://www.w3.org/1999/xhtml">
<head>
<title>Using Math method to fit a circle</title>
<style type="text/css">
#elem
{
    width: 400px;
    height: 200px;
    border: 1px solid #000;
}
</style>
<script type="text/javascript">
//<![CDATA[

function compStyle(elemId,property) {
    var elem = document.getElementById(elemId);
    var style;
    if (window.getComputedStyle)
      style=window.getComputedStyle(elem,null).getPropertyValue(property);
    else if (elem.currentStyle)
        style=elem.currentStyle[property];
    return style;
}
window.onload=function() {
  var height = parseInt(compStyle("elem","height"));
  var width = parseInt(compStyle("elem","width"));

  var x = width / 2;
  var y = height / 2;

  var circleRadius = Math.min(width,height) / 2;

  var circ = document.getElementById("circ");
  circ.setAttribute("r",circleRadius);
  circ.setAttribute("cx",x);
  circ.setAttribute("cy",y);
}
//--><!]]>
</script>

</head>
<body>
<div id="elem">
    <svg xmlns="http://www.w3.org/2000/svg" width="600" height="600">
      <circle id="circ" width="10" height="10" r="10" fill="red" />
    </svg>
</div>

</div>
</body>
```

Figure 4-1 shows the page once it's loaded. There are techniques in SVG that can accomplish the same procedure using the SVG element's `viewPort` setting, but even with these, at some point in time you'll need to polish off your basic geometry skills if you want to work with graphics. However, as the example demonstrates, most of the math you'll need is relatively simple, and basic.

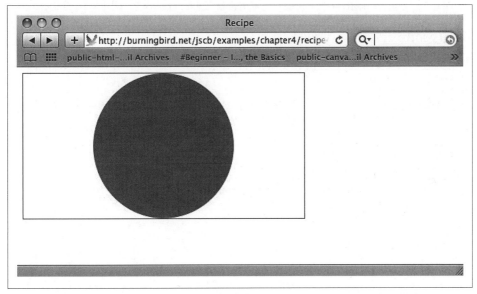

Figure 4-1. Page with SVG circle fit into rectangular div element

See Also

Finding a circle's radius and the center point of an element is important when working with both SVG and Canvas, covered in Chapter 15. The method used to find the computed width and height of the `div` element can be found in Recipe 13.2. Recipe 12.15 covers the `setAttribute` method.

SVG is not supported in IE8 and earlier, but should be supported in IE9.

4.9 Calculating the Length of a Circular Arc

Problem

Given the radius of a circle, and the angle of an arc in degrees, find the length of the arc.

Solution

Use `Math.PI` to convert degrees to radians, and use the result in a formula to find the length of the arc:

```
// angle of arc is 120 degrees, radius of circle is 2
var radians = degrees * (Math.PI / 180);
var arclength = radians * radius; // value is 4.18879020478...
```

Discussion

The length of a circular arc is found by multiplying the circle's radius times the angle of the arc, in radians.

If the angle is given in degrees, you'll need to convert the degree to radians first, before multiplying the angle by the radius.

See Also

The `Math` trigonometric methods provide essential functionality for creating various Canvas and SVG effects, discussed in Chapter 15. Recipe 4.7 covers how to convert between degrees and radians.

CHAPTER 5

Working with Arrays and Loops

5.0 Introduction

An array is an ordered collection of elements. In JavaScript, an array can be created using formal object notation, or it can be initialized using literal notation, as demonstrated in the following code:

```
var arrObject = new Array("val1", "val2"); // array as object
var arrLiteral = ["val1", "val2"]; // array literal
```

To the developer, there is no difference: you can invoke an **Array** method on both a literal and an object. However, to the JavaScript engine, an array literal has to be *reinterpreted* each time it's accessed, especially when used in a function call. On the positive side, though, array literals can replace the need for temporary variables, especially when sending values to a function.

A new **Array** object is created using the new operator, as follows:

```
var arrObject = new Array();
```

You can also create a new array that has some values:

```
var arrObject = new Array("val1","val2");
```

You can create an array literal by using square brackets to hold the array values. For instance, you can define an array literal and assign it to a variable:

```
var arrLiteral = ["val1","val2","val3"];
```

You can also create, and use, a literal array in a function or method call:

```
someFunction("param1", ["val1","val2"]);
```

Note, though, that when you pass a variable containing an array literal to a function, it is passed by reference—the same as passing a variable holding an **Array** object. Changes to the variable in the function are reflected outside of the function:

```
function chgArray(arr) {
    arr[0] = "surprise!";
}
```

```
var newArray = new Array("val1", "val2");
var newLiteral = ["val1","val2"];

chgArray(newArray);
chgArray(newLiteral);

alert(newArray); // prints surprise!,val2
alert(newLiteral); // prints surprise!,val2
```

An array, whether literal or object, can hold values of different data types:

```
var arrObject = new Array("val1", 34, true); // string, number, boolean
var arrLiteral = [arrObject, "val2", 18, false); // object, string, number, boolean
```

You can print out an array; the JavaScript engine will automatically convert the array into a string representation:

```
alert(arrLiteral); // prints out val1,34,true,val2,18,false
```

In this example, the JavaScript engine makes the array-to-string conversion for both the array literal and the array object contained as an element within the array literal.

Array elements can be accessed directly, using square brackets containing their *index* (position in the array). In addition, array elements can be set using the same index, which automatically creates the array element if it doesn't exist:

```
var arrObject = new Array();

arrObject[0] = "cat"; // array now has one element
alert(arrObject[0]); // prints cat
```

Arrays in JavaScript are zero-based, which means the first element index is zero, and the last element is at the array length, minus 1:

```
var farmAnimals = new Array("cat","dog","horse","pig");
alert(farmAnimals[0]); // print cat
alert(farmAnimals[3]); // print pig
```

Not all array elements have to be defined when created. For instance, if you create an array literal, you can use commas to delimit array elements that don't yet exist:

```
var arrLiteral = ["val1",,"val3"];
```

In this code, the second array element is currently `undefined`. You can't use the empty comma, though, to add an undefined array element to the end of the array: JavaScript will just ignore it.

To create an array of several undefined elements, you can provide an array length when creating an array:

```
var largeCollection = new Array(100); // a new array with 100 undefined elements
```

One you've created an array, using `Array` object or literal notation, you can access the array elements in a loop, or use any number of array methods.

5.1 Looping Through an Array

Problem

You want to easily access all elements of an array.

Solution

The most common approach to accessing an array is to use a `for` loop:

```
var mammals = new Array("cat","dog","human","whale","seal");
var animalString = "";
for (var i = 0; i < mammals. length; i++) {
   animalString += mammals[i] + " ";
}
alert(animalString);
```

Discussion

A `for` loop can be used to access every element of an array. The array begins at zero, and the array property `length` is used to set the loop end.

Sometimes, though, you don't want to access *every* element of the array. For instance, you might want to traverse an array until you find either a specific element, or any element that meets (or doesn't meet) a certain criteria. In these cases, you'll want to use a `while` loop and test the array elements:

```
var numArray = new Array(1,4,66,123,240,444,555);
var i = 0;

while (numArray[i] < 100) {
     alert(numArray[i++]);
}
```

Notice that the index counter, `i`, is incremented as it's used to access an array element. The use of `i++` means that the existing value of `i` is accessed first, and then the variable is incremented.

5.2 Creating a Multidimensional Array

Problem

You want to create a multidimensional array (an array of arrays).

Solution

Create an array in which each element is also an array. For example, to create an array with three elements, each of which is also an array of three elements containing, respectively, string, number, and array literals, use the code snippet in Example 5-1.

Example 5-1. Creating a multidimensional array

```
// set array length
var arrayLength = 3;

// create array
var multiArray = new Array(arrayLength);
for (var i = 0; i < multiArray.length; i++) {
  multiArray[i] = new Array(arrayLength);
}

// add items to first array index
multiArray[0][0] = "apple";
multiArray[0][1] = "banana";
multiArray[0][2] = "cherry";

// second
multiArray[1][0] = 2;
multiArray[1][1] = 56;
multiArray[1][2] = 83;

// third
multiArray[2][0] = ['test','again'];
multiArray[2][1] = ['Java','script'];
multiArray[2][2] = ['read','books'];

alert(multiArray); // printed out in first index order
alert(multiArray[2]); // prints out subarray
alert(multiArray[2][2][0]); // individual item
```

Discussion

Multidimensional arrays in JavaScript are managed by creating a new array as an element within an existing array. The new array can be created as an **Array** element, or as an array literal.

In Example 5-1, an array, *multiArray*, is created as an **Array** object with three members. Each of those three elements is also created as **Array** objects with three members. The array data is then set, with the first array member containing string literals, the second containing number literals, and the third array literals—themselves containing two array members, each with a string literal.

To access the array elements, use the square bracket notation, with each set of brackets used to address each level of the array. In the following code, the array contents are printed out via an alert window, after being converted to a string first, if necessary:

```
alert(multiArray[2]); // prints out test,again,Java,script,read,books
alert(multiArray[2][2]); // prints out read,books
alert(multiArray[2][2][1]); // prints out books
```

Multidimensional arrays are typically used to hold the data from a table structure, but how the structure is maintained is up to the developer. For instance, the developer can support an array structure in which the outer index reflects the columns, and the inner reflects the rows. As an example, Table 5-1 shows a simple five-column, three-row table containing a set of numbers.

Table 5-1. Simple table with five columns and three rows and sample data

45.89	4	34	9998.99	56
3	23	99	43	2
1	1	0	43	67

To create this in JavaScript using a multidimensional array, use the following code:

```
var table = new Array(5);

table[0] = [45.89, 4, 34, 9998.99, 56]; // first row
table[1] = [3, 23, 99, 43, 2]; // second row
table[2] = [1, 1, 0, 43, 67]; // third row
```

Of course, this doesn't take into account column and row headers. To add in the headers, just treat them as array data, making sure to incorporate them into the proper place in the array to reflect the table structure.

 In a multideveloper environment, it's essential that there is agreement among the developers about whether table structure data is stored column-centric or row-centric.

5.3 Creating a String from an Array

Problem

You want to create a single string from an array.

Solution

Use the `Array` object's built-in `join` method to join the array elements into a string:

```
var fruitArray = ['apple','peach','lemon','lime'];
var resultString = fruitArray.join('-'); // apple-peach-lemon-lime
```

Discussion

The `Array join` method takes one optional parameter, a delimiter used to separate the strings when joined—in this case, the dash (-). It returns a string with all of the array elements concatenated. If the array contains anything other than strings, the values are converted to a string equivalent:

```
var numberArray = [1,2,3,4,5]; // array literal containing number elements
var resultString = numberArray.join('+'); // returns string with 1+2+3+4+5
```

If the delimiter parameter isn't provided, a comma is inserted between array element values by default:

```
var numberArray = [1,2,3,4,5];
var resultString = numberArray.join(); // returns string with 1,2,3,4,5
```

5.4 Sorting an Array

Problem

You want to sort an array.

Solution

Use the Array object's sort method:

```
var fruitArray = ['strawberry','apple','orange','banana','lime'];
alert(fruitArray.sort()); // returns apple,banana,lime,orange,strawberry
```

Discussion

The Array object's sort method sorts the array elements alphabetically if no optional compare function parameter is provided. To facilitate the sort, all data types are converted to their string equivalent before sorting:

```
var numberArray = [4,13,2,31,5];
alert(numberArray.sort()); // returns  13,2,31,4,5
```

Though the array members in this example are numbers, they're sorted in lexicographical (dictionary) order, not numerically. To do an actual numeric sort, use a custom sort function:

```
function compareNumbers(a,b) {
   return a - b;
}
var numArray = [13,2,31,4,5];
alert(numArray.sort(compareNumbers)); // prints 2,4,5,13,31
```

The function subtracts the second parameter value from the first, and if the first is less than the second, a negative value is returned; otherwise, the value is positive. If the return value is less than zero, the sort index for the second parameter is set higher than the first parameter. If the value is greater than zero, the sort index for the first parameter is set higher than the other. If the value is exactly zero, the sort index for the two is unchanged.

If the array elements contain strings that could be converted to numbers, then the *compareNumbers* sort function still works, as number conversion is automatic:

```
var numberArray=["34","4","5"];
alert(numberArray.sort(compareNumbers)); // prints 4,5,34
```

The **sort** method sorts the elements in an ascending order. If you want to do a reverse sort, use the **sort** method to sort the elements, and then use the **reverse** method to reverse the array member order:

```
var numberArray = [4,5,1,3,2];
numberArray.sort();
numberArray.reverse(); // array now has 5,4,3,2,1
```

5.5 Store and Access Values in Order

Problem

You want to store values in such a way that you can access the values in the order in which they were stored.

Solution

To store and access values in the order in which they're received, create a FIFO (first-in, first-out) queue. Use the JavaScript **Array** object **push** method to add items to the queue, and **shift** to retrieve:

```
// create new array
var queue = new Array();

// push on three entries
queue.push('first');
queue.push('second');
queue.push('third');

// shift two entries
alert(queue.shift());  // returns first
alert(queue.shift());  // returns second
alert(queue);  // returns third
```

Discussion

A *queue* is an array of elements that are added one at a time, and retrieved in a first-in, first-out order (FIFO). Think of a line at the bank: people go to the end when they arrive at the bank, and tellers help those in the front of the line, who have been there the longest.

You could emulate this behavior using counter variables to hold the index of the last item added (the end), and the index of the last one retrieved (from the front), but luckily, the JavaScript **Array** object provides methods that handle this information for us, and also keep the array clean in the process.

The **Array push** method creates a new array element and adds it to the end of the array:

```
queue.push('first');
```

The array element count increments with each pushed element.

The `Array shift` method extracts the array element from the front of the array, removing it from the array, and returning the element:

```
var elem = queue.shift();
```

The array element count decreases by one with each shifted element, as `shift` also modifies the array in addition to returning the item.

5.6 Store and Access Values in Reverse Order

Problem

You want to store values in such a way that you can access the values in reverse order: access the most recently stored value first, then a LIFO (last-in, first-out) stack.

Solution

To access stored values in reverse order (last item added is accessed first), create a LIFO (last-in, first-out) stack. Use the JavaScript `Array` object's `push` method to add items to the stack, and the `pop` method to retrieve:

```
// create new array
var queue = new Array();

// push on three entries
queue.push('first');
queue.push('second');
queue.push('third');

// pop two entries
alert(queue.pop());  // returns third
alert(queue.pop());  // returns second
alert(queue); // returns first
```

Discussion

A *stack* is an array of elements, with each new element added to the top of the stack, and retrieved in a last-in, first-out (LIFO) order. Think of a stack of dishes: you add plates to the top as they're washed, and retrieve them from the top when needed. You could use a variable holding an integer that tracks the end of the array after each addition and retrieval, but JavaScript provides the functionality we need.

The `Array push` method creates a new array element and adds it to the end of the array:

```
queue.push('first');
```

The array element count increments with each pushed element.

The `Array pop` method extracts the array element from the end of the array, removing it from the array, and returning the element:

```
var elem = queue.pop();
```

The array element count decreases by one with each popped element, as `pop` modifies the array.

5.7 Create a New Array as a Subset of an Existing Array

Problem

You want to create a new array from a segment of an existing array. If the array elements are objects, you want to keep both arrays in sync.

Solution

Use the `Array` object `slice` method to create a new array based on elements within a given range:

```
var origArray = new Array(4);
origArray[0] = new Array("one","two");
origArray[1] = new Array("three","four");
origArray[2] = new Array("five","six");
origArray[3] = new Array("seven","eight");

// create new array using slice
var newArray = origArray.slice(1,3);
```

Discussion

The `Array slice` method is a simple way of building a new array from a consecutive sequence of elements in another array. The parameters are the beginning and ending index for the sequence of elements to copy. A negative value for either index indicates that `slice` should work from the end of the array.

If the copied elements are literal values, such as strings, numbers, and Booleans, they're copied *by value*—changing the value in the old array has no impact on the same values in the new array, and vice versa.

When objects are copied, though, they're copied *by reference*, whether they're copied via `slice` or by direct variable assignment:

```
var first = new Array("one","two","three");
var second = first; // copied by reference
second[1] = "apple"; // first and second arrays now have "one","apple","three"
```

The code that follows demonstrates the object syncing when used with slice. A section of one array is used to create a new array with `slice`. The elements in the first array are `Array` objects. In the code, when the value of one of the objects in the first array is changed, the change is reflected in the new array. Conversely, when a value is changed in the new array, the change is reflected in the original array:

```
var origArray = new Array(4);
origArray[0] = new Array("one","two");
```

```
origArray[1] = new Array("three","four");
origArray[2] = new Array("five","six");
origArray[3] = new Array("seven","eight");

var newArray = origArray.slice(1,3);
alert(newArray); // prints out three,four,five,six

// modify original
origArray[1][0] = "octopus";

// print out new
alert(newArray); // prints out octopus,four,five,six

// modify new
newArray[1][1] = "kitten";

// print out old
alert(origArray); // prints out one,two,octopus,four,five,kitten,seven,eight
```

Another handy use for slice is to convert the function arguments property into a proper array:

```
var args = Array.prototype.slice.call(arguments);
```

Using slice to create a subset of an array is a way of quickly copying a subset of an array and, if the values are objects, ensure both arrays are in sync. Be aware, though, that IE8 doesn't support slice.

5.8 Searching Through an Array

Problem

You want to search an array for a specific value and get the array element index if found.

Solution

Use the new (ECMAScript 5) Array object methods indexOf and lastIndexOf:

```
var animals = new Array("dog","cat","seal","elephant","walrus","lion");
alert(animals.indexOf("elephant")); // prints 3
```

Discussion

Though support for both indexOf and lastIndexOf has existed in browsers for some time, it's only been formalized with the release of ECMAScript 5. Both methods take a search value, which is then compared to every element in the array. If the value is found, both return an index representing the array element. If the value is not found, −1 is returned. The indexOf method returns the first one found, the lastIndexOf returns the last one found:

```
var animals = new Array("dog","cat","seal","walrus","lion", "cat");
```

```
alert(animals.indexOf("cat")); // prints 1
alert(animals.lastIndexOf("cat")); // prints 5
```

Both methods can take a starting index, setting where the search is going to start:

```
var animals = new Array("dog","cat","seal","walrus","lion", "cat");

alert(animals.indexOf("cat",2)); // prints 5
alert(animals.lastIndexOf("cat",4)); // prints 1
```

Currently, all of the book's target browsers support indexOf and lastIndexOf, except for IE8.

See Also

As mentioned, not all browsers support indexof and lastIndexOf. A cross-browser method to implement like functionality in these browsers is given in the Mozilla documentation, at *https://developer.mozilla.org/en/Core_JavaScript_1.5_Reference/Global _Objects/Array/indexOf*. Since IE8 doesn't support indexOf, here's the Mozilla workaround for the function:

```
if (!Array.prototype.indexOf)
{
  Array.prototype.indexOf = function(elt /*, from*/)
  {
    var len = this.length >>> 0;

    var from = Number(arguments[1]) || 0;
    from = (from < 0)
         ? Math.ceil(from)
         : Math.floor(from);
    if (from < 0)
      from += len;

    for (; from < len; from++)
    {
      if (from in this &&
          this[from] === elt)
        return from;
    }
    return -1;
  };
}
```

5.9 Flatten a Multidimensional Array

Problem

You want to flatten a multidimensional array into a single dimensional array.

Solution

Use the `Array` object `concat` method to merge the array dimensions into a single dimensional array:

```
var origArray = new Array();
origArray[0] = new Array("one","two");
origArray[1] = new Array("three","four");
origArray[2] = new Array("five","six");
origArray[3] = new Array("seven","eight");

// flatten array
var newArray = origArray[0].concat(origArray[1],origArray[2],origArray[3]);
alert(newArray[5]); // prints six
```

Discussion

The `Array` object `concat` method takes one or more arrays, and appends the array elements on to the end of the contents of the parent array on which the method was called. The merged array is then returned as a new array.

One use for this type of functionality is to return a single dimensional array made up of elements from a multidimensional array, as shown in the solution.

5.10 Search and Remove or Replace Array Elements

Problem

You want to find occurrences of a given value in an array, and either remove the element or replace with another value.

Solution

Use the `Array` methods `indexOf` and `splice` to find and remove/replace array elements:

```
var animals = new Array("dog","cat","seal","walrus","lion", "cat");

// remove the element from array
animals.splice(animals.indexOf("walrus"),1); // dog,cat,seal,lion,cat

// splice in new element
animals.splice(animals.lastIndexOf("cat"),1,"monkey"); // dog,cat,seal,lion,monkey
```

Discussion

The `splice` method takes three parameters. The first parameter is required; it's the index where the splicing is to take place. The other two parameters are optional: the number of elements to remove, and a substitute. If the index is negative, the elements will be spliced from the end, not from the beginning of the array:

```
var animals = new Array("cat","walrus","lion", "cat");

// splice in new element
animals.splice(-1,1,"monkey"); // cat,walrus,lion,monkey
```

If the number of elements to splice is not provided, all elements from the index to the end will be removed:

```
var animals = new Array("cat","walrus","lion", "cat");

// remove all elements after second
animals.splice(2); // cat,walrus
```

The last parameter, the replaced value, can be a set of replacement values, separated by commas:

```
var animals = new Array("cat","walrus","lion", "cat");

// replace second element with two
animals.splice(2,1,"zebra","elephant"); // cat,walrus,zebra,elephant,cat
```

Removing or replacing one element is handy, but being able to remove or replace all instances of a particular element is even handier. In Example 5-2, an array is created with several elements, including multiple instances of a specific value. The `splice` method is then used in a loop to replace all of the elements with this one value with elements with a new value. The `splice` method is used again, in a separate loop, to remove the newly spliced elements.

Example 5-2. Using looping and splice to replace and remove elements

```
<!DOCTYPE html>
<head>
<title>Looping and Splicing</title>
<meta http-equiv="Content-Type" content="text/html;charset=utf-8" >
<script>

var charSets = new Array("ab","bb","cd","ab","cc","ab","dd","ab");

// replace element
while (charSets.indexOf("ab") != -1) {
    charSets.splice(charSets.indexOf("ab"),1,"**");
}
alert(charSets); // **,bb,cd,**,cc,dd,**

// delete new element
while(charSets.indexOf("**") != -1) {
    charSets.splice(charSets.indexOf("**"),1);
}
alert(charSets); // bb,cd,cc,dd

</script>

</head>
<body>
</body>
```

The example works with all of this book's target browsers except for IE8, which doesn't currently support either indexOf or splice.

See Also

See Recipe 5.8 for a workaround for indexOf.

5.11 Applying a Function Against Each Array Element

Problem

You want to use a function to check an array value, and replace it if it matches a given criterion.

Solution

Use the new ECMAScript 5 Array object forEach to attach a *callback* function to each array element:

```
var charSets = new Array("ab","bb","cd","ab","cc","ab","dd","ab");

function replaceElement(element,index,array) {
   if (element == "ab") array[index] = "**";

}

// apply function to each array element
charSets.forEach(replaceElement);
alert(charSets); // prints **,bb,cd,**,cc,**,dd,**
```

Discussion

In the last section, we used a while loop to traverse an array to find and replace a value, but how much more helpful is it to use the forEach method?

The forEach method takes one parameter, the function. The function itself has three parameters: the array element, the index of the element, and the array. All three were used in the function, *replaceElement*.

First, the element's value is tested to see if it matches a given string, *ab*. If matched, the array element's index is used to modify the array element's value with the replacement string, **.

 Don't return a value from the function passed to the forEach method, as the value will be discarded.

Chrome, Firefox, Opera, and Safari support forEach, but IE8 does not.

See Also

The concept of callback functions is covered in more detail in Chapter 6.

Most modern browsers support forEach. However, for those that don't, you can emulate the forEach behavior using the Array.prototype property. Mozilla provides a description about how to emulate forEach at *https://developer.mozilla.org/en/Core_Java Script_1.5_Reference/Global_Objects/Array/forEach*. For completeness, I've duplicated the code below. To use, add the code into a library function and make sure it's processed before the forEach method is needed:

```
if (!Array.prototype.forEach)
{
  Array.prototype.forEach = function(fun /*, thisp*/)
  {
    var len = this.length >>> 0;
    if (typeof fun != "function")
      throw new TypeError();

    var thisp = arguments[1];
    for (var i = 0; i < len; i++)
    {
      if (i in this)
        fun.call(thisp, this[i], i, this);
    }
  };
}
```

5.12 Applying a Function to Every Element in an Array and Returning a New Array

Problem

You want to convert an array of decimal numbers into a new array with their hexadecimal equivalents.

Solution

Use the Array object map method to create a new array consisting of elements from the old array that have been modified via a callback function passed to the map method:

```
// function to convert decimal to hexadecimal
function convertToHex(element,index,array) {
   return element.toString(16);
}

var decArray = new Array(23, 255, 122, 5, 16, 99);

var hexArray = decArray.map(convertToHex);
alert(hexArray); // 17,ff,a,5,10,63
```

Discussion

Like the forEach method in Recipe 5.11, the ECMAScript 5 map method allows us to attach a callback function that is applied to each array element. Unlike forEach, though, the map method results in a new array rather than modifying the original array. Therefore, you won't return a value when using forEach, but you must return a value when using map.

The function that's passed to the map method has three parameters: the current array element, the index for the array element, and the array. The forEach and map methods are currently not supported by IE8.

See Also

Most modern browsers support the Array object map method, but to ensure that the functionality is present, you can use the Array.prototype property to emulate the method's behavior. See how at the Mozilla website (*https://developer.mozilla.org/en/Core_JavaScript_1.5_Reference/Global_Objects/Array/map*).

For comprehensiveness, I've included the code for the workaround below. To use, include the code in a library function that is processed before the map method is needed:

```
if (!Array.prototype.map)
{
  Array.prototype.map = function(fun /*, thisp*/)
  {
    var len = this.length >>> 0;
    if (typeof fun != "function")
      throw new TypeError();

    var res = new Array(len);
    var thisp = arguments[1];
    for (var i = 0; i < len; i++)
    {
      if (i in this)
        res[i] = fun.call(thisp, this[i], i, this);
    }

    return res;
  };
}
```

5.13 Creating a Filtered Array

Problem

You want to filter element values in an array and assign the results to a new array.

Solution

Use the `Array` object `filter` method:

```
function removeChars(element,index,array) {
   return (element !== "**");
}

var charSet = new Array("**","bb","cd","**","cc","**","dd","**");

var newArray = charSet.filter(removeChars);
alert(newArray); // bb,cd,cc,dd
```

Discussion

The `filter` method is another ECMAScript 5 addition, like `forEach` and `map`, covered in Recipes 5.11 and 5.12, respectively. Like them, the method is a way of applying a callback function to every array element.

The function passed as parameter to the `filter` method returns a Boolean value, true or false, based on some test against the array elements. This returned value determines if the array element is added to a new array: it is added if the function returns true; otherwise, it is not added. In the solution, the character string "**" is filtered from the original array when the new array is created.

The function has three parameters: the array element, the index for the element, and the array, itself. The `filter` method is not supported by IE8.

See Also

Support for `filter` is fairly broad, but to ensure access to the functionality, there is a way to emulate the filter method using `Array.prototype`. Mozilla details the approach at *https://developer.mozilla.org/en/Core_JavaScript_1.5_Reference/Global_Objects/Array/filter*, but I've copied the technique below. To use, include the function in your code, and run the function before you need to access the `filter` method:

```
if (!Array.prototype.filter)
{
  Array.prototype.filter = function(fun /*, thisp*/)
  {
    var len = this.length >>> 0;
    if (typeof fun != "function")
      throw new TypeError();

    var res = new Array();
    var thisp = arguments[1];
    for (var i = 0; i < len; i++)
    {
      if (i in this)
      {
        var val = this[i]; // in case fun mutates this
        if (fun.call(thisp, val, i, this))
```

```
            res.push(val);
        }
    }

    return res;
  };
}
```

5.14 Validating Array Contents

Problem

You want to ensure that an array meets certain criteria.

Solution

Use the `Array` object's **every** method to check that every element passes a given criteria. For instance, the following code checks to ensure that every element in the array is an alphanumeric character:

```
var elemSet = new Array("**",123,"aaa","abc","-",46,"AAA");

// testing function
function textValue (element,index,array) {
   var textExp = /^[a-zA-Z]+$/;
   return textExp.test(element);
}

// run test
alert(elemSet.every(textValue)); // false
```

Or use the `Array` object's **some** method to ensure that at least some of the elements pass the criteria. As an example, the following code checks to ensure that at least some of the array elements are alphanumeric strings:

```
var elemSet = new Array("**",123,"aaa","abc","-",46,"AAA");

// testing function
function textValue (element,index,array) {
   var textExp = /^[a-zA-Z]+$/;
   return textExp.test(element);
}

// run test
alert(elemSet.some(textValue)); // true
```

Discussion

The **every** and **some** `Array` object methods are the last of the ECMAScript 5 `Array` methods I'll be covering in this book. Unlike the `Array` callback function methods I covered in previous recipes in this chapter, **every** and **some** functions do not work against all array elements; they only process as many array elements as necessary to fulfill their functionality.

The solution demonstrates that the same callback function can be used for both the every and the some Array object methods. The difference is that when using the every method, as soon as the function returns a false value, the processing is finished, and the method returns false. The some method, though, will continue to test against every array element until the callback function returns true. At that time, no other elements are validated, and the method returns true. However, if the callback function tests against all elements, and doesn't return true at any point, the some method returns false.

Which method to use depends on your needs. If all array elements must meet certain criteria, then use every; otherwise, use some.

The callback function takes three parameters: the element, the index for the element, and the array. Neither the some or every method are supported by IE8, but they are supported by the other target browsers for this book.

See Also

Most modern browsers support every and some, but for those browsers that don't (such as most versions of Internet Explorer), you can emulate the behavior using the Array.prototype. Mozilla covers how to do this at *https://developer.mozilla.org/en/Core _JavaScript_1.5_Reference/Global_Objects/Array/some* and *https://developer.mozilla .org/en/Core_JavaScript_1.5_Reference/Global_Objects/Array/every*.

For comprehensiveness, I've also included the functionality below. To use, ensure that the script provided is processed before the methods are needed.

Here's how to emulate some:

```
if (!Array.prototype.some)
{
  Array.prototype.some = function(fun /*, thisp*/)
  {
    var i = 0,
        len = this.length >>> 0;

    if (typeof fun != "function")
      throw new TypeError();

    var thisp = arguments[1];
    for (; i < len; i++)
    {
      if (i in this &&
          fun.call(thisp, this[i], i, this))
        return true;
    }

    return false;
  };
}
```

Here's how to emulate **every**:

```
if (!Array.prototype.every)
{
  Array.prototype.every = function(fun /*, thisp*/)
  {
    var len = this.length >>> 0;
    if (typeof fun != "function")
      throw new TypeError();

    var thisp = arguments[1];
    for (var i = 0; i < len; i++)
    {
      if (i in this &&
          !fun.call(thisp, this[i], i, this))
        return false;
    }

    return true;
  };
}
```

5.15 Using an Associative Array to Store Form Element Names and Values

Problem

You want to store form element names and values, for later validation purposes.

Solution

Use an associative array to store the elements, using the element identifiers as array index:

```
var elemArray = new Object(); // notice Object, no Array
var elem = document.forms[0].elements[0];
elemArray[elem.id] = elem.value;
```

Iterate over the array using the **for...in** statement:

```
for (var key in elemArray) {
  str+=key + "," + elemArray[key] + " ";
}
```

Discussion

Most JavaScript arrays use a numeric index, such as the following:

```
arr[0] = value;
```

However, you can create an *associative array* in JavaScript, where the array index can be a string representing a keyword, mapping that string to a given value. In the solution, the array index is the identifier given the array element, and the actual array value is the form element value.

You *can* create an associative array, but you're not using the `Array` object to do so. Using the `Array` object is risky and actively discouraged—especially if you're using one of the built-in libraries that use the `prototype` attribute for extending objects, as people discovered when the popular Prototype.js library was first released several years ago.

The earlier Prototype.js library made an assumption that most array use in JavaScript is numeric index–based, like most of the earlier examples in this chapter. The library extended the `Array` object functionality via `Array.prototype`, based on this assumption. But extending `Array` objects in this way breaks the `for...in` loop functionality used to traverse an associative array created from an `Array` object.

It's not that Prototype.js was "breaking" JavaScript. The `for...in` loop was intended for one purpose: iterating over an object's properties, such as being able to loop through the `String` object's properties, or your own custom object properties.

When we use an `Array` object to create an associative array, what we're really doing is adding new properties to the array object, rather than adding new array elements. You could actually create an associative array with a `RegExp` or `String`, as well as an `Array`. The reason is that in JavaScript objects *are* associative arrays. When you're adding a new array, *element*:

```
obj[propName] = "somevalue";
```

what you're really doing is adding a new object property:

```
obj.propName = "somevalue";
```

To further demonstrate how different the associative array is from a numeric-based array, when you use an `Array` to create an associative array, you can't access the array "elements" by index, and the length property returns zero.

Instead of using an `Array` object to create the associative array, use the JavaScript `Object` directly. You get the exact same functionality, but avoid the clashes with libraries that extend the base `Array` object using `prototype`.

Example 5-3 shows a web page. Here, when the form is submitted, all of the form elements of type text are accessed and stored in an associative array. The element IDs are used as the array keyword, and the values assigned to the array elements. Once collected, the associative array is passed to another function that could be used to validate the values, but in this case just creates a string of keyword/value pairs, which is then displayed.

Example 5-3. Demonstrating associative array with form elements

```
<!DOCTYPE html>
<html xmlns="http://www.w3.org/1999/xhtml">
<head>
<title>Associative Array</title>
<script type="text/javascript">
//<![CDATA[

// get the form element names and values
function getVals() {
  var elems = document.getElementById("picker").elements;
  var elemArray = new Object();
  for (var i = 0; i < elems.length; i++) {
    if (elems[i].type == "text")
        elemArray[elems[i].id] = elems[i].value;
  }
  checkVals(elemArray);
  return false;
}

// check values
function checkVals(elemArray) {

  var str = "";
  for (var key in elemArray) {
    str+=key + "," + elemArray[key] + " ";
  }

 document.getElementById("result").innerHTML = str;
}

//--><!]]>
</script>
</head>
<body>
<form id="picker" onsubmit="return getVals()">
<label>Value 1:</label> <input type="text" id="first" /><br />
<label>Value 2:</label> <input type="text" id="second" /><br />
<label>Value 3:</label> <input type="text" id="third"  /><br />
<label>Value 4:</label> <input type="text" id="four"   /><br />
<input type="submit" value="Validate" />
</form>
<div id="result"></div>
</body>
</html>
```

In the example, notice that the array index is formed by the form element's id. When the array is traversed, the for loop syntax used is:

```
for (keyword in array)
```

This syntax accesses the array index, which is then assigned to the keyword variable that can be used to access the array value:

```
for (keyword in array)
    var a = array[keyword];
```

Figure 5-1 shows the example after values are typed into the form fields and the form is submitted.

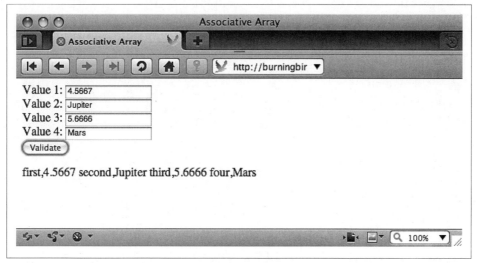

Figure 5-1. Demonstration of associative array and traversing form elements

This type of keyword/value pairing is commonly referred to as a *hash map* or *hash table*, though the JavaScript functionality isn't a true hash map functionality. The reason why it isn't a true hash map is that it doesn't account for the fact that the same keyword could be used with multiple values, and the JavaScript version only accepts strings as keywords.

See Also

See Chapter 16 for more on the object nature of JavaScript, and Recipe 16.3 for more information about extending the built-in objects, such as `Array`, using the `prototype` property. For more on the risks associated with associative arrays in JavaScript, read "JavaScript 'Associative Arrays' Considered Harmful" (*http://andrewdupont.net/2006/05/18/javascript-associative-arrays-considered-harmful/*), by Andrew Dupont.

CHAPTER 6

Building Reusability with JavaScript Functions

6.0 Introduction

JavaScript functions provide a way to encapsulate a block of code in order to reuse the code several times. They're typically created using the `function` statement and syntax similar to the following:

```
function functionname(arg1, arg2, ..., argn) {
    function body
}
```

JavaScript functions have `Function` objects, which can be constructed the same as a `String` or `Number`, using the `new` operator:

```
var fn = new Function (arg1, arg2, ..., argn, functionbody);
```

However, using this syntax is not as efficient as using the `function` statement, because using a function constructor requires that the function be parsed each time it's called. Functions defined with the `function` statement are parsed once, when the code is loaded.

There are three basic kinds of functions:

Declarative function
> A declarative function is a statement triggered by the use of the function keyword, and parsed when the JavaScript application is first loaded.

Anonymous function or function constructor
> An anonymous function is constructed using the new operator and referencing the `Function` object. It's anonymous because it isn't given a name, and access to the function occurs through a variable or another object property. It's parsed each time it's accessed.

Function literal or function expression
> As with other JavaScript objects, functions can be both object and literal. A literal function is a function expression, including parameter and body, which is used in place—such as in an argument to another function. Like a declarative function, it's also parsed only once, when the JavaScript application is loaded. Like the function created as an object, it can also be anonymous.

6.1 Creating a Block of Reusable Code

Problem

You want to create a block of code that you can use several times.

Solution

Create a simple, named, parameter-less function using the `function` statement:

```
function simpleFunction() {
    alert("Hello, function!");
};

simpleFunction();
```

Discussion

A function created using the `function` keyword and given a name is known as both a *declarative function* and a *static function*. The basic structure is:

```
function functionName() {
    // JavaScript statements
}
```

This type of function is parsed when the page containing the JavaScript application is loaded, and the parsed results are used whenever the function name is referenced. It's an efficient way of reusing the same code.

Any name that would be valid for a variable would work for a function. Variable names can be any combination of characters, numbers, and underscores, as long as the variable name starts with a character or underscore and case-sensitivity is preserved.

However, functions typically perform some action, and best practices suggest that the function name should be descriptive. For instance, a function that sums the numbers in an HTML table might be named *sumTableValues*.

6.2 Passing Single Data Values to and from a Function

Problem

You need to pass data values into a named function and get a result back.

Solution

Provide arguments for the incoming data, and return the result:

```
function makeHello(strName) {
   return ("Hello " + strName);
}

window.onload=function() {
   var name = prompt("What's your name?","");
   var greeting = makeHello(name);
   alert(greeting);
}
```

Discussion

Function arguments are a way to pass data to a function. The arguments are separated by commas and included in the parentheses following the function name:

```
var firstName = "Shelley":
var lastName = "Powers";

makeHello(firstName, lastName);
```

The function then processes the arguments, as needed:

```
function makeHello(firstName, lastName) {
    alert("Hello " + firstName + " " + lastName);
}
```

Data is returned from the function to the calling program using the **return** statement:

```
function makeHello(firstName, lastName) {
   return "Hello " + firstName + " " + lastName;
}
```

You can pass several arguments to the function, but only one return value. If you want to return more than one value, you can pass more complex objects, such as an array, to and from a function.

Unless you're sure about the type of data coming from the user, you'll want to also test the data first. For instance, if you want to ensure that a value passed to the function is a number, you could do the following:

```
function someFunc(num) {
   if (typeof num == "number") {
      ...
   }
}
```

You also don't have to provide a one-to-one mapping between the value passed to the object, and the number of function parameters. Every function has an `arguments` object which contains all of the arguments passed to the function. It's not a true function, but you can use array index notation to access the argument, and it does provide a length property for the number of arguments:

```
function sumNums() {
   var sum = 0;
   for (var i = 0; i < arguments.length; i++) {
      var num = parseFloat(arguments[i]);
      if (!isNaN(num)) {
         sum+=num;
      }
   }
   return sum;
}
...
var sum = sumNums(4.55, 3.0,1, "apple", 56.33);
```

See Also

Recipe 6.3 demonstrates passing more complex objects as arguments.

6.3 Passing Complex Data Objects to a Function

Problem

You need to pass more complex data to a function.

Solution

You can use objects, such as arrays, as function arguments:

```
function makeHello(name) {
   name[name.length] = "Hello " + name[0] + " " + name[1];
}
var name = new Array('Ima','Reader');
makeHello(name);
alert(name[2]); // displays "Hello Ima Reader"
```

Discussion

Function arguments in JavaScript can be scalar values, such as a string or number, or complex objects, such as arrays. Arrays are a simple way to pass many values to a function without having to create separate parameters for each. It's also a way to pass an unknown number of values to a function, such as an array of numbers to be summed:

```
function addNumbers(nums) {
   var total = 0;
   for (var i = 0; i < nums.length; i++) {
      total+=nums[i];
```

```
      }
      return total;
   }
```

A complex object is treated differently than a scalar argument in a function. In the solution, an array is passed to the *makeHello* function, but isn't returned from the function. However, the generated value added to the array in the function is still accessible to the calling program, because objects are passed into functions *by reference*.

Scalar arguments are passed *by value*, which means that a copy of the argument is made for processing in the function and changes to the argument in the function won't be reflected back to the calling program. Objects, though, are passed by reference: any changes to them in the function are reflected in the calling program.

Example 6-1 demonstrates the differences between scalar and complex objects when used as function arguments. The function takes two parameters, a string literal and an array. Both are modified in the function, and the contents of both are printed after the function returns control to the calling program.

Example 6-1. Functional differences between scalar and array arguments

```
<!DOCTYPE html>
<html xmlns="http://www.w3.org/1999/xhtml">
<head>
<title>Function test</title>
<script>
//<![CDATA[

window.onload=function() {
  var items = new Array('apple','orange','cherry','lime');
  var sep = '*';
  concatenateString(items,sep);

  alert(items);
  alert(sep);
}

function concatenateString(strings, separator) {
  var result="";
  for (var i = 0; i < strings.length; i++) {
    result+=strings[i] + separator;
  }

  // assign result to separator
  separator = result;

  // and array
  strings[strings.length]=result;
}


//--><!]]>
</script>
</head>
```

```
<body>
</body>
</html>
```

The array reflects the change that occurred in the function:

```
apple,orange,cherry,lime,apple*orange*cherry*lime*
```

While the string argument does not reflect the change, and consists only of the asterisk separator string (*).

6.4 Creating a Dynamic Runtime Function

Problem

You need to create a function, but you won't know its structure until runtime.

Solution

Use an anonymous function, created using the `Function` object constructor:

```
// two parameters and one function body string
var functionName = new Function (x, y, functionBody);
functionName(varA, varB); // two parameters are processed by function
```

Discussion

Functions created using the new `Function` object constructor are called *anonymous* functions because they're not given a function name when they're created. Instead, they're assigned to a variable. You then use the variable as you would a function call.

Anonymous functions are parsed at runtime, which makes them inefficient for general purposes. However, they allow us to define both parameters and function body at runtime, which is handy if you're not sure what the function body is going to be until runtime.

To demonstrate an anonymous function, I'm going to borrow an example from another of my books, *Learning JavaScript (http://oreilly.com/catalog/9780596521882/)* (O'Reilly), replicated in Example 6-2. This JavaScript application prompts the web page reader to provide a function that takes two parameters, as well as the value of the parameters. The application then uses these values to create the function and invoke it.

Example 6-2. Using an anonymous function

```
<!DOCTYPE html>
<html xmlns="http://www.w3.org/1999/xhtml">
<head>
<title>Anonymous Function</title>
<script>
//<![CDATA[
```

```
window.onload=function() {

    var func = prompt("Enter function body:","");
    var x = prompt("Enter value for x:","");
    var y = prompt("Enter value for y:","");

    var newFun = new Function("x","y",func);
    var result = newFun(x,y);

}


//--><!]]>
</script>
</head>
<body>
</body>
</html>
```

When prompted for the function body, use something simple such as this (shown in Figure 6-1):

```
alert(x + " " + y)
```

If you pass in *Hello* and *World* for the next two prompts, the result is an alert message with "Hello World".

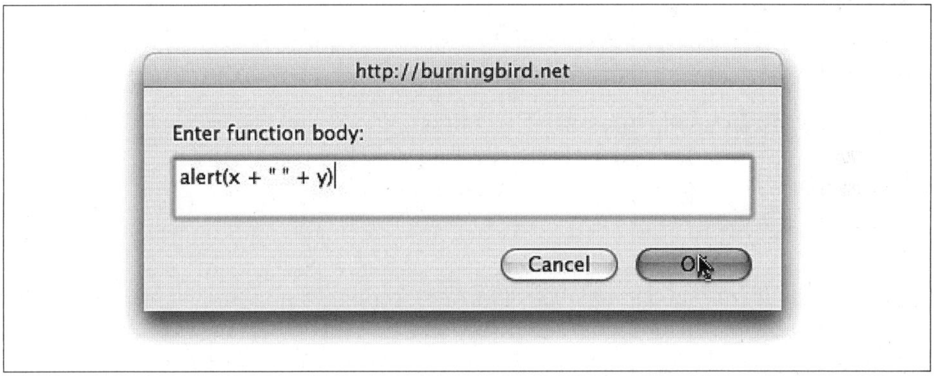

Figure 6-1. Entering function body for anonymous function

The function return value is assigned a variable, just in case the dynamic function body returns a value. If no value is returned, then the returned value is undefined.

Of course, using an anonymous function like this isn't the safest thing to do, because you can't control what the person enters as function body. And it's not particularly useful either.

Anonymous functions can be useful when passing functions as arguments, or assigning them to object properties. However, in most of these cases a literal function is preferred over a function object, because function literals are parsed once, when the application is loaded.

See Also

Literal functions are covered in Recipe 6.5.

6.5 Passing a Function As an Argument to Another Function

Problem

You want to pass a function as an argument to another function.

Solution

For the following function:

```
function otherFunction(x,y,z) {
   x(y,z);
}
```

use a *literal function*:

```
var param = function(arg1, arg2) { alert(arg1 + " " + arg2); };
otherFunction(param, "Hello", "World");
```

or a *function expression* as a function argument:

```
otherFunction(function(arg1,arg2) { alert(arg1 + ' ' + arg2); }, "Hello","World");
```

Discussion

The `function` keyword is an operator as well as a statement, and can be used to create a function as an expression. Functions created this way are called *function expressions*, *function literals*, and *anonymous functions*, though "anonymous functions" is an overloaded term since it applies to functions as objects, as well as functions as expressions.

A function name can be provided with literal functions, but it's only accessible within the function:

```
var param = function inner() { return typeof inner; }
alert(param()); // prints out "function"
```

This functionality may not seem useful, but it's essential if you want to implement recursion.

You can pass a function as an argument to another function as a named variable, or even directly within the argument list, as shown in the solution. Unlike functions constructed as objects, function literals are parsed when the page is loaded, rather than each time they're accessed.

See Also

See Recipe 6.6 for a demonstration of using a named function literal in recursion.

6.6 Implementing a Recursive Algorithm

Problem

You want to implement a function that will recursively traverse an array and return a reversed array string.

Solution

Use a function literal recursively until the end goal is met:

```
var reverseArray = function(x,indx,str) {
   return indx == 0 ? str : reverseArray(x,--indx,(str+= " " + x[indx]));;
}

var arr = new Array('apple','orange','peach','lime');
var str = reverseArray(arr,arr.length,"");
alert(str);

var arr2 = ['car','boat','sun','computer'];
str = reverseArray(arr2,arr2.length,"");
alert(str);
```

Discussion

Before looking at the solution, I want to cover the concept of recursion first, and the look at functional recursion.

Recursion is a well-known concept in the field of mathematics, as well as computer science. An example of recursion in mathematics is the *Fibonacci Sequence*:

$f_n = f_{n-1} + f_{n-2}$, for n= 2,3,4,...,n and $f_0 = 0$ and $f_1 = 1$

A Fibonacci number is the sum of the two previous Fibonacci numbers.

Another example of mathematical recursion is a *factorial*, usually denoted with an exclamation point (4!). A factorial is the product of all integers from 1 to a given number *n*. If *n* is 4, then the factorial (4!) would be:

$24 = 1 \times 2 \times 3 \times 4$

These recursions can be coded in JavaScript using functional recursion. A common example of JavaScript recursion is the solution for a Fibonacci:

```
var fibonacci = function (n) {
   return n < 2 ? n : fibonacci(n - 1) + fibonacci(n - 2);
}
```

or a factorial:

```
function Factorial(n) {
   return n == 1 ? 1 : n * Factorial(n -1);
}
var val = Factorial(4);
```

In the Fibonacci example, *n* is tested to see if it is less than 2. If it is, the value of *n* (2) is returned; otherwise the Fibonacci function is called again with (*n* – 1) and with (*n* – 2), and the sum of both is returned.

A little convoluted? The second example with the `Factorial` might be clearer. In this example, when the function is first called, the value passed as argument is compared to the number 1. If *n* is less than or equal to 1, the function terminates, returning 1.

However, if *n* is greater than 1, what's returned is the value of *n* times a call to the `Factorial` function again, this time passing in a value of *n* – 1. The value of *n*, then, decreases with each iteration of the function, until the terminating condition (or base) is reached.

What happens is that the interim values of the function call are pushed onto a stack in memory and kept until the termination condition is met. Then the values are popped from memory and returned, in a state similar to the following:

```
return 1;           // 0!
return 1;           // 1!
return 1 * 2;       // 2!
return 1 * 2 * 3;   // 3!
return 1 * 2 * 3 * 4;  // 4!
```

In the solution, we reverse the array elements by using a recursive function literal. Instead of beginning at index zero, we begin the array from the end length, and decrement this value with each iteration. When the value is zero, we return the string.

If we want the reverse, to concatenate the array elements, in order, to a string, we modify the function:

```
var orderArray = function(x,indx,str) {
  return indx == x.length-1 ? str : orderArray(x,++indx,(str+=x[indx] + " "));
}

var arr = new Array('apple','orange','peach','lime');
var str = orderArray(arr,-1,"");
```

Rather than the length of the array, we start with an index value of –1, and continue the loop until one less than the length of the array. We increment the index value, rather than decrement with each loop.

Most recursive functions can be replaced with code that performs the same function linearly, via some kind of loop. The advantage of recursion is that recursive functions can be fast, and efficient. The downside, though, is that recursive functions can be very memory-intensive.

See Also

Some of the negative consequences of recursive functions can be mitigated via *memoization*, covered in Recipe 6.9. Accessing the outer variable internally with the recursive function is covered in Recipe 6.7, which goes into function scope.

6.7 Create a Function That Remembers Its State

Problem

You want to create a function that can remember static data, but without having to use global variables and without resending the same data with each function call.

Solution

Create an outer function that takes one or more parameters, and then an inner function that also takes one or more parameters but uses both its and its parent function's parameters in order to perform its functionality. Return the inner function from the outer function, and assign it to a variable. From that point, use the variable as a function:

```
function greetingMaker(greeting) {
   function addName(name) {
      return greeting + " " + name;
   }
   return addName;
}

// Now, create new partial functions
var daytimeGreeting = greetingMaker("Good Day to you");
var nightGreeting = greetingMaker("Good Evening");

...

// if daytime
alert(daytimeGreeting(name));

// if night
alert(nightGreeting(name));
```

Discussion

We want to avoid global variables as much as possible because of potential clashes between libraries. However, there are times when you need to store data to be used across several function calls, and you don't want to have to repeatedly send this information to the function each time.

A way to persist this data from one function to another other is to create one of the functions within the other, so both have access to the data, and then return the inner function from the outer. Returning one function from another is known as a *function closure*. Before I get into the specifics of function closure, I want to spend a few minutes on functions and scope.

> This type of function closure is also known as a *partial function*, or *currying*, which is covered in detail in Recipe 6.8.

In the solution, the *inner function* `addName` is defined in the *outer function* `greeting Maker`. Both of the functions have one argument. The inner function has access to both its argument and the outer function's argument, but the outer function cannot access the argument passed to the inner function. The inner function can operate on the outer function's parameters because it is operating within the same context, or *scope*, of the outer function.

In JavaScript, there is one scope that is created for the outermost application environment. All global variables, functions, and objects are contained within this outer scope.

When you create a function, you create a new scope that exists as long as the function exists. The function has access to all variables in its scope, as well as all of the variables from the outer scope, but the outer scope does not have access to the variables in the function. Because of these scoping rules, we can access window and document objects in all of our browser applications, and the inner function in the solution can also access the data passed to, or originating in, the outer function that wraps it.

> This also explains how the recursive functions in Recipe 6.6 can internally access the variables they're assigned to in the outer application scope.

However, the outer function cannot access the inner function's arguments or local data, because they exist in a different scope.

An inner function doesn't have to be returned from the outer function. It could be an invoked direction in the code in the outer function. When it is returned, like in the solution, and the following code:

```
function outer (x) {
  return function(y) { return x * y; };
}

var multiThree = outer(3);
alert(multiThree(2)); // 6 is printed
alert(multiThree(3)); // 9 is printed
```

the returned function forms a *closure*. A JavaScript closure is a variable local to a function that remains alive when the function returns.

When the inner function is returned from the outer function, its application scope at the time, including all references to the outer function's variables, is now passed to the outer, global scope. So even though the outer function's application scope no longer exists, the inner function's scope exists *at the time the function was returned*, including a snapshot of the outer function's data. It will continue to exist until the application is finished, and the outer, global scope is released.

 Another way a closure can be made is if an inner function is assigned to a global variable.

So what happens to these variables when an application scope is released? JavaScript supports automatic garbage collection. What this means is you and I don't have to manually allocate or deallocate memory for our variables. Instead, the memory for variables is created automatically when we create variables and objects, and deallocated automatically when the variable scope is released.

In the solution, the outer function `greetingMaker` takes one argument, which is a specific greeting. It also returns an inner function, `addName`, which itself takes the person's name. In the code, `greetingMaker` is called twice, once with a daytime greeting, assigned to a variable called `daytimeGreeting`, and once with a nighttime greeting, assigned to a variable called `nightGreeting`.

Now, whenever we want to greet someone in daytime, we can use the daytime greeting function, `daytimeGreeting`, passing in the name of the person. The same applies to the nighttime greeting function, `nightGreeting`. No matter how many times each is used, the greeting string doesn't need to be respecified: we just pass in a different name. The specialized variations of the greeting remain in scope until the page that contains the application is unloaded from the browser.

Closures are interesting and useful, especially when working with JavaScript objects, as we'll see later in the book. But there is a downside to closures that turns up when we create accidental closures.

An accidental closure occurs when we code JavaScript that creates closures, but aren't aware that we've done so. Each closure takes up memory, and the more closures we create, the more memory is used. The problem is compounded if the memory isn't released when the application scope is released. When this happens, the result is a persistent memory leak.

Here's an example of an accidental closure:

```
function outerFunction() {
    var doc = document.getElementById("doc");
    var newObj = { 'doc' : doc};
    doc.newObj = newObj;
}
```

The newObj contains one property, doc, which contains a reference to the page element identified by doc. But then, this element is given a new property, newObj, which contains a reference to the new object you just created, which in turn contains a reference to the page element. This is a circular reference from object to page element, and page element to object.

The problem with this circular reference is exacerbated in earlier versions of IE, because IE does not release memory associated with DOM objects (such as the doc element) if application scope is released. Even leaving the page does not reclaim the memory: you have to close the browser.

 Other browsers detected this type of situation and performed a cleanup when the user left the application (the web page where the JavaScript resided).

Luckily, newer versions of IE don't have this problem. However, function closures should be deliberate, rather than accidental.

See Also

More on function closures and private function methods in Chapter 16. An excellent overview of function scope and closure is "JavaScript Closures" (*http://www.jibbering .com/faq/faq_notes/closures.html*), by Richard Cornford. Though written in 2004, it's still one of the best descriptions of closures. Mozilla provides a nice, clean description of closures at *https://developer.mozilla.org/en/Core_JavaScript_1.5_Guide/Working _with_Closures*.

Recipe 6.8 also makes use of specialized function closure, specifically for simplifying the number of arguments that have to be passed to functions, an effect called *currying*.

6.8 Improving Application Performance with a Generalized Currying Function

Problem

You have several functions you want to simplify by attaching recurring argument values to the functions, so the arguments don't have to be repeated.

Solution

Use the concept of *currying*, a specialized form of function closure, to create a function generator that takes the function name and the persisted arguments, and returns a new partial function that only needs the remaining arguments. Here is the **curry** function I adapted from a function created by Dustin Diaz, which works in all of this book's target browsers:

```
function curry (fn, scope) {
    var scope = scope || window;
    var args = [];
    for (var i=2, len = arguments.length; i < len; ++i) {
        args.push(arguments[i]);
    };
    return function() {
        var args2 = [];
        for (var i = 0; i < arguments.length; i++) {
            args2.push(arguments[i]);
        }
        var argstotal = args.concat(args2);
        return fn.apply(scope, argstotal);
    };
}
```

When you want to *curry* a function, you pass the function name, and whatever values you want statically assigned to the returned function:

```
function diffPoint (x1, y1, x2, y2) {
    return [Math.abs(x2 - x1), Math.abs(y2 - y1)];
}
var diffOrigin = curry(diffPoint, null, 3.0, 4.0);
var newPt = diffOrigin(6.42, 8.0); // array with 3.42, 4
```

Discussion

A typical function could be like the following, which takes two pairs of numbers (an origin and a new location) and returns an array with the difference between the two:

```
function diffPoint (x1, y1, x2, y2) {
    return [x2 - x1, y2 - y1];
}
```

The function is fine, but if the origin is going to be the same across many calls to the function, wouldn't it be nice to somehow attach this information to the function? Currying is the process that allows us to do this.

Currying is a way of statically attaching more than one argument to a function, so the argument doesn't have to be duplicated. We demonstrated one form of currying in Recipe 6.7, but in that case, we created a single purpose outer function in order to provide the currying functionality for the inner function.

In the solution, what I've done is create a multipurpose currying function that can perform this functionality for any method in which we want to split parameters between those repeated and those not. In the `curry` method, I capture the arguments for the first function call, and those from the second, concatenate the two, and then use the `Function apply` method to return a function with the combined set of arguments.

The code then uses the `curry` method to create a new function, `diffOrigin`, that finds the difference between the point and a given origin, in this case, where origin is at x = 3, y = 4:

```
var diffOrigin = curry(diffPoint, null, 3.0, 4.0);
var newPt = diffOrigin(6.42, 8.0); // array with 3.42, 4
```

We can use the same curry method with `diffPoint` and another set of origin points:

```
var farPoint = curry (diffPoint, null, 183.66, 98.77);
```

and then use it as many times as needed:

```
var ptA = farPoint(1.33, 2.11);
var point0 = genFunction(0,0);  // 182.329999..., 96.66
```

The curry method can also take a scope as an argument. In the example, there is no specialized scope, so the window object is used. However, I could also have passed in a reference to an element or other object, and then the inner function would have access to that object's context.

See Also

A `curry` method is provided in many JavaScript libraries, such as Dojo, jQuery, and Prototype.js, either directly or as an extension. The `Function apply` method is demonstrated in Chapter 16, beginning with Recipe 16.5. See another example of function closure and currying in Recipe 6.7.

6.9 Improve Application Performance with Memoization (Caching Calculations)

Problem

You want to optimize your JavaScript applications and libraries by reducing the need to repeat complex and CPU-intensive computations.

Solution

Use function *memoization* in order to cache the results of a complex calculation. Here, I'm borrowing an example from Douglas Crockford's book, *JavaScript: The Good Parts (http://oreilly.com/catalog/9780596517748/)* (O'Reilly), as applied to the code to generate a Fibonacci number:

```
var fibonacci = function () {
    var memo = [0,1];
    var fib = function (n) {
        var result = memo[n];
        if (typeof result != "number") {
    result = fib(n -1) + fib(n - 2);
      memo[n] = result;
        }
        return result;
    };
    return fib;
}();
```

Discussion

Memoization is the process where interim values are cached, rather than recreated, cutting down on the number of iterations and computation time. It works especially well with something like the Fibonacci numbers, or factorials, both of which operate against previously calculated values. For instance, we can look at a factorial, 4!, as follows:

return 1;	// 0!
return 1;	// 1!
return 1 * 2;	// 2!
return 1 * 2 * 3;	// 3!
return 1 * 2 * 3 * 4;	// 4!
But we can also view it as:	3! * 4 // 4!

In other words, if we cache the value for 2! when creating 3!, we don't need to recalculate 1 * 2; and if we cache 3! when calculating 4!, we don't need 1 * 2 * 3, and so on.

Memoization is built into some languages, such as Java, Perl, Lisp, and others, but not into JavaScript. If we want to memoize a function, we have to build the functionality ourselves. The key to the effective use of memoization is being aware that the technique doesn't result in performance improvements until the number of operations is significant enough to compensate for the extra effort.

Example 6-3 shows the memoized and nonmemoized versions of the Fibonacci function that Crockford provided in his book. The example also uses the Console API to record times, so you'll need to run the application in Firefox or Safari. Make sure the tool's Console is open. Note that the calculations are intense and can take a considerable time. Save any work you have in other tabs. You may have to override a message given by the browser, too, about killing a script that's running a long time.

Example 6-3. A demonstration of memoization

```
<!DOCTYPE html>
<html xmlns="http://www.w3.org/1999/xhtml">
<head>
<title>Testing Memoization</title>
<script>
//<![CDATA[

window.onload=function() {

// Memoized Function
var fibonacci = function () {
    var memo = [0,1];
    var fib = function (n) {
        var result = memo[n];
        if (typeof result != "number") {
            result = fib(n -1) + fib(n - 2);
            memo[n] = result;
        }
        return result;
    };
    return fib;
}();

// nonmemoized function
var fib = function (n) {
    return n < 2 ? n : fib(n - 1) + fib(n - 2);
};
// run nonmemo function, with timer
console.time("non-memo");
for (var i = 0; i <= 10; i++) {
    console.log(i + " " + fib(i));
}
console.timeEnd("non-memo");

// now, memo function with timer
console.time("memo");
for (var i = 0; i <= 10; i++) {
    console.log(i + " " + fibonacci(i));
```

```
}
console.timeEnd("memo");

}
//--><![]]>
</script>
</head>
<body>
<p>content</p>
</body>
</html>
```

First, the code is run against a number of 10. The result is as follows, and as shown in Figure 6-2:

```
non-memo: 39ms
memo: 38ms
```

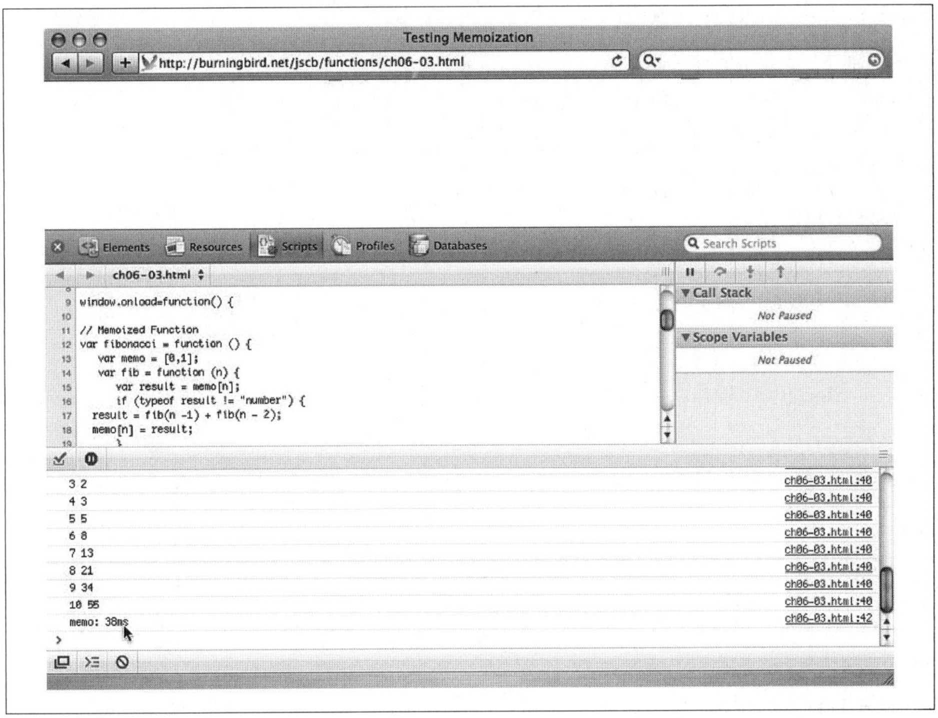

Figure 6-2. Memoization program running in Safari, with debugger and console displayed

The result generates one big "meh." In the second run, though, the code is edited to run the code in a `for` loop of 30. The result is as follows:

```
non-memo: 54761ms
memo: 160ms
```

A major change.

See Also

There's little information on JavaScript memoization online. There has been effort to create memoize functions that can work with all functions that would benefit. Crockford provided one in his book, *JavaScript: The Good Parts (http://oreilly.com/catalog/9780596517748/)* (O'Reilly). Other discussions on the topic can be found by searching for "JavaScript memoization" in your favorite search engine.

6.10 Using an Anonymous Function to Wrap Global Variables

Problem

You need to create a variable that maintains state between function calls, but you want to avoid global variables.

Solution

Use an anonymous function to wrap variables and functions both:

```
<!DOCTYPE html>
<head>
<title>faux Global</title>
<script>

(function() {
  var i = 0;

  function increment() {
    i++;
    alert("value is " + i);
  }

  function runIncrement() {
    while (i < 5) {
      increment();
    }
  }

  window.onload=function() {
    runIncrement();
  }
})();

</script>
</head>
<body>
</body>
```

Discussion

The functionality demonstrated in the solution has existed for some time, but I've only seen anonymous functions as a way to scope what would normally be global variables in John Resig's work with the jQuery framework library. It's used as a way of wrapping jQuery plug-in functions so that the code can use the jQuery dollar sign function ($) when the jQuery plug-in is used with another framework library, such as Prototype, which also uses the dollar sign function:

```
// swap colors, blue and red
(function($) {
    $.fn.flashBlueRed = function() {
        return this.each(function() {
          var hex = $.bbConvertRGBtoHex($(this).css("background-color"));
          if (hex == "#0000ff") {
              $(this).css("background-color", "#ff0000");
            } else {
              $(this).css("background-color", "#0000ff");
            }
        });
    };
})(jQuery);
```

The approach consists of surrounding the code block with parentheses, beginning with the anonymous function syntax, and following up with the code block and then the final function closure. It could be the following, if there's no parameter passed into the code block:

```
})();
```

or the following, if you are passing a parameter into the function:

```
})(jQuery);
```

Now you can use as many "global" variables as you need without polluting the global space or colliding with global variables used in other libraries.

See Also

Recipe 17.7 covers writing jQuery plug-ins.

CHAPTER 7

Handling Events

7.0 Introduction

Events, especially within an interactive environment such as a browser, are what make JavaScript essential. There is very little JavaScript functionality that isn't triggered by *some* event, even if the only event that occurs is a web page being loaded. Event handling in JavaScript depends on determining which event or events you want to trigger some activity, and then attaching JavaScript functionality to the event.

The earliest form of event handling is still one of the most common: the use of an event handler. An event handler is an element property that you can assign a function, such as the following, which assigns a function to the `window.onload` event handler:

```
window.onload=someFunction;
```

You can also assign an event handler directly in an element, such as in the opening `body` tag:

```
<body onload="someFunction()">
```

However, I don't recommend embedding events directly in page elements, as it makes it difficult to find and change the event handling routines later. If you use the first approach, which is to assign a function to an event handler in script element or in a JavaScript library, you only have to look in one place in order to make changes.

 JavaScript lives in an enormous number of environments, as Chapter 21 demonstrates. Most of this chapter is focused on JavaScript within a browser or browser-like environment.

Some Common Events

There are several events that can be captured via JavaScript, though not all are available to all web page elements. The `load` and `unload` events are typically used with the window object to signal when the page is finished loading, and just before the page is unloaded because the web page reader is navigating away from the page. The submit and reset events are used with forms to signal when the form is submitted, or has been reset by the reader.

The blur and focus events are frequently used with form elements, to determine when an element gets focus, and loses it. Changing a form value can trigger the change event. The blur and change events are especially handy if you need to validate the form values.

Most web page elements can receive the click or dblclick event. Other mouse events include mousedown, mousemove, mouseout, mouseover, and mouseup, which can be used to track the cursor and mouse activity.

You can also track keyboard activity with events such as keydown and keyup, as well as keypress. If something can be scrolled, you can typically capture a scroll event.

Event History and New Event Handling

There's a history to event handling with JavaScript. The earliest form of event handling is frequently termed "DOM Level 0" event handling, even though there is no DOM Level 0. It involves assigning a function directly to an event handler.

You can assign the event handler in the element directly:

```
<div onclick="clickFunction()">
```

or assign a function to the event handler in a script element or JavaScript library:

```
window.onload=someFunction;
```

In the last several years, a newer DOM Level 2 event handling system has emerged and achieved widespread use. With DOM Level 2 event handling, you don't assign a function to an event handler directly; instead, you add the function as an event listener:

```
window.addEventListener("load",loadFunction,false);
```

The general syntax is:

```
targetElement.addEventListener(typeOfEvent,listenerFunction,
                  useCapture);
```

The last parameter in the function call has to do with how events are handled in a stack of nested elements. For example, if you're capturing an event for a link within a div element, and you want both elements to do some processing based on the event, when you assign the event listener to the link, set the last parameter to false, so the event bubbles up to the div element.

You can also remove event listeners, as well as cancel the events themselves. You can also prevent the event from propagating if the element receiving the event is nested in another element. Canceling an event is helpful when dealing with form validation, and preventing event propagation is helpful when processing click events.

It's up to you to decide which level of event handling meets your needs. If you're doing simple event handling—not using any external JavaScript libraries and not worried about canceling events, or whether events bubble up in a stack of elements—you can use DOM Level 0 events. Most of the examples in this book use `window.onload` to trigger the demonstration JavaScript.

If you need the more sophisticated event handling, including the ability to more easily control events, you'll want to use DOM Level 2 events. They can be easily encapsulated into a JavaScript library, and can be safely integrated into a multi-JavaScript library environment. However, the fly in this little event handling pie is that the DOM Level 2 event handling isn't supported universally by all browsers: Microsoft has not implemented DOM Level 2 event handling with IE8 or earlier. However, it's fairly simple to work around the cross-browser issues, as detailed in Recipe 7.3.

 There's ongoing work to create a new DOM Level 3 event handling, which builds on the work of the DOM Level 2 event handling and is included as part of the Web Applications work at the W3C. However, implementation of the newer material is sparse, at best.

New Events, New Uses

There are newer events to go with the newer models, and to go with a nonbrowser-specific DOM. As examples of DOM events, the `DOMNodeInserted` and `DOMNodeRe moved` events are triggered when a node is added or removed from the page's document tree. However, I don't recommend using the W3C event for general web pages, as these events are not supported in the current versions of IE, and only partially supported in most other browsers. Most web application authors wouldn't need these events, anyway.

There are also events associated with the increasingly popular mobile and other hand-held computing environments. For instance, Firefox has a nonstandard set of events having to do with *touch swiping*, which Mozilla calls the *mouse gesture events*. It's interesting, but use with caution until there's wider acceptance of the newer events. We'll take a look at one type of mobile device event handling towards the end of the chapter.

See Also

See Recipe 7.3 for a demonstration of handling cross-browser event handling.

7.1 Detecting When the Page Has Finished Loading

Problem

You want to run a function after the page is finished loading.

Solution

Capture the load event via the `onload` event handler on the window:

```
window.onload=functionName;
```

Or:

```
window.onload=function() {
    var someDiv = document.getElementById("somediv");
    ...
}
```

Discussion

Prior to accessing any page element, you have to first make sure it's been loaded into the browser. You could add a script block into the web page after the element. A better approach, though, is to capture the window `load` event and do your element manipulation at that time.

This recipe uses the DOM Level 0 event handling, which assigns a function or functionality to an event handler. An event handler is an object property with this syntax:

```
element.onevent=functionName;
```

Where `element` is the target element for the event, and `onevent` is the specific event handler. Since the event handler is a property of the window object, as other objects also have access to their own event handler properties, it's accessed using *dot notation* (`.`), which is how object properties are accessed in JavaScript.

The window `onload` event handler in the solution is assigned as follows:

```
window.onload=functionName;
```

You could also use the `onload` event handler directly in the element. For the window load event, attach the `onload` event handler to the body element:

```
<body onload="functionName()">
```

Use caution with assigning event handlers directly in elements, though, as it becomes more difficult to find them if you need to change them at a later time. There's also a good likelihood of element event handlers eventually being deprecated.

See Also

See Recipe 7.3 for a discussion about the problems with using this type of DOM Level 0 event handling.

7.2 Capturing the Location of a Mouse Click Event Using the Event Object

Problem

You need to discover the location in the web page where a mouse click occurred.

Solution

Assign the `onclick` event handler to the `document` object, and when the event handler function is processed, access the click location from the `Event` object:

```
document.onclick=processClick;
...
function processClick(evt) {

   // access event object
   evt = evt || window.event;
   var x = 0; var y = 0;

   // if event object has pageX property
   // get position using pageX, pageY
   if (evt.pageX) {
      x = evt.pageX;
      y = evt.pageY;

   // else if event has clientX property
   } else if (evt.clientX) {
      var offsetX = 0; offsetY = 0;

      // if documentElement.scrollLeft supported
      if (document.documentElement.scrollLeft) {
          offsetX = document.documentElement.scrollLeft;
          offsetY = document.documentElement.scrollTop;
      } else if (document.body) {
          offsetX = document.body.scrollLeft;
          offsetY = document.body.scrollTop;
      }

      x = evt.clientX + offsetX;
      y = evt.clientY + offsetY;
   }

   alert ("you clicked at x=" + x + " y=" + y);
}
```

Discussion

Whoa! We didn't expect all of this for a simple task such as finding the location in the page of a mouse click. Unfortunately, this recipe is a good demonstration of the cross-browser challenges associated with JavaScript event handling.

From the top: first, we need to find information about the event from the *event object*. The event object contains information specific to the event, such as what element received the event, the given location relative to the event, the key pressed for a key press event, and so on.

In the solution, we immediately run into a cross-browser difference in how we access this object. In IE8 and earlier, the Event object is accessible from the Window object; in other browsers, such as Firefox, Opera, Chrome, and Safari, the Event object is passed, by default, as a parameter to the event handler function.

The way to handle most cross-browser object differences is to use a conditional OR (||) operator, which tests to see if the object is not null. In the case of the event object, the function argument is tested. If it is null, then window.event is assigned to the variable. If it isn't, then it's reassigned to itself:

```
evt = evt || window.event;
```

You'll also see another approach that's not uncommon, and uses the *ternary operator*, to test to see if the argument has been defined and is not null. If it isn't, the argument is assigned back to the argument variable. If it is, the window.event object is accessed and assigned to the same argument variable:

```
evt = evt ? evt : window.event;
```

Once we've worked through the event object difference, we're on to the next. Firefox, Opera, Chrome, and Safari both get the mouse location in the web page via the nonstandard event pageX and pageY properties. However, IE8 doesn't support these properties. Instead, your code can access the clientX and clientY properties, but it can't use them as is. You have to adjust the value to account for any offset value, due to the window being scrolled.

Again, to find this offset, you have to account for differences, primarily because of different versions of IE accessing your site. Now, we could consider disregarding anything older than IE6, and that's an option. For the moment, though, I'll show support for versions of IE both older and newer than IE6.

For IE6 strict and up, you'll use document.documentElement.scrollLeft and document.documentElement.scrollTop. For older versions, you'll use document.body.scrollLeft and document.body.scrollTop. Here's an example of using conditional statements:

```
var offsetX = 0; offsetY = 0;
if (document.documentElement.scrollLeft) {
    offsetX = document.documentElement.scrollLeft;
    offsetY = document.documentElement.scrollTop;
} else if (document.body) {
    offsetX = document.body.scrollLeft;
    offsetY = document.body.scrollTop;
}
```

Once you have the horizontal and vertical offsets, add them to the `clientX` and `clientY` values, respectively. You'll then have the same value as what you had with `pageX` and `pageY`:

```
x = evt.clientX + offsetX;
y = evt.clientY + offsetY;
```

To see how all of this holds together, Example 7-1 shows a web page with a red box. When you click anywhere in the web page, the box is moved so that the top-left corner of the box is positioned exactly where you clicked. The example implements all of the various cross-browser workarounds, and operates safely in all the main browser types, even various older browsers.

Example 7-1. Capturing the mouse-click location and moving element to location

```
<!DOCTYPE html>
<head>
<title>Box Click Box Move</title>
<style type="text/css">

#info
{
  width: 100px; height: 100px;
  background-color: #ff0000;
  position: absolute;
  top: 0;
  left: 0;
}
</style>
<script>

window.onload=function() {
  document.onclick=processClick;
}

function processClick(evt) {
  evt = evt || window.event;
  var x = 0; var y = 0;
  if (evt.pageX) {
    x = evt.pageX;
    y = evt.pageY;
  } else if (evt.clientX) {
    var offsetX = 0; offsetY = 0;
    if (document.documentElement.scrollLeft) {
      offsetX = document.documentElement.scrollLeft;
      offsetY = document.documentElement.scrollTop;
    } else if (document.body) {
      offsetX = document.body.scrollLeft;
      offsetY = document.body.scrollTop;
    }

    x = evt.clientX + offsetX;
    y = evt.clientY + offsetY;
  }
```

```
    var style = "left: " + x + "px; top: " + y + "px";
    var box = document.getElementById("info");
    box.setAttribute("style", style);
}
</script>
</head>
<body>
<div id="info"></div>
</body>
```

Cross-browser differences may seem overwhelming at times, but most of the code can be packaged into a library as a reusable event handler. However, there is a good likelihood that many of these browser differences will vanish with IE9.

 The example doesn't work with IE7 because of the use of setAttribute with the style attribute. The downloaded example contains a workaround.

See Also

Mozilla has, as usual, excellent documentation on the event object at *https://developer .mozilla.org/En/DOM/Event*. See Recipe 12.15 for a description of setAttribute.

7.3 Creating a Generic, Reusable Event Handler Function

Problem

You want to implement DOM Level 2 event handling, but the solution needs to be reusable and cross-browser friendly.

Solution

Create a reusable event handler function that implements DOM Level 2 event handling, but is also cross-browser friendly. Test for object support to determine which functions to use:

```
function listenEvent(eventTarget, eventType, eventHandler) {
   if (eventTarget.addEventListener) {
      eventTarget.addEventListener(eventType, eventHandler,false);
   } else if (eventTarget.attachEvent) {
      eventType = "on" + eventType;
      eventTarget.attachEvent(eventType, eventHandler);
   } else {
      eventTarget["on" + eventType] = eventHandler;
   }
}
```

```
...
listenEvent(document, "click", processClick);
```

Discussion

The reusable event handler function takes three arguments: the target object, the event (as a string), and the function name. The object is first tested to see if it supports addEventListener, the W3C DOM Level 2 event listener method. If it is supported, this method is used to map the event to the event handler function.

The first two arguments to addEventListener are the event string and the event handler function. The last argument in addEventListener is a Boolean indicating how the event is handled with nested elements (in those cases where more than one element has an event listener attached to the same event). An example would be a div element in a web page document, where both the div and document have event listeners attached to their click events.

In the solution, the third parameter is set to false, which means that the listener for an outer element (document) doesn't "capture" the event, but allows it to be dispatched to the nested elements (the div) first. When the div element is clicked, the event handler function is processed for the div first, and then the document. In other words, the event is allowed to "bubble up" through the nested elements.

However, if you set the third parameter to true, the event is captured in the outer element, and then allowed to "cascade down" to the nested elements. If you were to click the div element, the document's click event would be processed first, and then the div.

Most of the time, we want the events to bubble up from inner nested elements to outer elements, which is why the generic function is set to false by default. However, to provide flexibility, you could add a third parameter to the reusable function, allowing the users to determine whether they want the default bubble-up behavior or the cascade-down instead.

 Most JavaScript libraries, applications, and developers assume that events are processed in a bubble-up fashion. If you are using external material, be very cautious about setting events to be cascade-down.

To return to the solution, if addEventListener is not supported, then the application checks to see if attachEvent is supported, which is what Microsoft supports in IE8. If this method is supported, the event is first modified by prepending "on" to it (required for use with attachEvent), and then the event and event handler function are mapped.

Notice that attachEvent doesn't have a third parameter to control whether the event is bubble-up or cascade-down. That's because Microsoft only supports bubble-up.

Lastly, in the rare case where neither `addEventListener` nor `attachEvent` is supported, the fallback method is used: the DOM Level 0 event handling. If we're not worried about very old browsers, such as IE5, we can leave off the last part.

Why go through all of this work when we can just use the simpler DOM Level 0 event handling? The quick answer is *compatibility*.

When we use DOM Level 0 event handling, we're assigning an event handler function to an object's event:

```
document.onclick=functionName;
```

If we're using one or more JavaScript libraries in addition to our code, we can easily wipe out the JavaScript library's event handling. The only way to work around the overwriting problem is the following, created by highly respected developer Simon Willison:

```
function addLoadEvent(func) {
  var oldonload = window.onload;
  if (typeof window.onload != 'function') {
    window.onload = func;
  } else {
    window.onload = function() {
      if (oldonload) {
        oldonload();
      }
      func();
    }
  }
}
```

In the function, whatever the `window.onload` event handler is assigned, is assigned to a variable. The type is checked and if it's not a function, we can safely assign our function. If it is, though, we assign an anonymous function to the event handler, and in the anonymous function, invoke both our function and the one previously assigned.

However, a better option is to use the more modern event listeners. With DOM Level 2 event listeners, each library's function is added to the event handler without over-writing what already exists; they're even processed in the order they're added.

 The differences in how browsers handle events goes much deeper than what method to use. Recipes 7.5 and 7.7 cover other differences associated with the cross-browser event handling.

To summarize, if you're just doing a quick and dirty JavaScript application, without using any libraries, you can get away with DOM Level 0 events. I use them for most of the small examples in this book. However, if you're building web pages that could use libraries some day, you're better off using DOM Level 2. Luckily, most JavaScript libraries already provide the cross-browser event handling functions.

Reusable, DOM Level 2 event handling: piece of cake. Except that we're not finished.

Creating a universal stop-listening function

There will be times when we want to stop listening to an event, so we need to create a cross-browser function to handle stopping events:

```
function stopListening (eventTarget,eventType,eventHandler) {
    if (eventTarget.removeEventListener) {
        eventTarget.removeEventListener(eventType,eventHandler,false);
    } else if (eventTarget.detachEvent) {
        eventType = "on" + eventType;
        eventTarget.detachEvent(eventType,eventHandler);
    } else {
        eventTarget["on" + eventType] = null;
    }
}
```

Again, from the top: the W3C DOM Level 2 method is removeEventListener. If this method exists on the object, it's used; otherwise, the object is tested to see if it has a method named detachEvent, Microsoft's version of the method. If found, it's used. If not, the final DOM Level 0 event is to assign the event handler property to null.

Now, once we want to stop listening to an event, we can just call stopListening, passing in the same three arguments: target object, event, and event handler function.

> IE8 does not support DOM Level 2 event handling, but IE9 will. However, until older versions of IE, such as IE7 and IE8, vanish from use, you'll most likely need to continue using the cross-browser technique covered in this recipe.

7.4 Canceling an Event Based on Changed Circumstance

Problem

You need to cancel an event, such as a form submission, before the event propagates to other elements.

Solution

Create a reusable function that will cancel an event:

```
// cancel event
function  cancelEvent (event) {
    if (event.preventDefault) {
        event.preventDefault();
    } else {
        event.returnValue = false;
    }
}
```

```
...
function validateForm(evt) {
    evt = evt || window.event;
    cancelEvent(evt);
}
```

Discussion

You may want to cancel an event before it completes processing, such as preventing the default submission of a form, if the form elements don't validate.

If you were using a purely DOM Level 0 event handling procedure, you could cancel an event just by returning false from the event handler:

```
function formSubmitFunction() {
...
if (bad)
    return false
}
```

However, with the new, more sophisticated event handling, we need a function like that shown in the solution, which cancels the event, regardless of event model.

In the solution, the event is passed as an argument to the function from the event handler function. If the event object has a method named `preventDefault`, it's called. The `preventDefault` method prevents the default action, such as a form submission, from taking place.

If `preventDefault` is not supported, the event property `returnValue` is set to `false` in the solution, which is equivalent to what we did with returning false from the function for DOM Level 0 event handling.

7.5 Preventing an Event from Propagating Through a Set of Nested Elements

Problem

You have one element nested in another. Both capture the click event. You want to prevent the click event from the inner element from bubbling up or propagating to the outer event.

Solution

Stop the event from propagating with a generic routine that can be used with the element and any event:

```
// stop event propagation
function cancelPropagation (event) {
```

```
        if (event.stopPropagation) {
            event.stopPropagation();
        } else {
            event.cancelBubble = true;
        }
    }
```

In the event handler for the inner element click event, call the function, passing in the event object:

```
cancelPropagation(event);
```

Discussion

If we don't want to cancel an event, but do want to prevent it from propagating, we need to stop the event propagation process from occurring. For now, we have to use a cross-browser method, since IE8 doesn't currently support DOM Level 2 event handling.

In the solution, the event is tested to see if it has a method called stopPropagation. If it does, this event is called. If not, then the event cancelBubble property is set to true. The first method works with Chrome, Safari, Firefox, and Opera, while the latter property works with IE.

To see this work, Example 7-2 shows a web page with two div elements, one nested in another and both assigned a click event handler function. When the inner div element is clicked, two messages pop up: one for the inner div element, one for the other. When a button in the page is pressed, propagation is turned off for the event. When you click the inner div again, only the message for the inner div element is displayed.

Example 7-2. Preventing an event from propagating among nested elements

```
<!DOCTYPE html>
<head>
<title>Prevent Propagation</title>
<style>
#one
{
   width: 100px; height: 100px; background-color: #0f0;
}
#two {
   width: 50px; height: 50px; background-color: #f00;
}
#stop
{
  display: block;
}
</style>
<script>

// global for signaling propagation cancel
var stopPropagation = false;
```

```
function listenEvent(eventTarget, eventType, eventHandler) {
    if (eventTarget.addEventListener) {
        eventTarget.addEventListener(eventType, eventHandler,false);
    } else if (eventTarget.attachEvent) {
        eventType = "on" + eventType;
        eventTarget.attachEvent(eventType, eventHandler);
    } else {
        eventTarget["on" + eventType] = eventHandler;
    }
}

// cancel propagation
function  cancelPropagation (event) {
    if (event.stopPropagation) {
        event.stopPropagation();
    } else {
        event.cancelBubble = true;
    }
}

listenEvent(window,"load",function() {
    listenEvent(document.getElementById("one"),"click",clickBoxOne);
    listenEvent(document.getElementById("two"),"click",clickBoxTwo);
    listenEvent(document.getElementById("stop"),"click",stopProp);
  });

function stopProp() {
    stopPropagation = true;
}

function clickBoxOne(evt) {
  alert("Hello from One");
}

function clickBoxTwo(evt) {
  alert("Hi from Two");
  if (stopPropagation) {
     cancelPropagation(evt);
  }
}
</script>

</head>
<body>
<div id="one">
<div id="two">
<p>Inner</p>
</div>
</div>
<button id="stop">Stop Propagation</button>
</body>
```

The button event handler only sets a global variable because we're not worried about
its event propagation. Instead, we need to call cancelPropagation in the click event

handler for the div elements, when we'll have access to the actual event we want to modify.

Example 7-2 also demonstrates one of the challenges associated with cross-browser event handling. There are two click event handler functions: one for the inner div element, one for the outer. Here's a more efficient click handler method function:

```
function clickBox(evt) {
    evt = evt || window.event;
    alert("Hi from " + this.id);
    if (stopPropagation) {
        cancelPropagation(evt);
    }
}
```

This function combines the functionality contained in the two functions in the example. If stopPropagation is set to false, both elements receive the event. To personify the message, the identifier is accessed from the element context, via this.

Unfortunately, this won't work with IE8. The reason is that event handling with attachEvent is managed via the window object, rather than the DOM. The element context, this, is not available. You can access the element that receives the event via the event object's srcElement property. However, even this doesn't work in the example, because the srcElement property is set to the first element that receives the event, and isn't updated when the event is processed for the next element as the event propagates through the nested elements.

When using DOM Level 0 event handling, these problems don't occur. Microsoft has access to the element context, this, in the handler function, regardless of propagation. We could use the above function only if we assign the event handler for the two div elements using DOM Level 0:

```
document.getElementById("one").onclick=clickBox;
document.getElementById("two").onclick=clickBox;
```

7.6 Capturing Keyboard Activity

Problem

You want to capture keyboard events for a textarea, and look for specific character uses.

Solution

Capture the keyboard activity for a textarea element and check the ASCII value of the character to find the character or characters of interest:

```
var inputTextArea = document.getElementById("source");
listenEvent(inputTextArea,"keypress",processKeyStroke);
function processKeyStroke(evt) {
```

```
evt = evt ? evt : window.event;
var key = evt.charCode ? evt.charCode : evt.keyCode;
// check to see if character is ASCII 38, or the ampersand (&)
if (key == "38")
    ...
```

Discussion

There are multiple events associated with the keyboard:

keydown
> Key is pressed down.

keyup
> Key is released.

keypress
> Follows keydown.

textInput
> Follows keypress (Safari only).

Let's look more closely at keypress and keydown.

When a key is pressed down, it generates a keydown event, which records that a key was depressed. The keypress event, though, represents the character being typed. If you press the Shift key and the "L" key to get a capital letter L, you'll get two events if you listen to keydown, but you only get one event if you listen with keypress. The only time you'll want to use keydown is if you want to capture every key stroke.

In the solution, the keypress event is captured and assigned an event handler function. In the event handler function, the event object is accessed to find the ASCII value of the key pressed (every key on a keyboard has a related ASCII numeric code). Cross-browser functionality is used to access this value: IE and Opera do not support char Code, but do support keyCode; Safari, Firefox, and Chrome support charCode.

 Not listed in the possible keyboard events is the textInput event, which is part of the new DOM Level 3 event specification currently in draft state. It also represents a character being typed. However, its implementation is sparse, and based on an editor draft, not a released specification. Stick with keypress for now.

To demonstrate how keypress works, Example 7-3 shows a web page with a textarea. When you open the page, you'll be prompted for a "bad" ASCII character code, such as 38 for an ampersand (&). When you start typing in the textarea, all of the characters are reflected in the textarea *except* for the "bad" character. When this character is typed, the event is canceled, the default keypress behavior is interrupted, and the character doesn't appear in the textarea.

Example 7-3. Preventing a keyboard value based on ASCII value of key

```html
<!DOCTYPE html>
<head>
<title>Filtering Input</title>
<script>

var badChar;

function listenEvent(eventTarget, eventType, eventHandler) {
    if (eventTarget.addEventListener) {
        eventTarget.addEventListener(eventType, eventHandler,false);
    } else if (eventTarget.attachEvent) {
        eventType = "on" + eventType;
        eventTarget.attachEvent(eventType, eventHandler);
    } else {
        eventTarget["on" + eventType] = eventHandler;
    }
}

// cancel event
function  cancelEvent (event) {
    if (event.preventDefault) {
        event.preventDefault();
        event.stopPropagation();
    } else {
        event.returnValue = false;
        event.cancelBubble = true;
    }
}

window.onload=function() {
    badChar = prompt("Enter the ASCII value of the keyboard
key you want to filter","");
    var inputTA = document.getElementById("source");
    listenEvent(inputTA,"keypress",processClick);
}
function processClick(evt) {
    evt = evt || window.event;
    var key = evt.charCode ? evt.charCode : evt.keyCode;

    // zap that bad boy
    if (key == badChar) cancelEvent(evt);
}

</script>
</head>
<body>
<form>
<textarea id="source" rows="20" cols="50"></textarea>
</form>
</body>
```

Other than being a devious and rather nasty April Fool's joke you can play on your blog commenters, what's the purpose of this type of application?

Well, a variation of the application can be used to filter out nonescaped characters such as ampersands in comments for pages served up as XHTML. XHTML does not allow for nonescaped ampersands. The program could also be adapted to listen for ampersands, and replace them with the escaped versions (&). Normally, you would escape text as a block on the server before storing in the database, but if you're doing a live echo as a preview, you'll want to escape that material before you redisplay it to the web page.

And it makes a wicked April Fool's joke on your blog commenters.

 The use of the prompt can trigger a security warning with IE.

See Also

See Recipes 7.3 and 7.4 for an explanation of the event handler functions shown in Example 7-2.

7.7 Using the New HTML5 Drag-and-Drop

Problem

You want to incorporate the use of drag-and-drop into your web page, and allow your users to move elements from one place in the page to another.

Solution

Use the new HTML5 native drag-and-drop, which is an adaptation of the drag-and-drop technique supported in Microsoft Internet Explorer. Example 7-4 provides a demonstration.

Example 7-4. Using the new HTML5 drag-and-drop

```
<!DOCTYPE html>
<head>
<title>HTML5 Drag-and-Drop</title>
<style>
#drop
{
  width: 300px;
  height: 200px;
  background-color: #ff0000;
  padding: 5px;
  border: 2px solid #000000;
}
#item
```

```
{
    width: 100px;
    height: 100px;
    background-color: #ffff00;
    padding: 5px;
    margin: 20px;
    border: 1px dashed #000000;
}
*[draggable=true] {
  -moz-user-select:none;
  -khtml-user-drag: element;
  cursor: move;
}

*:-khtml-drag {
  background-color: rgba(238,238,238, 0.5);
}

</style>
<script>

function listenEvent(eventTarget, eventType, eventHandler) {
    if (eventTarget.addEventListener) {
        eventTarget.addEventListener(eventType, eventHandler,false);
    } else if (eventTarget.attachEvent) {
        eventType = "on" + eventType;
        eventTarget.attachEvent(eventType, eventHandler);
    } else {
        eventTarget["on" + eventType] = eventHandler;
    }
}

// cancel event
function  cancelEvent (event) {
    if (event.preventDefault) {
        event.preventDefault();
    } else {
        event.returnValue = false;
    }
}

// cancel propagation
function  cancelPropagation (event) {
    if (event.stopPropagation) {
        event.stopPropagation();
    } else {
        event.cancelBubble = true;
    }
}

window.onload=function() {
    var target = document.getElementById("drop");
    listenEvent(target,"dragenter",cancelEvent);
    listenEvent(target,"dragover", dragOver);
    listenEvent(target,"drop",function (evt) {
```

```
                cancelPropagation(evt);
                evt = evt || window.event;
                evt.dataTransfer.dropEffect = 'copy';
                var id = evt.dataTransfer.getData("Text");
                target.appendChild(document.getElementById(id));
                });

    var item = document.getElementById("item");
    item.setAttribute("draggable", "true");
    listenEvent(item,"dragstart", function(evt) {
                evt = evt || window.event;
                evt.dataTransfer.effectAllowed = 'copy';
                evt.dataTransfer.setData("Text",item.id);
                });

};

function dragOver(evt) {
  if (evt.preventDefault) evt.preventDefault();
  evt = evt || window.event;
  evt.dataTransfer.dropEffect = 'copy';
  return false;
}
</script>
</head>
<body>
<div>
<p>Drag the small yellow box with the dash border to the larger
red box with the solid border</p>
</div>
<div id="item" draggable="true">
</div>
<div id="drop">
</div>
</body>
```

Discussion

As part of the HTML5 specification, drag-and-drop has been implemented natively, though Opera doesn't currently support drag-and-drop and it can be a bit tricky in Firefox, Chrome, Safari, and IE8. The example does not work with IE7, either.

 Currently, implementations of HTML5 drag-and-drop are not robust or consistent. Use with caution until the functionality has broader support.

Drag-and-drop in HTML5 is not the same as in previous implementations, because what you can drag is mutable. You can drag text, images, document nodes, files, and a host of objects.

To demonstrate HTML5 drag-and-drop at its simplest, we'll explore how Example 7-4 works. First, to make an element draggable, you have to set an attribute, `draggable`, to `true`. In the example, the `draggable` element is given an identifier of `item`. Safari also requires an additional CSS style setting:

```
-khtml-user-drag: element;
```

The allowable values for `-khtml-user-drag` are:

element
> Allows element to be dragged.

auto
> Default logic to determine whether element is dragged (only images, links, and text can be dragged by default).

none
> Element cannot be dragged.

Since I'm allowing a `div` element to be dragged, and it isn't a link, image, or text, I needed to set `-khtml-user-drag` to `element`.

The element that can be dragged must have the `draggable` attribute set to `true`. It could be set in code, using `setAttribute`:

```
item.setAttribute("draggable","true");
```

However, IE doesn't pick up the change in state; at least, it doesn't pick up the CSS style change for a `draggable` object. Instead, it's set directly on the object:

```
<div id="item" draggable="true">
</div>
```

The `dragstart` event handler for the same element is where we set the data being transferred with the drag operation. In the example, since I'm dragging an element node, I'm going to set the data type to "text" and provide the identifier of the element (accessible via `target`, which has the element context). You can specify the element directly, but this is a more complex operation. For instance, in Firefox, I could try the following, which is derived from the Mozilla documentation:

```
evt.dataTransfer.setData("application/x-moz-node",target);
```

and then try to process the element at the drop end:

```
var item = evt.dataTransfer.getData("application/x-moz-node");
target.appendChild(item);
```

However, the item gets set to a serialized form of the `div` element, not an actual reference to the `div` element. In the end, it's easier just to set the data transfer to text, and transfer the identifier for the element, as shown in Example 7-4.

You can also set several different kinds of data to be transferred, while your drop targets only look for specific types. There doesn't have to be a one-to-one mapping. Also note that WebKit/Safari doesn't handle the MIME types correctly unless you use getData and setData specifically.

The next part of the drag-and-drop application has to do with the drag receiver. In the example, the drag receiver is another `div` element with an identifier of "drop". Here's another instance where things get just a tad twisted.

There are a small group of events associated with HTML5 drag-and-drop:

dragstart
> Drag event starts.

drag
> During the drag operation.

dragenter
> Drag is over the target; used to determine if target will accept drop.

dragover
> Drag is over target; used to determine feedback to user.

drop
> Drop occurs.

dragleave
> Drag leaves target.

dragend
> Drag operation ends.

The dragged item responds to `dragstart`, `drag`, and `dragend`. The target responds to `dragenter`, `dragover`, `dragleave`, and `drop`.

When the dragged object is over the target, if the target wants to signal it can receive the drop, it must cancel the event. Since we're dealing with browsers that implement DOM Level 2 event handling, the event is canceled using the `cancelEvent` reusable function created in an earlier recipe. The code also returns false:

```
function dragOver(evt) {
  if (evt.preventDefault) evt.preventDefault();
  evt = evt || window.event;
  evt.dataTransfer.dropEffect = 'copy';
  return false;
}
```

In addition, the `dragenter` event must also be canceled, either using `preventDefault` or returning false in the inline event handler, as shown in the example.

Both **dragenter** and **dragover** *must* be canceled if you want the **target** element to receive the **drop** event.

When the **drop** event occurs, the **drop** event handler function uses **getData** to get the identifier for the element being dragged, and then uses the DOM **appendChild** method to append the element to the new target. For a before and after look, Figure 7-1 shows the page when it's loaded and Figure 7-2 shows the page after the drag-and-drop event.

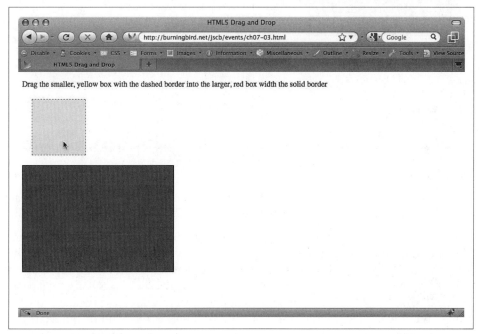

Figure 7-1. Web page with drag-and-drop enabled; before drag-and-drop

I also had to cancel event propagation with the receiver element, though it's not required in all browsers.

In the example, I use an anonymous function for the **dragstart** and **drop** event handler functions. The reason is that, as mentioned in Recipe 7.5, the **attachEvent** method supported by Microsoft does not preserve element context. By using an anonymous function, we can access the element in the other function scope, within the event handler functions.

I haven't been a big fan of drag-and-drop in the past. The operation requires a rather complex hand-and-mouse operation, which limits the number of people who can take advantage of this interactive style. Even if you have no problems with fine motor skills,

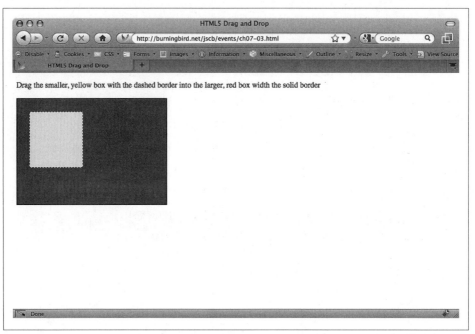

Figure 7-2. Web page after drag-and-drop operation

using drag-and-drop with a touch screen or mouse pad can be cumbersome. It's also been extremely problematic to implement.

The current HTML5 specification details newly standardized drag-and-drop functionality, though not everyone is pleased by the capability. Peter-Paul Koch (PPK) of the well-known Quirksblog describes the current implementation of drag-and-drop in HTML5 as the "HTML5 drag-and-drop disaster" (*http://www.quirksmode.org/blog/archives/2009/09/the_html5_drag.html*), and be aware that the article may not be safe for work). Why? According to PPK, there are several things wrong with the implementation: too many events, confusing implementation details, and inconsistencies.

One of the biggest concerns PPK mentions is the requirement that if an element is to receive a drop, when it receives either the **dragenter** or **dragover** event, it has to cancel the events.

I sympathize, but I understand some of the decisions that went into the current implementation of drag-and-drop in HTML5. For instance, we're dealing with a legacy event handling model, so we can't invent new event triggers just for drag-and-drop. If, by default, an element is not a valid drag-and-drop target, then the drag-and-drop operation must continue as another target is sought. If the dragged element enters or is over a valid target, though, by canceling the **dragenter** and **dragover** events, the target is signaling that yes, it is interested in being a target, and doing so using the only means available to it: by canceling the **dragenter** and **dragover** events.

PPK recommends using what he calls "old school" implementations of drag-and-drop. The only issue with those is they aren't cross-browser friendly, and can be complicated to implement. They're also not accessible, though accessibility can be added.

Gez Lemon wrote an article for Opera on using the WAI-ARIA (Web Accessibility Initiative–Accessible Rich Internet Applications) accessible drag-and-drop features. It's titled "Accessible drag and drop using WAI-ARIA" (*http://dev.opera.com/articles/view/accessible-drag-and-drop/*). He details the challenges associated with making accessible drag-and-drop, as well as the two drag-and-drop properties associated with WAI-ARIA:

aria-grabbed
> Set to true when element is selected for dragging.

aria-dropeffect
> Effect that happens when source is released on drag target.

The `aria-dropeffect` has the following values:

copy
> Source is duplicated and dropped on target.

move
> Source is removed and moved to target.

reference
> A reference or shortcut to source is created in target.

execute
> Function is invoked, and source is input.

popup
> Pop-up menu or dialog presented so user can select an option.

none
> Target will not accept source.

In the article, Gez provides a working example using the existing drag-and-drop capability, and also describes how ARIA can be integrated into the new HTML5 drag-and-drop. The example provided in the article currently only works with Opera, which hasn't implemented HTML5 drag-and-drop. Yet. But you can check out Figure 7-3 to see how drag-and-drop would look from a keyboard perspective.

Though old school drag-and-drop is complicated, several libraries, such as jQuery, provide this functionality, so you don't have to code it yourself. Best of all, ARIA accessibility is being built into these libraries. Until the HTML5 version of drag-and-drop is widely supported, you should make use of one of the libraries.

In addition, as the code demonstrates, drag-and-drop can follow the old school or the new HTML5 method, and the libraries can test to see which is supported and provide the appropriate functionality. We can use the jQuery script.aculo.us, or Dojo drag-and-drop, now and in the future, and not worry about which implementation is used.

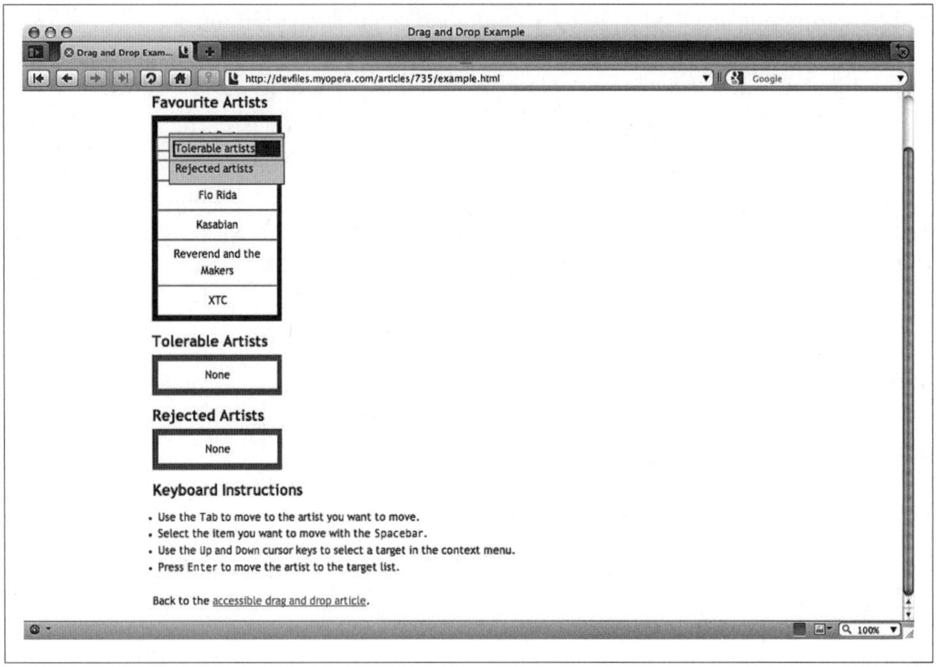

Figure 7-3. What a keyboard-enabled drag-and-drop operation could look like

See Also

Safari's documentation on HTML5 drag-and-drop can be found at *http://developer.ap ple.com/mac/library/documentation/AppleApplications/Conceptual/SafariJSProgTopics/ Tasks/DragAndDrop.html*. Mozilla's documentation is at *https://developer.mozilla.org/ en/Drag_and_Drop*. The HTML5 specification section related to drag-and-drop can be accessed directly at *http://dev.w3.org/html5/spec/Overview.html#dnd*.

See Recipe 7.5 for more on the complications associated with advanced cross-browser event listening, and Recipes 7.3, 7.4, and 7.5 for descriptions of the advanced event listening functions. Recipe 12.15 covers `setAttribute`.

7.8 Using Safari Orientation Events and Other Mobile Development Environments

Problem

You want to determine if the Safari browser accessing your web page has changed its orientation from portrait to landscape.

Solution

Use the proprietary orientation events for Safari:

```
window.onorientationchange = function () {
    var orientation = window.orientation;
    switch(orientation) {
        case 0:
            // portrait orientation
            break;
        case 90:
        case -90:
            // landscape orientation
            break;
    }
}
```

Discussion

We're not going to spend a great deal of time on mobile devices—in this chapter, or in the rest of the book. The primary reason is that most mobile devices either react to your web page as any other browser would react, albeit in miniature, or the requirements for mobile development are so extensive as to warrant a separate book.

In addition, many small device and touch screen events are proprietary to the browser, such as the one demonstrated in the solution for this recipe.

In the solution, we want to capture an orientation change, since devices like the iPhone can flip from portrait to landscape. In the solution, we use the `iPhoneOrientation` events to first capture the orientation change, and then determine the new orientation.

Based on orientation, we can do things such as swap a portrait thumbnail for a landscape-based image, or even activate some form of motion. When Apple rolled out the `iPhoneOrientation` example, it provided a snow globe that would "shake" when orientation changed.

Typically, though, sophisticated mobile applications, such as many of those for the iPhone/iPod touch, are not web-based. They use a SDK provided by the company, which may actually require that you purchase a subscription. As for general web access for mobile devices, you're better off providing mobile CSS files for mobile devices. Use proportional sizes for any pop ups and code your page regardless of device. In fact, many mobile devices turn off JavaScript for web pages automatically. As long as you ensure your web page is based on progressive enhancement (fully functional without script), you should be set for the mobile world.

See Also

Apple's `iPhoneOrientation` script can be found at *http://developer.apple.com/safari/library/samplecode/iPhoneOrientation/index.html*. XUI is a JavaScript framework for mobile devices currently under development, and is accessible at *http://xuijs.com/*.

jQTouch is a jQuery plug-in for mobile devices, at *http://www.jqtouch.com/*. I also recommend Jonathan Stark's book, *Building iPhone Apps with HTML, CSS, and JavaScript (http://oreilly.com/catalog/9780596805791/)* (O'Reilly).

CHAPTER 8

Browser Pieces

8.0 Introduction

The browser objects include the `window`, `navigator`, `screen`, `history`, and `location`. They're part of what is known as the Browser Object Model (BOM), or the DOM Level 0 set of objects, which also includes the `document`, frames, and various other elements. Typically though, when we think of browser objects, we think of the first five elements I just mentioned. In the HTML5 specification, these are known as the *browsing context*.

The topmost element is the `window`, and all the other browser objects are children. You can access the children elements using the window:

```
var browser = window.navigator.userAgent;
```

Or you can access the objects directly:

```
var browser = navigator.userAgent;
```

When working with the browser objects, be aware that until very recently, none of the objects was covered by a standard specification, and a consistent implementation was not guaranteed. Though most browsers share the same methods and properties, there are also browser-specific properties with each object. Make sure to check your target browsers' documentation when you work with the objects, and test the pages in all of the browsers.

Work is underway with the W3C HTML5 effort to provide a user application object model, which does include all of the browser objects covered in this chapter. However, it's all very new, and not broadly implemented at the time of this writing. It's also subject to change, since the HTML5 effort is still ongoing. Where possible, I'll note how an object or method is changing because of this new work.

8.1 Ask the Web Page Reader to Confirm an Action

Problem

You want to confirm an action with the web page reader.

Solution

Use the `confirm` pop-up box:

```
var answer = confirm("Are you sure you want to do that?");
if (answer == true) {
   alert("You're sure");
} else {
   alert("You decided against");
}
```

Discussion

There are three types of pop-up boxes in JavaScript. The `alert` pop up just provides a message, with an OK button to close the pop up:

```
alert("You're sure");
```

The `confirm` pop up, demonstrated in the solution, asks a question that is answered `true` by pushing the OK button, `false` if the Cancel button is pressed:

```
var answer = confirm("Are you sure?");
```

The last pop up is the `prompt`. You supply a string used for the prompt message, and can optionally provide a default response. The web page reader is given an input field to type a response, which is returned:

```
var answer = prompt("What's your name", "anonymous");
```

You'll want to provide a default response, even if it's only an empty string (""). Use caution when using the prompt pop up, as browser security could block the small window, or require user permission in order to work. Based on the newer levels of security, consider using forms, even for simple, one-answer questions.

8.2 Creating a New, Stripped-Down Browser Window

Problem

You want to open a web page in a new, stripped-down, fixed-size browser window.

Solution

Open a new browser window using the `window.open` method, passing in optional parameters: a URL to load, and a window name:

```
var newWindow = window.open("http://oreilly.com", "namedWindow");
```

Discussion

In older implementations, the `window.open` method takes three parameters: the URL, the window name, and the window features as a string of comma-delimited options. If the URL is omitted, the window opens with "about:blank". If the name is not given, the default "_blank" is used, which means each window is a new window. If the features string is omitted, default formatting is used.

However, the `window.open` method is changing with HTML5. At the time this was written, the features string was no longer supported, and a fourth parameter, `replace`, is a Boolean value that indicates whether the URL replaces the contents in an open window, and removes the existing URL from the window's history.

 Opening a new window can trigger pop up window prevention, and the default behavior can change from browser to browser. For instance, in Firefox 3.x, the new window is opened as a new tab by default, though you can configure it differently in the user preferences.

8.3 Finding Out About the Browser Accessing the Page

Problem

You want to determine information about the browser accessing the web page.

Solution

Use the `Navigator` object to discover information about the browser and browser environment:

```
var browser = navigator.userAgent;
var info = "<p>Browser: " + browser + "</p>";

var platform = navigator.platform;
info+="<p>Platform: " + platform + "</p>";
```

Discussion

The `Navigator` object has a wealth of information about the web page reader's browser, as well as the operating system. The supported properties change from browser to browser, and several properties aren't of much interest to the average JavaScript developer. At a minimum, most support the helpful properties shown in Table 8-1.

Table 8-1. Navigator properties

Property	Purpose	Example
appCodeName	Code name for the browser	Mozilla
appName	Official name of the browser	Netscape
appVersion	Browser version	5.0 (Macintosh; U; PPC Mac OS X 10_4_11; en) AppleWebKit/531.9 (KHTML, like Gecko) Version/4.0.3 Safari/531.9
cookieEnabled	Whether cookies are enabled	`true` if enabled, otherwise `false`
language	Language supported	en-US or en
platform		MacPPC
product		Gecko
userAgent		Mozilla/5.0 (Macintosh; U; PPC Mac OS X 10.4; en-US; rv:1.9.1.3) Gecko/20090824 Firefox/3.5.3
vendor	Vendor for browser	Apple Computer, Inc.

There are also some collections, such as `mimeTypes` and `plugins`.

It's interesting to look at the `Navigator` object contents, and useful for checking important information such as whether cookies are enabled or not. It's a bad decision, though, to use the `Navigator` object to detect the browser to determine which code to run.

Most browsers are constantly releasing new versions with new functionality. If you code for a browser, you have to change your code each time a browser releases a new browser. Plus it's very easy to spoof a browser string, so the value is very unreliable. You're better off using object, rather than browser, detection when coding cross-browser applications.

See Also

To see object detection in action, see Chapter 7, which focuses on event handling and features several instances of using object detection.

8.4 Warning the Web Page Reader About Leaving a Page

Problem

Your web page reader has clicked a link that takes him out of your website. Because of the sensitive nature of your site, such as a government, bank, or medical organization site, you want to make sure that the person is aware that he's leaving your site and going to an external site.

Solution

Add an event listener for the window `unload` event and then provide a prompt to the web page reader that he's leaving the site:

```
window.onunload=goodbye;

function goodbye() {
    alert("You're leaving our site. Thanks for stopping by!");
}
```

Discussion

We don't want to indiscriminately throw up pop ups, or intervene with links or people going about their business, but there are times when we want to ensure that people know that when they click a link, type in a new domain, or even close the browser, they're leaving the current site.

I've seen such actions in bank websites, the IRS's site (U.S. tax organization), and other sites where the type of information being gathered can be quite confidential. You want people to be aware of the fact that they're leaving the previously secure website and going somewhere that may be less than secure.

In particular, providing this functionality is helpful behavior if you provide links to external sites within your web pages. Because the link is in your pages, your web page readers may assume the external site is an offshoot of your own. If the other site resembles your site enough, the confusion can be exacerbated. Your readers may provide information to the new site only because they think there is a connection between your site and the external one.

8.5 Changing Stylesheets Depending on Color Support

Problem

You want to change your site's stylesheet if the device viewing the page only supports 4-bit grayscale, or 8-bit color.

Solution

Use the `Screen` object to check the `colorDepth` property, and change either a CSS rule or an entire stylesheet based on the findings:

```
if (window.screen.colorDepth <= 8) {
    var style = document.documentElement.style ?
document.documentElement.style : document.body.style;
    style.backgroundColor="#ffffff";
}
```

Or:

```
function setActiveStyleSheet(title) {
  var a;
  for(var i=0; (a = document.getElementsByTagName("link")[i]); i++) {
    if(a.getAttribute("rel").indexOf("style") != -1
      && a.getAttribute("title")) {
      a.disabled = true;
      if(a.getAttribute("title") == title) a.disabled = false;
    }
  }
}
if (window.screen.colorDepth <= 4) {
  setActiveStyleSheet("dull");
}
```

Discussion

Once upon a time, most computer monitors only supported 8-bit, or 256-color monitors. If you used a CSS style color that was beyond what was considered a "web-safe" color, you couldn't depend on the end result. Where you expected a delicate violet, you might get a washed-out, gray-like color instead.

How important is it to support web-safe colors these days? Not too important. Computer systems have been beyond the 256-color limit for well over a decade now, and most old 8-bit systems have gone on to their reward or been repurposed into nongraphical Linux boxes.

Still, there is a whole new breed of web-accessible tools now, including eReaders, like the Kindle, that are redefining what we think of when it comes to web display. The Kindle supports 4-bit grayscale, and it allows web access.

You can either change colors directly, as the solution demonstrates, or you can change the stylesheet. The latter is a better option if you use color and graphics extensively in your website.

The stylesheet switcher code in the solution was from an example I provided in my O'Reilly book *Painting the Web* (*http://oreilly.com/catalog/9780596515096*), which is adapted from an article at A List Apart (*http://www.alistapart.com/articles/alternate/*). The technology is very mature, as the date of the article (2001) demonstrates. Nowadays, people provide different stylesheets based on the use of the media attribute. Some examples of the media attribute are:

- `print`, for printing
- `handheld`, for handheld devices
- `screen`, for typical computer monitors
- `tv`, for television
- `braille`, for Braille tactile devices

In addition, there's an @media rule you can use directly in stylesheets to modify values based on media types. However, there may be cases where there is no media type or @media rule that works—or the result is quirky, at best.

Let's examine the stylesheet switcher from the top. The `for` loop is controlled by accessing all of the link elements in the web page, which are then assigned, in turn, to a variable, `a`. In the loop, each is checked to see if it has a `rel` attribute set to `style`. If it does, and it has a `title`, and the `title` doesn't match the stylesheet we want, we disable the stylesheet. However, if the title does match, then we enable the stylesheet.

See Also

For more on the `getAttribute` method, see Recipe 11.12. Lynda Weinmann is generally regarded as the first person who provided documentation of web-safe colors. You can see the web-safe palette and read more of the history of web-safe colors at *http://www .lynda.com/resources/webpalette.aspx*.

8.6 Modifying Image Dimensions Depending on Page Size

Problem

You want to set the screen width and serve up an appropriately sized photo.

Solution

Use the `Screen` object's `availWidth` or `width` values to determine available space:

```
window.onload=function() {
  if (window.screen.availWidth >= 800) {
    var imgs = document.getElementsByTagName("img");
    for (var i = 0; i < imgs.length; i++) {
      var name = imgs[i].src.split("-");
      var newname = name[0] + "-big.jpg";
      imgs[i].src = newname;
    }
  }
}
```

Discussion

The ability to swap images in and out of the page has been around for years, and was a very common form of dynamic HTML at one time. It's still popular with Ajax-based image libraries and slideshows.

The solution assumes that the website can be accessed in browsers or other user agents that are less than 800 pixels in width. It also assumes the images are provided in two sizes, and the names of the images are differentiated between those that are large (`imgname-big.jpg`), and small (`imgname-thumb.jpg`).

There are two horizontal properties available with `Screen`: `availWidth` and `width`. The `width` property provides information about the screen `width`, while the `availWidth` property provides information about the browser width. In the solution, I'm using `availWidth`.

In the solution, all of the `img` elements in the page are accessed, and for each, the name of the current image is accessed. The `String split` method is used to find the unique part of the image filename (before the dash), which is then concatenated to `-big.jpg` to set the image `src` attribute to the larger-sized image.

One of the disadvantages to this approach is that the person will see this switching going on. A way around this is to use CSS to modify the width of the image, say to 90% of the page size:

```
img
{
    max-width: 90%;
}
```

However, this doesn't always generate a good image, as browsers don't do the best job of creating smaller versions of images.

The solution also doesn't take into account the bandwidth necessary to, first, load the larger image. That's why it's not unusual for websites just to load the smallest image into the web page by default, and then provide a link to the larger image, or use an image management JavaScript library to load larger images inline when clicking the thumbnail.

See Also

Probably one of the more popular image JavaScript libraries in use is LightBox2, available at *http://www.huddletogether.com/projects/lightbox2/*.

8.7 Creating Breadcrumbs in a CMS Template Page

Problem

You want to display footprint information based on the page URL for use in a Content Management System (CMS) template.

Solution

Use the `window.location` object to get information about the current page's URL, and then break it down to provide the footprint information:

```
var items = location.pathname.substr(1).split("/");
var breadcrumbTrail = "<p>";
for (var i = 0; i < items.length; i++) {
  breadcrumbTrail+=" -> " + items[i];
```

```
        }
        breadcrumbTrail+="</p>";
```

Discussion

The `window.location` object can be accessed in JavaScript as just `location`. It has eight properties, all of which describe one aspect of the web page URL, as listed in Table 8-2.

Table 8-2. window.location object properties

Property	Description	Example
hash	Part of URL following #, including the #	#mysection
host	Hostname and optional port	burningbird.net or [burningbird.net]:80
hostname	Hostname	burningbird.net
href	Full URL	http://burningbird.net/jscb#test
pathname	Relative path name	/jscb#test
port	Port number	80
protocol	URL protocol	http:
search	Part of the URL following ?, including ?	?q=username

A breadcrumb trail is a reprint of the path relative to the `hostname`, broken into pieces that can then be accessed directly.

You could embed the breadcrumb directly into a web page, but many Content Management Systems (CMS), such as Drupal or Wordpress, use one page as a template for most of the site contents. For instance, Drupal has one page called *page.tmpl.php*, which serves as the template for most of the content of a Drupal site.

Though there are plug-ins and other applications that can embed a breadcrumb, sometimes it's just as easy to use JavaScript to create the breadcrumb—especially if the navigation to the separate site components is also available in a menu (for accessibility purposes, or if JavaScript is turned off).

To demonstrate how to create a breadcrumb, Example 8-1 shows a breadcrumb application that not only parses out the different relative path components, but surrounds them with a subpath link and adds an arrow annotation.

Example 8-1. Building a breadcrumb trail with window.location

```
<!DOCTYPE html>
<html xmlns="http://www.w3.org/1999/xhtml">
<head>
<title>breadcrumb trail</title>
<script>
//<![CDATA[


window.onload=function() {
```

```
  // split relative path
  var items = location.pathname.substr(1).split("/");

  // build main path
  var mainpath = "<a href='" + location.protocol + "//" +
   location.hostname + "/";

  // begin breadcrumb
  var breadcrumbTrail = "<p>";
  for (var i = 0; i < items.length; i++) {

    // trailing slash
    if (items[i].length == 0 ) break;

    // extend main path for new level
    mainpath+=items[i];

    // add slash after all but last item
    if (i < items.length-1)
      mainpath+="/";

    // create breadcrumb component
    // add arrows for interior items only
    if (i > 0 && i < items.length)
      breadcrumbTrail+=" -> ";

    // add crumb
    breadcrumbTrail+= mainpath + "'>" + items[i] + "</a>";
  }

  // insert into page
  breadcrumbTrail+="</p>";
  document.getElementById("breadcrumb").innerHTML=breadcrumbTrail;

}

//--><![]]>
</script>
</head>
<body>
<div id="breadcrumb"></div>
</body>
</html>
```

The application adjusts for the first item in the list (no arrow), as well as the last (no final slash [/]), and includes handling cases where subdirectories have a trailing slash in the URL. There would be no list items for the main page, so no breadcrumb is printed out. You could adjust the script even further to not insert the empty paragraph element into the script when there are no items, or use different markup.

The script is simple, and works whether the page is statically or dynamically generated, as shown in Figure 8-1.

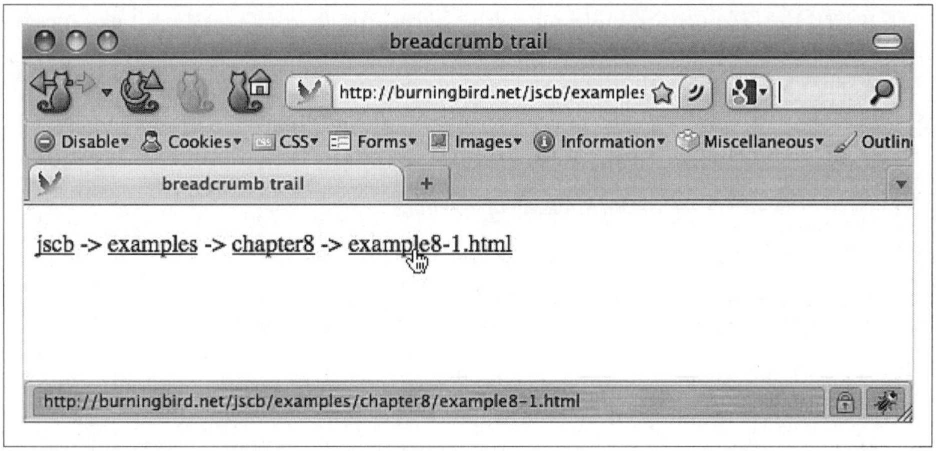

Figure 8-1. A JS-enabled breadcrumb application

8.8 Bookmarking a Dynamic Page

Problem

You have a dynamic application in which updates occur in the page rather than when the page refreshes. You want to provide a link to your web page reader that not only takes the user back to the page, but returns it to a given state.

Solution

Use the `Location` object's `hash` property in order to return to the state directly:

```
var someval = window.location.hash.split("#")[1];
if (someval == "state1") {
...
}
```

Discussion

A page fragment (*#somevalue*) isn't just a way to annotate an in-page link; it can also be a way to restore a state for an application. If dynamic effects are being made in a web page, and you want to preserve state at any time in such a way that a person can return to that state, you can create a unique hash for it and then provide the link to your web page reader.

To demonstrate, Example 8-2 is a web page that has a `div` wrapping a `button` and another `div`, and which changes various CSS-style property attributes with each click of the button. Since we want to give the web page reader the ability to return to a state at any time, a link is generated for that the person.

Why don't I use a stylesheet class and change the class name, rather than set the attributes individually? And why call all of the functions in order, rather than directly call each one? The reason is I'm building on the style settings from each previous function call, rather than resetting the style with each. If I used a class setting with the values, the results would be vastly different, because the style attributes not set would be returned to their inherited values. That's the major difference between using a class setting and changing individual style attributes.

Example 8-2. Preserving page state through hash on link

```
<!DOCTYPE html>
<head>
<title>Remember me?</title>
<script>

    window.onload=function() {

        // set up button
        document.getElementById("next").onclick=nextPanel;

        // check for hash, if found, reload state
        var hash = window.location.hash.split("#")[1];
        switch (hash) {
          case "one" :
             functionOne();
             break;
          case "two" :
             functionOne();
             functionTwo();
             break;
          case "three" :
             functionOne();
             functionTwo();
             functionThree();
        }

    }

    // display next panel, based on button's class
    function nextPanel() {
        var classNm = this.getAttribute("class");
        switch(classNm) {
           case "zero" :
              functionOne();
              break;
           case "one" :
              functionTwo();
              break;
           case "two" :
              functionThree();
        }
    }
    // set both the button class, and create the state link,
    // add to page
    function setPage(page) {
        document.getElementById("next").setAttribute("class",page);
```

```
        var link = document.getElementById("link");
        var path = location.protocol + "//" + location.hostname + "/" +
                   location.pathname + "#" + page;
        link.innerHTML="<p><a href='" + path + "'>link</a></p>";

    }

    // function one, two, three - change div, set button and link
    function functionOne() {
        var square = document.getElementById("square");
        square.style.backgroundColor="#ff0000";
        square.style.width="200px";
        square.style.height="200px";
        square.style.padding="10px";
        square.style.margin="20px";
        setPage("one");
    }

    function functionTwo() {
        var square = document.getElementById("square");
        square.style.backgroundColor="#ffff00";
        square.style.position="absolute";
        square.style.left="200px";
        setPage("two");
    }

    function functionThree() {
        var square = document.getElementById("square");
        square.style.width="400px";
        square.style.height="400px";
        square.style.backgroundColor="#00ff00";
        square.style.left="400px";
        setPage("three");
    }
</script>
</head>
<body>
<button id="next" class="zero">Next Action</button>
<div id="square">
<p>This is the object</p>
<div id="link"></div>
</div>
</body>
```

In the code, if there is a hash mark given in the window.object, the functions to set the state of the page are called. Since, in this example, each is dependent on what's happened in the other state functions, they'll need to be called before the end state. So if the hash mark is three (#three), both functionOne and functionTwo need to be called before functionThree, or the div element's state will be different (the style settings won't be the same).

The use of set- and getAttribute with the style attribute won't work with IE7. The downloadable example contains a workaround.

See Also

Recipe 12.15 provides a detailed discussion about changing CSS properties for elements. Chapters 13 and 14 demonstrate other dynamic page effects created by setting CSS-style attributes or changing an element's class name. Recipe 20.1 covers another example in which information can be persisted using the URL. Recipe 20.3 demonstrates state persistence using new HTML5 functionality.

Recipe 8.9 extends the concept of state from Example 8-2, so that the example can also work with page refreshes and after the use of the back button. Recipe 11.12 covers the getAttribute method.

8.9 Preserving State for Back Button, Page Refresh

Problem

You want to store a dynamic page's effects in such a way that if the web page reader accidentally hits the page refresh or back button, the effects aren't lost.

Solution

You set the location object's hash to preserve state automatically, so a dynamic effect is preserved:

```
// get state
var someval = window.location.hash.split("#")[1];
if (someval == "state1") {
...
}
// set state
function setPage(page) {
  location.hash=page;
}
```

Discussion

In Recipe 8.8, links are provided for the web page reader to return to a page state at a later time. The same principle can be used to capture a page state at any time, in case the person accidentally refreshes a page.

To modify Example 8-2 to maintain state automatically, all you need to do is modify the `setPage` function:

```
function setPage(page) {
  document.getElementById("next").setAttribute("class",page);
  location.hash=page;
}
```

Rather than build a link and add to the page, the page is added as a hash to `location`, which also serves to add the link, with hash, to the page history. With this change, if the person accidentally does a refresh at any point in time, the page will be returned to the exact state it was in before she did the refresh.

The use of `location` and unique hashes to record dynamic state has also been used for the infamous back button problem when it comes to dynamic or Ajax-based applications.

With most browsers, if you add a new hash with each state change, and then click the back button, you'll see the address bar reflect the change. What you probably won't see, though, is the actual state of the change reflected in the page. That's because even if you change the location in the address bar, you're not triggering a page reload. And there is no way to capture an address change in order to reload the page.

A workaround to this problem is to add a timer that fires at certain intervals, triggering code that checks the current `location` object and, in turn, triggers a page reload so the page reflects the address bar. Frankly, I'm not overly fond of this approach.

I do like the idea of capturing state because of accidental page refreshes, or providing a bookmark link. I haven't found repairing the back button to be a serious concern. At least, not until the state of technology is such that it can occur without having to use such things as timers.

See Also

See Recipe 8.8 for Example 8-2.

Speaking of the state of technology, Recipe 20.3 introduces the new HTML5 history object method, `pushState`, and associated `window.onpopevent` event handler. These maintain state and were created to help resolve the back button problem mentioned in this recipe. Recipe 12.15 covers the `setAttribute` method.

CHAPTER 9

Form Elements and Validation

9.0 Introduction

Outside of hypertext links, form elements were the very first form of interaction between web developers and web page readers, and were also one of the first reasons for interest in a scripting language.

With the advent of JavaScript, form elements could be validated before the data was sent to the server, saving the reader time and the website extra processing. JavaScript can also be used to modify form elements based on the data the web reader provides, such as filling a selection list with the names of cities when a certain state is selected.

The important point to remember when using JavaScript with form elements is that people turn JavaScript off, so it can't be a dependency for any form action. JavaScript enhances, not replaces.

Though validating the form on the client can save a round trip, as a sound design practice, you'll still want to validate the data on the server.

9.1 Accessing Form Text Input Values

Problem

You need to access the contents of a text input form element using JavaScript.

Solution

Use the DOM to access the form element:

```
var formValue = document.forms["formname"].elements["elementname"].
value;
```

Discussion

Forms in a web page can be accessed through an object collection (`forms`) via the `document` object. Each form has its own collection (`elements`) of `form` elements.

Accessing the `form` element's value varies, based on the type of `form` element. For instance, a text input or `textarea form` element's value can be accessed using the `value` attribute. To access the following `form` input element's data:

```
<form id="textsearch">
<input type="text" id="firstname" />
</form>
```

use the following JavaScript:

```
txtValue = document.forms["textsearch"].elements("pattern").value;
```

As demonstrated earlier in the book, you can also access the input `form` element directly, via its identifier:

```
var txtValue = document.getElementByid("pattern").value;
```

However, when you're working with a larger form, you're more likely going to want to work with the DOM Level 0 form collections, in order to be consistent.

You can also access the `form` element using an integer representing the form and the element's position in the page. The first `form` that appears in the page is given an array index of zero, the second an index of one, and so on. The same with the elements. So to access the example `form` element, use the following:

```
var txtValue = document.forms[0].elements[1].value;
```

Using an array index is tricky, since it may be difficult to determine the location of a specific form and element. In addition, adding a new form or element can make for incorrect JavaScript, or a web page application that doesn't perform as expected. However, it's also a simple way to process all `form` elements in a loop:

```
while (var i = 0; i < document.forms[0].elements.length; i++) {
   var val = document.forms[0].elements[i].value;
}
```

 Whenever you're accessing data from a text or other field where the user can input whatever value he wants, before sending to the database or displaying in the page, you will want to strip or encode any harmful SQL, markup, or script that may be embedded in the value. You can use `encodeURI` and `encodeURIComponent` in JavaScript for encoding.

See Also

See Recipe 2.4 for another demonstration of accessing a form and elements.

The solution uses the ECMAScript Binding for the DOM Level 2 HTML API, which can be found at *http://www.w3.org/TR/DOM-Level-2-HTML/ecma-script-binding .html*. For more on how to secure form input and the challenges of input security, read Jeff Atwood's "Protecting Your Cookies: HttpOnly" (*http://www.codinghorror.com/ blog/2008/08/protecting-your-cookies-httponly.html*).

9.2 Dynamically Disabling and Enabling Form Elements

Problem

Based on some action or event, you want to disable, or enable, one or more `form` elements.

Solution

Use the `disabled` property to enable or disable `form` element(s), accessing the element via the forms/elements collections:

```
document.forms["formname"].elements["elementname"].disabled=true;
```

or via direct access to an element with an identifier:

```
document.getElementById("elementname").disabled=true;
```

Discussion

It's not unusual to disable some fields in a `form` until information is provided or a specific event occurs. An example would be clicking a radio button enabling or disabling other `form` elements, such as input text fields.

See Also

See Recipe 9.4 for an example of clicking radio buttons and enabling or disabling specific `form` elements. See Recipe 9.8 for another approach to providing access to `form` elements based on activity (hiding or showing `form` elements).

9.3 Getting Information from a Form Element Based on an Event

Problem

You need to access information from a `form` element after an event.

Solution

Depending on the form element, you can capture any number of events, and based on the event, process the form element data.

If you want to validate a form field after the data in the field has changed, you can assign a function to the onchange event handler function for the element:

```
document.getElementById("input1").onchange=textChanged;
```

In the related function, access the form element's value:

```
var value = this.value;
```

You can also attach a function to a form element based on whether it gets or loses focus, using the onfocus and onblur event handlers. The onblur event handler can be handy if you want to ensure a form field has data:

```
document.getElementById("input2").onblur=checkValue;
```

In the function that checks to ensure some value is provided, you'll first need to trim any whitespace. Since the String trim method is not supported in IE8, the following code uses a variation of the regular expression String.replace method covered in Chapter 2:

```
var val = this.value;
val = val.replace(/^\s\s*/, '').replace(/\s\s*$/, '')
if (val.length == 0) alert("need value!");
```

You can capture keyboard events for form elements, such as onkeypress for a checkbox, but a click event is triggered for most form elements whether the element is clicked on by a mouse or the spacebar is clicked when the element has keyboard focus:

```
document.getElementById("check1").onclick=getCheck;
```

In the function, you can then access the checkbox checked property:

```
var checked = this.checked;
if (checked) { ...}
```

Discussion

There are several different events based on the type of form element. Each can be captured, and the appropriate event handler assigned a function.

Table 9-1 contains a list of form elements and the events most commonly captured for the element.

Table 9-1. Form elements and commonly occurring events

Elements	Events
button, submit	click, keypress, focus, blur
checkbox	click, keypress
radiobutton	click, keypress

Elements	Events
textarea	select, change, focus, blur, click, keypress, mousedown, mouseup, keydown, keyup
password, text	change, focus, blur, keypress, select
selection	change, focus, blur
file	change, focus, blur

The list of elements isn't exhaustive, nor is the list of events, but this gives you an idea of the more commonly occurring form element/event pairings.

In the form event handler function, you can access both the event and the element to get information about both. How you do this depends on your browser, and also how you assign the events.

For instance, if you use the DOM Level 0 event handling in which you assign the event handler function directly to the event handler property:

```
document.getElementById("button1").onclick=handleClick;
```

In all browsers, you can access the element using the element context this. However, if you use DOM Level 2 and up event handling, such as the following function, which provides cross-browser event handling:

```
function listenEvent(eventObj, event, eventHandler) {
    if (eventObj.addEventListener) {
        eventObj.addEventListener(event, eventHandler,false);
    } else if (eventObj.attachEvent) {
        event = "on" + event;
        eventObj.attachEvent(event, eventHandler);
    } else {
        eventObj["on" + event] = eventHandler;
    }
}
```

You can access the element context with this for Firefox, Opera, Chrome, Safari, but not for IE8. For IE8, you'll have to access the element using the event object:

```
function handleClick(evt) {
    // cross browser event access
    evt = evt || window.evt;

    // cross browser element access
    var elem;
    if (evt.srcElement)
        elem = evt.srcElement;
    else
        elem = this;
```

See Also

See Chapter 2 for using regular expressions with form elements, and Chapter 7 for more on event handling, including with form elements.

9.4 Performing an Action When a Radio Button Is Clicked

Problem

You want to perform an action based on which radio button is clicked.

Solution

Attach an `onclick` event handler to each of the radio buttons; in the event handler function, perform whatever action you need:

```
window.onload=function() {
  var radios = document.forms[0].elements["group1"];
  for (var i = 0; i < radios.length; i++)
    radios[i].onclick=radioClicked;
}

function RadioClicked() {
    if (this.value == "one") {
      document.forms[0].elements["line_text"].disabled=true;
    }
}
```

Discussion

One relatively common use for JavaScript is to modify `form` elements based on actions taken elsewhere in the form. For example, clicking a specific radio button may disable some elements, but enable others. To do this, you need to assign an event handler function to a `form` element's event handler, and then find out information about the element that received the event.

In the solution, a set of radio buttons with the name of `group1` are accessed from the form, and the `onclick` event handler for each is assigned to a function named `function RadioClicked`. In the function, properties associated with the clicked radio button are accessible via `this`, which is a proxy for the owner of the event. Via `this`, we can find out information about the event's owner, including the type of element receiving the event ("radio"), the `tagName` ("input"), and the `value` ("one").

With this information, we can determine which of the radio buttons was clicked, and perform whatever action we need based on this information.

One action associated with radio buttons is to enable or disable other `form` elements when one or another of the radio buttons is clicked. Example 9-1 shows a more complete demonstration of this type of activity. In the example, three radio buttons are paired with three text input fields. All three text input fields are disabled when the web page is loaded. Clicking any one of the radio buttons enables one input field and disables the other two.

Example 9-1. Disabling/enabling input elements based on a clicked radio button

```
<!DOCTYPE html>
<head>
<title>Radio Click Pick</title>

<style>
:enabled {
    border: 4px solid #ff0000;
    padding: 5px 5px 5px 15px;
}

:disabled {
    border: 2px solid #cccccc;
}

</style>
<script>

window.onload=function() {

  // first, disable all the input fields
  document.forms[0].elements["intext"].disabled=true;
  document.forms[0].elements["intext2"].disabled=true;
  document.forms[0].elements["intext3"].disabled=true;

  // next, attach the click event handler to the radio buttons
  var radios = document.forms[0].elements["group1"];
  for (var i = [0]; i < radios.length; i++)
    radios[i].onclick=radioClicked;
}
function radioClicked() {

  // find out which radio button was clicked and
  // disable/enable appropriate input elements
  switch(this.value) {
    case "one" :
       document.forms[0].elements["intext"].disabled=false;
       document.forms[0].elements["intext2"].disabled=true;
       document.forms[0].elements["intext3"].disabled=true;
       break;
    case "two" :
       document.forms[0].elements["intext2"].disabled=false;
       document.forms[0].elements["intext"].disabled=true;
       document.forms[0].elements["intext3"].disabled=true;
       break;
    case "three" :
       document.forms[0].elements["intext3"].disabled=false;
       document.forms[0].elements["intext"].disabled=true;
       document.forms[0].elements["intext2"].disabled=true;
       break;
  }

}

</script>
```

```
</head>
<body>
<form id="picker">
Group 1: <input type="radio" name="group1" value="one" /><br />
Group 2: <input type="radio" name="group1" value="two" /><br />
Group 3: <input type="radio" name="group1" value="three" /><br />
<br />
<input type="text" id="intext" />
<input type="text" id="intext2"  />
<input type="text" id="intext3"  />
</form>
</body>
```

The nonassociated text input fields are disabled with each new clicked event, in order to clear previous activity. In addition, to add a little flair to the example, new CSS3 functionality to style enabled and disabled attributes is used in the example, as shown in Figure 9-1. The CSS3 setting works with all of the book target browsers except IE8.

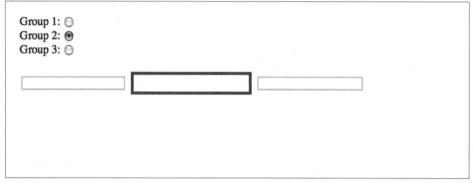

Figure 9-1. Modifying a form element based on a radio button click

See Also

See Recipe 9.2 for more information about attaching event handlers to form elements, and getting information from the elements in an event handler function.

9.5 Checking for a Valid Phone Number

Problem

You want to validate form information that requires a certain format, such as a valid phone number.

Solution

Access the form field value, and then use a regular expression to validate the format. To validate a U.S.-based phone number (area + prefix + digits):

```
// filter out anything but numbers to
// standardize input
var phone = document.forms[0].elements["intext"].value;
var re = /\D+/g;
var cleanphone = phone.replace(re,"");

// check length
if (cleanphone.length < 10) alert("bad phone");
```

Discussion

To validate form fields, you need to strip out any extraneous material first, and then test only what is necessary. Phone numbers can be provided using different formats:

(314) 555-1212

314-555-1212

314.555.1212

3145551212

All you really need are the numbers; everything else is just syntactic sugar. To validate a phone number, strip out anything that isn't a number, and then check the length, as shown in the solution.

Once validated, you can then reformat into a standard format, though usually if you're going to store a phone number in a database, you want to store it in the smallest form possible (all numbers).

Another way to ensure that the data is correct is to provide three fields for the number, and only allow the number of characters for each field (3-3-4). But it's probably simpler for you and for your users to use just one field.

See Also

There are any number of regular expression formulas that work for various validation purposes. See more on regular expressions in Chapter 2. Also note that many JavaScript frameworks and libraries provide simple-to-use validation routines, where all you have to do is give each input element a class name or some other indicator in order to trigger proper validation.

See Recipe 14.2 for integrating accessibility into your forms using ARIA.

9.6 Canceling a Form Submission

Problem

You want to cancel a form submission if you find the data entered into the form fields invalid.

Solution

If the form fields don't validate, cancel the form submission event using the technique appropriate to the event handling technique you're using. Here, we're borrowing from Chapter 7 (where we covered events):

```
// listen to an event
function listenEvent(eventObj, event, eventHandler) {
   if (eventObj.addEventListener) {
      eventObj.addEventListener(event, eventHandler,false);
   } else if (eventObj.attachEvent) {
      event = "on" + event;
      eventObj.attachEvent(event, eventHandler);
   } else {
      eventObj["on" + event] = eventHandler;
   }
}


// cancel event
function  cancelEvent (event) {
   if (event.preventDefault) {
      event.preventDefault();
   } else {
      event.returnValue = false;
   }
}

window.onload=function() {
   var form = document.forms["picker"];
   listenEvent(form,"submit",validateFields);
}

function validateFields(evt) {
   evt = evt ? evt : window.event;
   ...

   if (invalid) {
      cancelEvent(evt);
   }
}
```

Discussion

In the same function you use to validate the form field(s), cancel the event. In the event function, the `cancelEvent` function checks to see if the `preventDefault` method is supported. If it is, it's called. If not, the event's `returnValue` is set to false (cancel event).

See Also

See Chapter 7 for more information on event handling.

9.7 Preventing Duplicate Form Submissions

Problem

Potential harm could occur if a user submits the same form multiple times. You want to prevent duplicate form submissions.

Solution

One approach is to provide a message that the form has been submitted, and then provide some means to prevent the web page reader from submitting the form again. In its simplest variation, the following would work:

```
function validateSubmission(evt) {
...
alert("Thank you, we're processing your order right now");
document.getElementById("submitbutton").disabled=true; // disable
```

Discussion

Multiple concurrent form submissions are one of the worst problems that can occur in a user interface. Most people would be unhappy if, say, they found they had purchased two of the same item when they were only expecting to purchase one.

There are several different approaches you can take to prevent duplicate form submissions, and how strict you want to be depends on the seriousness of the double submission.

For example, comment forms don't usually restrict form submission. Duplicate submissions may result in a message that duplicate comments have posted, and the first has been rejected. Even if the duplicate comment is posted, it's a minor nuisance, rather than a serious problem.

However, it's essential to prevent duplicate form submission with any kind of storefront, and anything that could result in unexpected charges to your web customers.

If you do restrict duplicate form submissions, provide some form of feedback to the customer. In the solution, I took a simple approach, popping up a message providing feedback to the users that the form has been submitted, and then disabling the submit button so they can't click it again.

It's an OK approach, but we can take the security a little further. Instead of a pop up, we can embed a message directly into the page. Instead of just disabling the submit button, we can also use a flag to doubly ensure that a submission can't be initiated while an existing form submission is being processed. Example 9-2 demonstrates a safer way to prevent duplicate form submissions.

Example 9-2. Demonstrating prevention of duplicate form submissions

```html
<!DOCTYPE html>
<html xmlns="http://www.w3.org/1999/xhtml">
<head>
<title>Prevent Duplication Form Submission</title>

<style>
#refresh
{
    display: none;
    width: 200px; height: 20px;
    background-color: #ffff00;
}
</style>
<script>
//<![CDATA[

var inprocess=false;

window.onload=function() {
    document.forms["picker"].onsubmit=validateSubmit;
    document.getElementById("refresh").onclick=startOver;
}

function validateSubmit() {

  // prevent duplicate form submission
  if (inprocess) return;
  inprocess=true;
  document.getElementById("submitbutton").disabled=true;

  // for example only
  document.getElementById("refresh").style.display="block";
  document.getElementById("message").innerHTML=
"<p>We're now processing your request, which can take a minute.</p>";

  // validation stuff
  return false;
}

function startOver() {
    inprocess=false;
    document.getElementById("submitbutton").disabled=false;
    document.getElementById("message").innerHTML="";
    document.getElementById("refresh").style.display="none";
}
//--><!]]>
</script>
</head>
<body>
<form id="picker" method="post" action="">
Group 1: <input type="radio" name="group1" value="one" />
Group 2: <input type="radio" name="group1" value="two" />
Group 3: <input type="radio" name="group1" value="three" /><br />
<br />
```

```
Input 1: <input type="text" id="intext" />
Input 2: <input type="text" id="intext2"  />
Input 3: <input type="text" id="intext3"  /><br /><br />
<input type="submit" id="submitbutton" value="Send form" />
</form>
<div id="refresh">
<p>Click to reset example</p>
</div>
<div id="message">
</div>
</body>
</html>
```

If you load the example into a browser and click the Send Form button, it will become disabled and two new elements will display: a processing message and a button to refresh the page. The latter is included only because this is an example, as a way to reset the example.

Normally, in a form, a post-processing web page will display with a confirmation of the action and a message of thanks, or whatever is appropriate. If Ajax is used to make the update, the form can be reenabled once the Ajax processing is complete.

9.8 Hiding and Displaying Form Elements

Problem

You want to hide form elements until some event.

Solution

Surround the form elements that will be hidden with a div element:

```
<form id="picker" method="post" action="">
Item 1: <input type="radio" name="group1" value="one" />
Item 2: <input type="radio" name="group1" value="two" />
Item 3: <input type="radio" name="group1" value="three" /><br />
<br />
<div id="hidden_elements">
Input 1: <input type="text" id="intext" />
Input 2: <input type="text" id="intext2"  />
Input 3: <input type="text" id="intext3"  /><br /><br />
</div>
<input type="submit" id="submitbutton" value="Send form" />
</form>
```

Change the div's display to none when the page loads:

```
window.onload=function() {

    document.getElementById("hidden_elements").style.display="none";

    //  attach the click event handler to the radio buttons
```

```
    var radios = document.forms[0].elements["group1"];
    for (var i = [0]; i < radios.length; i++)
        radios[i].onclick=radioClicked;
}
```

When the event to display the form elements occurs, change the div element's display
so that the form elements are displayed:

```
function radioClicked() {
    if (this.value == "two") {
        document.getElementById("hidden_elements").style.display="block";
    } else {
        document.getElementById("hidden_elements").style.display="none";
    }
}
```

Discussion

In the solution, the hidden form elements are surrounded by a div element in order to
make it easier to work with them as a group. However, you could also control the
display for elements individually.

The CSS display property allows you to completely remove elements from the page
(display="none"), as shown in Figure 9-2. This makes it an ideal CSS property to use;
the visibility property will only hide the elements, but it doesn't remove them from
the display. If you used visibility, you'd have a gap between the displayed elements
and the form button.

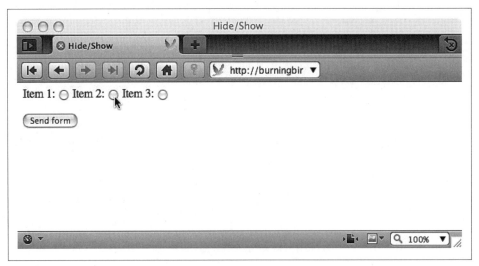

Figure 9-2. Page with form elements removed from display

In the solution, clicking the second radio button displays the input fields, as shown in
Figure 9-3. Notice in the code that if you click on the first or third radio button, the

display for the hidden elements is set to none, just in case it is currently displayed after a previous second radio button selection.

You always want to take into account the state of the page whenever you're processing an event that changes the makeup of a form. If certain elements are only displayed for given form values, then any activity in the form should either check the current state of the form or just reissue either the hide or show functionality, because it doesn't hurt to reshow a shown element or rehide one already hidden.

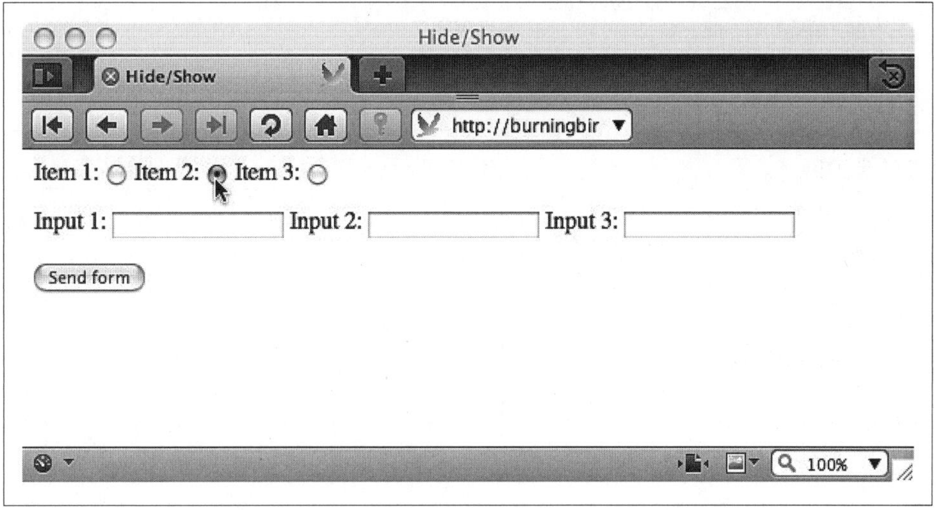

Figure 9-3. Page with hidden form elements displayed

See Also

See a full-page example of the hidden/displayed form element example in Recipe 10.1 (Example 10-1).

9.9 Modifying a Selection List Based on Other Form Decisions

Problem

You want to modify the contents of a second selection list based on the choice made in a first selection list.

Solution

You have two options when it comes to modifying the contents of one selection list, based on the choice in another selection list.

The first is to query a database and build the selection list based on the choice. This is demonstrated in Recipe 18.9, which covers Ajax.

The second approach is to maintain a static copy of the second selection list options:

```
var citystore = new Array();
citystore[0] = ['CA','San Francisco'];
citystore[1] = ['CA','Los Angeles'];
citystore[2] = ['CA','San Diego'];
citystore[3] = ['MO','St. Louis'];
citystore[4] = ['MO','Kansas City'];
citystore[5] = ['WA','Seattle'];
citystore[6] = ['WA','Spokane'];
citystore[7] = ['WA','Redmond'];
//And use this copy to rebuild the selection list:
function filterCities() {
  var state = this.value;
  var city = document.getElementById('cities');
  city.options.length=0;

  for (var i = 0; i < citystore.length; i++) {
    var st = citystore[i][0];
    if (st == state) {
      var opt = new Option(citystore[i][1]);
      try {
        city.add(opt,null);
      } catch(e) {
        city.add(opt);
      }
    }
  }
}
```

Discussion

Selection lists are often built from direct database queries. To prevent the lists from being too large, they may be built based on choices in other **form** elements, from an Ajax-enabled query, an array, or even a hidden selection list.

As the solution demonstrates, regardless of approach, the simplest and quickest way to populate the selection list is to first set the options array list to zero, which deletes everything from the list; then go through the available option data, and based on whatever criteria, create new options with the option data and append to the empty selection list.

To see this type of functionality in action, Example 9-3 shows an entire application that incorporates the code in the solution. Clicking a state will populate the second selection list with cities for that state. A **try...catch** block is used when adding the new option to the selection list, because IE8 does not support the second parameter for the element's position in the **add** method. If the first **add** method fails, the second is used.

Example 9-3. Populating a selection list

```
<!DOCTYPE html>
<html xmlns="http://www.w3.org/1999/xhtml">
<head>
```

```
<title>Populating Selection Lists</title>
<script>
//<![CDATA[

var citystore = new Array();
citystore[0] = ['CA','San Francisco'];
citystore[1] = ['CA','Los Angeles'];
citystore[2] = ['CA','San Diego'];
citystore[3] = ['MO','St. Louis'];
citystore[4] = ['MO','Kansas City'];
citystore[5] = ['WA','Seattle'];
citystore[6] = ['WA','Spokane'];
citystore[7] = ['WA','Redmond'];

window.onload=function() {
  document.getElementById("state").onchange=filterCities;
}

function filterCities() {
  var state = this.value;
  var city = document.getElementById('cities');
  city.options.length=0;

  for (var i = 0; i < citystore.length; i++) {
    var st = citystore[i][0];
    if (st == state) {
      var opt = new Option(citystore[i][1]);
      try {
        city.add(opt,null);
      } catch(e) {
        city.add(opt);
      }
    }
  }
}

//--><!]]>
</script>
</head>
<body>
<form id="picker" method="post" action="">
<select id="state">
<option value="">--</option>
<option value="MO">Missouri</option>
<option value="WA">Washington</option>
<option value="CA">California</option>
</select>
<select id="cities">
</select>
</form>
</body>
</html>
```

If scripting is disabled in an application like this one, the best option is to hide the city selection list by default and display a button (again by default) that submits the form and populates the city selection on a second page.

See Also

See Recipe 18.9 for a demonstration of using Ajax to populate a selection list. More on the `try...catch` error handling in Recipe 10.4.

CHAPTER 10

Debugging and Error Handling

10.0 Introduction

It would be wonderful if we could, by some miracle, manage to create JavaScript applications that never fail, never have errors, never go wrong. Then we would have perfection and wouldn't need things like debuggers and error handling. But what would be the fun in that?

There are two types of errors in JavaScript. The first is a programming error, where we, the JavaScript developers, do something wrong. These types of errors are typically found using our favorite browser and our favorite debugger.

At a minimum, what we need from a debugger is the ability to stop program execution and then examine variables and objects at that point. It also helps if we can continue the program by steps, drill into functions, and examine network activity and the state of the DOM at any time. However, we can usually manage debugging if we have the ability to stop a program and examine object values.

The second type of error occurs when the web page reader answers a question incorrectly, pushes the wrong button, or tries to type in a Social Security number when we're expecting a name. Or the error can happen when we're mixing libraries and something goes wrong between them. We'll look at these kinds of errors first, and then we'll get into the various browsers and their debugging capabilities.

10.1 Gracefully Handling No JavaScript Support

Problem

You want to ensure your pages work as well with JavaScript turned off as when it's turned on.

Solution

One approach is to the use the `noscript` element to provide alternative functionality:

```
<script type="text/javascript">
document.writeln("<p>Some content</p>");
</script>
<noscript><p>Fall back account</p></noscript>
```

However, more modern applications make an assumption that JavaScript is turned off, and ensure the page works correctly script-free. Once that's taken care of, we add script to make the page more interactive.

Discussion

Several years ago, it wasn't uncommon to find script blocks scattered about a page, generating web page content on the fly. To ensure that something showed up even if scripting was turned off, the developers would match the script with a `noscript` element. This `noscript` element would provide fallback page content or information. The `noscript` element has gone out of favor, and is listed as obsolete in HTML5. Now, web developers create the entire page and all of its content without any scripting enabled. Then, and only then, they'll add script to make the page more helpful, interactive, or even fun.

For example, a web page can have several `form` elements. It's workable, but having many `form` elements can take up a lot of space. However, the `form` elements have to be available if scripting is turned off.

To solve the problem, the developer can style the form elements to be displayed by default, and then use JavaScript to turn off the display of some of the elements when the page loads. Based on the web page reader's actions, `form` elements will be displayed and hidden as needed. This ensures that the `form` elements are always available and only hidden when support for scripting is ensured.

Example 10-1 shows a very simple implementation of this type of functionality. If scripting is turned off, all of the `form` elements display by default. If scripting is turned on, however, the text input elements in the lower part of the form are hidden when the page is loaded (note emphasized code), and only displayed when the second radio button is clicked.

Example 10-1. Form elements set to display by default if scripting is disabled, hidden if scripting is enabled

```
<!DOCTYPE html>
<html xmlns="http://www.w3.org/1999/xhtml">
<head>
<title>Hide/Show</title>
<style>
</style>
<script>
//<![CDATA[
```

```
var inprocess=false;

window.onload=function() {

  document.getElementById("hidden_elements").style.display="none";

  //  attach the click event handler to the radio buttons
  var radios = document.forms[0].elements["group1"];
  for (var i = [0]; i < radios.length; i++)
    radios[i].onclick=radioClicked;
}

function radioClicked() {
   if (this.value == "two") {
    document.getElementById("hidden_elements").style.display="block";
   } else {
    document.getElementById("hidden_elements").style.display="none";
   }
}

//--><!]]>
</script>
</head>
<body>
<form id="picker" method="post" action="">
Item 1: <input type="radio" name="group1" value="one" />
Item 2: <input type="radio" name="group1" value="two" />
Item 3: <input type="radio" name="group1" value="three" /><br />
<br />
<div id="hidden_elements">
Input 1: <input type="text" id="intext" />
Input 2: <input type="text" id="intext2"  />
Input 3: <input type="text" id="intext3"  /><br /><br />
</div>
<input type="submit" id="submitbutton" value="Send form" />
</form>
</body>
</html>
```

Figure 10-1 shows what the page looks like if scripting is disabled, and Figure 10-2 shows what the page looks like with scripting enabled.

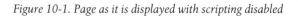

Figure 10-1. Page as it is displayed with scripting disabled

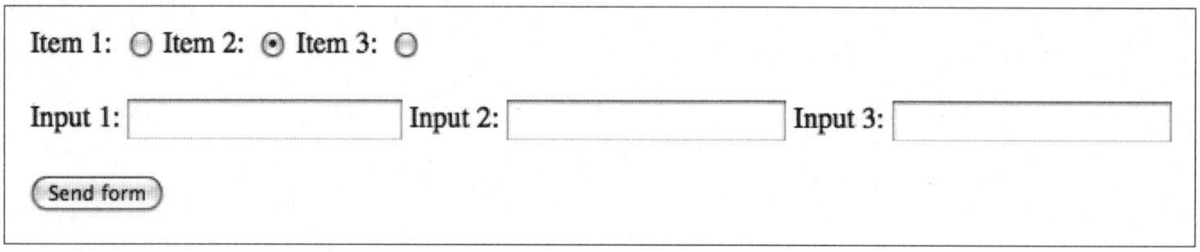

Item 1: ◯	Item 2: ◉	Item 3: ◯

Input 1: [ ]	Input 2: [ ]	Input 3: [ ]

(Send form)

Figure 10-2. Page with scripting enabled

 This concept of adding scripting after the page is fully constructed is known as *progressive enhancement*. It was the brain child of Steven Champeon of *http://hesketh.com*.

See Also

There are several good articles on progressive enhancement. You can start with:

- "Progressive Enhancement: Paving the Way for Future Web Design" (*http://www.hesketh.com/publications/articles/progressive-enhancement-paving-the-way-for/*)
- "Understanding Progressive Enhancement" (*http://www.alistapart.com/articles/understandingprogressiveenhancement*)
- "Progressive Enhancement: What It Is, and How to Use It?" (*http://www.smashingmagazine.com/2009/04/22/progressive-enhancement-what-it-is-and-how-to-use-it/*)

To ensure the accessibility of this effect, check out the use of ARIA in Chapter 14.

10.2 Checking for Errors in Functions

Problem

You want to signal to the calling application that an error happened in a function.

Solution

The simplest approach to signaling an error in a function is through the returned result:

```
function sumNumbers(numArray) {
  var result = 0;

  // sum numbers in array
  // unless array is empty, or nonnumber reached
  if (numArray.length > 0) {
    for (var i = 0; i < numArray.length; i++) {
      if (typeof numArray[i] == "number") {
        result+=numArray[i];
      }
```

```
      else {
        result = NaN;
        break;
      }
    }
  }
  else {
    result = NaN;
  }
  return result;
}
...
  var ary = new Array(1,15,"three",5,5);
  var res = sumNumbers(ary); // res is NaN
  if (isNaN(res)) alert("Encountered a bad array or array element");
```

Discussion

A simple way to return an error from a function is through the result. The important point to remember is that the return value and type need to match what you would expect from the data type of the result if things had gone well.

In the solution, the global NaN value is returned if the array was empty, or has at least one entry that isn't a number. The result is tested with the isNaN function, and if the result is NaN, a message to that effect is given.

10.3 Using an Alert for Simple Debugging

Problem

You want a simple way to check the value of a variable.

Solution

Use an alert message box to output the value of a variable:

```
alert(someVariable);
```

Discussion

Most developers use what I call the poor man's debugging tool: printing out the value of a variable using whatever output functionality is available. With JavaScript, the poor man's debugging usually occurs through an alert message box or with the JavaScript console, if the console is supported by the browser.

To use an alert message box to debug, just provide the variable in the function call:

```
alert(variableName);
```

If the variable is a simple scalar value, the result of this function call is a printout of the string value of the object's contents. If the object is more complex, the print results will vary. For instance, an array will have a print out value like the following:

```
var fruit = ['apple','cherry','pear'];
alert(fruit); // prints out apple, cherry, pear
```

The array values are all printed out, in order, with a comma between the entries.

Using an object with the alert can have interesting effects. If you pass a variable containing a reference to a web page element, you may get unpredictable results depending on the browser used, its age, the DOM the browser supports, and so on. For the most part, though, and for most web page elements, the object printouts will be the same. In Safari 4, a variable with a reference to a `div` element:

```
alert(divElement);
```

prints out as:

```
[object HTMLDivElement]
```

Not particularly useful. However, the following could provide useful information:

```
alert(divElement.innerHTML); // prints out contents of div element
```

Anything beyond these simple printouts, though, should be left for browser debuggers.

10.4 Catching an Error and Providing Graceful Error Handling

Problem

You want to incorporate helpful error handling into your JavaScript.

Solution

Use the `try...catch` exception handling technique:

```
try {
  someFunction(var1);
} catch (e) {
  alert (e.message);
}
finally {
  j = null;
}
```

Discussion

In the solution, the code accesses a function that hasn't been defined. Normally, this would trigger a JavaScript error, resulting in an error message like that shown in the Firefox JavaScript console in Figure 10-3. It would also cause the script to fail at that point. It's an effective error-handling mechanism, but not a particularly graceful or helpful one.

When the code that could result in an error is contained in a `try` statement, the associated `catch` statement handles the exception it causes. After the error is processed, the program control then skips to the first statement that follows the exception handling statements.

Figure 10-3. Firefox console error when accessing a nonexistent function

You can also use an optional `finally` statement with code that you want to process regardless of the success of the `try` statement. You'll most likely want to use the `finally` statement to do any necessary cleanup.

The exception in the solution is an `Error` object, and it comes with useful information. In the solution, the error message is accessed and printed out to an alert message box. Peering into the exception in Firefox, we find the following properties:

`fileName`
    Name of file where exception occurred

`lineNumber`
    Number of the line where exception occurred

`message`
    The exception message

`name`
    The name of the exception (i.e., `ReferenceError`)

`stack`
    A stack trace of the exception

The `fileName`, `lineNumber`, and `stack` are nonstandard Firefox extensions and aren't guaranteed to exist between browsers. The `message` and error `name` are standard, and should always be available if the application or browser implements JavaScript exception handling.

10.5 Initiating Manageable Errors

Problem

You want to incorporate custom exceptions into your applications or libraries that provide useful information to calling applications.

Solution

Use the `throw` statement, and create a custom object as an exception:

```
if (typeof value == "number") {
    sum+=number;
} else {
    throw "NotANumber";
}
```

Discussion

The `throw` statement is partner to `try...catch`. With `throw`, you can throw exceptions rather than returning error values from functions or setting some global error value. The advantage to using `throw` and `try...catch` is that it doesn't matter how deeply nested the error occurs, as the exception can ensure that the error is reflected to the calling application, and cleanly, too.

In the solution, the exception is thrown as a string. You can also throw an integer, Boolean, or object. If you only need to provide an exception message, use the string—or an integer if you're using an array of exceptions, and the integer is used to look up the error. Otherwise, either create and throw a specific exception, or create a new `Error` object, providing your own error message:

```
if (typeof value == "number") {
    sum+=number;
} else {
    throw new Error("NotANumber");
}
```

The existing exception types are `Error`, as demonstrated, and:

EvalError
    Used when `eval` is used improperly

RangeError
    Used when the number is out of range

ReferenceError
> Used when a nonexistent variable is referenced

SyntaxError
> Used when there's a syntax error

TypeError
> Indicates an unexpected type

URIError
> Used when a malformed URI is encountered

DOMException
> Indicates a DOM error

EventException
> Indicates a DOM event exception

RangeException
> Indicates a DOM range exception

The last three exceptions are related to the DOM API. All the errors take a custom message as a `string` parameter.

10.6 Using Firebug with Firefox

Problem

You want to set up Firefox for debugging JavaScript.

Solution

Use Firebug, the popular Firefox add-on development tool.

Discussion

Unlike other development tools, Firebug is a Firefox add-on, which you'll need to download and install. However, it installs very easily, and new releases update through Firefox automatically.

To start Firebug, look for the little bug in the status bar, on the right of the browser. Clicking the bug opens Firebug, as shown in Figure 10-4.

The Firebug tab pages include the Console, the HTML element inspector, the CSS panel, the Script tab, the DOM tree tab, and the Net tab. The Net tab will be handy later in the book when we're working with Ajax, but for now, we'll take a look at the HTML, DOM, and CSS tabs before going into more detail on the Script debugger and Console.

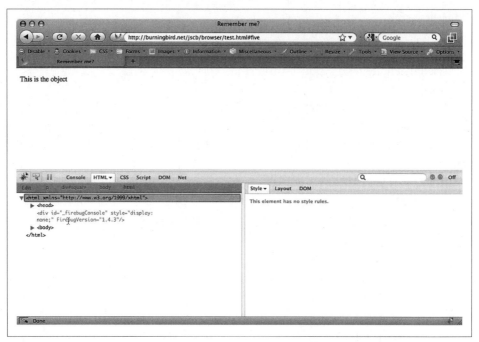

Figure 10-4. The Firebug tabbed pages

In the HTML tab, you can view the page's element tree, clicking any element in the tree to highlight the element in the page, as shown in Figure 10-5. Notice the Style, Layout, and DOM options in the right panel. The Layout tab is currently checked, and shows the width, borders, and padding.

The HTML tab is a good way to check your web page to see which element you need to access or modify with your JavaScript application.

The CSS tab shows the CSS currently set for the web page. You can also edit the CSS by clicking the Edit option, as shown in Figure 10-6. Again, handy if you're setting CSS to work with your JavaScript application. If there is more than one CSS stylesheet, you can select which one to display from a drop-down menu.

The DOM inspector provides descriptions of the DOM for all of the page elements. This includes all the properties and methods, which makes a terrific in-page reference for all the functionality you need when you're building your dynamic page applications, as shown in Figure 10-7.

If the Panels are not enabled when you open Firebug, you can enable them by right-clicking the little Firebug icon in the status bar. Once they are enabled, you can control what shows up in each panel with drop-down menus.

Figure 10-5. The Firebug HTML tab, with the Layout option selected

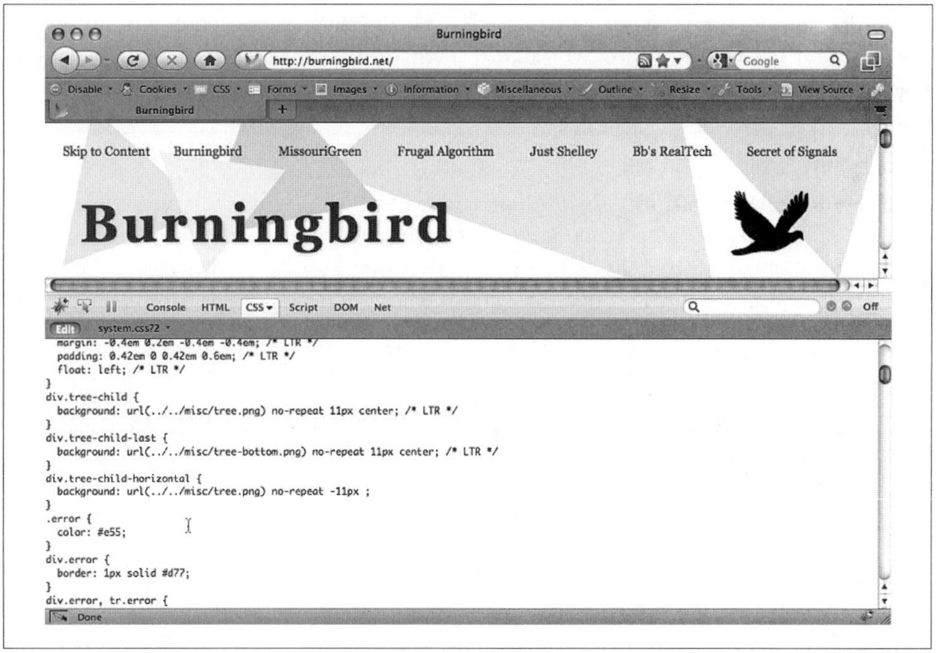

Figure 10-6. The Firebug CSS tab, with editing turned on

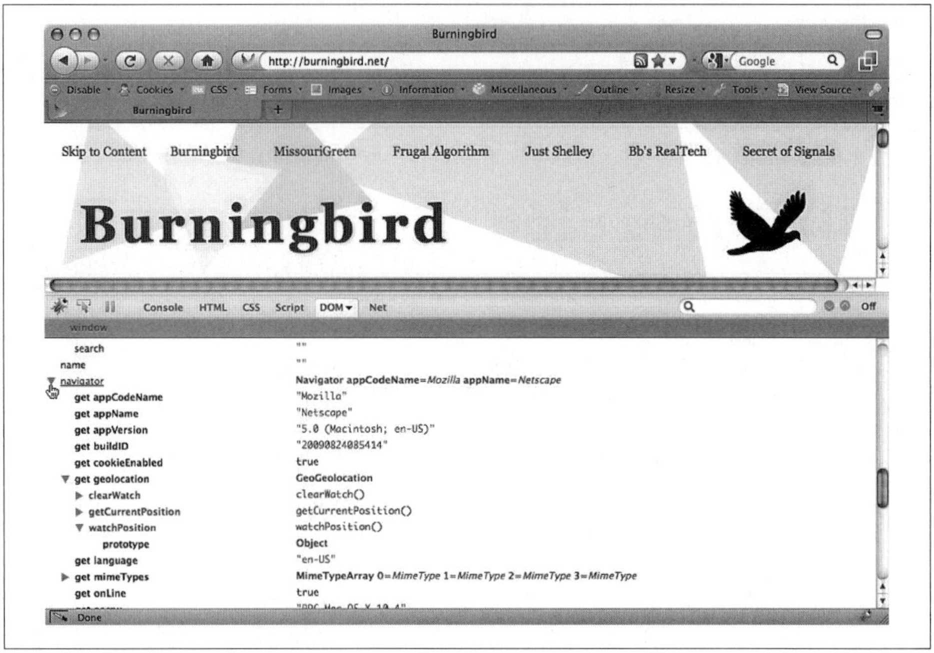

Figure 10-7. The Firebug DOM inspector

You can also open Firebug in a separate window, via the Firebug icon menu. Opening the debugger in a separate window is handy if you don't want to take up page real estate with a debugger.

See Also

Download Firebug from *http://getfirebug.com/*. Estelle Weyl wrote a nice tutorial on Firebug at *http://www.evotech.net/blog/2007/06/introduction-to-firebug/*. There's also a Firebug Lite for use with other browsers, but I've found that each browser's one native debugger to be sufficient. If you want to try it, though, download it from *http://getfire bug.com/lite.html*.

10.7 Setting a Breakpoint and Examining Data with Firebug

Problem

You want to stop program execution in Firefox and check out the program variables at the time.

Solution

Set a breakpoint in Firebug and use the Watch Expression panel to examine the data.

Discussion

JavaScript breakpoints can be set by clicking the line where you want the breakpoint to be set, as shown in Figure 10-8.

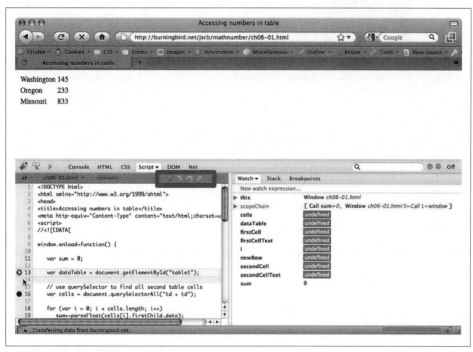

Figure 10-8. Setting a breakpoint in Firebug

In Figure 10-8, a dark box surrounds the debugging flow controls. From left to right, the first control continues execution of the program until another breakpoint, or the application ends. The next control is Step Into, which causes the debugger to drill into any function. The next is Step Over, which would step over a function. The last is Step Out, to step out of a function.

When you set a breakpoint, you can set it to stop the program execution every time the line is reached, or you can specify a constraint by right-clicking the breakpoint and providing a constraint on the breakpoint, as shown in Figure 10-9. Most of the time, though, you'll probably want to stop execution with each iteration.

When a breakpoint is reached in Firebug, you can examine the Watch expressions, variables, and objects, the execution stack, or where current breakpoints are set (handy for very large applications) in the left panel.

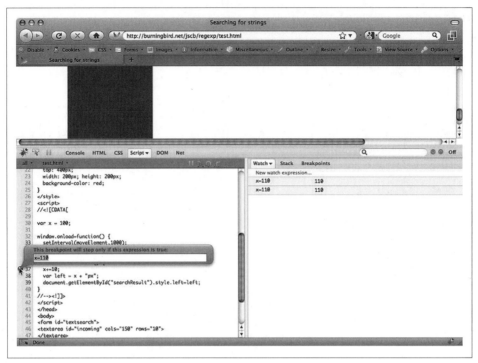

Figure 10-9. Setting a conditional breakpoint in Firebug

Figure 10-10 shows the Watch panel open, with several objects showing. If any of the variables have a drop-down arrow next to it, clicking the arrow displays any properties and methods of the object directly beneath the object. As you step through program execution, the objects are updated according to the program.

10.8 Firefox and the Console

Problem

You want to profile a JavaScript application's performance in Firefox.

Solution

Use Firebug and the Console commands to profile the JavaScript application.

Discussion

The Firebug Console object, its associated panel, and its API, are handy not only for JavaScript profiling, but for program logging, performing a trace, and other debugging.

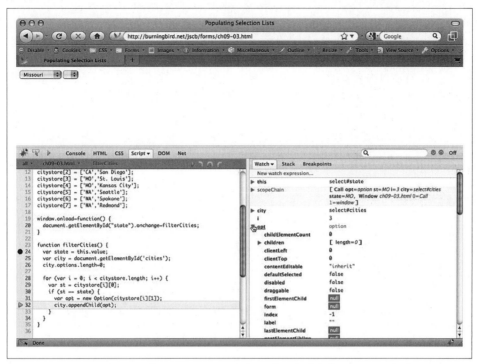

Figure 10-10. Examining watch expressions in Firebug after the breakpoint is reached

When the Console panel is enabled in Firebug, there's a drop-down menu at the top of the panel that controls what shows up in the Console, such as CSS and XML errors, whether to turn on strict warnings, or to open a larger command line. The command line is a small line at the bottom of the Console panel, as shown in Figure 10-11.

The Console command line is a way to enter Console commands (naturally). The command line isn't for the inexperienced, but it can be a quick way to work your way around the DOM. It also has an "autofill" capability: if you start to type in a DOM element, as shown in Figure 10-12, and hit the tab, you can cycle through options at any point, hitting the return when you find one you want.

Returning to the solution, to profile JavaScript, you'll use the Console object API, not the Command Line API. The Console object API is actually controlled in your Java-Script, with commands given directly in the script. For instance, to start a JavaScript profile and give it a name of test, use the following:

```
console.profile('test');
```

When you want to finish the profile, use:

```
console.profileEnd();
```

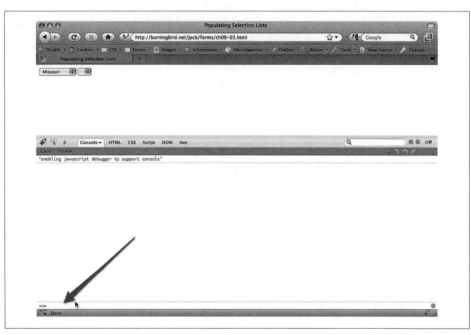

Figure 10-11. The Firebug Console, including command line

Figure 10-12. Using the Firebug Console command line

In the profile tab for the Console panel, you can see the named profiles, and if you click on each, see where time was spent in the application, as shown in Figure 10-13.

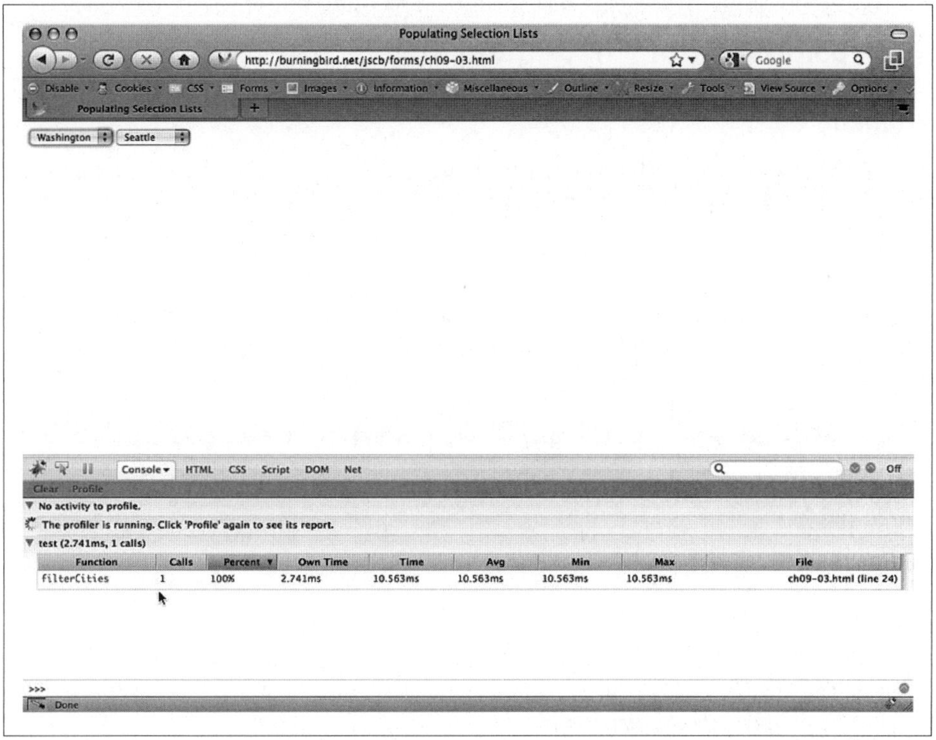

Figure 10-13. Using the Console object's profile methods to profile the JavaScript

There are other Console object API methods, including `console.log` to log messages, `console.count`, which prints out the number of times the line with this command is executed, `console.time` and `console.timeEnd`, to set up a timer to test execution time for a block of code, and so on.

Best of all, as we'll see later, other browser debuggers have also implemented at least partial support for the Console API.

> As with all debugging aids built into an application, make sure you re-move console inline code commands before rolling your application out for beta or release.

See Also

The Console command line documentation can be found at *http://getfirebug.com/cl .html*, and the command line API at *http://getfirebug.com/wiki/index.php/Command*

_Line. The console object API documentation can be found at *http://getfirebug.com/
wiki/index.php/Console*.

10.9 Using IE's Built-in Debugger

Problem

You're using Internet Explorer and you want to debug your JavaScript application.
You need to turn on the IE Developer Tools.

Solution

The Developer Tools, including a JavaScript debugger, can be found under
Tools→Developer Tools, or by pressing F12, as shown in Figure 10-14.

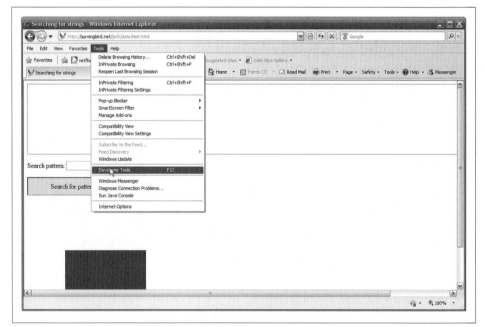

Figure 10-14. Finding the Developer Tools in IE8

Discussion

The Developer Tools that come with IE8 are as featured as you would need and provide
tabbed panels for inspecting HTML, CSS, JavaScript, and JavaScript application Profiling, as shown in Figure 10-15. Don't let references to "JScript" intimidate you: this is
Microsoft's term for JavaScript, but is more or less the same thing as "JavaScript" or
even "ECMAScript" to everyone else.

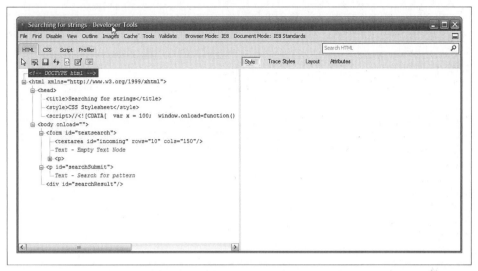

Figure 10-15. The IE Developer Tools interface

The HTML and CSS Developer Tools provide displays of HTML or CSS for the current web page. In the left panel is a display of markup or CSS for the page, and if you click on an object, properties for what you clicked display in the right panel.

As with Firebug, you can examine the layout for the page or the CSS attributes for an element. You can modify both or choose a new stylesheet, and save any edits to a new HTML or CSS file. The Profile panel is a great way of testing your web page and application performance to see where a script may be dragging, as shown in Figure 10-16.

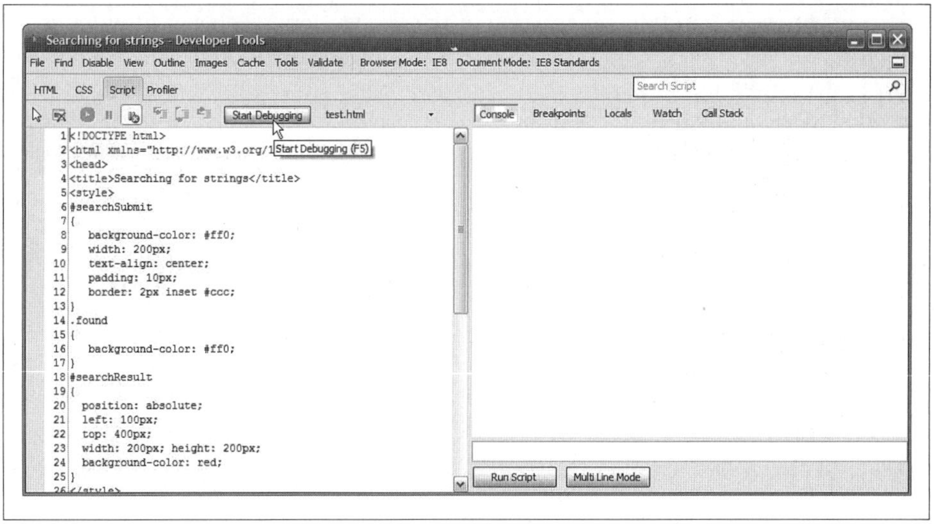

Figure 10-16. Using the IE Developer Tools profile feature

Microsoft does support a Console API, but be forewarned: it does not operate the same as the Console API defined with Firebug and also used by WebKit. It's only available when typing script into the Console pane; you can't use it within the actual script itself. Handy, but not as handy as being able to place console calls into the code itself.

As for the Console pane, Figure 10-17 shows it open, with errors displayed.

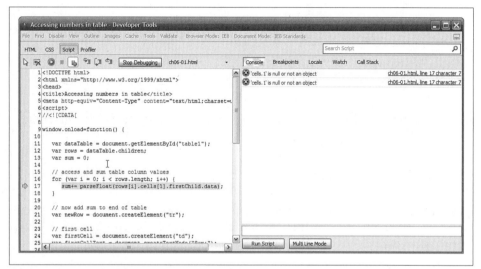

Figure 10-17. Examining JavaScript errors in the IE Developer Tools Console pane

See Also

Microsoft provides good documentation of the IE Developer Tools at *http://msdn.mi crosoft.com/en-us/library/dd565622(VS.85).aspx*. Be aware, though, that Microsoft moves pages around a lot, and doesn't provide redirection in most cases. If the link provided in this book dies, try searching for "IE8 Developer Tools" to find the documentation. The high-level IE Developer page is at *http://msdn.microsoft.com/en-us/ie/ default.aspx*. This will probably be a safe URL.

10.10 Setting a Breakpoint with IE Developer Tools

Problem

You want to halt execution of a JavaScript application at specific lines, and examine the application data at that point.

Solution

Use the IE Developer Tools Script debugger to set breakpoints in your code and then examine the data, as well as the Call Stack and Watch expressions in the right side of the script debugger.

Discussion

The IE Developer Tools Script debugger isn't turned on until you do so explicitly, or you hit an error in the JavaScript and the browser asks if you want to debug the script. When you open the script, you can set a breakpoint by clicking to the left of the line where you want the breakpoint to stop, as shown in Figure 10-18.

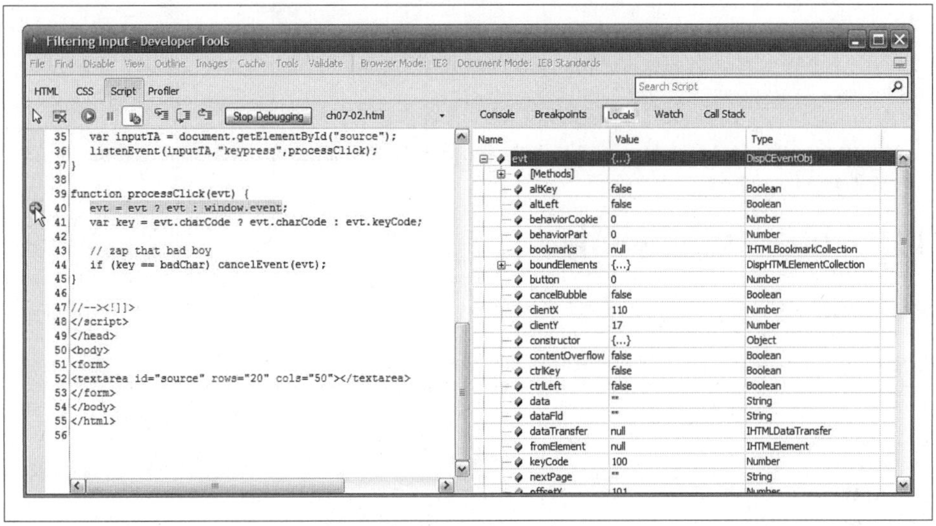

Figure 10-18. The Script Debugger with a breakpoint set and code execution stopped

Next to the Start/Stop Debugging button shown in Figure 10-18, you can see the options that control program flow (Step Into, Step Over, Step Out). In the right side of the debugger is a display of the local variables at that point in the code execution. Currently the Event object is open, and all of its properties and methods are displayed.

Clicking any of the methods or properties that have a plus (+) next to the name pops open the additional properties and methods nested next to the property, as shown in Figure 10-19. This nesting is typical for all of the debuggers. Otherwise, the displays could get too cluttered to see what's happening.

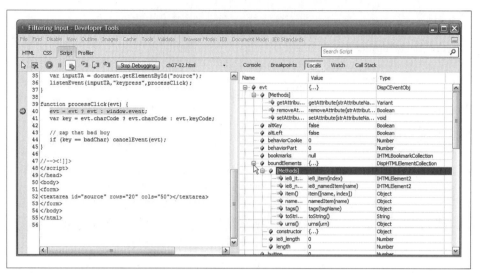

Figure 10-19. The Script Debugger Locals panel with additional properties displayed below their parent element or object

10.11 Opera's Dragonfly

Problem

Your favorite browser is Opera and you want to see what kind of debugging capability this browser has.

Solution

Use Opera's Dragonfly for JavaScript and other debugging.

Discussion

I will say one thing: Opera has the prettiest named debugger.

As with most of the browsers these days, Dragonfly is built into Opera. You can access the tool by selecting the Tools menu, then Advanced, and Developer Tools. Dragonfly opens in the bottom half of the web page, as shown in Figure 10-20.

As with Firebug and IE's Developer Tools, Dragonfly provides a panel for examining and working with HTML (DOM), an Error Console, a place to control the settings for the tool, a Network page, and a script debugger.

The Settings panel is rather nice, because it's quite simple to see where to make changes, as shown in Figure 10-21.

The Error Console will show JavaScript errors, CSS errors, or both, as shown in Figure 10-22. Unfortunately, at this time, Dragonfly does not support the Console API.

Figure 10-20. Opera's Dragonfly opened into browser

Figure 10-21. Dragonfly's Settings page

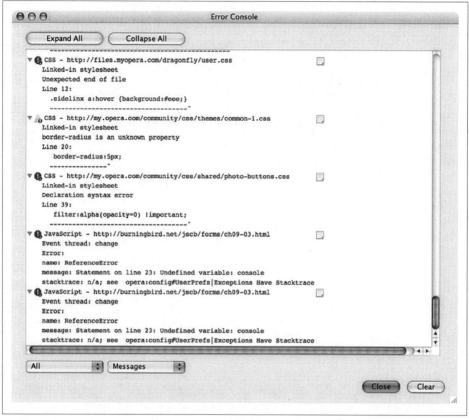

Figure 10-22. Showing both CSS and JavaScript errors in the Dragonfly Error Console

The Network page shows how long each component of the page took to load and the component's size, as shown in Figure 10-23. Though not as colorful as Safari's setup (as you'll see later in this chapter), it's nicely organized and easy to read.

As with other developing tools (except for IE's), you can unlock the Dragonfly frame into a separate window by clicking the double window icon next to the Dragonfly icon at the top of the pane.

Clicking the Dragonfly icon reloads the debugging context, and clicking the red X closes Dragonfly.

See Also

Opera has provided a nice set of documentation for DragonFly at *http://www.opera .com/dragonfly/documentation/*.

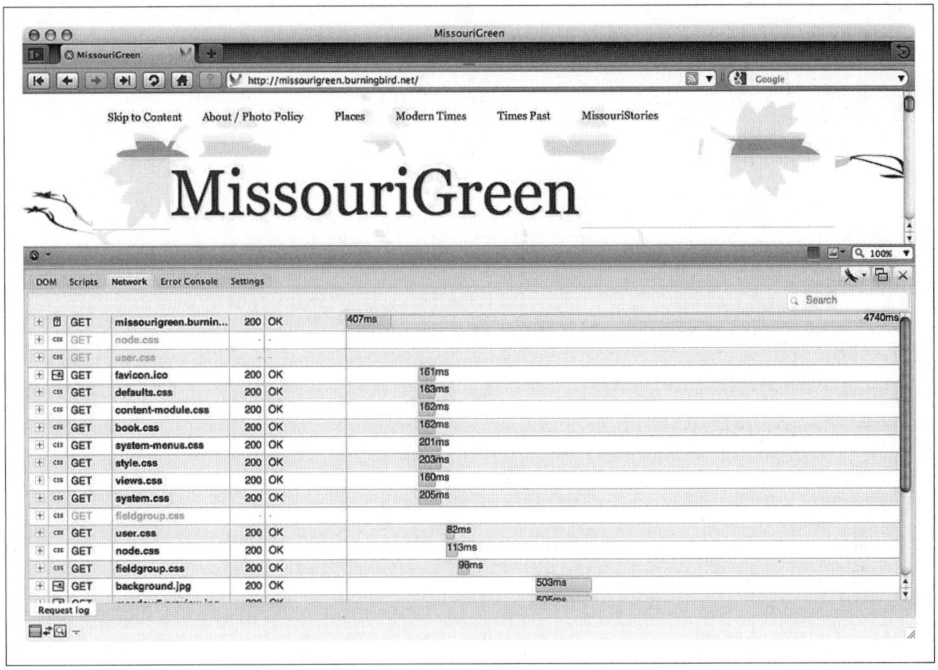

Figure 10-23. Dragonfly's Network page

10.12 Setting a Breakpoint with Dragonfly

Problem

You want to set a breakpoint and examine program state in Opera.

Solution

Use Dragonfly's Scripts panel. Click the line to the left of where you want the breakpoint to be. As with all other debuggers, you have options at the top to continue script processing: Step Over, Step Into, and Step Out, as shown in Figure 10-24.

Notice the right panel in Figure 10-24. Currently, it's set to display the current call stack. You can click the Inspection tab to view local variables as they're set while you walk through the code, as shown in Figure 10-25.

10.13 Turning on Safari's Development Tools

Problem

You need to find the development tools available for Safari 4.

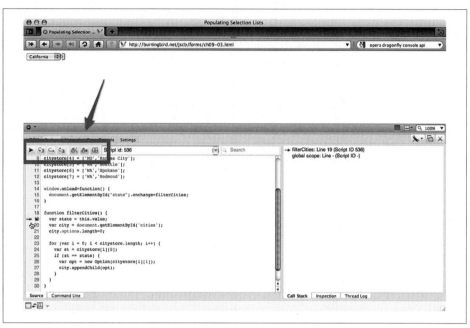

Figure 10-24. Stopping at a breakpoint in Dragonfly

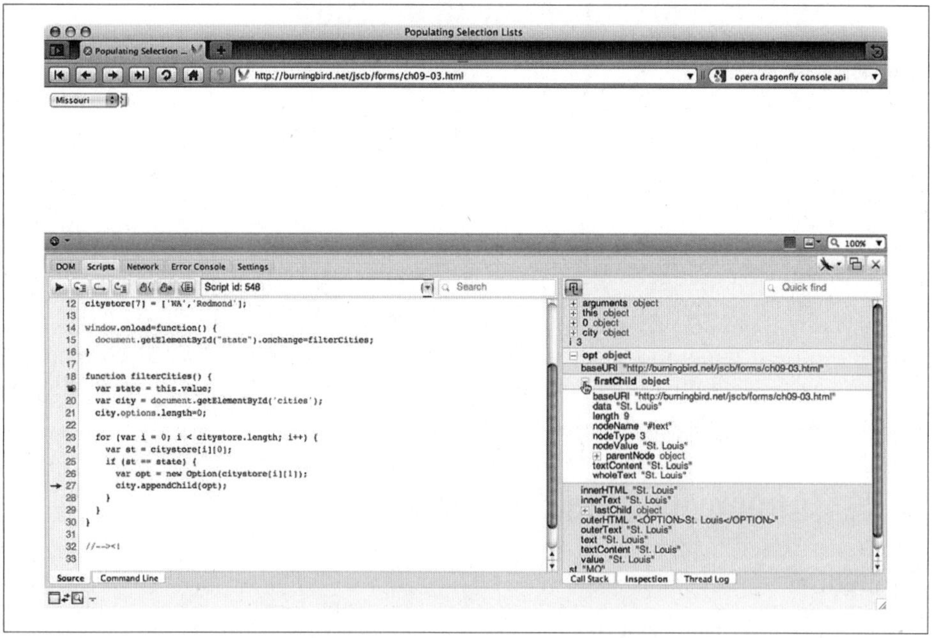

Figure 10-25. Inspecting local variables using Dragonfly

Solution

In the Preferences menu, select the Advanced option and check the option to "Show Develop menu" in menu bar.

Discussion

Safari 4 and up feature a wide variety of helpful tools for the web developer. Once you turn on the Develop menu, you'll see options to:

- Open the page in another browser
- Change the User Agent signature to others, to test applications
- Show Web Inspector
- Show Error Console
- Show Snippet Editor
- Start Debugging JavaScript
- Start Profiling JavaScript
- Disable Caches
- Disable Images
- Disable Styles
- Disable JavaScript
- Disable Runaway JavaScript Timer
- Disable Site-Specific Hacks

All of the options are handy, but I'll focus on those useful for the JavaScript developer.

The Show Web Inspector option opens the Web Inspector into the lower portion of the browser window.

The Web Inspector is a terrific way of examining the page elements, as well as checking resource use for pages and debugging script, as shown in Figure 10-26. Moving your mouse over any of the elements shades the element in the page, making it easier to spot. The right window shows the current style setting for the element.

Most of the other options work within the Web Inspector, including the Error Console.

The Show Error Console will open the Web Inspector if it's not already opened, and then an error message at the bottom. The Error Console reflects all of the JavaScript errors that occur, including the line number where the error occurred, as shown in Figure 10-27.

The ability to open the page in another browser provides a nice way to quickly open a page for testing in one of the other browsers currently available in the system. The ability to change the User Agent string is a way of testing JavaScript applications and libraries to see if the code or behavior changes based on the user agent.

Figure 10-26. The Web Inspector open in a Safari browser

Figure 10-27. The Error Console opened in the Web Inspector

The Snippet Editor is a cute little bugger. When you click on this option, a small, double-paned window opens. You can type HTML, CSS, or JavaScript in the upper pane, and the result is displayed in the bottom pane. It's a great way of trying out various pieces of markup or code, without having to create a web page, as shown in Figure 10-28.

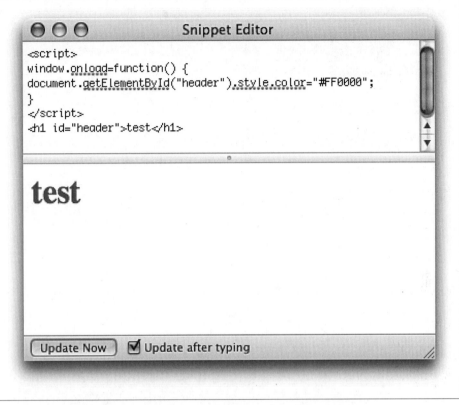

Figure 10-28. The Snippet Editor with a line of HTML and small piece of JavaScript

The JavaScript profile functionality provides information about where your application is spending its time. It is compatible with the `console.profile` methods described with Firefox, and provides a nice interface to view the results. Figure 10-29 demonstrates a profile of a small Canvas application.

I'll cover one last tool before getting into the JavaScript debugging in Safari: the resource window. Though not specific to JavaScript use, this handy window can provide you a good idea of why your pages may be loading slowly; it provides a breakdown of what's loaded, and how long it's taking. The resources tracked are JavaScript files, stylesheets, images, and the document, as shown in Figure 10-30.

See Also

The Firefox JavaScript profile functionality is covered in Recipe 10.9. For a detailed overview of the developer tools available with Safari 4, see *http://www.apple.com/safari/features.html#developer*.

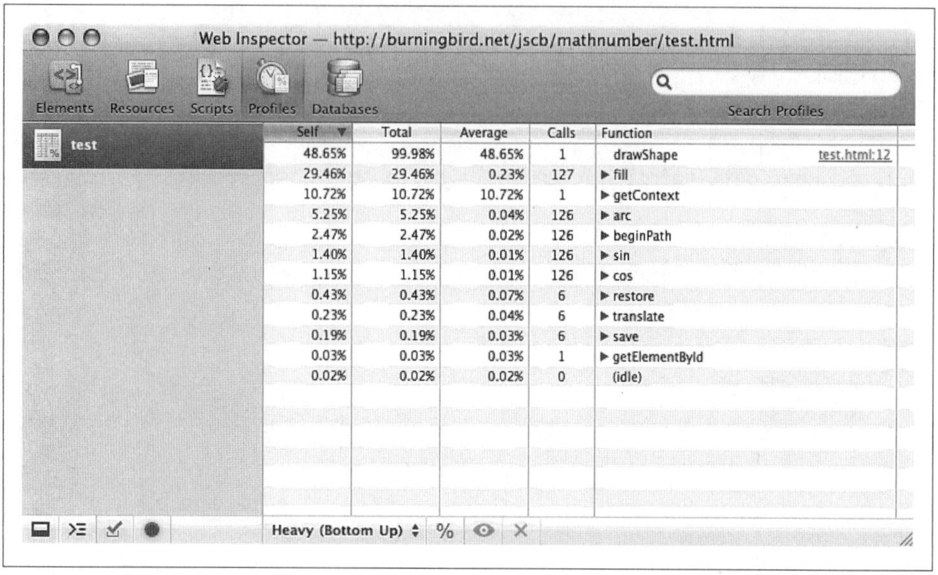

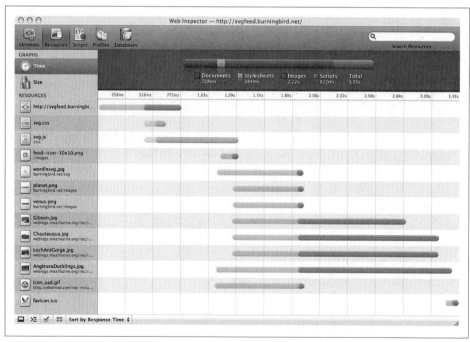

Figure 10-29. Snapshot of the Safari/WebKit JavaScript Profile window

Figure 10-30. Web Inspector Resources Panel

10.14 Setting a Breakpoint with Safari's Debugger

Problem

You want to stop program execution and investigate the state of variables.

Solution

Set a breakpoint in Safari's debugger, and when the breakpoint is reached, check out the program variables at that point.

Discussion

When the JavaScript debugger is open and JavaScript loaded, you can set a breakpoint by clicking to the left of the line number for the line where you want the breakpoint to occur, as shown in Figure 10-31.

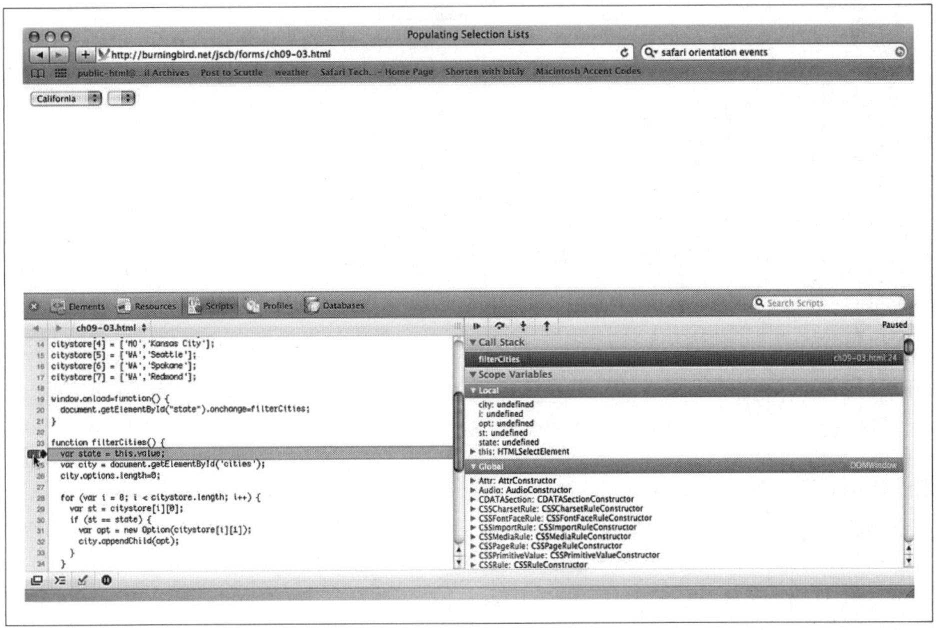

Figure 10-31. Setting a breakpoint and examining local variables in the Safari debugger

As shown in Figure 10-31, when the breakpoint is reached, you can check out both local and global variables, including those for DOM elements, such as document. Clicking the arrows next to any of the objects will open a display with the object's methods and properties.

Once you've reached the breakpoint, you can continue program execution by using the buttons above the data panel, as shown in Figure 10-32. From the left, the buttons represent the pause/run button (to continue execution), and the Step Over, Step Into, and Step Out Of buttons for controlling how you want to handle function calls in a line. Typically, I use Step Over, because I don't necessarily want to drill into a function: I want to see return values. However, it is a handy way of seeing what's happening when you're using JavaScript libraries.

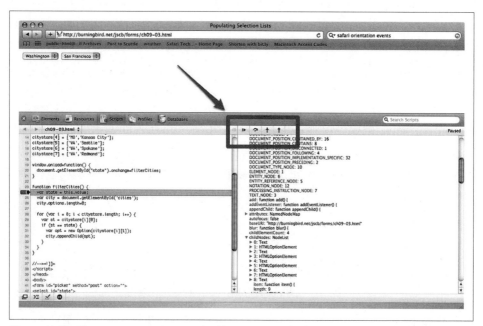

Figure 10-32. The program execution control buttons over the data panel in the script debugger

Safari (or, I should say, WebKit) is the only browser that implements the console API made popular by Firebug. If you want to start a JavaScript profile in Safari, insert a console command to start the profile, as well as the end profile command.

You can then check out the profile in the Profiles panel in the debugger, as shown in Recipe 10.12, in Figure 10-29.

10.15 Debugging in Chrome

Problem

You want to use a JavaScript debug tool in Google's Chrome.

Solution

The Developer Tools for Chrome are a little hard to find because of the user interface, but if you look under the Page icon on the menu bar, you'll see an option labeled Developer. Clicking it displays several options, including Debug JavaScript and JavaScript Console. Clicking the Debug JavaScript option opens the Web Inspector, including JavaScript Developer.

Discussion

Chrome is based on WebKit, so the same web inspector and debugging tools made available in WebKit are also available in Chrome. Once you've turned on the debug option, you'll see set of panels (as shown in Figure 10-33) that will look familiar if you've worked with recent versions of Safari.

Figure 10-33. The WebKit debugger toolset, open in Chrome

You can set breakpoints, examine data, inspect HTML and CSS, and create JavaScript profiles—basically, all of the functionality you expect from web developer tools.

See Also

The debugger for Chrome is the WebKit debugger, so I'll refer you to Recipe 10.13, on how the debugger is used to debug JavaScript in Safari.

CHAPTER 11

Accessing Page Elements

11.0 Introduction

A web document is organized like an upside-down tree, with the topmost element at the root and all other elements branching out, beneath. As you can see when you look at a web page within the Safari Web Developer Elements window (Figure 11-1), the top-level element is the `html` element, followed by the `head` and `body` elements. The `head` element contains `title`, `script`, and `meta` elements, while the body contains a couple of `div` elements, one containing paragraphs (`p`), the other containing an unordered list (`ul`) and list items (`li`)—one of which contains a paragraph, which contains a `span`.

Except for the root element (HTML), each element has a parent `node`, and all of the elements are accessible from one object: `document`.

There are several different techniques available for accessing these document elements, or *nodes* as they're called in the Document Object Model (DOM). Today, we access these nodes through standardized versions of the DOM, such as the DOM Levels 2 and 3, mentioned throughout the book. Originally, though, a de facto technique was to access the elements through the browser object model, sometimes referred to as DOM Level 0. The DOM Level 0 was invented by the leading browser company of the time, Netscape, and its use has been supported (more or less) in most browsers since. The key object for accessing web page elements in the DOM Level 0 is the `document` object.

The DOM Level 0 Document

In the earlier browser object model, page elements were accessed via the `document` object, via a set of element collections. For instance, to access an `img` element, we would access the `images` array, which contains entries for all images in the page, in order of their occurrence in the page:

```
var selectImage = document.images[1]; // get second image in page
```

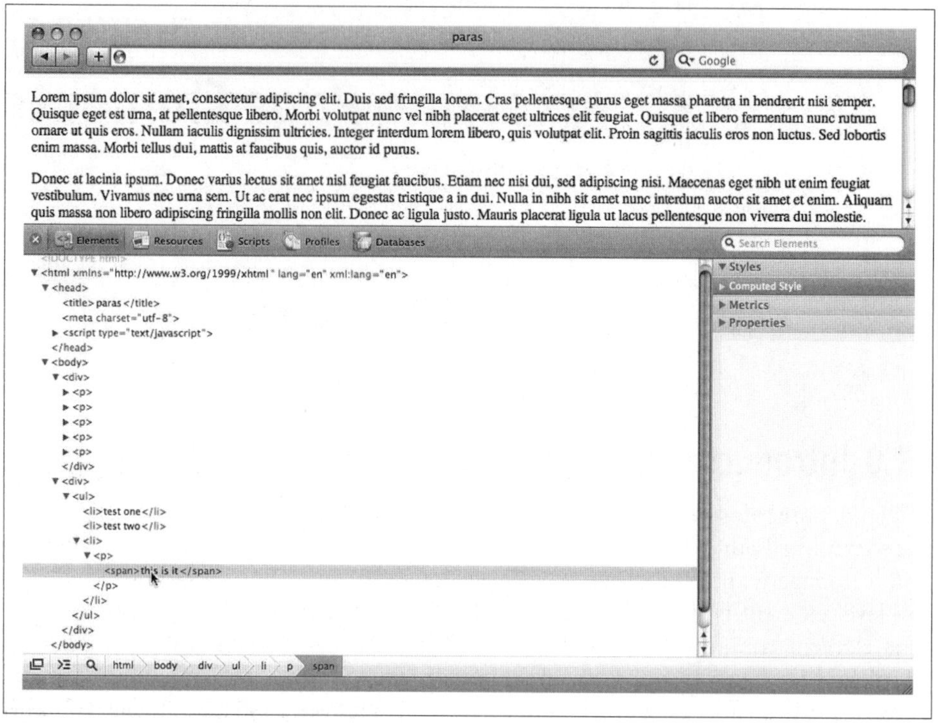
paras
Google
Lorem ipsum dolor sit amet, consectetur adipiscing elit. Duis sed fringilla lorem. Cras pellentesque purus eget massa pharetra in hendrerit nisi semper. Quisque eget est urna, at pellentesque libero. Morbi volutpat nunc vel nibh placerat eget ultrices elit feugiat. Quisque et libero fermentum nunc rutrum ornare ut quis eros. Nullam iaculis dignissim ultricies. Integer interdum lorem libero, quis volutpat elit. Proin sagittis iaculis eros non luctus. Sed lobortis enim massa. Morbi tellus dui, mattis at faucibus quis, auctor id purus.
Donec at lacinia ipsum. Donec varius lectus sit amet nisl feugiat faucibus. Etiam nec nisi dui, sed adipiscing nisi. Maecenas eget nibh ut enim feugiat vestibulum. Vivamus nec urna sem. Ut ac erat nec ipsum egestas tristique a in dui. Nulla in nibh sit amet nunc interdum auctor sit amet et enim. Aliquam quis massa non libero adipiscing fringilla mollis non elit. Donec ac ligula justo. Mauris placerat ligula ut lacus pellentesque non viverra dui molestie.
Elements
Resources
Scripts
Profiles
Databases
Search Elements
<html xmlns="http://www.w3.org/1999/xhtml" lang="en" xml:lang="en">
<head>
<title>paras</title>
<meta charset="utf-8">
<script type="text/javascript">
</head>
<body>
<div>
<p>
<p>
<p>
<p>
<p>
</div>
<div>
<ul>
<li>test one</li>
<li>test two</li>
<li>
<p>
<span>this is it</span>
</p>
</li>
</ul>
</div>
</body>
Styles
Computed Style
Metrics
Properties
html
body
div
ul
li
p
span

Figure 11-1. Example of a document tree

The earliest collections that can be accessed via the `Document` object are:

`images`
: All images in the page

`forms`
: Any forms in the page

`links`
: All links in the page (declared with `<a href="...">`)

`cookie`
: Access, add, and modify web page cookies

Some of the collection elements themselves had collections, such as being able to access all elements within a form via the form's `elements` property:

```
var elemOne = document.forms[0].elements[0]; // first element in first form
```

As with images, elements could be accessed by array entry, with position in the array determined by the position of the element in the web page. In addition, elements given an identifier could also be accessed directly via the collection:

```
<form id="new">
...
</form>
```

```
var newForm = document.forms["new"];
```

Forms also had name attributes as well as ids, either of which could be used to access the form. The form could also be accessed, via a shortcut, by its identifier/name:

```
var newForm = document.new; // form named "new"
```

Note, though, that this technique is not standardized via specification, though support for it is included in most (if not all) browsers.

 Also note that the name attribute is only supported in a limited set of web page elements. You're encouraged to use the id attribute instead.

In addition, all elements in the web page could be accessed via the document.all property, by specifying the identifier given the element:

```
<div id="test">
...
var tstElem = document.all["test"]; // returns ref to test div element
```

The all collection was created by Microsoft in Internet Explorer, and eventually became another de facto standard. The all property and the other collections are still available for use now, and many of the element collections are now in the DOM Level 2 HTML specification, but the all property's use is discouraged in favor of the techniques formalized under the DOM Level 1 specification.

The Standardized DOMs

The problem with the earliest techniques in accessing web page elements is that the browser companies didn't agree on any one technique, and to support all of the browsers we had to use a convoluted set of if statements, testing for browser support.

The W3C remedied this problem by releasing a new, standard approach to working with the web page document object model: the DOM Level 1. Since then, the organization has worked to refine the DOM with releases of DOM Level 2, DOM Level 3, and the current work associated with HTML5—demonstrated in this chapter and in the rest of this book.

The W3C specifications provide a core API that can be used for more generic documents, as well as APIs specific to HTML. These include a new events model, support for XPath, keyboard access, in addition to various methods to access existing elements, and to create new elements that can then be inserted into the document tree. The W3C documentation for the DOM consists of the standards specifications and language bindings. We're primarily interested in the ECMAScript language binding.

Be aware that at the time this book was written, implementation of DOM Level 3 Events functionality was sketchy, at best.

The most used method supported in the DOM Level 2 and up is the `document` object method `getElementById`:

```
<div id="test">
...
var testElement = document.getElementById("test");
```

The `document.getElementById` method originated in the DOM Level 1 HTML API, and then moved over as a more generalized method to DOM Level 2.

With `document.getElementById`, rather than have to access a specific element collection or determine if `document.all` was supported, we can use the standard method and be assured of accessing any page element by its given `id`.

The `getElementById` method was just the beginning, and this very helpful method has been joined by `getElementsByTagName`, to get all elements via a specific element tag; `getElementsByClassName`, to get all elements that share the same class name; and the very new `querySelector` and `querySelectorAll` methods, which allow us to use the CSS style selectors in order to make more sophisticated queries.

See Also

See Chapter 7 for coverage of event handling in DOM Level 2. The best way to find a summary of the different DOM specifications is via the W3C DOM Technical Reports page (*http://www.w3.org/DOM/DOMTR*). Mozilla also provides a nice DOM summary (*https://developer.mozilla.org/En/DOM_Levels*), as does the Wikipedia entry on the DOM (*http://en.wikipedia.org/wiki/Document_Object_Model*).

The ECMAScript binding for DOM Level 1 is at *http://www.w3.org/TR/REC-DOM -Level-1/ecma-script-language-binding.html*. DOM Level 2's ECMAScript binding is at *http://www.w3.org/TR/DOM-Level-2-Core/ecma-script-binding.html*. The binding for DOM Level 3 is at *http://www.w3.org/TR/DOM-Level-3-Core/ecma-script-binding .html*.

11.1 Access a Given Element and Find Its Parent and Child Elements

Problem

You want to access a specific `document` element, and find its parent and child elements.

Solution

Give the element a unique identifier, and use the `document.getElementById` method:

```
<div id="demodiv">

...
var demodiv = document.getElementById("demodiv");
```

Find its parent via the `parentNode` property:

```
var parent = demodiv.parentNode;
```

Find its children via the `childNodes` property:

```
var children = demodiv.childNodes;
```

Discussion

The most commonly used DOM method is `getElementById`. It takes one parameter: a case-sensitive string with the element's identifier. It returns an `element` object, which is referenced to the element if it exists; otherwise, it returns null.

The returned `element` object has a set of methods and properties, including several inherited from the `node` object. The `node` methods are primarily associated with traversing the document tree. For instance, to find the parent node for the element, use the following:

```
var parent =demodiv.parentNode; // parent node property
```

If you want to find out what children an element has, you can traverse a collection of them through the `childNodes` property:

```
if (demodiv.hasChildNodes()) {
   var children =demodiv.childNodes;
   for (var i = 0; i < children.length; i++) {
      outputString+=" has child " + children[i].nodeName + "<br />";
   }
}
```

You can find out the type of element for each node through the `nodeName` property:

```
var type = parent.nodeName; // BODY
```

You also might be surprised at what appears as a child node. For instance, whitespace before and after an element is, itself, a child node, with a `nodeName` of #text. For the following `div` element:

```
<div id="demodiv" class="demo">
<p>Some text</p>
<p>Some more text</p>
</div>
```

The `demodiv` element (node) has five children, not two:

```
has child #text
has child P
```

```
has child #text
has child P
has child #text
```

However, IE8 only picks up the two paragraph elements, which demonstrates why it's important to be specific with the queries and check nodeName to ensure you're accessing the correct elements.

11.2 Accessing All Images in the Web Page

Problem

You want to access all img elements in a given document.

Solution

Use the document.getElementsByTagName method, passing in img as the parameter:

```
var imgElements = document.getElementsByTagName('img');
```

Discussion

The getElementsByTagName returns a collection of nodes (a NodeList) of a given element type, such as the img tag in the solution. The collection can be traversed like an array, and the order of nodes is based on the order of the elements within the document: the first img element in the page is accessible at index 0, and so on:

```
var imgElements = document.getElementsByTagName('img');
for (var i = 0; i < imgElements.length; i++) {
   var img = imgElements[i];
   ...
}
```

Though the NodeList collection can be traversed like an array, it isn't an Array object— you can't use Array object methods, such as push() and reverse(), with a NodeList. NodeList's only property is length, which contains the number of elements in the collection. The only method is item, which takes the index of the item, beginning with the first element at index 0:

```
var img = imgElements.item(1); // second image
```

NodeList is an intriguing object because it's a live collection, which means changes made to the document after the NodeList is retrieved are reflected in the collection. Example 11-1 demonstrates the NodeList live collection functionality, as well as getElementsByTagName.

In the example, three images in the web page are accessed as a NodeList collection using the getElementsByTagName method. The length property, with a value of 3, is output in an alert. Immediately after the alert, a new paragraph and img elements are created, and the img appended to the paragraph. To append the paragraph following the others in the page, getElementsByTagName is used again, this time with the paragraph tags (p). We're not really interested in the paragraphs, but in the paragraphs' parent element, found via the **parentNode** property on each paragraph.

The new paragraph element is appended to the paragraph's parent element, and the previously accessed **NodeList** collection variable's length property again printed out. Now, the value is 4, reflecting the addition of the new img element.

Example 11-1. Demonstrating getElementsByTagName and the NodeList live collection property

```
<!DOCTYPE html>
<html xmlns="http://www.w3.org/1999/xhtml" xml:lang="en" lang="en">
<head>
<title>NodeList</title>
<script type="text/javascript">
//<![CDATA[

window.onload=function() {
   var imgs = document.getElementsByTagName('img');
   alert(imgs.length);
   var p = document.createElement("p");
   var img = document.createElement("img");
   img.src="orchids4.preview.jpg";
   p.appendChild(img);

   var paras = document.getElementsByTagName('p');
   paras[0].parentNode.appendChild(p);

   alert(imgs.length);
}
//]]>
</script>
</head>
<body>
<p><img src="orchids12.preview.jpg"
  alt="Orchid from MBG 2009 orchid show" /></p>
<p><img src="orchids6.preview.jpg"
  alt="Orchid from MBG 2009 orchid show" /></p>
<p><img src="orchids9.preview.jpg"
  alt="Orchid from MBG 2009 orchid show" /></p>
</body>
</html>
```

In addition to using getElementsByTagName with a specific element type, you can also pass the universal selector (*) as a parameter to the method to get all elements:

```
var allelems = document.getElementsByTagName('*');
```

 IE7, or IE8 running in IE7 mode, will return an empty nodelist if you use the universal selector with the getElementsByTagName method.

Namespace Variation

There is a variation of getElementsByTagName, getElementsByTagNameNS, which can be used in documents that support multiple namespaces, such as an XHTML web page with embedded MathML or SVG.

In Example 11-2, an SVG document is embedded in XHTML. Both the XHTML document and the embedded SVG make use of the title element. The title element in the XHTML document is part of the default XHTML namespace, but the title in the SVG is part of the Dublin Core namespace.

When the title element is accessed, information about the title, including its namespace, the prefix, the localName and the textContent are printed out. The prefix is the dc component of dc:title, and the localName is the title part of dc:title. The text Content is a new property, added with the DOM Level 2, and is the text of the element. In the case of title (either the XHTML or the Dublin Core element), it would be the title text.

Example 11-2. The differences between the namespace and nonnamespace variation of getElementsByTagName

```
<!DOCTYPE html PUBLIC
    "-//W3C//DTD XHTML 1.1 plus MathML 2.0 plus SVG 1.1//EN"
    "http://www.w3.org/2002/04/xhtml-math-svg/xhtml-math-svg.dtd">
<html xmlns="http://www.w3.org/1999/xhtml" xml:lang="en">
<head>
<title>Namespace</title>
<script type="text/javascript">
//<![CDATA[

window.onload=function () {

   var str = "";
   var title = document.getElementsByTagName("title");
   for (var i = 0; i < title.length; i++) {
      str += title.item(i).namespaceURI + " " +
             title.item(i).prefix + " " +
             title.item(i).localName + " " +
             title.item(i).text + " ";
   }
   alert(str);

   str = "";
   if (!document.getElementsByTagNameNS) return;
   var  titlens =
document.getElementsByTagNameNS("http://purl.org/dc/elements/1.1/",
"title");
   for (var i = 0; i < titlens.length; i++) {
      str += titlens.item(i).namespaceURI + " " +
             titlens.item(i).prefix + " " +
             titlens.item(i).localName + " " +
             titlens.item(i).textContent + " ";
   }
```

```
     alert(str);}
//]]>

</script>
</head>
<body>
<h1>SVG</h1>
<svg id="svgelem"
     height="800" xmlns="http://www.w3.org/2000/svg">
          <circle id="redcircle" cx="300" cy="300" r="300"
           fill="red" />
  <metadata>
    <rdf:RDF xmlns:cc="http://web.resource.org/cc/"
xmlns:dc="http://purl.org/dc/elements/1.1/"
xmlns:rdf="http://www.w3.org/1999/02/22-rdf-syntax-ns#
">
      <cc:Work rdf:about="">
        <dc:title>Sizing Red Circle</dc:title>
        <dc:description></dc:description>
        <dc:subject>
          <rdf:Bag>
            <rdf:li>circle</rdf:li>
            <rdf:li>red</rdf:li>
            <rdf:li>graphic</rdf:li>
          </rdf:Bag>
        </dc:subject>
        <dc:publisher>
          <cc:Agent rdf:about="http://www.openclipart.org">
            <dc:title>Testing RDF in SVG</dc:title>
          </cc:Agent>
        </dc:publisher>
        <dc:creator>
          <cc:Agent>
            <dc:title id="title">Testing</dc:title>
          </cc:Agent>
          </dc:creator>
        <dc:rights>
          <cc:Agent>
            <dc:title>testing</dc:title>
          </cc:Agent>
          </dc:rights>
        <dc:date></dc:date>
        <dc:format>image/svg+xml</dc:format>
        <dc:type
            rdf:resource="http://purl.org/dc/dcmitype/StillImage"/>
        <cc:license
            rdf:resource="http://web.resource.org/cc/PublicDomain"/>
        <dc:language>en</dc:language>
      </cc:Work>
      <cc:License
          rdf:about="http://web.resource.org/cc/PublicDomain">
        <cc:permits
            rdf:resource="http://web.resource.org/cc/Reproduction"/>
        <cc:permits
            rdf:resource="http://web.resource.org/cc/Distribution"/>
```

```
        <cc:permits
            rdf:resource="http://web.resource.org/cc/DerivativeWorks"/>
        </cc:License>
      </rdf:RDF>
    </metadata>
    </svg>
  </body>
</html>
```

The result of the application can vary between browsers. When using Firefox and accessing `title` without using the namespace variation, the only `title` returned is the XHTML document `title`. However, when using the namespace variation (`getElements ByTagNameNS`), and specifying the Dublin Core namespace (*http://purl.org/dc/elements/1.1/*), all of the Dublin Core titles in the RDF within the SVG are returned.

When accessing the nonnamespaced version of `getElementsByTagName` in Safari, Chrome, and Opera, both the XHTML title and the Dublin Core titles are returned, as shown in Figure 11-2.

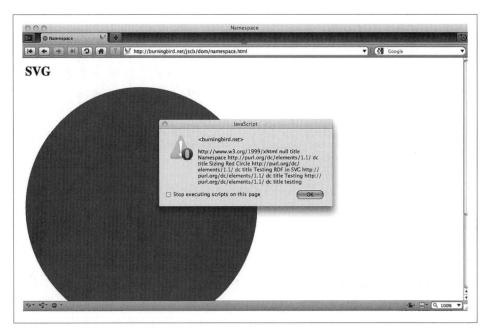

Figure 11-2. Using getElementsByTagNameNS to get namespaced elements

Though IE8 doesn't directly support the XHTML MIME type, if the page is served as `text/html` using some form of content negotiation, IE will process the page as HTML. However, though the `getElementsByTagName` works with IE, the *namespaced* version of the method, `getElementsByTagNameNS`, does not. All of the values are returned as `undefined`. IE8 doesn't return the `dc:title` entries in the SVG, either.

If the Dublin Core namespace is declared in the `html` element, instead of in the `svg` element, IE8 *does* return all of the `dc:title` entries, as well as the XHTML title:

```
<html xmlns="http://www.w3.org/1999/xhtml"
                    xmlns:dc="http://xml:lang="en">
```

An alternative approach consists of using a tag name string that concatenates the `prefix` and `localName`. All of the browsers will find the `dc:title` using the following:

```
var titles = document.getElementsByTagName("dc:title");
```

However, you can't access the namespace-specific properties using the pseudonamespace method. Your applications can't access the namespace properties using the IE approach of embedding all of the namespace declarations in the `html` tag, but you can find out the namespace URI via Microsoft's `tagURN` property:

```
alert(title[i].tagURN); // for dc:title
```

Browsers can use the following to get all elements with a given tag, regardless of namespace, if the document is served as `application/xhtml+xml` or other XML type:

```
var titles = document.getElementsByTagNameNS("*","title");
```

This JavaScript returns both the default XHTML namespace title and the titles in the Dublin Core namespace.

 As mentioned earlier, IE8 doesn't properly support namespaces, but IE9 should with its new support for XHTML.

See Also

Using `getElementsByTagName` to get all the paragraphs just to find their parent in Example 11-1 is overkill. Recipe 11.5 demonstrates how to use the Selectors API to directly access just the parent element for the paragraphs. The `parentNode` property is introduced in Recipe 11.1.

11.3 Discover All Images Within an Article

Problem

You want to access all images within article elements only.

Solution

Find all `article` elements in the web page. Once they are found, find the `img` elements for each one:

```
var imgString = "";

// find all articles
var articles = document.getElementsByTagName('article');

// find all images in articles
for (var i = 0; i < articles.length; i++) {
  var imgs = articles[i].getElementsByTagName('img');

  // print out src
  for (var j = 0; j < imgs.length; j++) {
    var img = imgs[j];
    imgString+=img.src + "<br />";
  }
}
document.getElementById("result").innerHTML=imgString;
```

Discussion

The DOM method getElementsByTagName is available for the element object, as well as the document object. This is handy if you want to look for elements of a certain type throughout the document or within a specific subtree of the document, with a given element as its root.

In the solution, the first use of getElementsByTagName returns a nodeList, which is a collection of article elements for the entire document. This collection is traversed like an array, and the getElementsByTagName is used again, this time with each of the article elements, to look for any img elements within the subtree formed by the article.

The example works with all of the book target browsers except IE8. IE8 does pick up the articles from the first use of document.getElementsByTagName. However, IE8 does not support the use of getElementsByTagName with an element, so it doesn't pick up the images.

See Also

In order to access the new HTML5 article element with IE8, you'll need to use an HTML5 *shim*. IE8 and earlier versions don't correctly process the new HTML5 elements, such as article, without this additional assistance. Recipe 12.4 has more discussion on using an HTML5 shim.

Recipe 11.3 provides in-depth coverage of the getElementsByTagName method.

11.4 Discover all Images in Articles Using the Selectors API

Problem

You want to get a list of all img elements that are descendants of article elements, but not have to traverse HTML collection objects, which can be a slow operation.

Solution

Use the newer Selectors API and access the `img` elements contained within article elements using CSS-style selector strings:

```
var imgs = document.querySelectorAll("article img");
```

Discussion

Once you've worked with the Selectors API, you'll never look for another way to access `document` elements. The Selectors API is a new specification that is undergoing work at the time this was written. It has broad implementation across browsers, though there are some differences in implementation support.

 Earlier versions of browsers, such as IE7, Firefox 2, and so on, do not support the Selectors API. You'll have to use fallback methods to perform the same queries. In addition, IE8 does not support many selector variations.

There are two selector query API methods. The first, `querySelectorAll`, was demonstrated in the solution. The second is `querySelector`. The difference between the two is `querySelectorAll` returns all elements that match the selector criteria, while `querySelector` only returns the first found result.

The selectors syntax is derived from those that support CSS selectors. In the example, all `img` elements that are descendants of article elements are returned. To access all `img` elements, regardless of parent element, use:

```
var imgs = document.querySelectorAll("img");
```

In the solution, you'll get all `img` elements that are direct or indirect descendants of a `article` element. This means that if the `img` element is contained within a `div` that's within an article, this `img` element will be among those returned:

```
<article>
   <div>
      <img src="..." />
   </div>
</article>
```

If you want only those `img` elements that are direct children of an `article` element, you would use the following:

```
var imgs = document.querySelectorAll("article> img");
```

If you're interested in accessing all `img` elements that are immediately followed by a paragraph, you would use:

```
var imgs = document.querySelectorAll("img + p");
```

If you're interested in an `img` element that has an empty `alt` attribute, you can use the following:

```
var imgs = document.querySelectorAll('img[alt=""]');
```

If you're only interested in `img` elements that don't have an empty `alt` attribute, use the following:

```
var imgs = document.querySelectorAll('img:not([alt=""])');
```

The negation pseudoselector (`:not`) is used to find all `img` elements with `alt` attributes that are not empty.

For these queries, which are looking for all `img` elements that meet the given selectors, you should get the same result with the more modern browsers, such as Firefox 3.x, Opera 10.x, Safari 4.x, and Chrome 4.x. Unfortunately, IE8 has only limited support for selectors—the code in the solution does not work.

The collection of elements returned from `querySelectorAll` is not a "live" collection, unlike the collection of objects returned from `getElementsByTagName`. Updates to the page are not reflected in the collection if the updates occur after the collection is retrieved.

 Though the Selectors API is a wonderful creation, it shouldn't be used for every document query. For instance, it's not efficient for accessing elements by a specific identifier, so you're still better off using `getElementById` for this purpose. Best bet is to test your application using the Selectors API and a variety of other methods and see which provides best performance and broadest support.

Namespace Variation

CSS3 provides syntax for handling namespaces. This is how to define a namespace in CSS3, via the Namespace module:

```
@namespace svg "http://www.w3.org/2000/svg";
```

If an element is given with a namespace prefix, such as the following:

```
<q:elem>...</q:elem>
```

to style the element, you would use:

```
@namespace q "http://example.com/q-markup";
q|elem { ... }
```

and to style an attribute, you could use:

```
@namespace foo "http://www.example.com";
[foo|att=val] { color: blue }
```

Recipe 11.2 covered the concept of namespaces when querying against the document, and introduced the first of the namespace-specific methods: `getElementsByTagNameNS`.

Since the CSS selectors allow for resolving namespaces, we might assume we could use namespaces with `querySelector` and `querySelectorAll`. In fact we could, with earlier iterations of the API Selectors draft, but there is no way to do so now.

Now, a namespace error will be thrown if the namespace is not resolved before using the Selectors API methods. Unfortunately, the Selectors API doesn't provide an approach to resolve the namespace before using one of the methods.

Instead, the Selectors API specification recommends using JavaScript processing to handle namespaces. For instance, to find all of the `dc:title` elements within an SVG element in a document, you could use the following:

```
var list = document.querySelectorAll("svg title");
var result = new Array();
var svgns = "http://www.w3.org/2000/svg"

for(var i = 0; i < list.length; i++) {
  if(list[i].namespaceURI == svgns) {
    result.push(list[i]);
  }
}
```

In the example code, querying for all of the titles that are descendants of the **svg** element will return both SVG titles and any Dublin Core or other titles used in the SVG block. In the loop, if the title is in the Dublin Core namespace, it's pushed on to the new array; otherwise, if the title is in some other namespace, including the SVG namespace, it's disregarded.

It's not an elegant approach, but it is serviceable, and also the only option available for namespaces and the Selectors API at this time.

 IE8 and earlier do not support the `namespaceURI` property, nor do they support XHTML or SVG, where you would most likely need to use namespaces. IE9 should provide support for namespaces, XHTML, and SVG.

See Also

JavaScript access of the new HTML5 elements, such as `article`, requires the use of a HTML5 *shim*: a small JavaScript application that enables the use of these elements in IE8. Recipe 12.4 has more on the use of the HTML5 shim.

There are three different CSS selector specifications, labeled as Selectors Level 1, Level 2, and Level 3. You can access CSS Selectors Level 3 at *http://www.w3.org/TR/css3 -selectors/*, a site which contains links to the documents defining the other levels. These documents provide the definitions of, and examples for, the different types of selectors. In addition, the CSS3 Namespace module can be found at *http://www.w3.org/TR/css3 -namespace/*, and is currently a Candidate Recommendation.

There are currently two Selectors API specifications under development: the Selectors API Level 1 (*http://www.w3.org/TR/selectors-api/*), which is a Candidate Recommendation, and the Selectors API Level 2 (*http://www.w3.org/TR/selectors-api2/*), which is a working draft.

John Resig, the creator of the popular jQuery library, has provided a comprehensive test suite for selectors at *http://ejohn.org/apps/selectortest/*. The source for the test suite can be found at *http://github.com/jeresig/selectortest/tree/master*. The CSS3.info site also has a nice selectors test at *http://tools.css3.info/selectors-test/test.html*. This one is a little easier to view, and provides links with each test to the example code.

As noted, Selectors API support isn't universal. However, many of the popular Java-Script framework libraries, such as jQuery, Prototype, and Dojo, provide workarounds so you can use the selector and it offers a fallback, if necessary.

Chapter 17 introduces using jQuery and other libraries with your application code.

11.5 Finding the Parent Element for a Group of Elements

Problem

You want to access the parent element for a group of paragraphs.

Solution

Use the `querySelector` method to access the first paragraph in the set, and then access the `parentNode` property for this element:

```
var parent = document.querySelector("body p").parentNode;
```

Discussion

With all the ways we can access child nodes and siblings, not to mention descendants to many depths, you'd think we'd also be able to directly query for parent elements. Unfortunately, there is nothing in CSS comparable to `:parent` to return a parent element. However, we can fake it by accessing a known child element and then accessing the parent via the `parentNode` property.

In the solution, the `querySelector` method will return the first paragraph element that is a descendant of the body element. Since `querySelector` only returns one element, you don't have to use array reference to access an individual element. Once we have one of the child elements, the parent is accessed via the `parentNode` property.

See Also

See Recipe 11.4 for more details on the Selectors API and the `querySelector` and `querySelectorAll` methods.

11.6 Highlighting the First Paragraph in Every Element

Problem

Based on some user event, you want to dynamically change the background color to yellow for the first paragraph in every `div` element.

Solution

Use the `document.querySelectAll` with the appropriate CSS selector in order to reference all first paragraphs in `div` elements, and then modify the paragraph's CSS background color:

```
var paras = document.querySelectorAll('div p:first-of-type');
for (var i = 0; i < paras.length; i++) {
    paras[i].setAttribute("style","background-color: #ffff00");
}
```

If the specific pseudoselector syntax is not supported, use an alternative, such as the following:

```
var divs = document.querySelectorAll("div");
for (var j = 0; j < divs.length; j++) {
    var ps = divs.item(j).getElementsByTagName("p");
    if (ps.length > 0) {
        ps[0].setAttribute("style","background-color: #ffff00");
    }
}
```

Discussion

We're only interested in selectors where the paragraph element is a descendant of a `div` element:

```
var paras = document.querySelectorAll('div p');
```

In addition, we're interested in the first paragraph element in the `div`, so at first glance, the following looks acceptable:

```
var paras = document.querySelectorAll('div p:first-child');
```

However, there's no guarantee that the `div` element won't contain elements of other types, and if the first element is not a paragraph, the first paragraph won't be found. Instead, as shown in Example 11-3, the `:first-of-type` CSS selector is used so that the first paragraph in the `div` element is highlighted when the document is clicked, even if it isn't the first element in the `div`. The code is included in a `try...catch` block in order to provide an alternative if the type of selector syntax isn't supported.

Example 11-3. Using the first-of-type selector in order to highlight the first paragraph element in a div

```
<!DOCTYPE html>
<head>
<title>paras</title>
<meta charset="utf-8" />
<style>
div
{
  padding: 10px;
  border: 1px solid #000000;
}
</style>
<script type="text/javascript">

window.onload=function() {
    document.onclick=function() {
      try {
        var paras = document.querySelectorAll('div p:first-of-type');
        for (var i = 0; i < paras.length; i++) {
          paras[i].setAttribute("style","background-color: #ffff00");
        }
      } catch(e) {
        var divs = document.querySelectorAll("div");
        for (var j = 0; j < divs.length; j++) {
          var ps = divs.item(j).getElementsByTagName("p");
          if (ps.length > 0) {
            ps[0].setAttribute("style","background-color: #ffff00");
          }
        }
      }
    }
  };
}
</script>
</head>
<body>
  <div>
     <p>Paragraph one</p>
     <p>Paragraph two</p>
     <p>Paragraph three</p>
  </div>
  <div>
     <p>Paragraph one</p>
     <p>Paragraph two</p>
  </div>
  <div>
     <ul>
        <li>List item one</li>
        <li>List item two</li>
     </ul>
     <p>Paragraph one</p>
     <p>Paragraph two</p>
  </div>
</body>
```

Figure 11-3 shows that even though the first element in the third `div` is an unordered list, the first paragraph that follows is still highlighted. Another CSS selector that provides the same functionality is `:nth-of-type(1)`, where parentheses are used to wrap the number of the target element.

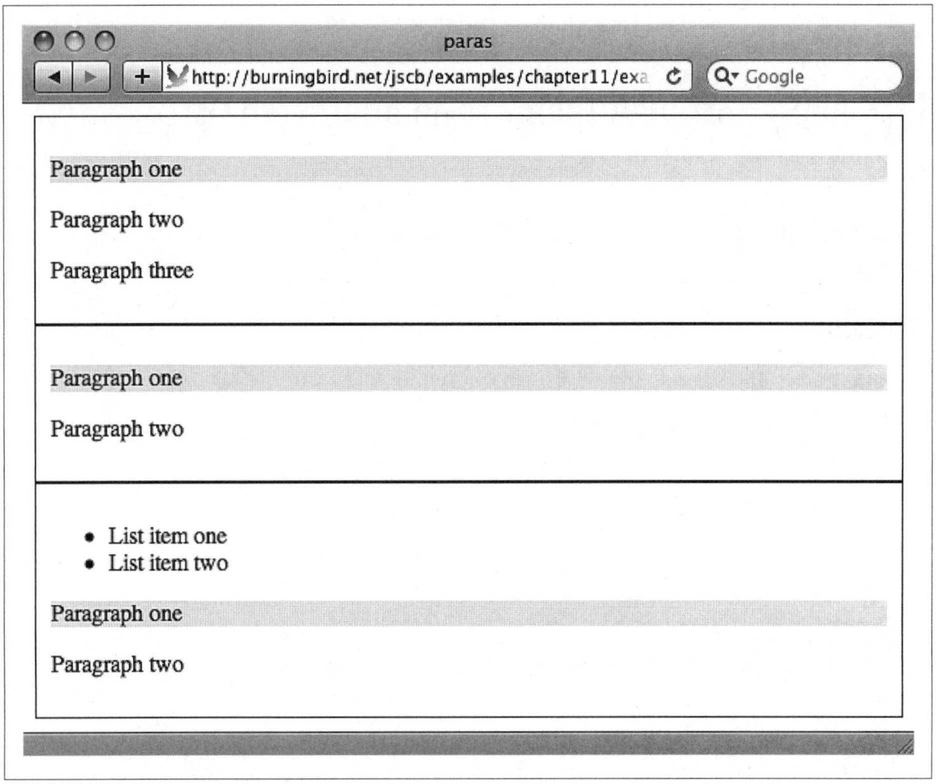

Figure 11-3. Page displaying highlighted first paragraphs in every div element

Firefox, Safari, Chrome, and Opera support `:first-of-type`. IE8 doesn't, but it does support `:first-child`. However, as the example demonstrates, we can't count on the paragraph being the first element. Instead, we use a more generalized query for all `div` elements, and then access all the paragraphs with `getElementsByTagName`.

We could use the `getElementsByTagName` for the first query, except that this method returns a live collection, and the first approach doesn't. We want the functionality to be the same for both approaches, as much as possible. If you need to support IE7, though, you should use `getElementsByTagName`, as this browser doesn't support `querySelectorAll`.

See Also

See Recipe 11.2 for more on `getElementsByTagName` and live collections, and Recipe 11.4 for an in-depth introduction to the Selectors API. Microsoft provides a page for the CSS selectors it supports at *http://msdn.microsoft.com/en-us/library/cc351024(VS.85).aspx*. Note, though, that Microsoft does have a habit of changing its URLs, so this web page address may not work in the future.

11.7 Apply a Striping Theme to an Unordered List

Problem

You want to modify the appearance of unordered list items so that the list appears striped.

Solution

Use the Selectors API to query for every other item in the list, and then change the background color:

```
var lis = document.querySelectorAll('li:nth-child(2n+1)');
for (var i = 0; i < lis.length; i++) {
   lis[i].setAttribute("style","background-color: #ffeeee");
}
```

or:

```
var lis = document.querySelectorAll('li:nth-child(odd)');
for (var i = 0; i < lis.length; i++) {
   lis[i].setAttribute("style","background-color: #eeeeff");
}
```

or access the list parent element and then traverse its child nodes, changing the background color of every other element, using the arithmetic modulo operator:

```
var parentElement = document.getElementById("thelist");
var lis = parentElement.getElementsByTagName("li");
for (var i = 0; i < lis.length; i++) {
   if (i % 2 == 0) {
      lis[i].setAttribute("style","background-color: #eeffee");
   }
}
```

Discussion

The `:nth-child()` pseudoclass allows us to specify an algorithm pattern, which can be used to find elements that match a certain pattern, such as `2n+1`, to find every other element. You can also use the **odd** and **even** arguments to access the odd or even elements of the type:

```
var lis = document.querySelectorAll('li:nth-child(odd)');
```

Not all browsers support this relatively new selector type. Firefox, Opera, Safari, and Chrome do, but IE8 doesn't support the first two approaches given in the solution, and older versions of most other browsers don't. In these situations, you'll want to use the third approach in the solutions: get access to all of the elements using whatever method, and then use the `modulo` arithmetic operator to filter the elements. The `modulo` operator returns the remainder of dividing the first operand by the second. Dividing the numbers 0, 2, 4, 6, and so on by 2 returns 0; the condition is successful, and the element is affected.

In the solution, the even elements are the ones affected. To access the odd elements, use the following:

```
if ((i + 1) % 2) {
    ...
}
```

The `setAttribute` with the style property also doesn't work for IE7 for the third approach. The downloadable example code contains a workaround for this browser.

See Also

See Recipe 11.4 for more details on the Selectors API and the `querySelector` and `querySelectorAll` methods. See Recipe 12.15 for more on `setAttribute`.

11.8 Creating an Array of All Elements of a Given Class

Problem

You want to retrieve a collection of elements that have a specific class name within the document.

Solution

Use the `getElementsByClassName` method to retrieve a collection of all elements in the document that share the same class name:

```
var elems = document.getElementsByClassName("classname");
```

or use the Selectors API to get the class-named items:

```
var elems = document.querySelectorAll(".classname");
```

Discussion

The method, `getElementsByClassName`, goes beyond one element type to find all elements that share the same class value. It can also work with multiple classes:

```
var elems = document.getElementsByClassName("firstclass secondclass");
```

Chrome, Safari, Firefox, and Opera support `getElementsByClassName`, but IE8 doesn't. The second approach using `querySelectorAll` is a good alternative option. It, too, can search for multiple class names:

```
var elems = document.querySelectorAll(".firstclass, .secondclass");
```

See Also

See Recipe 11.4 for more details on the Selectors API and the `querySelector` and `querySelectorAll` methods.

11.9 Finding All Elements That Share an Attribute

Problem

You want to find all elements in a web document that share the same attribute.

Solution

Use the universal selector (*) in combination with the attribute selector to find all elements that have an attribute, regardless of its value:

```
var elems = document.querySelectorAll('*[class]');
```

The universal selector can also be used to find all elements with an attribute that's assigned the same value:

```
elems = document.querySelectorAll('*[class="red"]');
```

Discussion

The solution demonstrates a rather elegant query selector. All elements are analyzed because of the use of the universal selector (*). To test the existence of an attribute, all you need do is list the attribute name within square brackets (*[attrname]*).

In Recipe 11.8, a couple approaches were demonstrated for finding all elements that have a specific class name. The query selector used in the solution could be modified to do the same:

```
var elems = document.querySelectorAll('*[class"=test"]');
```

If you're not sure of the class name, you can use the substring-matching query selector:

```
var elements = document.querySelectorAll('*[class*="test"]');
```

Now any class name that contains the substring test matches.

You could also modify the syntax to find all elements that don't have a certain value. For instance, to find all `div` elements that don't have the target class name, use the `:not` negation operator:

```
var elems = document.querySelectorAll('div:not(.test)');
```

This and the selector syntax examples given in the solution work with Opera, Chrome, Firefox, and Safari. Both of the selector syntax examples in the solution work with IE8, but the use of the negation operator, :not, does not. The querySelectorAll method does not work with IE7.

See Also

See Recipe 11.4 for more details on the Selectors API and the querySelector and querySelectorAll methods.

11.10 Finding All Checked Options

Problem

You want to find all checkbox input elements that are selected (checked):

Solution

Use a :checked pseudoclass selector to directly query all checked checkbox input elements:

```
var checked = document.querySelectorAll("#checks
input[type='checkbox']:checked");
for (var i = 0; i < checked.length; i++) {
  str+=checked[i].value + " ";
}
```

If the :checked selector fails, use the following, which accesses all of the input elements, checks their type, and then checks to see if they're selected:

```
var inputs = document.querySelectorAll("#checks input");
for (var j = 0; j < inputs.length; j++) {
   if (inputs.item(j).type == "checkbox" && inputs.item(j).checked) {
     str+=inputs.item(j).value + " ";

   }
}
```

Discussion

The :checked pseudoselector will only return those checkbox or radio elements that are checked. Since we only want the checkbox input types, we further refined the selector syntax to look for a specific type of input element.

The use of the :checked pseudoclass selector is a nicely targeted approach, though it's only supported in Safari, Firefox, Chrome, and Opera, and not in IE8. The alternative does work in IE8, but not IE7, which doesn't support the querySelectorAll method.

When working with these new selectors, a good approach is to wrap the selector query in a **try** statement and then provide an alternative in the **catch** statement. Incorporating this into the solution gives us:

```
var str = "checked values ";
try {
   var checked = document.querySelectorAll("#checks
input[type='checkbox']:checked");
   for (var i = 0; i < checked.length; i++) {
      str+=checked[i].value + " ";
   }
} catch(e) {
   var inputs = document.querySelectorAll("#checks input");
   for (var j = 0; j < inputs.length; j++) {
      if (inputs.item(j).type == "checkbox" &&
                          inputs.item(j).checked) {
         str+=inputs.item(j).value + " ";
      }
   }
}
document.getElementById("results").innerHTML=str;
```

See Also

Recipe 11.4 includes more details on the Selectors API and the `querySelector` and `querySelectorAll` methods.

11.11 Summing All the Values in a Table Row

Problem

You want to sum the numbers in table cells per row (or per column).

Solution

Use the Selectors API to access the specific table row cells directly, or retrieve a collection of all table rows, access the target row from the returned collection, and then access the table row's cells. Once retrieved by either method, traverse the cells, accessing the cell data and converting the data to a number:

```
try {
   var cells = document.querySelectorAll("tr:nth-child(3) td");
} catch(e) {
   var tableElement = document.getElementById("thetable");
   var trs = tableElement.getElementsByTagName("tr");
   var cells = trs[2].getElementsByTagName("td");
}

// process cell data
var sum = 0;
for (var i = 0; i < cells.length; i++) {
```

```
          var val = parseFloat(cells[i].firstChild.data);
          if (!isNaN(val)) {
              sum+=val;
          }
      }
  }

  // output the sum
  alert("sum " + sum);
```

Discussion

There are several ways to get all the cells for a table row, including adding a click event handler to the rows, and then processing all of the cells when the row is clicked.

In the solution, we looked at two different approaches. The first approach uses the Selectors API querySelectorAll with a selector that targets all table cells in the third table row. The second approach is to access all of the table rows, using getElementsBy TagName, and then access all the table cells using the same method, against the target row. I prefer the first approach, because it reduces the processing involved and provides better, targeted results. However, tr:nth-child(3) td isn't supported in IE8. To prevent problems where the selector syntax or querySelectorAll aren't supported, the code is wrapped in a try...catch block, with the second approach as the fallback option.

What if we want to sum a column of table cells, rather than a row? In this case, what we really want is every table cell in a specific position for every table row. For this type of functionality, especially in light of some of the quirks with querySelectorAll, we'll need to use another approach, such as getElementsByTagName. Example 11-4 shows an example that sums values from the third column—skipping the first row, which consists of column headers.

Example 11-4. Application that sums cells in third table column

```
<!DOCTYPE html>
<html xmlns="http://www.w3.org/1999/xhtml" lang="en" xml:lang="en">
<head>
<title>Sum Table Column</title>
<script>
//<![CDATA[

window.onload=function() {
  var table = document.querySelector("table");
  table.onclick=sum;
}

function sum() {
  var rows =
      document.getElementById("sumtable").getElementsByTagName("tr");
  var sum = 0;

  // start with one to skip first row, which is col headers
  for (var i = 1; i < rows.length; i++) {
    sum+=parseFloat(rows[i].childNodes[2].firstChild.data);
```

```
  }
  alert(sum);
}


//]]>
</script>

</head>
<body>
<table id="sumtable">
<tr><th>Value 1</th><th>Value 2</th><th>Value 3</th><th>Value 4</th>
</tr>
<tr><td>--</td><td>**</td><td>5.0</td><td>nn</td></tr>
<tr><td>18.53</td><td>9.77</td><td>3.00</td><td>153.88</td></tr>
<tr><td>Alaska</td><td>Montana</td><td>18.33</td><td>Missouri</td>
</tr>
</table>
</body>
</html>
```

The actual data value is accessed via the `data` property of the `Text` node that is the `td` child element. The `parseFloat` method is used to convert the text to a number. If you're not sure that the table cells contain numbers, you'll want to test the value first, or you could up with a result of `NaN`.

In the example, the table rows are accessed using `getElementsByTagName` directly on the `table` element, which is retrieved using the `getElementById` method on the `document` object. Rather than have to use all of these methods individually, I *chain* the methods one after another. *Method chaining* doesn't work with all JavaScript object methods, but it does work with many among the DOM objects.

You probably wouldn't use a `querySelector` or `getElementsByTagName` with a static web table, because you can create the sums as you're building the table (if the table is built via an Ajax call). However, if you're using something like *editing in place* to add or modify table values, this isn't a bad approach to update column or row sums after the edit.

The example works with all the book's target browsers, but does not work with IE7 because of the use of `querySelector`.

See Also

`ParseFloat` is covered in Recipe 4.5. Recipe 16.13 has a demonstration and a more in-depth explanation of method chaining. Recipe 11.4 includes more details on the Selectors API and the `querySelector` and `querySelectorAll` methods.

11.12 Get Element Attributes

Problem

You want to access the information contained in an element attribute.

Solution

If the attribute is defined as a standard attribute in the DOM by the user agent (browser), you can access the attribute directly on the element:

```
<input id="field" type="check" checked="checked" value="test" />
...

var field = document.getElementById("field");
alert(field.checked); // true
alert(field.value);  // test
alert(field.type);   // text
```

Some attributes are renamed when you access them in JavaScript, such as the `class` attribute, which you access as `className`:

```
<div id="elem" class="test" role="article" data-index="1">
testing
</div>
...
    var elem = document.getElementById("elem");
    alert(elem.className);  // test
```

For nonstandard attributes, or ones that have been newly defined but are not considered standard by the specific browser, you need to use the `getAttribute` method:

```
var index = elem.getAttribute("data-index");
alert(index); // 1

var role = elem.getAttribute("role");
alert(role);  // article
```

Discussion

When elements are defined in various HTML specifications, such as HTML5, they're given a set of shared and/or unique attributes, which you can access directly from the object:

```
var id = elem.id;
```

Nonstandard or newly defined attributes have to be accessed using the `getAttribute` method:

```
var role = elem.getAttribute("role");
```

Since the `getAttribute` method works equally well with standard and nonstandard attributes, you should get in the habit of using the method to access all attributes.

If the attribute doesn't exist, the method returns a value of null or the empty string
(""). You can check to see if an attribute exists first, by using the `hasAttribute` method:

```
if (elem.hasAttribute(role)) {
  var role = elem.getAttribute("role");
    ...
}
```

This approach bypasses the problem that can occur when different user agents return
different values (empty string or null) when an attribute doesn't exist.

See Also

There is a namespace variation of `getAttribute`, `getAttributeNS`, which takes the namespace as the first parameter of the method. See Recipe 11.2 for more on working with
namespaces.

11.13 Get Style Information for an Element

Problem

You want to get one or more CSS style settings for an element.

Solution

If you want to access style information that's set inline or via JavaScript, and access it
directly on the element's style property, use:

```
var width = elem.style.width;
```

If you want to access the element's existing style information, regardless of how it's set,
you need to use a cross-browser approach:

```
function getStyle(elem, cssprop, cssprop2){

 // IE
 if (elem.currentStyle) {
   return elem.currentStyle[cssprop];

 // other browsers
 } else if (document.defaultView &&
                document.defaultView.getComputedStyle) {
   return document.defaultView.getComputedStyle(elem,
null).getPropertyValue(cssprop2);

 // fallback
 } else {
   return null;
 }
}

window.onload=function() {
```

```
    // setting and accessing style properties
    var elem = document.getElementById("elem");

    var color = getStyle(elem,"backgroundColor", "background-color");
    alert(color); // rgb(0,255,0)
}
```

Discussion

Every web page element has a set of properties and methods, some unique to the object, and some inherited from other objects, such as `Element` or `Node`, covered in earlier recipes. One of the properties elements share is the `style` object, representing the CSS style settings for the element.

There are a couple of ways you can get style information. The first is to directly access the `style` object, using the familiar *dot notation* used throughout the book to access object properties and methods:

```
    var elem = document.getElementById("elem");
    var width = elem.style.width;
```

All inline or dynamically set style settings can be accessed using this approach, but there is a special syntax you have to use. For nonhyphenated property values, such as `width`, you access the setting directly:

```
    var width = elem.style.width;
```

However, for property names with hyphens, such as `background-color`, use a *Camel-Case notation* such as the following:

```
    var bkcolor = elem.style.backgroundColor;
```

Using `background-color` doesn't work, because JavaScript interprets the hyphen as a subtraction operator. The new name is formed by removing the hyphen, and capitalizes the first letter of the word following the hyphen.

Another approach to accessing the style is to use the `getAttribute` method to access the `style` object:

```
    var style = elem.getAttribute("style");
```

However, you would then have to parse the values out of the string. You're better off just accessing the values directly on the `style` property.

 IE7 also returns an object, rather than a string with CSS values, when you access the style property using `getAttribute`.

Only those CSS values that are set *inline*, using the element's `style` attribute, or set dynamically using JavaScript, are accessible using either of the approaches just demonstrated. To access CSS values set by default by the user agent, via a stylesheet, dynamically, or inline, you'll need to use a cross-browser approach:

```
var style;
var cssprop = "fontFamily";
var cssprop2 = "font-family";
if (elem.currentStyle) {
  style = elem.currentStyle[cssprop];
} else if (document.defaultView &&
                  document.defaultView.getComputedStyle) {
  style = document.defaultView.getComputedStyle(elem,
null).getPropertyValue(cssprop2);
}
```

The `currentStyle` object is an IE-specific object that consists of a collection of all supported and applicable CSS style properties for an element. It expects values to be in CamelCase notation, such as `fontFamily`, rather than `font-family`.

The book's other target browsers support the `window.getComputedStyle` method, which can also be accessed as `document.defaultView.getComputedStyle`. This method takes two parameters: the element, and a pseudoelement, which is typically left null (or an empty string, `""`).

What's returned using the cross-browser approach is rather interesting. It's the computed style for the element, which is a combination of all CSS settings, including those that are set by default by the browser, set using a stylesheet, or set dynamically using CSS. What's returned when accessing the `font-family` depends on the circumstances:

- If the font-family is not set, you'll get the browser default value, if any
- If the font-family is set via a stylesheet, you'll get the stylesheet value
- If the font-family is set inline and in a stylesheet, you'll get the inline value
- If the font-family is set dynamically, regardless of whether it is set inline or in a stylesheet, you'll get the dynamic value

See Also

Example 12-7, in Recipe 12.15, demonstrates various techniques for setting and retrieving style information.

CHAPTER 12

Creating and Removing Elements and Attributes

12.0 Introduction

The existing Document Object Models provide a plethora of methods you can use to create new web document elements. Most of the methods I use in this chapter and in the following chapters are from the DOM Levels 1 and 2 and, since most of the examples in this chapter are specific to HTML or XHTML documents, the methods and objects described inherit functionality from both Core and HTML DOM specifications.

There is one older property, `innerHTML`, from the nonstandard DOM Level 0, that I'll also demonstrate, primarily because it's so popular, and also because of new support in HTML5.

Most of the methods and associated properties are available with all of the modern browsers. I'll make a note where a method or property isn't supported by one or more browsers.

See Also

See the Introduction to Chapter 11, for a more in-depth look at the Document Object Model and the DOM levels.

12.1 Using innerHTML: A Quick and Easy Approach to Adding Content

Problem

You want to add a couple of paragraphs with text to a `div` element, and you want to do so quickly and easily.

Solution

Use the `innerHTML` property to overwrite an element's existing contents, with new material:

```
var div = document.getElementById("target");
div.innerHTML = "<p>This is a paragraph</p><p>This is a second</p>";
```

Discussion

The `innerHTML` property has been around for a very long time, and is part of what is known as DOM Level 0—the first de facto API developed by the browser companies. It can be much faster when you're making complex additions to the web page, because its processing is handled by the HTML parser, rather than the DOM engine.

Because `innerHTML` was never part of a standard, there are some variations in how it's implemented. For instance, not all browsers support the use of `innerHTML` with tables, so you won't want to use the property for adding table rows. The use of `innerHTML` isn't standard with XML formats, such as XHTML, as there's no way to ensure that what is appended into the page is well formed. In earlier years, the use of `innerHTML` wasn't even supported with XHTML documents.

Now, though, `innerHTML` is becoming officially blessed by being defined within the HTML5 effort. In addition, the `outerHTML` property has also been formally defined in the HTML5 specification. It differs from `innerHTML` in that `outerHTML` represents both the element and the element's contents, while `innerHTML` only represents the element's contents.

 Currently, the HTML5 specification states that the use of `innerHTML` will abort the current X/HTML parsing process. And not all browsers allow `innerHTML` to be set until after the page is finished loading. Based on these restrictions, it's best to not use `innerHTML` until after the page is completely loaded.

12.2 Inserting Elements Before Existing Page Elements

Problem

You need to add a new `div` element to the web page before an existing `div` element.

Solution

Use the DOM method `createElement` to create a new `div` element. Once created, attach it to the web page before an existing element, using another DOM method, `insertBefore`:

```
// get the existing element
var refElement = document.getElementById("sister");

// get the element's parent node
var parent = refElement.parentNode;

// create new div element
var newDiv = document.createElement("div");

// attach to page before sister element
parent.insertBefore(newDiv, refElement);
```

Discussion

Adding a web page element is uncomplicated, as long as you keep in mind the tree-like structure of the web page. If you're interested in attaching a web page element before another element, you'll not only need to access this element, but also the target element's parent element, in order to create the actual placement.

The reason you need the parent element is that there is no functionality to insert an element before another, given just the target element. Instead, you have to access the target element's parent element, and use the insertBefore method to insert the new element before the existing one.

In Example 12-1, the solution for this recipe is embedded into a web page that originally consists only of one named div element. When this element receives a click event, a new sister div element is created and inserted into the document before the existing element.

Example 12-1. Inserting a div element into a web page

```
<!DOCTYPE html>

<head>
<title>object detection</title>
<style type="text/css">
div
{
  width: 50%;
  height: 20px;
  padding: 10px;
  margin: 10px 0;
}

#div1
{
  background-color: #ffff00;
  }

.divclass
{
  background-color: #ccffcc;
}
```

```
</style>
<script type="text/javascript">

window.onload=function() {
  document.getElementById("div1").onclick=addDiv;
}

function addDiv() {

  // get parent
  var parent = this.parentNode;

  // create new div
  var newDiv = document.createElement("div");
  newDiv.className = "divclass";
  newDiv.innerHTML = "<p>I'm here, I'm in the page</p>";

  // add to page
  parent.insertBefore(newDiv,this);
}
</script>
</head>
<body>
  <div id="div1">
      <p>Click me to add new element</p>
  </div>
</body>
```

In the example, since the event is attached to the original div element, a reference to it can be accessed using this within the event function, because the element is the owner of the onclick event handler function. You can then get the element's parent through the parentNode property. Once you have a reference to both the parent and the existing element, all you need to do is create the new div element and insert it.

Use the document.createElement method, passing in the type of element—in this case, div. Since the current document is an HTML document, the createElement method creates a new HTMLElement, which inherits all functionality of the more generic Element class, as well as additional methods and properties. The new element is assigned a CSS style through the className property, which is a standard property for all HTMLElement objects. It's given some content using the innerHTML property. The new div element is then added to the web page with insertBefore.

Each successive click of the original div element prepends a new div element to the original, each with the same class and content. Figure 12-1 shows the web page after the original div element has been clicked several times.

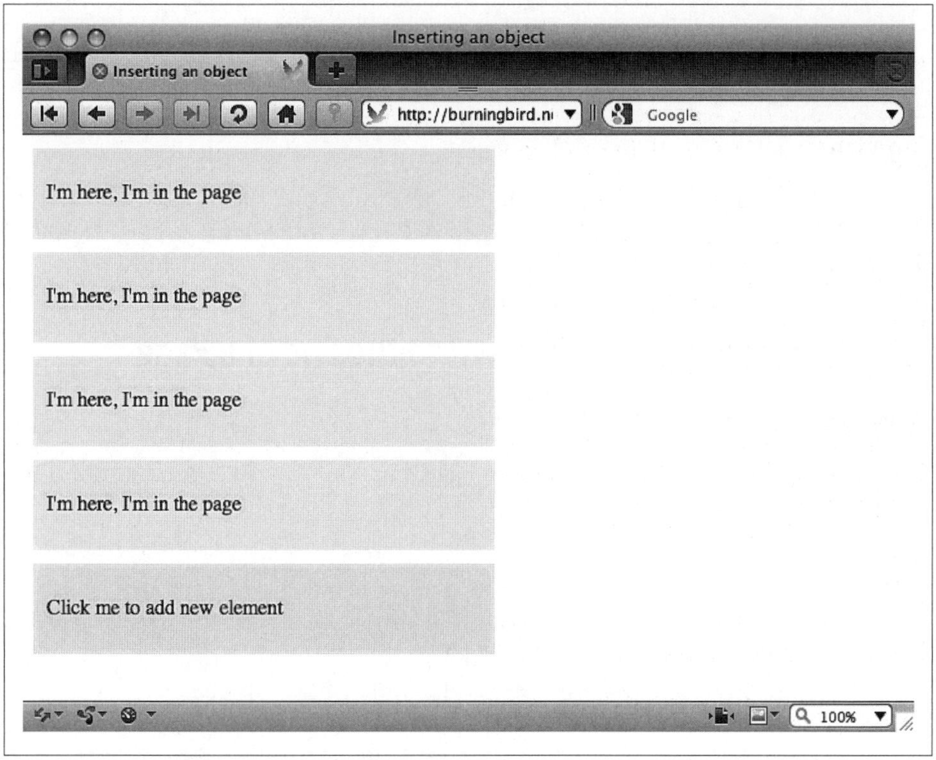

Figure 12-1. Inserting div elements into a web page

Namespace Variation

Recipe 11.2 included a discussion on namespaces and their impact on some of the DOM methods that allow us to query and add new web page elements in a document that can contain multiple namespaces. If you're working within an environment where namespaces are supported, such as an XHTML or SVG document, and you create a new element or attribute, it's automatically added to the document's default namespace unless you use one of the namespace-specific DOM methods.

Generally, the default behavior is sufficient. However, if you want to create an element within a specific namespace, such as creating a title in the Dublin Core namespace rather an XHTML title, use the namespace variation of `createElement`, `createElementNS`:

```
var dcTitle = document.createElementNS("http://purl.org/dc/elements/1.1/","title");
```

The `createElementNS` takes two parameters: the first is the namespace for the element; the second is the element tag.

The namespace method `createElementNS` is not supported in HTML currently, as namespaces aren't supported in HTML. The method is also not currently supported in IE8, but should be in IE9, when Microsoft adds support for XHTML.

See Also

See Recipe 11.2 for more information about namespaces and the DOM. For a specific description of the `HTMLElement`, see the related W3C page (*http://www.w3.org/TR/DOM -Level-2-HTML/html.html#ID-58190037*).

12.3 Appending a New Element to the End of a Page

Problem

You want to add a new element to a web page, but you want to append it to the end of the page.

Solution

Access the highest level web page element, the `body` element, and use the `appendChild` method to append the new element to the page:

```
var bdy = document.getElementsByTagName("body")[0]; // body element
var newDiv = document.createElement("div");

// append to body
bdy.appendChild(newDiv);
```

Discussion

Since we're appending the new element to the end of the page, it makes sense to access the top-level page element (the `body` element) directly, using the DOM `getElementsBy TagName` method. Since the method always returns an array (more properly, a `nodeList`), we get the individual element in the first array index:

```
var bdy = document.getElementsByTagName("body")[0];
```

Once we have the parent element, the `appendChild` method appends the new element to the end of the parent element. The method takes just one parameter: the newly created element.

Will a document always have a `body` element? Typically, yes, if the document is HTML or XHTML. However, if you're working with other document types, such as SVG or MathML, or are concerned about ensuring that the new element is appended to whatever is the top-level document element, you can use the approach demonstrated in Recipe 12.0 to get the parent of an existing element that will be a sibling to the new element:

```
var bdy = document.getElementById("div1").parentNode;
```

This sibling-parent approach ensures that the new element is appended as a sibling of the existing element, and at the same level in the document tree.

12.4 Triggering Older Versions of IE to Style New Elements

Problem

You want to use one of the new HTML5 elements, such as `article`, and have it styled or programmatically accessible in IE7/8.

Solution

Use `document.createElement` in order to trigger IE8 (and IE7) into properly handling new HTML5 elements:

```
// add article element
document.createElement("article");
```

Discussion

The `article` element is one of the new HTML5 elements, accessible via the DOM by all of the book's target browsers except for IE. In order to style or programmatically access `article` with IE8 or older, you need to apply an HTML5 *shim*. This shim introduces the `article` and other new elements to the IE DOM tree by using the `document.createElement` method to create one instance of the element:

```
document.createElement("article");
```

The element doesn't have to be assigned to a variable name or inserted into the web page—it just has to be created. Once an instance of the element type is created, IE can recognize the element. This step is essential not only for JavaScript applications, but to ensure the element can be styled with CSS.

Entire libraries now exist in order to define all of the HTML5 elements. All you need do is include the library before any other script in the page. The html5-shims page at Google Code (*http://code.google.com/p/html5-shims/*) maintains a list of HTML5 shims and other resources. The library I use in the book examples is the html5shiv, originally created by John Resig and now maintained by Remy Sharp, at *http://html5shiv.google code.com/svn/trunk/html5.js*.

See Also

See Recipes 11.3 and 11.4 for JavaScript applications that are dependent on the HTML5 shim.

12.5 Inserting a New Paragraph

Problem

You want to insert a new paragraph just before the third paragraph within a `div` element.

Solution

Use some method to access the third paragraph, such as `getElementsByTagName`, to get all of the paragraphs for a `div` element. Then use the `createElement` and `insertBefore` DOM methods to add the new paragraph just before the existing third paragraph:

```
// get the target div
var div = document.getElementById("target");

// retrieve a collection of  paragraphs
var paras = div.getElementsByTagName("p");

// if a third para exists, insert the new element before
// otherwise, append the paragraph to the end of the div
var newPara = document.createElement("p");
if (paras[3]) {
   div.insertBefore(newPara, paras[3]);
} else {
   div.appendChild(newPara);
}
```

Discussion

The `document.createElement` method creates any HTML element, which then can be assigned other elements or data and appended or inserted into the page. In the solution, the new paragraph element is inserted before an existing paragraph using the `insert Before` method.

Since we're interested in inserting the new paragraph before the existing third paragraph, we need to retrieve a collection of the `div` element's paragraphs, check to make sure a third paragraph exists, and then use the `insertBefore` method to insert the new paragraph before the old. If the third paragraph doesn't exist, we can append the element to the end of the `div` element using the `appendChild` method instead.

See Also

Chapter 11 demonstrates several techniques for accessing page elements, including `getElementsByTagName`. If your target browsers support it, you could also use the Selectors API to fine-tune the query.

The following recipe, Recipe 12.6, contains a complete example demonstrating how to access the `div` element and the paragraphs, and add a paragraph with text just before the second paragraph.

12.6 Adding Text to a New Paragraph

Problem

You want to create a new paragraph with text and insert it just before the second paragraph within a `div` element:

```
// use getElementById to access the div element
var div = document.getElementById("target");

// use getElementsByTagName and the collection index
// to access the second paragraph
var oldPara = div.getElementsByTagName("p")[1]; // zero based index

// create a text node
var txt =
 document.createTextNode("The new paragraph will contain this text");

// create a new paragraph
var para = document.createElement("p");

// append the text to the paragraph, and insert the new para
para.appendChild(txt);
div.insertBefore(para, oldPara);
```

Discussion

The text within an element is itself an object within the DOM. Its type is a `Text` node, and it is created using a specialized method, `createTextNode`. The method takes one parameter: the string containing the text.

Example 12-2 shows a web page with a `div` element containing four paragraphs. The JavaScript that runs after the page loads creates a new paragraph from text provided by the user via a prompt window. The text could just as easily have come from an Ajax application, as we'll see later in the book.

The provided text is used to create a text node, which is then appended as a child node to the new paragraph. The `paragraph` element is inserted in the web page before the first paragraph.

Example 12-2. Demonstrating various methods for adding content to a web page

```
<!DOCTYPE html>
<html xmlns="http://www.w3.org/1999/xhtml" xml:lang="en" lang="en">
<head>
<title>Adding Paragraphs</title>
<script type="text/javascript">
//<![CDATA[

window.onload=function() {

    // use getElementById to access the div element
```

```
    var div = document.getElementById("target");

    // get paragraph text
    var txt = prompt("Enter new paragraph text","");

    // use getElementsByTagName and the collection index
    // to access the first paragraph
    var oldPara = div.getElementsByTagName("p")[0]; //zero based index

    // create a text node
    var txtNode = document.createTextNode(txt);

    // create a new paragraph
    var para = document.createElement("p");

    // append the text to the paragraph, and insert the new para
    para.appendChild(txtNode);

    div.insertBefore(para, oldPara);

  }
//]]>
</script>
</head>
<body>
<div id="target">
  <p>
    There is a language 'little known,'<br />
    Lovers claim it as their own.
  </p>
  <p>
    Its symbols smile upon the land, <br />
    Wrought by nature's wondrous hand;
  </p>
  <p>
    And in their silent beauty speak,<br />
    Of life and joy, to those who seek.
  </p>
  <p>
    For Love Divine and sunny hours <br />
    In the language of the flowers.
  </p>
</div>
</body>
</html>
```

Figure 12-2 shows a web page after some text has been added.

 Inserting user-supplied text directly into a web page without scrubbing the text first is not a good idea. When you leave a door open, all sorts of nasty things can crawl in. Example 12-2 is for demonstration purposes only.

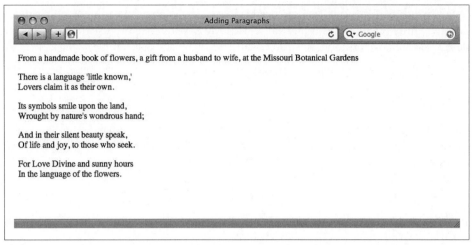

Figure 12-2. Demonstrating adding paragraphs and text to web page

See Also

See Chapter 18 for demonstrations of using Ajax to retrieve new page contents.

12.7 Adding Attributes to an Existing Element

Problem

You want to add one or more attributes to an existing element.

Solution

You can use the `createAttribute` method to create an `Attr` node, set its value using the `nodeValue` property, and then use `setAttribute` to add to an element:

```
var someElement = document.getElement("elem");
var newAttr = document.createAttribute("newAttribute");
newAttr.nodeValue = "testvalue";
someElement.setAttribute(newAttr);
```

or you can set the value directly with `setAttribute`, passing in the attribute name and value:

```
someElement.setAttribute("newAttribute","testvalue");
```

Discussion

You can add any number of attributes to a document element using either `createAttribute` and `setAttribute`, or `setAttribute` directly. Both approaches are equally efficient, so unless there's a real need, you'll most likely want to use the simpler approach of setting the attribute name and value directly in `setAttribute`.

When would you need to use `createAttribute`? If the attribute value is going to be another entity reference, as is allowable with XML, you'll need to use the `createAttribute` to create an `Attr` node, as `setAttribute` will only support simple strings.

You can also use `setAttribute` to modify the value for an existing attribute, such as the `id` or `class` attributes:

```
someElement.setAttribute("id", "newId");
```

Note, though, that some values have a different name when set directly, than when they're set using `setAttribute`. One such as is `class`, which is set directly using `className`:

```
someElement.className = "new";
someElement.setAttribute("class", "new");
```

If the attribute already exists, assigning a value to the attribute directly or using `setAttribute` modifies the attribute's value.

Namespace Variation

As discussed in Recipes 11.2 and 12.2, if you use the `createAttribute` or `setAttribute` methods in a document where multiple namespaces are supported (such as in an XHTML or SVG document), the engine processing the request sets the attribute without a namespace. If you mix `setAttribute` and `setAttributeNS` in the same document, you can end up with the same attribute in different namespaces.

If you're working in a document that's using elements and attributes from different namespaces, such as an XHTML document that incorporates SVG and MathML, you'll need to use the namespace-sensitive variants, `createAttributeNS` and `setAttributeNS`:

```
someElement.setAttributeNS("http://somecompany.com/namespace",
                           "class",
    "somename");
```

12.8 Testing for a Boolean Attribute

Problem

You want to test to see if an element has a Boolean attribute.

Solution

Use the `hasAttribute` method to check for the existence of the Boolean or any other attribute:

```
var targetNode = document.getElementById("target");
if (targetNode.hasAttribute("class")) {
    alert(targetNode.getAttribute("class"));
}
```

Discussion

Boolean attributes, referred to as *attribute minimization* in the XHTML specifications, are attributes in HTML where the attribute's presence signifies a state, and is assigned no value. An example is the use of the Boolean attribute `compact` with the `dl` element:

```
<dl compact>
```

In XHTML, these attributes have to be assigned a value, so they're assigned a value comparable to the name of the attribute:

```
<dl compact="compact">
```

You can check for the Boolean attribute (or any other) using `hasAttribute` or its namespace variation:

```
var res = div.hasAttributeNS("http://some.com/namespace","attrnm");
```

A value of `true` signifies the attribute is present; `false` that it is not.

 The `hasAttribute` method is not supported in IE7.

See Also

See Recipes 11.2 and 12.2 for more on namespace issues.

12.9 Removing an Attribute

Problem

You want to remove an attribute from an element.

Solution

Use the `removeAttribute` method:

```
if (targetNode.hasAttribute("class")) {
   targetNode.removeAttribute("class");
   alert(targetNode.getAttribute("class")); // null
}
```

Discussion

Most of the time, you're probably interested in changing an attribute's value, but there may be times when you want to remove an attribute completely. You might be tempted to set the value of the attribute to `null` to remove it:

```
div.setAttribute("class",null);
```

However, this is not correct. To remove any attribute, use the `removeAttribute` method, or its namespace variant, `removeAttributeNS`:

```
div.removeAttributeNS("http://somecom.com/namespace","customattr");
```

You don't technically have to use `hasAttribute` to check if the attribute exists first—using `removeAttribute` on a nonexistent attribute does not throw an exception. Handy, since IE7 does not support `hasAttribute`.

See Also

See Recipes 11.2 and 12.2 for more on namespace-specific methods.

12.10 Moving a Paragraph

Problem

You want to move the last paragraph to before the first.

Solution

Get a reference to the paragraph you want to move, the first paragraph, and the parent element for the first paragraph, and use `insertBefore` to insert the last paragraph before the first:

```
var para = document.getElementsByTagName("p");
var parent = para[0].parentNode;
parent.insertBefore(para[para.length-1], para[0]);
```

Discussion

An element exists only once in the DOM regardless of its location. When you insert or append the element in a new location, it's automatically removed from its previous position in the page layout.

See Also

See Recipe 12.2 for a description of `insertBefore`.

12.11 Replacing Links with Footnote Bullets

Problem

You want to scan a web page for links, remove the links from the page, and replace them with text-based footnote bullets at the end of the document.

Solution

You'll have to use a variety of techniques to accomplish this task. Example 12-3 demonstrates a full application that moves all of the links contained in a paragraph to a bulleted footnote list at the end of the document—copying the contents of the link to the original link position first, and adding a superscript to reference the new footnote.

Example 12-3. Application to pull links out of the web document and append in a list at the end

```
<!DOCTYPE html>
<head>
<title>Moving Links</title>
<style>
 ul li
  {
    list-style-type: none;
    padding-bottom: 5px;
  }
</style>
<script type="text/javascript">

window.onload=function() {

  var links = document.querySelectorAll("a");
  var footnote = document.createElement("ul");

  // for all links
  for (var i = 0; i < links.length; i++) {

    // get parent element
    var parent = links[i].parentNode;

    // create number index text
    var num = document.createTextNode(i+1);
    var sup = document.createElement("sup");
    sup.appendChild(num);

    // process the children
    var children = links[i].childNodes;
    for (var j = 0; j < children.length; j++) {
        var newChild = children[j].cloneNode(true);
        parent.insertBefore(newChild,links[i]);
    }

    // add number subscript
    var sup2 = sup.cloneNode(true);
    parent.insertBefore(sup2,links[i]);

    // add a link to footnote
    var li = document.createElement("li");
    li.appendChild(sup);
    li.appendChild(links[i]);

    footnote.appendChild(li);
```

```
    }
    document.getElementsByTagName("body")[0].appendChild(footnote);}
</script>
</head><body>  <div id="target">
    <p>A favorite place of mine to visit in St. Louis is the <a
href="http://http://www.mobot.org/">Missouri Botanical Gardens</a>.
Great flowers all year round, and one of the finest annual
orchid shows. My most visited places, though, are the <a
href="http://www.stlzoo.org/">St.
Louis Zoo</a>, the <a href="http://www.nps.gov/jeff/index.htm"><em>Gateway
Arch</em></a>,
 the new <a href="http://www.citygardenstl.org/">City Garden</a>,
and the <a href="http://mdc.mo.gov/areas/cnc/powder/">Powder
Valley Conservation Nature Center</a>.
    </p>
  </div>
</body>
```

Discussion

As demonstrated in the solution, you can use `querySelectorAll` to find all the links in
the page, passing in the anchor tag:

```
var links = document.querySelectorAll("a");
```

You can't use `getElementsByTagName` to get the links, and I'll explain why a little later
in the discussion. The solution also creates a new unordered list to contain the links
we pull out of the document.

Once you have a reference to all the links in the page, it's time for the fun part. One of
the interesting challenges with moving a link is that you typically want to preserve the
link's text in place—especially if the link references meaningful content—beyond the
to-be-discouraged "here" or "link".

You can't assume the link contents are text because a link can contain other elements
(though not another link). You could use `innerHTML` to access and copy the contents,
but `innerHTML` isn't well supported in XHTML.

Another approach is to move all of the child nodes out of the link. Now, you might
think a way to move the link contents out of the link is to use something like the
following:

```
var children = links[i].childNodes;
for (var j = 0; j < children.length; j++) {
    parent.insertBefore(children[j],links[i]);
}
```

The problem with this approach, though, is that `childNodes` points to a `nodeList`. In
Chapter 11, we learned that `nodeLists` are live collections, which means changes in the
page are reflected immediately in the `nodeList` in our code. So, if the link is something
like the following:

```
<a href="http://oreilly.com">O'Reilly sells <em>books!</em></a>
```

The childNodes collection would have a length of 2 for the text node and the em. However, in the first loop iteration, once the first element has been moved (in this case, inserted before the existing link's location, but it could be moved to the bullet list), the length of the childNodes value is now 1, but the for loop iterator has been incremented to 1—there is now only one child in the collection, and the for loop exits, leaving us with a link with the contents of the em element.

This is all really nice functionality, but it works against us sometimes. This is also the reason I didn't use the getElementsByTagName method to get a list of the anchor tags. The getElementsByTagName also returns a live nodeList, and when we append the links to the in-memory unordered list, the link is removed from the document, and the length of the collection is affected.

Luckily, as the solution demonstrates, we have other methods that do what we want, without the interesting side effects. The cloneNode method is used to clone the child elements, which the solution places just before the link. Once the children are taken care of, the entire link element is moved to the bulleted list using appendChild on a newly created list element (li), which is then appended to our unordered list (ul).

When using cloneNode, especially in a circumstance such as this, you'll want to pass a parameter of true when cloning the node:

```
var newElement = oldElement.cloneNode(true);
```

This ensures that all of the node's children are also cloned in place, in addition to the element. Once all of the links are processed in the document, the last act is to append the unordered list to the end of the document. Figure 12-3 shows the web page after the JavaScript is finished.

The application works with all the book's target browsers. It doesn't work with IE7, because that browser version does not support the querySelectorAll method.

12.12 Adding Rows to an Existing Table

Problem

You want to add one or more rows to an HTML table.

Solution

Adding table rows isn't complicated, but depending on the size of the table, it can be tedious. For each table cell, you have to create a textNode for the value, append the value to a new td element, append the element to a new tr element, and then append the whole thing to the table:

```
var table = document.getElementById("targettable");

var tr = document.createElement("tr");
var td = document.createElement("td");
```

```
var txt = document.createTextNode("some value");

td.appendChild(txt);
tr.appendChild(td);
table.appendChild(tr);
```

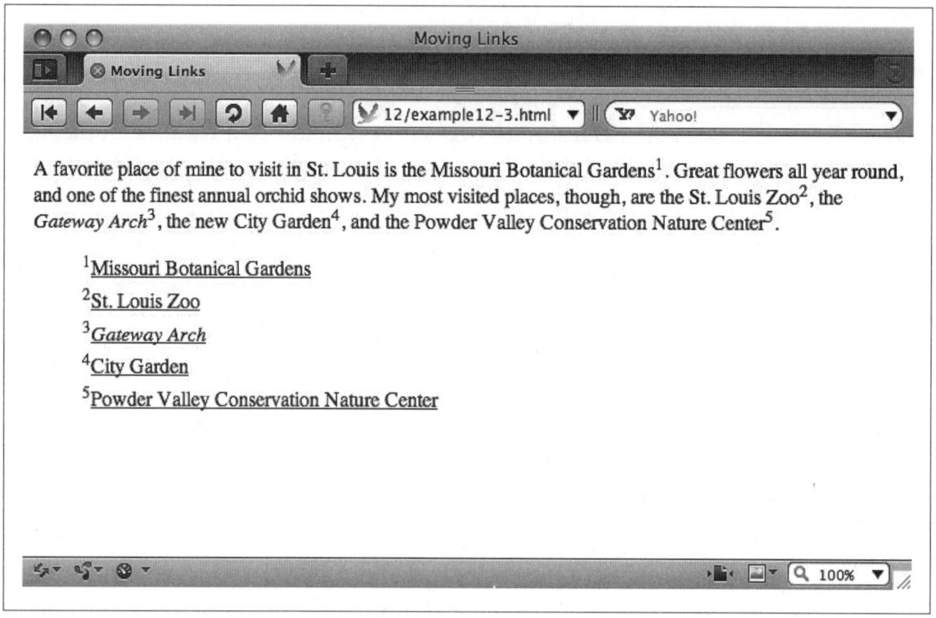

Figure 12-3. Web page after application has pulled all in-page links to a separate bulleted list

Discussion

Usually, when we're creating table rows it's because we've received data back from an Ajax function call. Typically, the data is organized in such a way that we can use loops of some form to process the data and simplify the process. Example 12-4 demonstrates how **for** loops can be used to process data in arrays, and to create all the necessary table elements.

Example 12-4. Extracting data from arrays and creating and appending table rows

```
<!DOCTYPE html>
<head>
<title>Sum Table Column</title>
<script>
window.onload=function() {

  var values = new Array(3);
  values[0] = [123.45, "apple", true];
  values[1] = [65, "banana", false];
  values[2] = [1034.99, "cherry", false];
```

```
    var mixed = document.getElementById("mixed");

    // IE7 only supports appending rows to tbody
    var tbody = document.createElement("tbody");

    // for each outer array row
    for (var i = 0 ; i < values.length; i++) {
      var tr = document.createElement("tr");

      // for each inner array cell
      // create td then text, append
      for (var j = 0; j < values[i].length; j++) {
        var td = document.createElement("td");
        var txt = document.createTextNode(values[i][j]);
        td.appendChild(txt);
        tr.appendChild(td);
      }

      // append row to table
      // IE7 requires append row to tbody, append tbody to table
      tbody.appendChild(tr);
      mixed.appendChild(tbody);
    }

}

</script>

</head>
<body>
<table id="mixed">
<tr><th>Value One</th><th>Value two</th><th>Value three</th></tr>
</table>
</body>
```

The data for the table is in static arrays, but could easily be XML or JSON returned from an Ajax call.

To repeat, the steps to create and add a table row are:

1. Create the table row (tr).
2. For each table cell, create a table cell element (td).
3. For each table cell, create a text node for its data, and set the data.
4. Append the text node to the table cell.
5. Append the table cell to the table row.
6. When all of the table cells have been appended to the table row, append the table row to the tbody element, and the tbody element to the table.

The application includes support for creating a tbody element and appending the table rows to this element, which is then appended to the table. IE7 does not allow for direct appending of table rows to the table. IE8 does, though, as do the other supported browsers.

See Also

Working with XML- and JSON-formatted data is covered in Chapter 19.

12.13 Removing a Paragraph from a div Element

Problem

You want to remove a paragraph from the web page.

Solution

You need to find the paragraph's parent and use the `removeChild` method to remove the paragraph:

```
var para = document.getElementById("thepara");
para.parentNode.removeChild(para);
```

Discussion

The DOM `removeChild` method removes the element from the display and the DOM tree. The element still remains in memory, though, and you can capture a reference to the element when you make the `removeChild` call:

```
var oldpara = paraParent.removeChild(child);
```

Example 12-5 demonstrates how to remove paragraphs from the page. When the page is first loaded, all of the paragraphs are accessed via `getElementsByTagName` and the `onclick` event handler for each assigned to the `pruneParagraph` function.

The `pruneParagraph` function references the element that received the click event, finds its parent node, and then removes the paragraph. You can continue to click paragraphs until they're all gone. After the paragraph is removed, the paragraphs in the page are queried again, and their count printed out.

Example 12-5. Removing paragraph elements from the page

```
<!DOCTYPE html>
<head>
<title>removeChild</title>
<style>
p
{
    padding: 20px;
    margin: 10px 0;
    width: 400px;
    background-color: #eeeeff;
}
```

```
</style>
<script>

window.onload=function() {

    var paras = document.getElementsByTagName("p");
    for (var i = 0; i < paras.length; i++)
      paras[i].onclick=pruneparagraph;
}

function pruneparagraph() {
  var parent = this.parentNode;
  parent.removeChild(this);

  alert("paras " + document.getElementsByTagName("p").length);
}

</script>

</head>
<body>
    <p>This is paragraph one</p>
    <p>This is paragraph two</p>
    <p>This is paragraph three</p>
    <p>This is paragraph four</p>
    <p>This is paragraph five</p>
</body>
```

Figure 12-4 shows the page after the second and fourth paragraphs have been removed.
Notice that the paragraphs that follow the removed elements move to fill in the space
newly freed.

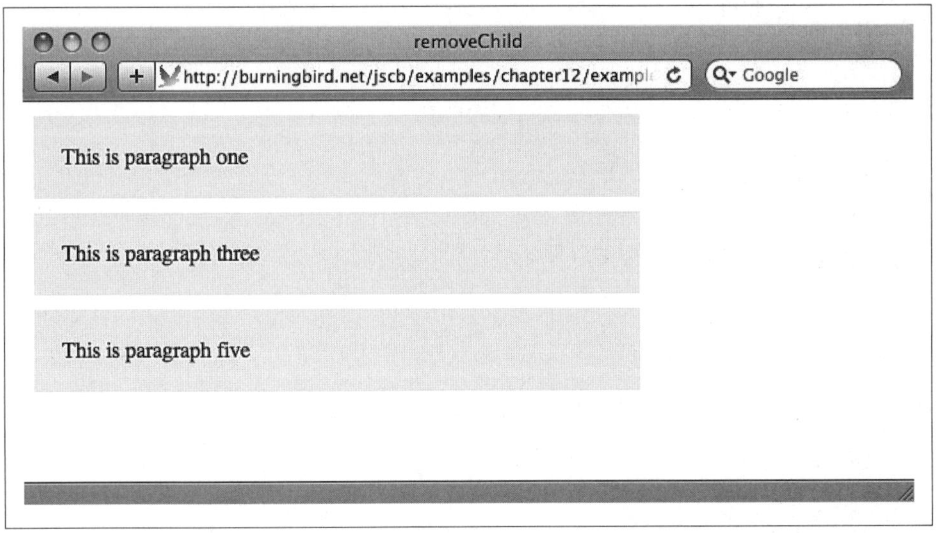

Figure 12-4. Page with two paragraphs removed

12.14 Deleting Rows from an HTML Table

Problem

You want to remove one or more rows from an HTML table.

Solution

You can use the DOM `removeChild` method on an HTML table row, and all of the child elements, such as the table cells, will also be removed:

```
var parent = row.parentNode;
var oldrow = parent.removeChild(parent);
```

Discussion

When you remove an element from the web document, you're not only removing the element, you're removing all child elements. You can also get a reference to the removed element if you want to process its contents before it's completely discarded. The latter is helpful if you want to provide an undo method in case the person accidentally selects the wrong table row.

To demonstrate the nature of DOM pruning, Example 12-6 is a modification of Example 12-4, except that before each new table row is added, the tr element's onclick event handler is assigned to a function. When any of the new table rows is clicked, it's removed from the table. The removed table row element is then traversed and the data in its cells is extracted and concatenated to a string, which is then printed out.

Example 12-6. Adding and removing table rows and associated table cells and data

```
<!DOCTYPE html>
<head>
<title>Adding and Removing Elements</title>
<style>
table {
    border-collapse: collapse;
}
td, th {
    padding: 5px;
    border: 1px solid #ccc;
}
tr:nth-child(2n+1)
{
    background-color: #eeffee;
}
</style>
<script>
window.onload=function() {

  var values = new Array(3);
  values[0] = [123.45, "apple", true];
  values[1] = [65, "banana", false];
```

```
      values[2] = [1034.99, "cherry", false];

      var mixed = document.getElementById("mixed");

      // IE 7 requires tbody
      var tbody = document.createElement("tbody");

      // for each outer array row
      for (var i = 0 ; i < values.length; i++) {
         var tr = document.createElement("tr");

         // for each inner array cell
         // create td then text, append
         for (var j = 0; j < values[i].length; j++) {
           var td = document.createElement("td");
           var txt = document.createTextNode(values[i][j]);
           td.appendChild(txt);
           tr.appendChild(td);
         }

         // attache event handler
         tr.onclick=prunerow;

         // append row to table
         tbody.appendChild(tr);
         mixed.appendChild(tbody);
      }
}

function prunerow() {
  var parent = this.parentNode;
  var oldrow = parent.removeChild(this);

  var datastring = "";
  for (var i = 0; i < oldrow.childNodes.length; i++) {
    var cell = oldrow.childNodes[i];
    datastring+=cell.firstChild.data + " ";
  }

  alert("removed " + datastring);
}
</script>

</head>
<body>
<table id="mixed">
<tr><th>Value One</th><th>Value two</th><th>Value three</th></tr>
</table>
</body>
```

The example demonstrates that it's a whole lot simpler to prune the DOM tree than to grow new branches.

See Also

Example 12-4 can be found in Recipe 12.12.

12.15 Changing the Element's CSS Style Properties

Problem

You want to modify one or more CSS properties for an element.

Solution

If you're only modifying a single property, you can change the CSS setting directly using the element's `style` property:

```
var elem = document.getElementById("elem");
elem.style.width = "500px";
```

If you're modifying one or more values, you can use the element's `setAttribute` method:

```
elem.setAttribute("style","width: 500px; background-color: yellow;");
```

Discussion

An element's CSS properties can be modified in JavaScript using one of two approaches. As the solution demonstrates, the simplest approach is to set the property's value directly using the element's `style` property:

```
elem.style.width = "500px";
```

If the CSS property contains a hyphen, such as `font-family` or `background-color`, use a CamelCase notation for the property:

```
elem.style.fontFamily = "Courier";
elem.style.backgroundColor = "rgb(255,0,0)";
```

You can also use the element's `setAttribute` method to set the style property:

```
elem.setAttribute("style","font-family: Courier; background-color: yellow");
```

However, when you set the style property using `setAttribute`, it erases any previously set values in the JavaScript.

Example 12-7 demonstrates how the style-setting techniques work, including the impact of using `setAttribute`. Various techniques are used to set and get style attributes, including a cross-browser approach to access the *computed style* for the attribute.

Example 12-7. Demonstrating setting and retrieving CSS style settings

```
<!DOCTYPE html>
<head>
<title>Changing style</title>
<meta charset="utf-8" />
```

```
<style>
#elem
{
  width: 200px; background-color: lime;
}
</style>
<script type="text/javascript">


function getStyle(elem, cssprop, cssprop2){

 // IE
 if (elem.currentStyle) {
   return elem.currentStyle[cssprop];

 // other browsers
 } else if (document.defaultView &&
                 document.defaultView.getComputedStyle) {
   return document.defaultView.getComputedStyle(elem,
null).getPropertyValue(cssprop2);

 // fallback
 } else {
   return null;
 }
}
window.onload=function() {

   // setting and accessing style properties
   var elem = document.getElementById("elem");

   var color = getStyle(elem,"backgroundColor", "background-color");
   alert(color); // rgb(0,255,0)

   elem.style.width = "500px";
   elem.style.backgroundColor="yellow";

   alert(elem.style.width); // 500px
   alert(elem.style.backgroundColor); // yellow

   // array notation
   elem.style["fontFamily"] = "Courier";

   // demonstrating overwriting properties
   var style = elem.getAttribute("style");
   alert(style); // should display color: purple; width: 500px;
                 // background-color: yellow;

   elem.setAttribute("style","height: 100px");
   var style = elem.getAttribute("style");
   alert(style); // now only displays height, resets styles

   var font = getStyle(elem,"fontFamily", "font-family");
   alert(font); // default font family
```

```
}
</script>
</head>
<body>
<div id="elem" style="color: purple">
testing
</div>
</body>
```

As soon as the page loads, the `div` element is accessed using `getElementById`, and its `background-color` is retrieved using a cross-browser function that gets the computed style for the attribute. The message output is "rgb(0,255,0)", representing the lime color set in the page's stylesheet.

Next, two CSS properties are set using the element's `style` property: the `width` and `background-color`. Now the `div` element has a yellow background and is 500, rather than 200, pixels wide. Both of the modified values are accessed and printed out, so we can confirm that yes, the values have changed.

Next, the `font-family` for the element is set to Courier, using the array notation, which is another approach you can use to set and get style property values. Now the `div` element is 500 pixels wide, with a yellow background, and its font family is Courier.

The style property is accessed using `getAttribute`. A string of the values set using the `style` property is returned for all browsers:

```
color: purple; width: 500px; background-color: yellow;
font-family: Courier;
```

The purple font color is set inline within a `style` attribute in the `div` element.

Next, I'm using the `setAttribute` method to change the element's height. A couple of things happen when I used the `setAttribute` method in the example. The height of the element is changed to 100 pixels, but the previously set style properties (`color`, `width`, `background-color`, and `font-family`) have been "erased," and revert back to the original settings in the stylesheet, or the defaults by the user agent. The element is now 200 pixels wide, 100 pixels tall, with a green background, and the font reverts back to the default font for the browser (typically a serif value), and the default font color, black.

As you can see, using `setAttribute` to change the `style` element property can significantly impact on previous settings, including any inline CSS settings. You should only use `setAttribute` if you're changing many values at once, and you don't use any inline style attributes or haven't modified the element's style settings previously in your application.

The effects demonstrated in this recipe work the same with all of the book's target browsers, except for IE7. The style property is an actual object in IE7, so when you access style with `getAttribute`, you'll get an object, not a string. Since it is an object, it's read only, which means you can't use `setAttribute` with IE7.

See Also

See Recipe 11.13 for more information about accessing the computed style for an element.

CHAPTER 13

Working with Web Page Spaces

13.0 Introduction

The web page space is all of the area contained within the browser's chrome: the outer edge of the browser, status, and menu bars. If the contents of the page are larger than the window area, vertical and horizontal scrollbars are added so you can scroll to see all of the page contents.

The web page size is determined by the page elements, in combination with the default and explicit styling for each. If there are no elements, or the elements don't participate in the page flow (if they're absolutely positioned, or in some other way removed from the flow), the area of the web page space is the size of the window minus the chrome.

Element sizes vary, based on their contents, but they can be resized or even clipped. If they are resized, setting the element's `overflow` alters what happens to their content if it is larger than the element's size. If the `overflow` is set to `scroll`, vertical and horizontal scrollbars are added to the element.

How the elements impact page flow is based on a number of factors. For instance, if the element is a block-level element, such as a `div`, header (`h1`), or paragraph (`p`), there's a new line before and after the element. An inline element, though, such as a `span`, is not surrounded by line breaks. The display for both types of elements can be changed by setting the CSS `display` or `float` property.

An element's positioning can also impact page flow. By default, elements have static positioning, where properties such as `top` and `left` have no impact. An element's position can be changed through the CSS `position` property, and through the use of positional properties such as `left` and `top`—either changing the element's position in the page, or removing it entirely out of the page flow.

All of the element properties just mentioned can be set in a stylesheet:

```
<style>
div#test
{
   position: absolute;
```

```
      left: 10px;
      top: 10px;
   }
```

In this chapter, we're more interested in the many ways of using JavaScript to dynamically manage the web page's space.

13.1 Determining the Area of the Web Page

Problem

You want to measure the width and height of the current web page window.

Solution

You'll need to use a cross-browser technique that ensures consistent results regardless of the browser used. The following is an example of a function that returns an object with the web page viewport's width and height:

```
function size()
{
  var wdth = 0;
  var hth = 0;

  if(!window.innerWidth)
  {
     wdth = (document.documentElement.clientWidth ?
document.documentElement.clientWidth :
document.body.clientWidth);
     hth = (document.documentElement.clientHeight ?
document.documentElement.clientWidth :
document.body.clientHeight);
  }
  else
  {
    wdth = window.innerWidth;
    hth = window.innerHeight;
  }
  return {width:wdth, height:hth};
}
```

Discussion

There is currently no standard approach to accessing the window viewport information, which is why we have to use a series of case statements.

Most major browsers, including Opera, Firefox, Chrome, and Safari, support window object properties called innerWidth and innerHeight, which return the window's viewport area, minus any scrollbar dimensions. However, Internet Explorer doesn't support innerWidth and innerHeight, which accounts for the first test case in the solution.

If the `innerWidth` property is supported, the width and height are accessed from `inner` `Width` and `innerHeight`, respectively. If it isn't supported, the ternary operator is used to test for a document property, `documentView`, and its property, `clientWidth`. If there is no `documentView` object, the `clientWidth` property is accessed on the document body property:

```
wdth = (document.documentElement.clientWidth ?
            document.documentElement.clientWidth :
            document.body.clientWidth);
```

IE provides viewport information through the `documentView` property *except* in IE6, when the application is run in *quirks mode*. Though support for IE6 is rapidly diminishing—major websites such as Google, YouTube, and Amazon no longer support it, and it isn't one of the supported browsers in this book—I've included the test to be comprehensive.

 Quirks mode is a way for browsers to provide backward version support. It's typically triggered with a special `DOCTYPE`, such as: `<!DOCTYPE HTML PUBLIC "-//W3C//DTD HTML 4.01 Transitional//EN">`.

After the tests, both the width and height values are assigned to appropriately named properties in a returned object, using JSON notation:

```
return {width:wdth, height: hth}
```

Once the viewport size object is returned, you can access the width and height using the following code:

```
var viewPort = size();
var w = viewPort.width;
var h = viewPort.height;
```

See Also

There is a draft for a CSS3 standards effort to define a CSSOM View module, in order to provide a standard set of CSS specifications for window viewports and other dimensional and view information. The current draft is at *http://www.w3.org/TR/cssom -view/*. However, the priority for this specification is low, and the cross-browser approach just demonstrated is widely adopted, so a standard approach is off in the distant future.

See Recipe 19.4 for more on the JSON notation.

13.2 Measuring Elements

Problem

You want to determine the current height of a web page element.

Solution

Call `getBoundingClientRect` for the element. If the returned `TextRectangle/ClientRect` object has a height property, use that. Otherwise, subtract the rectangle's bottom value from its top to derive the height:

```
var height = 0;
var rect = document.getElementById("it").getBoundingClientRect();
if (rect.height) {
    height = rect.height;
} else {
    height = rect.bottom - rect.height; // derive height
}
alert(rect.height);
```

Discussion

The `getBoundingClientRect` method is based on a method that Microsoft implemented for IE5, and is now being standardized in the W3C CSSOM View module. The W3C CSSOM View module specification provides a standardized way of getting information about the web page viewport, and the element's spatial arrangement within the viewport.

The `element.getBoundingClientRect` method returns a `ClientRect` object (`TextRectangle` in implementations) that contains information about the bounding rectangle for the element. Most implementations support four properties on the object: `top`, `bottom`, `right`, and `left`. Firefox also includes `width` and `height`, though both can be derived from the other values.

When I mention the bounding rectangle for the element, the dimensions returned include any `padding` and `border` values. If an element has the following stylesheet setting:

```
#elem
{
   height: 400px;
 }
```

and you access the bounding rectangle's height, it is 400 pixels. However, if the element has the following stylesheet:

```
#elem
{
   height: 400px;
   padding: 10px;
   border: 5px solid red;
```

```
    margin: 20px;
}
```

the bounding rectangle's height would be 430 pixels: 400 for the height setting, plus 10 pixels each side for the padding, and 5 pixels each side for the border. The margin doesn't figure into the calculation.

If you don't provide any stylesheet setting, the height depends on the viewport size; changing the viewport will also change the element's dimensions, including its height.

The values for each of the `ClientRect/TextRectangle` dimensions are floating-point numbers.

 Another impact on the element's bounding rectangle position is if it's in a `foreignObject` element in embedded SVG, in which case the top-left is relative to `foreignObject`'s container and other contents.

13.3 Locating Elements in the Page

Problem

You want to know the exact position of an element in the page.

Solution

Use `getBoundingClientRect` to get the dimensions and position of the bounding rectangle for the element, and then access its `top` and `left` values to find position:

```
function positionObject(obj) {
    var rect = obj.getBoundingClientRect();
    return [rect.left,rect.top];
}
```

Discussion

Element positioning is based on the position, or *offset*, of the element's top-left corner relative to its viewport and ancestor elements. The position of the element is relative to other elements, and is dependent on whether its position is static (by default), relative, fixed, or absolute. The margin also affects the element's position.

The `element.getBoundingClientRect` method returns the rectangle for the element, including the `top`, `left`, `right`, and `bottom` positions, regardless of stylesheet setting.

To demonstrate how the method can be used to find element positions, Example 13-1 contains a web page with three nested `div` elements and a separate `div` element acting as cursor. Each nested `div` element is labeled and outlined, and the separate element is a solid color. When the page loads, the user is prompted for a box label, and if the label matches one of the `div` elements, the solid cursor `div` element is positioned over the specified `div` element. The prompt/move continues until canceled.

Example 13-1. Moving elements over others based on location position and absolute positioning

```
<!DOCTYPE html>
<head>
<title>Locating Elements</title>
<style type="text/css">
div#a
{
    width: 500px;
}
div
{
  border: 1px solid #000;
  padding: 10px;
}
#cursor
{
  position: absolute;
  background-color: #ffff00;
  width: 20px;
  height: 20px;
  left: 50px;
  top: 300px;
}
</style>
<script type="text/javascript">

function positionObject(obj) {
    var rect = obj.getBoundingClientRect();
    return [rect.left,rect.top];
}
window.onload=function() {
    var tst = document.documentElement.getBoundingClientRect();
    alert(tst.top);
    var cont = "A";
    var cursor = document.getElementById("cursor");
    while (cont) {
        cont = prompt("Where do you want to move the cursor block?",
                        "A");
        if (cont) {
           cont=cont.toLowerCase();
           if (cont == "a" || cont == "b" || cont == "c") {
              var elem = document.getElementById(cont);
              var pos = positionObject(elem);
              cursor.setAttribute("style","top: " + pos[1] +
                                    "px; left : " + pos[0] + "px");
           }
        }
     }
}
</script>
</head>
```

```
<body>
  <div id="a">
    <p>A</p>
    <div id="b">
      <p>B</p>
      <div id="c">
        <p>C</p>
      </div>
    </div>
  </div>
  <div id="cursor"></div>
</body>
```

Figure 13-1 shows the page after I selected the "B" div element. The application works with all of this book's target browsers.

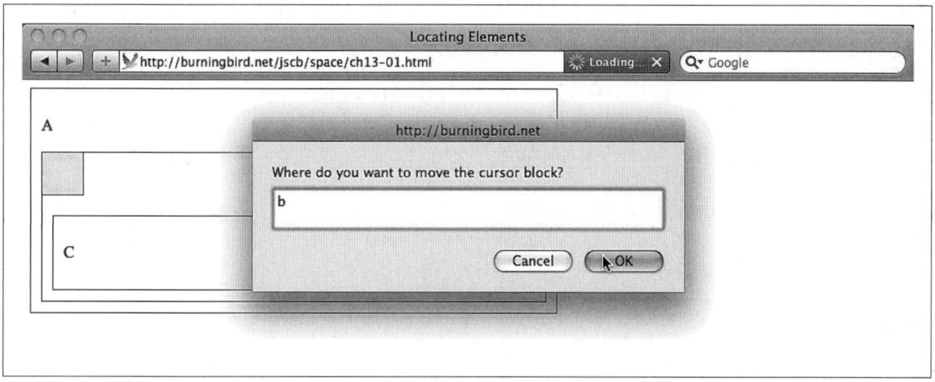

Figure 13-1. Showing element position in action

An interesting little quirk with getBoundingClientRect and positioning is that Microsoft originally added a two-pixel margin around the document element, which affected the getBoundingClientRect values. If you test the method with the document element:

```
var tst = document.documentElement.getBoundingClientRect();
alert(tst.top);
```

You get a value of 0 for Firefox, Safari, Chrome, and Opera, but you get a value of 2 for IE7, and –2 for IE8. If you run the application in IE7 compatibility mode and reposition the cursor element using code that's compatible for IE7 (IE7 doesn't like the setAttribute technique when used with the style attribute):

```
var pos = positionObject(elem);
cursor.style.top = pos[1] + "px";
cursor.style.left = pos[0] + "px";
```

The cursor is exactly 2 pixels off—both from the top and the left. With IE8, Microsoft "regularized" the margin for the document element, offsetting it –2 pixels. Now, when you use getBoundingClientRect with any element in the page, IE8 returns the same results as the other browsers.

If you need to support IE7, you'll need to adjust the `getBoundingClientRect` values accordingly, and also use the older approach of setting style values. The downloadable example code contains a workaround for this older browser.

See Also

See Recipe 12.15 for more on using `setAttribute` to change style settings.

13.4 Hiding Page Sections

Problem

You want to hide an existing page element and its children until needed.

Solution

You can set the CSS `visibility` property to hide and show the message:

```
msg.style.hidden="visible"; // to display
msg.style.hidden="hidden"; // to hide
```

or you can use the CSS `display` property:

```
msg.style.display="block"; // to display
msg.style.display="none"; // to remove from display
```

Discussion

Both the CSS `visibility` and `display` properties can be used to hide and show elements. There is one major difference between the two that impacts on which you'll use.

The `visibility` property controls the element's visual rendering, but its physical presence still affects other elements. When an element is hidden, it still takes up page space. The `display` property, on the other hand, removes the element completely from the page layout. The property can take several values, but there are four of interest to us:

none
: When display is set to `none`, the element is removed completely from display.

block
: When display is set to `block`, the element is treated like a `block` element, with a line break before and after.

inline-block
: When display is set to `inline-block`, the contents are formatted like a `block` element, which is then flowed like inline content.

inherit
: This is the default display, and specifies that the `display` property is inherited from the element's parent.

There are other values, but these are the ones we're most likely to use within JavaScript applications.

Unless you're using absolute positioning with the hidden element, you'll want to use the CSS `display` property. Otherwise, the element will affect the page layout, pushing any elements that follow down and to the right, depending on the type of hidden element.

There is another approach to removing an element out of page view, and that is to move it totally offscreen using a negative left value. This could work, especially if you're creating a slider element that will slide in from the left. It's also an approach that the accessibility community has suggested using when you have content that you want rendered by Assistive Technology (AT) devices, but not visually rendered.

To just hide an element, I generally use the `hidden` attribute, and to remove the element from the page display, I use the `display` attribute.

See Also

See Recipe 14.1 on accessible approaches to hiding and displaying page elements. See Recipe 13.4 for a demonstration of the `display` attribute.

13.5 Creating Collapsible Form Sections

Problem

You have a large form that takes up a lot of space. You only want to display sections of the form as they are needed.

Solution

Split the form into display blocks using `div` elements, and then change the block's styling to control the display of the form section. When the page is loaded, hide all of the form blocks by changing the display value to `none` using JavaScript:

```
theformblock.setAttribute("style","display: none");
```

or:

```
theformblock.style.display="none";
```

To expand the section, change the display setting to `block` using `setAttribute`:

```
theformblock.setAttribute("style","block");
```

or set the value directly:

```
theformblock.style.display="block";
```

Discussion

There are multiple ways you can prevent **form** elements from taking up page space. For one, you can clip the element by setting the clipping area. Another approach is to resize the element to zero height. The best approach, though, and the one most applications use, is to employ a *collapsible section*.

A collapsible section is a form of widget—a set of elements, CSS, and JavaScript packaged together and generally considered one object. The typical implementation consists of one element that acts as a label that is always displayed, another element that holds the content, and all contained within a third, parent element.

The collapsible section may or may not be used with other collapsible sections to form a higher level widget, the *accordion*. The accordion widget is a grouping of collapsible sections with an additional behavior: depending on preference, any number of collapsible sections can be expanded, or only one section can be expanded at a time.

To demonstrate how collapsible sections can be used with forms, Example 13-2 shows a form that's split into two sections. Notice that each **form** block has an associated label that expands the collapsed **form** section when clicked. When the label is clicked again, the form section is collapsed again.

Example 13-2. Collapsed form element

```
<!DOCTYPE html>
<head>
<title>Collapsed Form Elements</title>
<style>
.label
{
  width: 400px;
  margin: 10px 0 0 0;
  padding: 10px;
  background-color: #ccccff;
  text-align: center;
  border: 1px solid #ccccff;
}
.elements
{
  border: 1px solid #ccccff;
  padding: 10px;
  border: 1px solid #ccccff;
  width: 400px;
}
button
{
    margin: 20px;
}
</style>
</head>
<body>
<form>
  <div>
```

```
      <div id="section1" class="label">
        <p>Checkboxes</p>
      </div>
      <div id="section1b" class="elements">
        <input type="checkbox" name="box1" /> - box one<br />
        <input type="checkbox" name="box1" /> - box one<br />
        <input type="checkbox" name="box1" /> - box one<br />
        <input type="checkbox" name="box1" /> - box one<br />
        <input type="checkbox" name="box1" /> - box one<br />
      </div>
      </div>
    <div>

    <div id="section2" class="label">
      <p>Buttons</p>
    </div>
    <div class="elements">
      <input type="radio" name="button1" /> - button one<br />
      <input type="radio" name="button1" /> - button one<br />
      <input type="radio" name="button1" /> - button one<br />
      <input type="radio" name="button1" /> - button one<br />
      <input type="radio" name="button1" /> - button one<br />
      <button>Submit</button>
    </div>
</div>
</form>
<script type="text/javascript">

var elements = document.getElementsByTagName("div");

// collapse all sections
for (var i = 0; i < elements.length; i++) {
  if (elements[i].className == "elements") {
    elements[i].style.display="none";
  } else if (elements[i].className == "label") {
    elements[i].onclick=switchDisplay;
  }
}

//collapse or expand depending on state
function switchDisplay() {

  var parent = this.parentNode;
  var target = parent.getElementsByTagName("div")[1];

  if (target.style.display == "none") {
    target.style.display="block";
  } else {
    target.style.display="none";
  }
  return false;
}
</script>
</body>
```

There are numerous ways you can map the click activity in one element by changing the display in another. In Example 13-2, I wrapped both the `label` and the `content` elements in a parent element. When you click on a label, the parent to the `label` element is accessed in JavaScript and its children returned as an HTML collection. The second element's display toggles—if the element's display is `none`, it's changed to `block`; if `block`, changed to `none`. Figure 13-2 shows the page, with one form section expanded.

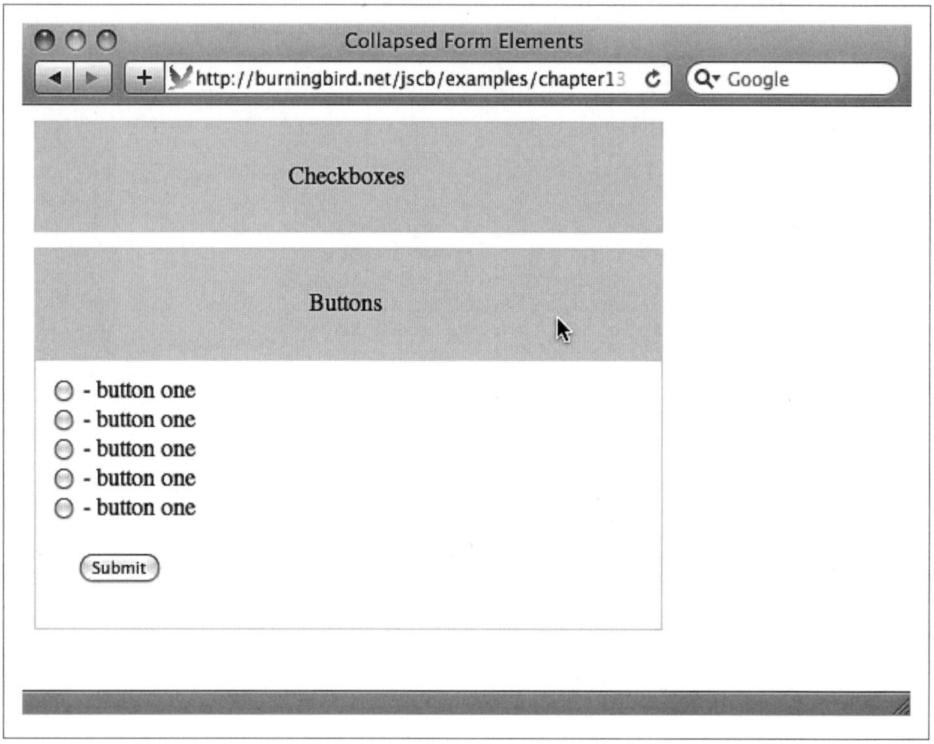

Figure 13-2. Form split over collapsible accordion sections, with one section expanded

In the example, notice that the `form` elements are displayed when the page loads, and only collapsed after the elements are loaded. The reason for this is if JavaScript is turned off, the `form` elements are displayed by default.

See Also

See Recipe 14.5 for how to make a collapsible section/accordion widget accessible with ARIA attributes.

13.6 Adding a Page Overlay

Problem

You want to overlay the web page in order to display a message, or provide an expanded photo.

Solution

Provide a stylesheet setting for a `div` element that is sized and positioned to cover the entire web page:

```
.overlay
{
   background-color: #000;
   opacity: .7;
   filter: alpha(opacity=70);
   position: absolute; top: 0; left: 0;
   width: 100%; height: 100%;
   z-index: 10;
}
```

Create the div element on demand, adding whatever other content is to be displayed to the div element:function expandPhoto() {

```
   var overlay = document.createElement("div");
   overlay.setAttribute("id","overlay");
   overlay.setAttribute("class", "overlay");
   document.body.appendChild(overlay);
}
```

When the overlay is no longer needed, remove it from the page:

```
function restore() {
   document.body.removeChild(document.getElementById("overlay"));
}
```

Discussion

Creating an overlay in a web page consists of creating a `div` element set to a `z-index` higher than anything else in the page, absolutely positioned at the upper left of the page, and sized 100%.

In the solution, this is achieved more easily by created a CSS style setting for the `overlay` class that manages the appearance of the element, and then using `document.createElement` and `appendChild` to add it to the page. To restore the page, the `overlay` element is removed.

Page overlays are popular for displaying ads, logins, or providing important site messages. They are also useful with photos. Example 13-3 contains a web page with four photo thumbnails. Clicking any of the thumbnails opens an overlay, and displays a larger size photo.

Example 13-3. Creating an overlay for displaying a larger photo

```
<!DOCTYPE html>
<head>
<title>Overlay</title>
<style>
img
{
  padding: 5px;
}

#outer
{
  width: 100%; height: 100%;
}
.overlay
{
   background-color: #000;
   opacity: .7;
   filter: alpha(opacity=70);
   position: fixed; top: 0; left: 0;
   width: 100%; height: 100%;
   z-index: 10;
}
.overlayimg
{
  position: absolute;
  z-index: 11;
  left: 50px;
  top: 50px;
}
</style>
<script>

function expandPhoto() {

    // create overlay and append to page
    var overlay = document.createElement("div");
    overlay.setAttribute("id","overlay");
    overlay.setAttribute("class", "overlay");
    document.body.appendChild(overlay);

    // create image and append to page
    var img = document.createElement("img");
    img.setAttribute("id","img");
    img.src = this.getAttribute("data-larger");
    img.setAttribute("class","overlayimg");

    // click to restore page
    img.onclick=restore;

    document.body.appendChild(img);

}
// restore page to normal
function restore() {
```

```
  document.body.removeChild(document.getElementById("overlay"));
  document.body.removeChild(document.getElementById("img"));
}


window.onload=function() {
  var imgs = document.getElementsByTagName("img");
  imgs[0].focus();
  for (var i = 0; i < imgs.length; i++) {
    imgs[i].onclick=expandPhoto;
    imgs[i].onkeydown=expandPhoto;
  }
}

</script>

</head>
<body>
<div id="outer">
  <p>Mouse click on image to expand the photo. To close expanded
photo, mouse click on image.</p>
  <img src="dragonfly2.thumbnail.jpg" data-larger="dragonfly2.jpg"
alt="image of common dragonfly on bright green and pink flowers" />
  <img src="dragonfly4.thumbnail.jpg" data-larger="dragonfly4.jpg"
alt="Dark orange dragonfly on water lily" />
  <img src="dragonfly6.thumbnail.jpg" data-larger="dragonfly6.jpg"
alt="Dark orange dragonfly on purple water lily" />
  <img src="dragonfly8.thumbnail.jpg" data-larger="dragonfly8.jpg"
alt="Dragonfly on bright pink water lily" />
</div>
</body>
```

Example 13-3 creates an overlay that fits the size of the page as it's currently opened. Note the CSS setting for the overlay, in particular the `fixed` positioning. This ensures that the overlay fits the window even if the contents require you to scroll to the right, or down, to see all of the contents.

Figure 13-3 shows the page with the overlay and one of the photos displayed.

The application works with Firefox, Opera, Chrome, Safari, and IE8. IE7 doesn't like the use of `setAttribute` with the `class` attribute. If you need to support IE7, set the `className` attribute directly:

```
overlay.className = "overlay";
```

See Also

See Recipe 12.15 for more on using `setAttribute` with CSS styles.

Figure 13-3. Demonstration of an overlap and photo

13.7 Creating Tab Pages

Problem

You have divided content that you want to hide or display based on the web page reader's actions.

Solution

Create a tabbed page effect and hide or display tab pages based on clicking the tab label:

```
// click on tab
function displayPage() {
  var current = this.parentNode.getAttribute("data-current");
  document.getElementById("tabnav_" + current).setAttribute("style",
                          "background-color: #fff");
  document.getElementById("tabpage_" + current).style.display="none";

  var ident = this.id.split("_")[1];
  this.setAttribute("style","background-color: #f00");
  document.getElementById("tabpage_" + ident).style.display="block";
  this.parentNode.setAttribute("data-current",ident);
}
```

Discussion

Tabbed pages have been popular for some time, and rightfully so. They're a great way to make use of limited web page space in a manner that's intuitive—we're all familiar with tabs from other applications, including browsers.

The tabbed page concept is simple: display a list of tabs to click on the top, and pages underneath. All tabs are shown, but only one page is shown at a time. Clicking any of the tabs resets the page:

- The highlighted tab is changed to the one just clicked.
- The currently displayed page is hidden or set to nondisplay.
- The clicked tab's style is changed (so it's highlighted).
- The associated content page is displayed.

In the solution, part of a tabbed page application is shown: the part that demonstrates what happens when you click the tab. In this case, the tab is associated by an identifier number attached to the end of the tab identifier for the associated tab page, so there doesn't have to be any form of container relation between the two. You want to avoid a container relationship between tab and page as much as possible, because it makes it difficult to ensure the page displays well when JavaScript is turned off.

The current tab picked is stored in the parent node's custom data attribute, `data-current`. Using a custom `data-*` attribute, as these values are called, means we can avoid global variables. The next time a tab is clicked, it's easy to find the current selection in order to reset the page.

 The custom `data-*` attributes were introduced with HTML5. You can use any name that begins with `data-`, and the page is still considered conforming to HTML5.

There are probably dozens of different approaches you can use to create tabbed pages, including making your own library, or using another that can be dropped into a page to automatically build the pages based on `class` settings.

The approach in Example 13-4 incorporates the approach outlined in the solution. It also makes use of the fact that elements form their own document trees, and that we can query an element tree the same as we can query the document tree. Using this approach, we can add as many tabbed page containers to the page as we wish. For each container, the application displays the navigation bar, turns off the display for all of the pages except the first, and highlights the first tab, and then adds the `onclick` event handler to each tab.

Example 13-4. Creating a reusable, multiple-count, tabbed page application

```html
<!DOCTYPE html>
<head>
<title>Tabbed Pages</title>
<style>
  .tabcontainer
  {
    padding: 5px; width: 500px;
    margin: 20px;
  }
  .tabnavigation ul
  {
    padding: 0; margin: 0; display: none;
  }
  .tabnavigation ul li
  {
    padding: 3px; display: inline;
    border: 1px solid #000; background-color: #fff;
  }
  .tabnavigation ul li:hover
  {
    cursor: pointer;
  }
  .tabpages
  {
    position: relative; z-index: 2;
    border: 1px solid #000; background-color: #fff;
  }
  .tabpage
  {
    margin: 0 10px;
  }
</style>
<script>

// set up display
// for each container display navigation
// hide all but first page, highlight first tab
window.onload=function() {

  // for each container
  var containers = document.querySelectorAll(".tabcontainer");
  for (var j = 0; j < containers.length; j++) {

    // display and hide elements
    var nav = containers[j].querySelector(".tabnavigation ul");
    nav.style.display="block";

    // set current tab
    var navitem = containers[j].querySelector(".tabnavigation ul li");
    var ident = navitem.id.split("_")[1];
    navitem.parentNode.setAttribute("data-current",ident);
    navitem.setAttribute("style","background-color: #f00");

    var pages = containers[j].querySelectorAll(".tabpage");
```

```
      for (var i = 1; i < pages.length; i++) {
        pages[i].style.display="none";
      }

      var tabs = containers[j].querySelectorAll(".tabnavigation ul li");
      for (var i = 0; i < tabs.length; i++) {
        tabs[i].onclick=displayPage;
      }
    }
  }
}

// click on tab
function displayPage() {
  var current = this.parentNode.getAttribute("data-current");
  document.getElementById("tabnav_" + current).setAttribute("style",
"background-color: #fff");
  document.getElementById("tabpage_" + current).style.display="none";

  var ident = this.id.split("_")[1];
  this.setAttribute("style","background-color: #f00");
  document.getElementById("tabpage_" + ident).style.display="block";
  this.parentNode.setAttribute("data-current",ident);
}
</script>
</head>
<body>
<div class="tabcontainer">
    <div class="tabnavigation">
        <ul>
            <li id="tabnav_1">Page One</li>
            <li id="tabnav_2">Page Two</li>
            <li id="tabnav_3">Page Three</li>
        </ul>
    </div>

    <div class="tabpages">
        <div class="tabpage" id="tabpage_1">
            <p>page 1</p>
        </div>
        <div class="tabpage" id="tabpage_2">
            <p>page 2</p>
        </div>
        <div class="tabpage" id="tabpage_3">
            <p>page 3</p>
        </div>
    </div>
</div>
<div class="tabcontainer">
    <div class="tabnavigation">
        <ul>
            <li id="tabnav_4">Page Two One</li>
            <li id="tabnav_5">Page Two Two</li>
        </ul>
    <div>
```

```
    <div class="tabpages">
        <div class="tabpage" id="tabpage_4">
            <p>Page 4</p>
        </div>
        <div class="tabpage" id="tabpage_5">
            <p>Page 5</p>
        </div>
    </div>
</div>
</body>
```

Figure 13-4 shows the application with two containers, different tabbed pages open in
each. The application works with Chrome, Firefox, Opera, Safari, and IE8. It doesn't
work with IE7 because of the use of querySelectorAll.

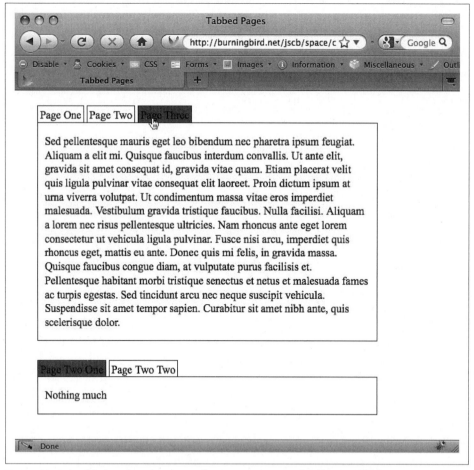

Figure 13-4. A tabbed page application with two containers, and different tabbed pages open in each

See Also

See Recipe 14.8 for how to make tabbed pages accessible using ARIA roles and attributes.

13.8 Creating Hover-Based Pop-up Info Windows

Problem

You like the Netflix web site's pop-up window that displays when the mouse cursor is over a movie thumbnail, and you want to incorporate this functionality into your own application.

Solution

The Netflix-style of pop-up info window is based on four different functionalities.

First, you need to capture the mouseover and mouseout events for each image thumbnail, in order to display or remove the pop-up window, respectively. Using a function that manages cross-browser event handling for every object that has an info bubble, assign a function to both the onmouseover and onmouseout event handlers. In the following code, the event handlers are attached to all images in the page:

```
function manageEvent(eventObj, event, eventHandler) {
    if (eventObj.addEventListener) {
        eventObj.addEventListener(event, eventHandler,false);
    } else if (eventObj.attachEvent) {
        event = "on" + event;
        eventObj.attachEvent(event, eventHandler);
    }
}

window.onload=function() {
  var imgs = document.getElementsByTagName("img");
  for (var i = 0; i < imgs.length; i++) {
     manageEvent(imgs[i],"mouseover",getInfo);
     manageEvent(imgs[i],"mouseout",removeWindow);
  }
}
```

Second, you need to access something about the item you're hovering over in order to know what to use to populate the pop-up bubble. The information can be in the page, or you can use Ajax to get the information:

```
function getInfo() {

  // prepare request
  if (!xmlhttp) {
    xmlhttp = new XMLHttpRequest();
  }
  var value = this.getAttribute("id");
```

```
var url = "photos.php?photo=" + value;
xmlhttp.open('GET', url, true);
xmlhttp.onreadystatechange = showWindow;
xmlhttp.send(null);

return false;
}
```

Third, you need to either show the pop-up window, if it already exists and is not displayed, or create the window. In the following code, the pop-up window is created just below the object, and just to the right when the Ajax call returns with the information about the item. The `element.getBoundingClientRect` method is used to determine the location where the pop up should be placed, and the DOM methods `document.crea teElement` and `document.createTextNode` are used to create the pop up:

```
// compute position for pop up
function compPos(obj) {
    var rect = obj.getBoundingClientRect();
    var height;
    if (rect.height) {
      height = rect.height;
    } else {
      height = rect.bottom - rect.top;
    }
    var top = rect.top + height + 10;
    return [rect.left, top];
}

// process return
function showWindow() {
   if(xmlhttp.readyState == 4 && xmlhttp.status == 200) {
      var response = xmlhttp.responseText.split("#");
      var img = document.getElementById(response[0]);

      if (!img) return;

      // derive location for pop up
      var loc = compPos(img);
      var left = loc[0] + "px";
      var top = loc[1] + "px";

      // create pop up
      var div = document.createElement("popup");
      div.id = "popup";
      var txt = document.createTextNode(response[1]);
      div.appendChild(txt);

      // style pop up
      div.setAttribute("class","popup");
      div.setAttribute("style","left: " + left + "; top: " + top);
      document.body.appendChild(div);
   }
}
```

Lastly, when the `mouseover` event fires, you need to either hide the pop-up window or remove it—whichever makes sense in your setup. Since I created a new pop-up window in the `mouseover` event, I'll remove it in the `mouseout` event handler:

```
function removeWindow() {
   var popup = document.getElementById("popup");
   if (popup)
     popup.parentNode.removeChild(popup);

   return false;
}
```

Discussion

Creating a pop-up information or help window doesn't have to be complicated, if you keep the action simple and follow the four steps outlined in the solution. If the pop up is help for `form` elements, then you might want to cache the information within the page, and just show and hide pop-up elements as needed. However, if you have pages like the ones at Netflix, which can have hundreds of items, you'll have better performance if you get the pop-up window information on demand using Ajax. The solution demonstrates that using Ajax doesn't add significant additional complexity to the application.

When I positioned the pop up in the example, I didn't place it directly over the object, as shown in Figure 13-5. The reason is that I'm not capturing the mouse position to have the pop up follow the cursor around, ensuring that I don't move the cursor directly over the pop up. But if I statically position the pop up partially over the object, the web page readers could move their mouse over the pop up, which triggers the event to hide the pop up...which then triggers the event to show the pop up, and so on. This creates a flicker effect, not to mention a lot of network activity.

If, instead, I allowed the mouse events to continue by returning `true` from either event handler function, when the web page readers move their mouse over the pop up, the pop up won't go away. However, if they move the mouse from the image to the pop up, and then to the rest of the page, the event to trigger the pop-up event removal won't fire, and the pop up is left on the page.

The best approach is to place the pop up directly under (or to the side, or a specific location in the page) rather than directly over the object. This is the approach Netflix uses on its site.

IE7 doesn't like the use of `setAttribute` with the `class` or `style` attributes. To modify the code so it also works with IE7, replace the `setAttribute` with:

```
// IE7
div.className="popup";
div.style.left=left;
div.style.top = top;
```

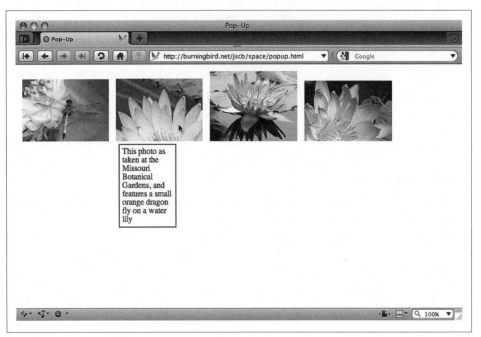

Figure 13-5. Demonstrating a pop-up mouseover information window

See Also

See Recipes 13.2 and 13.3 for more information about using `element.getBoundingClien tRect`. Chapter 12 provides coverage of creating new `page` elements, and Chapter 18 of using Ajax. Recipe 12.15 covers using `setAttribute` with CSS style settings.

13.9 Collapsing or Resizing the Sidebar

Problem

You have a website that has a main column and one or more side columns, as shown in Figure 13-6. You want to provide a way for your web page readers to control the width of the main column, without having to resize the browser.

Solution

Use a collapsible sidebar.

Add an X in a `span` element at the top of the sidebar. Include a custom `data-expand` attribute set to `"true"`, to track whether the column is expanded or not. Also include `tabindex="0"`, so that the element can receive `keypress` events:

```
<div>
  <p id="x" data-expand="true" tabindex="0">
```

```
<span style="text-decoration: underline">X</span>
Collapse sidebar</p>
</div>
```

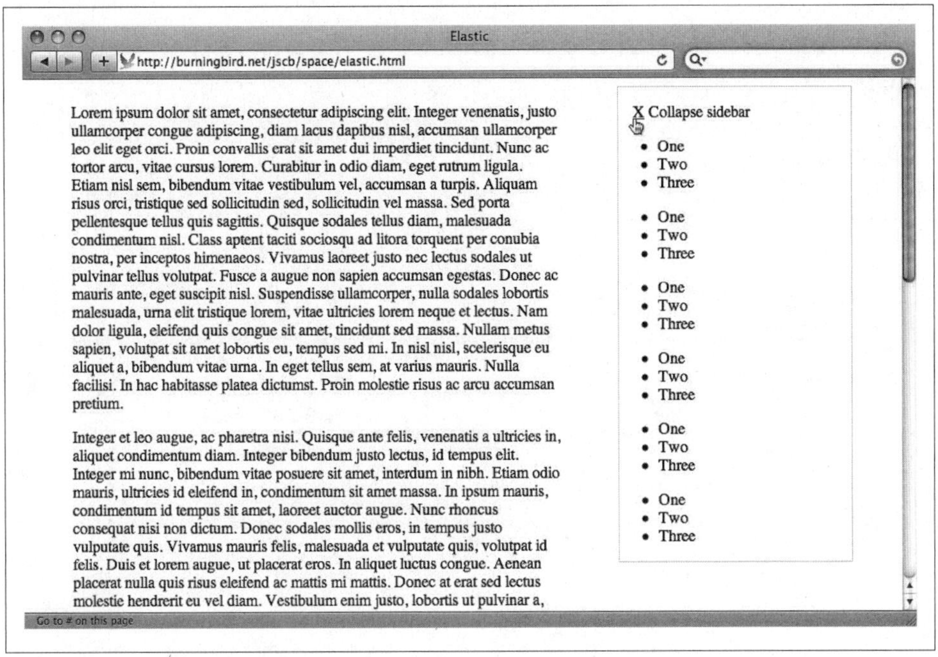

Figure 13-6. Collapsible sidebar page before sidebar is collapsed

Add a method handler to the element's click and **keypress** events that checks the **data-expand** attribute to see if the column is currently expanded or not. If it is expanded, the column is collapsed, and the main column expanded; if not, the sidebar and main column are returned to their regular dimensions:

```
window.onload=function() {

    var x = document.getElementById("x");
    x.setAttribute("style","display: block");
    x.onclick=expandOrShrink;
    x.onkeypress=expandOrShrink;
}

function expandOrShrink() {
    if (this.getAttribute("data-expand") == "true") {
        document.getElementById("sidebar").setAttribute("style",
                "width: 50px");
        document.getElementById("main").setAttribute("style",
                "width: 700px");
        this.setAttribute("data-expand", "false");
    } else {
        document.getElementById("sidebar").setAttribute("style",
                "width: 240px");
```

```
    document.getElementById("main").setAttribute("style",
            "width: 500px");
    this.setAttribute("data-expand", "true");
    }
}
```

Discussion

Working with page space doesn't mean that the JavaScript has to be complex or involved. The collapsible sidebar is very simple. The key to making it work is to ensure
that the sidebar contents are clipped when the sidebar is shrunk (as shown in Figure 13-7), rather than overflowing the sidebar dimensions.

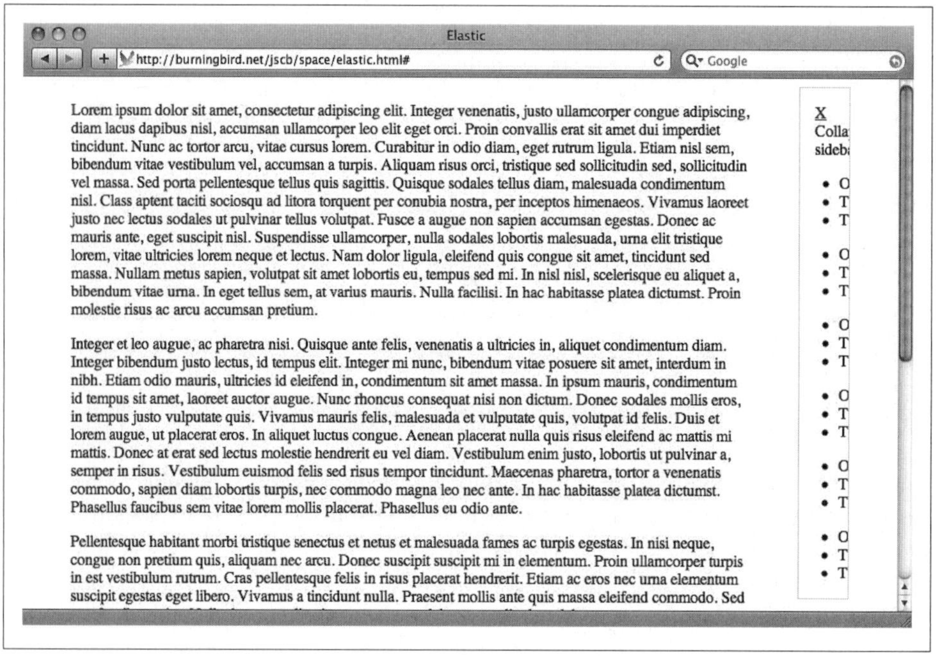

Figure 13-7. Collapsible sidebar page after sidebar is collapsed

To ensure the page works if JavaScript is disabled, the default CSS for the X element is
set to display none. When the page loads, JavaScript changes the X to display.

Since IE7 doesn't like the use of setAttribute with the style attribute, you can modify
the application to support this older browser by using direct attribute assignment:

```
function expandOrShrink() {
    if (this.getAttribute("data-expand") == "true") {
        document.getElementById("sidebar").setAttribute("style",
                "width: 50px");
        document.getElementById("main").setAttribute("style",
                "width: 700px");
```

```
    // IE7
    // document.getElementById("sidebar").style.width="50px";
    // document.getElementById("main").style.width="700px";

    this.setAttribute("data-expand", "false");
} else {
    document.getElementById("sidebar").setAttribute("style",
            "width: 240px");
    document.getElementById("main").setAttribute("style",
            "width: 500px");

    // IE7
    // document.getElementById("sidebar").style.width="240px";
    // document.getElementById("main").style.width="500px";

    this.setAttribute("data-expand", "true");
    }
}
```

IE7 does support the use of `getAttribute` and `setAttribute` with custom `data-*` attributes.

CHAPTER 14

Creating Interactive and Accessible Effects with JavaScript, CSS, and ARIA

14.0 Introduction

Using JavaScript with HTML and CSS to enable more interactive web pages has been around for over a decade. We've used the techniques to provide just-in-time help when people are submitting forms, highlight page sections, cue the users that something important has happened, or respond to mouse hover events.

These venerable techniques are now joined with a new capability: Accessible Rich Internet Applications (ARIA), a set of accessibility attributes that add accessibility to Rich Internet Applications.

This chapter is going to focus on classic interactive JavaScript techniques used across most of the Web, and requiring only basic HTML, CSS, and JavaScript skills. They'll be freshened for modern times with the use of the ARIA functionality.

Byte for byte, the effects described in this chapter can provide the most impact with the least effort. Best of all, the effects described in this chapter are probably the most cross-browser-friendly techniques in use today. They're certainly the most user-friendly techniques available.

The examples in this chapter work in all of the book's target browsers. To test the screen-reader-specific accessibility components, you can install a screen reader that provides a free testing option (such as Windows-Eyes, which allows 30 minutes of testing between reboots), or a free, fully functional screen reader such as NVDA, which unfortunately only works on Windows. The Mac has built-in screen reader support with VoiceOver, but it has only limited ARIA support at this time. The Linux environment has Orca, another free option. When testing for this chapter, I used Firefox 3.5 and NVDA in Windows XP.

I've long known that accessibility is an important feature for web applications, but I didn't realize until I was working on the examples for this chapter how fun developing for accessibility can be. Seeing previously silent, verbally unresponsive applications suddenly come alive when I turned on NVDA was rather amazing, and I must confess to going a little crazy trying out as many ARIA roles, relationships, and statuses as I could given the book deadline and size considerations.

 The ARIA capabilities are described in a set of documents created via the WAI-ARIA (Web Accessibility Initiative-Accessible Rich Internet Applications), an initiative under the auspices of the W3C. For more information on WAI-ARIA, see the WAI-ARIA overview page (*http://www.w3.org/WAI/intro/aria.php*).

Though much of the effort for accessibility has been focused on those needing to use screen readers, the concept of accessibility covers a broad range of impairments:

- Visual impairment, covering complete loss of vision, but can also include partial loss of vision, eye strain, monitors that are too large or too small, color blindness, and fatigue.

- Hearing loss, ranging from difficulty in hearing to complete deafness.

- Motor impairment, covering complete immobility, where the use of a mouse is impossible, to some fine-motor impairment, where the use of the mouse in coordination with the mouse button can be a problem.

- Cognitive impairment, covering a range of issues related to reading comprehension, reading ability and experience, memory, as well as experience with devices and with terminology.

As we go through the recipes, I'll try to tie what I've covered back to these broad groupings.

See Also

Recipe 7.7 also discusses ARIA related to the drag-and-drop event handling, and the new HTML5 native drag-and-drop support.

Two Windows-based commercial screen readers are JAWS (*http://www.freedomscientific.com/products/fs/jaws-product-page.asp*) and Window-Eyes (*http://www.gwmicro.com/Window-Eyes/*), both of which provide limited time-based testing without having to purchase the product. NVDA (*http://www.nvda-project.org/*) also works only on Windows, and is free. Orca, which works on Linux, can be found at *http://live.gnome.org/Orca*. VoiceOver is built-into the Mac environment, and can be controlled via System Preferences→System→Universal Access.

A nice overview in how to work with Firefox and NVDA can be found at Marco's Accessibility Blog (*http://www.marcozehe.de/articles/how-to-use-nvda-and-firefox-to-test-your-web-pages-for-accessibility/*). A good overview on setting up a screen reader test environment can be found at *http://www.iheni.com/screen-reader-testing/*.

The WebAIM website (*http://www.webaim.org/intro/*) provides a good overview of the different forms of disability types.

14.1 Displaying a Hidden Page Section

Problem

You want to hide or show a page section, as needed.

Solution

If there's a good likelihood of the page section being needed, you can embed it in the page and display it when needed:

```
var msg = document.getElementById("msg");
msg.style.display="block";
msg.setAttribute("aria-hidden", "false");
```

and hide it, when not:

```
var msg = document.getElementById("msg");
msg.style.display="none";
msg.setAttribute("aria-hidden", "true");
```

Discussion

Elements have different CSS `display` settings, depending on the type of element, and to some extent, the user agent. For browsers like Opera or Firefox, a `span` has an `inline` display value, while a `div` element has a `block` display value. Regardless of element type, though, setting the `display` to `none` removes the element completely from the document layout. Visually, this means the element is removed from view and does not take up any page space or affect how any other element displays, other than its own child elements.

Assistive Technology devices also understand and support the `display` property, though there are some inconsistencies in AT support. The `aria-hidden` attribute is a way of providing precise instructions to the AT device: when `true`, don't display/speak the text; if `false`, display/speak the text. It can be used in combination with the CSS `display` property to ensure the same result in visual and nonvisual environments.

Using `aria-hidden` with the CSS `display` property doesn't require any additional work. If the browser supports attribute selectors, you can set the element's visual display using the `aria-hidden` attribute:

```
#msg[aria-hidden=true]
{
   display: none;
}
```

With this CSS, when you change an element's `aria-hidden` attribute, you're also changing the CSS `display` property.

 Using this CSS style setting causes IE8 to lock up when it's running in IE7 compatibility mode.

Being able to hide sections of a page is useful not only for hiding and displaying messages, but also for hiding form elements, especially in a form that has a lot of elements. By hiding sections of the page and displaying them only as needed, you help to create an uncluttered web page. An uncluttered page helps everyone accessing your page, but is especially helpful for those who have cognitive disabilities and who may have challenges comprehending a mess of words and form controls all at once.

However, use this functionality with care. Providing a page with labels that a person can click to reveal the form elements underneath is helpful; unexpectedly popping up new controls can both surprise and irritate the user.

To ensure the page is always accessible even with JavaScript turned off, set the material you want available to be displayed by default, and hide the sections using JavaScript when the page is loaded. Set the messages you don't want displayed if JavaScript is disabled to be hidden by default.

See Also

See Recipe 14.5 for an example of a good implementation of hidden form content.

14.2 Creating an Alert Message

Problem

You want to alert the reader to important information.

Solution

Create a visually distinctive alert message in the web page, and ensure it's noticed by AT devices:

```
function addPopUp(txt) {
   // remove old alert, in case
   var msg = document.getElementById("msg");
   if (msg)
      document.body.removeChild(msg);

   // create new text and div elements and set
   // ARIA and class values and id
   var txtNd = document.createTextNode(txt);
```

```
msg = document.createElement("div");
msg.setAttribute("role","alert");
msg.setAttribute("id","msg");
msg.setAttribute("class","alert");

// append text to div, div to document
msg.appendChild(txtNd);
document.body.appendChild(msg);
}
```

Discussion

Unless a message is going to be displayed frequently, in my opinion it's better to create the message and add it to the page only when needed. That way your web page is uncluttered both physically and visually, and isn't taking up more bandwidth than necessary.

Creating a new text message is a simple four-step process:

1. Create the new `textNode`.
2. Create the parent element.
3. Append the new `textNode` to the parent element.
4. Append the parent element to the document.

In the solution, the message is going to be incorporated into a newly created `div` element. After the `div` element is created, three attributes are added. The first is the ARIA attribute `role`, set to `alert`. This should cause an AT device to interrupt what it's doing and immediately speak the message. The second attribute is the element `id`, so the element can be accessed at a later time. The last is a CSS style `class` name. The `class` ensures that the message is very easy to spot in the page visually. An example of a CSS setting could be:

```css
.alert
{
    background-color: #ffcccc; // pink
    font-weight: bold;
    padding: 5px;
    border: 1px dashed #000;
}
```

You can also use an attribute selector on the `role` attribute to style the CSS, and forgo the `class` name:

```css
[role="alert"]
{
  background-color: #ffeeee;
  font-weight: bold;
  padding: 5px;
  border: 1px dashed #000;
  width: 300px;
  margin: 20px;
}
```

Now the element's visual appearance matches the urgency of the ARIA `role`'s setting.

To ensure that messages don't visually pile up in the page before a new alert is created, any previously created alert is removed using the `removeChild` method on the message element's parent (in this example, the `body` element).

An `alert` lets people know that there's something they need to pay attention to, whether it's incorrect data or a session that's about to time out. Providing simple, specific messages to the user is also going to be helpful for those who use visual assistance devices such as screen magnifiers, or have some cognitive difficulties when it comes to web form use. This includes the inexperienced user, as well as those who may be fatigued or have other comprehension problems.

Another key aspect to messages such as these is ensuring that they can be easily dismissed using both keyboard and mouse movements, as we'll examine in more detail in later recipes.

See Also

The function to add the text demonstrated in the solution was derived from a tip in Marco's Accessibility blog (*http://www.marcozehe.de/2008/07/16/easy-aria-tip-3-aria-invalid-and-role-alert/*).

See Recipe 14.4 for a discussion about integrating keyboard access into mouse-based applications.

14.3 Highlighting Form Field with Missing or Incorrect Data

Problem

You want to highlight missing or incorrectly entered information in a form field.

Solution

For the fields that need to be validated, assign a function to the form field's `onchange` event handler that checks whether the field value is valid. If the value is invalid, pop up an alert with information about the error, and highlight the field using a contrasting color:

```
document.getElementById("elemid").onchange=validateField;
...
function validateField() {

  // check for number
  if (isNaN(parseFloat(this.value))) {
    this.parentNode.setAttribute("style",
"background-color: #ffcccc");
    this.setAttribute("aria-invalid", "true");
    generateAlert("You entered an invalid value in Third Field.
```

```
    Only numeric values such as 105 or 3.54 are allowed");
    }
}
```

For the fields that need a required value, assign a function to the field's **onblur** event handler that checks whether a value has been entered:

```
document.getElementById("field").onblur=checkMandator;
...
function checkMandatory() {
  // check for data
  if (this.value.length === 0) {
    this.parentNode.setAttribute("style",
"background-color: #ffcccc");
    this.setAttribute("aria-invalid", "true");
    generateAlert("A value is required in this field");
  }
}
```

If any of the validation checks are performed as part of the form submittal, make sure to cancel the submittal event if the validation fails.

Discussion

You can't depend on visual indicators to highlight errors, but they can be a useful extra courtesy.

Highlighting an error with color is good, but you should avoid colors that are hard to differentiate from the background. If the form background is white, and you use a dark yellow, gray, red, blue, green, or other color, there's enough contrast that it doesn't matter if the person viewing the page is color blind or not. In the example, I used a darker pink around the incorrect field, against a white page.

Using a color highlight for form errors is good, but it isn't enough: you also need to provide a text description of the error, so there's no question in the user's mind about what the problem is.

How you display the information is also an important consideration. None of us really like to use alert boxes, if we can avoid them. Alert boxes can obscure the form, and the only way to access the form element is to dismiss the alert, with its error message. A better approach is to embed the information in the page, near the form. Fortunately, with the new ARIA roles, we can create an alert message and assign it an ARIA **role** of **alert**, alerting those using screen readers or other AT devices.

One final touch: to ensure there's no confusion about which field is invalid, the solution also sets the **aria-invalid** attribute to **true** on the field. Not only does this provide useful information for AT device users immediately, it can be used to discover all incorrect fields when the form is submitted.

Example 14-1 demonstrates how to highlight an invalid entry on one of the form elements, and highlight missing data in another. The example also traps the form submit, and checks whether there are any invalid form field flags still set. Only if everything is clears is the form submittal allowed to proceed.

Example 14-1. Providing visual and other cues when validating form fields

```
<!DOCTYPE html>
<head>
<title>Validating Forms</title>
<style>
[role="alert"]
{
  background-color: #ffcccc;
  font-weight: bold;
  padding: 5px;
  border: 1px dashed #000;
}
div
{
  margin: 10px 0;
  padding: 5px;
  width: 400px;
  background-color: #ffffff;
}
</style>
<script>

window.onload=function() {

  document.getElementById("thirdfield").onchange=validateField;
  document.getElementById("firstfield").onblur=mandatoryField;
  document.getElementById("testform").onsubmit=finalCheck;
}

function removeAlert() {

    var msg = document.getElementById("msg");
    if (msg) {
       document.body.removeChild(msg);
    }
}

function resetField(elem) {
    elem.parentNode.setAttribute("style","background-color: #ffffff");
    var valid = elem.getAttribute("aria-invalid");
    if (valid) elem.removeAttribute("aria-invalid");
}

function badField(elem) {
  elem.parentNode.setAttribute("style", "background-color: #ffeeee");
  elem.setAttribute("aria-invalid","true");
}
function generateAlert(txt) {

    // create new text and div elements and set
    // Aria and class values and id
```

```
    var txtNd = document.createTextNode(txt);
    msg = document.createElement("div");
    msg.setAttribute("role","alert");
    msg.setAttribute("id","msg");
    msg.setAttribute("class","alert");

    // append text to div, div to document
    msg.appendChild(txtNd);
    document.body.appendChild(msg);
}

function validateField() {

    // remove any existing alert regardless of value
    removeAlert();

    // check for number
    if (!isNaN(parseFloat(this.value))) {
        resetField(this);
    } else {
        badField(this);
        generateAlert("You entered an invalid value in Third Field.
Only numeric values such as 105 or 3.54 are allowed");
    }
}

function mandatoryField() {

    // remove any existing alert
    removeAlert();

    // check for value
    if (this.value.length > 0) {
        resetField(this);
    } else {
        badField(this);
        generateAlert("You must enter a value into First Field");
    }
}
function finalCheck() {

    removeAlert();

    var fields = document.querySelectorAll("[aria-invalid='true']");
    if (fields.length > 0) {
        generateAlert("You have incorrect fields entries that must be
fixed before you can submit this form");
        return false;
    }
}

</script>
</head>
<body>
```

```
<form id="testform">
    <div><label for="firstfield">*First Field:</label><br />
        <input id="firstfield" name="firstfield" type="text"
aria-required="true" /></div>
    <div><label for="secondfield">Second Field:</label><br />
        <input id="secondfield" name="secondfield" type="text" /></div>
    <div><label for="thirdfield">Third Field (numeric):</label><br />
        <input id="thirdfield" name="thirdfield" type="text" /></div>
    <div><label for="fourthfield">Fourth Field:</label><br />
        <input id="fourthfield" name="fourthfield" type="text" /></div>

<input type="submit" value="Send Data" />
</form>

</body>
```

If either of the validated fields is incorrect in the application, the parent element's background color is set to pink and an error message is displayed. In addition, the `aria-invalid` attribute is set to `true` in the field, and an ARIA `role` is set to `alert` on the error message, as shown in Figure 14-1.

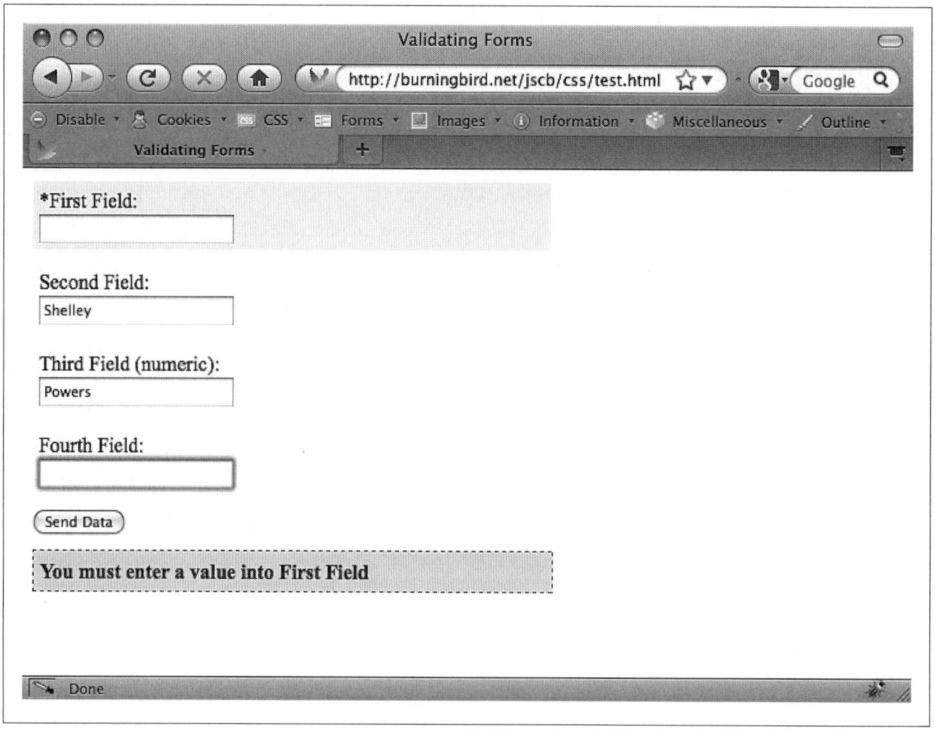

Figure 14-1. Highlighting an incorrect form field

Notice in the code that the element wrapping the targeted form field is set to its "correct state" when the data entered is correct, so that when a field is corrected it doesn't show up as inaccurate or missing on the next go-round. Regardless of what event happens, I remove the existing message alert, as it's no longer valid once the event that triggered it has been handled.

When the form is submitted, the application uses a `querySelectorAll` method call to check for all instances of `aria-invalid` set to `true`, and rejects the submission until these are corrected, as shown in Figure 14-2:

```
var badFields = document.querySelectorAll("[aria-invalid='true']");
```

You can also disable or even hide the correctly entered form elements, as a way to accentuate those with incorrect or missing data. However, I don't recommend this approach. Your users may find as they fill in the missing information that their answers in other fields were incorrect. If you make it difficult for them to correct the fields, they're not going to be happy with the experience—or the company, person, or organization providing the form.

Another approach you can take is to only do validation when the form is submitted. Most built-in libraries, such as the jQuery Validation plug-in, operate this way. Rather than check each field for mandatory or correct values as your users tab through, you only apply the validation rules when the form is submitted. This way people who want to fill out the form in a different order may do so without getting hit with irritating validation messages as they tab through. This approach is a friendlier technique for those people using a keyboard, rather than a mouse, to fill in the form. Or you can use a mix of both: field-level validation for correct data type and format, form-level validation for required values.

Using JavaScript to highlight a form field with incorrect and missing data is only one part of the form submission process. You'll also have to account for JavaScript being turned off, which means you have to provide the same level of feedback when processing the form information on the server, and providing the result on a separate page.

It's also important to mark if a form field is required ahead of time. Use an asterisk in the form field label, with a note that all form fields with an asterisk are required. Use the `aria-required` attribute to ensure this information is communicated to those using assistive devices.

See Also

See Recipe 14.1 for more information about displaying and hiding page sections, such as messages, and Recipe 14.2 for information about displaying error messages and other alerts.

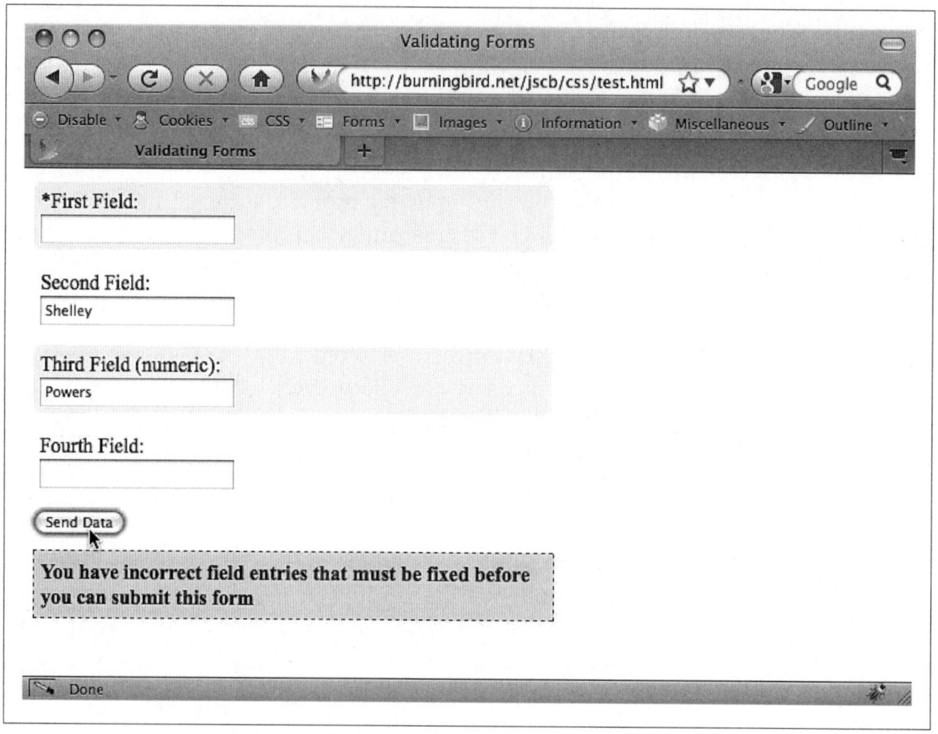

Figure 14-2. Attempting to submit a form with inaccurate form field entries

14.4 Adding Keyboard Accessibility to a Page Overlay

Problem

You've created a page overlay in order to display a larger image (or text, or other content), and you want it to be keyboard accessible.

Solution

Add keyboard listening to the page to complement the mouse events:

```
// mouse click on image within link
function imgClick() {
   var img = this.firstChild;
   expandPhoto(img.getAttribute("data-larger"));
   return false;
}

// key press on image within link
function imgKeyPress(evnt) {
   evnt = (evnt) ? evnt : ((window.event) ? window.event : "");
   var keycode = (evnt.which) ? evnt.which : evnt.keyCode;
   if (document.getElementById("overlay")) {
```

```
      if (keycode == 27) {
        restore();
        return false;
      }
    } else {
      if (keycode == 13) {
        var img = this.firstChild;
        var src = img.getAttribute("data-larger");
        expandPhoto(src);
        return false;
      }
    }
  }
```

Discussion

The first step to adding keyboard accessibility into a web page is to either use elements that can receive keyboard focus (a, area, button, input, object, select, and textarea), or use the tabindex="0" setting on the element, which will make the element focusable.

The second step is to capture keyboard activity in addition to the mouse events. In Example 14-2, I've taken Example 13-3 from Recipe 13.6, and modified what was a mouse-event-only application to also accept keyboard events. The example creates a page overlay and displays a larger image when a person either clicks on a thumbnail image in the original page, or presses the Enter (Return) key when the image has the focus. Clicking the expanded image or pressing the Esc key removes the overlay, and returns the page to its original state.

Example 14-2. Making an overlay/photo display page keyboard accessible

```
<!DOCTYPE html>
<head>
<title>Overlay</title>
<style>
img
{
  padding: 5px;
  border-style: none;
}

.overlay
{
  background-color: #000;
  opacity: .7;
  filter: alpha(opacity=70);
  position: absolute; top: 0; left: 0;
  width: 100%; height: 100%;
  z-index: 10;
}
.overlayimg
{
  position: absolute;
  z-index: 11;
```

```
      left: 50px;
      top: 50px;
}
</style>
<script>

// expand photo when a/img is clicked
function imgClick() {
    var img = this.firstChild;
    expandPhoto(img.getAttribute("data-larger"));
    return false;
}

// if overlay is open, and ESC, close overlay
// account for keydown event in page
function imgKeyDown(evnt) {
    evnt = (evnt) ? evnt : ((window.event) ? window.event : "");
    var keycode = (evnt.which) ? evnt.which : evnt.keyCode;
    if (document.getElementById("overlay")) {
        if (keycode === 27) {
          restore();
          return false;
        }
    } else {
        if (keycode == 13) {
            var img = this.firstChild;
            var src = img.getAttribute("data-larger");
            expandPhoto(src);
            return false;
        }
    }
    return true;
}
// create overlay, expand photo
function expandPhoto(src) {

    // create overlay element
    var overlay = document.createElement("div");
    overlay.setAttribute("id","overlay");
    overlay.setAttribute("class", "overlay");

    // IE7
    // overlay.id="overlay";
    // overlay.className = "overlay";

    document.body.appendChild(overlay);

    // add image
    var img = document.createElement("img");
    img.src = src;
    img.setAttribute("id","img");

    // set tabindex, for focus
    img.setAttribute("tabindex","-1");
```

```
    // style image
    img.setAttribute("class","overlayimg");

    // IE7
    // img.className = "overlayimg";

    img.onclick=restore;
    img.onkeydown=imgKeyDown;

    document.body.appendChild(img);

    // focus on image in overlay
    img.focus();
}

// remove overlay and image
function restore() {

 document.body.removeChild(document.getElementById("overlay"));
 document.body.removeChild(document.getElementById("img"));
}

// add click and keyboard events
window.onload=function() {
    var aimgs = document.getElementsByTagName("a");
    aimgs[0].focus();
    for (var i = 0; i < aimgs.length; i++) {
      aimgs[i].onclick=imgClick;
    }
}

</script>

</head>
<body>
<p>Mouse click on image, or use keyboard to move to photo and hit
ENTER to expand the photo. To close expanded photo, hit ESC or
mouse click on image.</p>
<a href="dragonfly2.jpg"><img src="dragonfly2.thumbnail.jpg" data-larger="dragonfly2.jpg"
alt="image of common dragonfly on bright green and pink flowers" /></a>
<a href="dragonfly4.jpg"><img src="dragonfly4.thumbnail.jpg" data-larger="dragonfly4.jpg"
alt="Dark orange dragonfly on water lily" /></a>
<a href="dragonfly6.jpg"><img src="dragonfly6.thumbnail.jpg" data-larger="dragonfly6.jpg"
alt="Dark orange dragonfly on purple water lily" /></a>
<a href="dragonfly8.jpg"><img src="dragonfly8.thumbnail.jpg" data-larger="dragonfly8.jpg"
alt="Dragonfly on bright pink water lily" /></a>
</body>
```

When I opened the new image, I assigned it tabindex of –1, to set keyboard focus. To ensure the application works with scripting disabled, the link references the larger image. When scripting is enabled, the image shows in the overlay; with scripting disabled, it opens in a separate page.

A click (rather than keypress) event is triggered when the Enter key is pressed and the focus is on one of the standard focusable elements: a, area, button, input, object, select, and textarea.

The tabbing did not work with Firefox on the Mac. It does work with Firefox on Windows, and hopefully, eventually, will work on the Mac, too. I also tested the application with Opera, Safari, and Chrome, and it worked fine. You do have to use Shift + the arrow keys to move among the images with Opera.

Safari overhauled its event system with Safari 3.1, and you no longer get a keypress event when clicking a noncharacter key. When the overlay is open, rather than capture the keypress event, you need to capture the keydown event if you're using the Esc key to return the page to normal.

The application worked out of the box for IE8. To make the page work with IE7, the use of setAttribute and getAttribute with the class attribute should be changed to direct assignment (the downloadable example code contains a workaround).

As you can see, using tabbing within a web page is somewhat challenging. However, the future looks bright for this capability, with the new tabindex instructions in HTML5 that clarify tabbing and tabindex behavior. Instead of having to wrap images in links to make them accessible, we can just assign them a tabindex="0". However, for non-focusable elements such as img, you do need to capture keypress and click events.

Providing keyboard access is absolutely essential for folks using AT devices, as well as people who have impaired movement. It's also an important capability for those who are using devices that may have limited mouse capability, such as some phones. And it's a nice enhancement for people who just prefer to use the keyboard whenever possible.

See Also

See Recipe 13.6 for a more in-depth explanation of the mouse events for the application. John Resig has an interesting post on the Safari 3.1 event-handling decision at *http://ejohn.org/blog/keypress-in-safari-31/*. Recipe 12.15 has more information on using setAttribute with CSS style properties.

14.5 Creating Collapsible Form Sections

Problem

You want to encapsulate form elements into collapsible sections, and expand when a label is clicked.

Solution

Use an *accordion* widget in combination with the `aria-hidden` and `aria-expanded` states, the `tablist`, `tab`, and `tabpanel` roles, and the `aria-labeledby` relationship indicator.

The entire set of accordion label/panel pairs is surrounded by one element, given a role of `tablist` and an attribute of `aria-multiselect` set to `true` to indicate that the element is a container for an accordion or `multiselectable tablist`. The text for the label is enclosed in a link to make it keyboard-accessible. Since these are groupings of `form` elements, the `label`/`elements` pair are surrounded by a `fieldset`, and the `label` is a `legend` element. If this application were a menu, these elements would most likely be `div` elements. The processing would, however, remain the same:

```
<form>
<div role="tablist" aria-multiselectable="true">
<fieldset>
<legend class="label" aria-controls="panel1" role="tab"
aria-expanded="true" id="label_1" >
<a href="">Checkboxes</a>
</legend>
<div  class="elements" id="panel_1" role="tabpanel"
aria-labeledby="label_1">
<input type="checkbox" name="box1" id="box1" value="one" />
<label for="box1">One</label><br />
<input type="checkbox" name="box2" id="box2" value="two" />
<label for="box2">Two</label><br />
<input type="checkbox" name="box3" id="box3" value="three" />
<label for="box3">Three</label><br />
<input type="checkbox" name="box4" id="box4" value="four" />
<label for="box4">Four</label><br />
<input type="checkbox" name="box5" id="box5" value="five" />
<label for="box5">Five</label><br />
</div>
</fieldset>
<fieldset>
<legend class="label" aria-controls="panel2" role="tab"
aria-expanded="true" id="label_2" >
<a href="">Buttons</a></legend>
<div class="elements" id="panel_2" role="tabpanel"
aria_labeledby="label_2">
<input type="radio" name="button1" id="b1" value="b one" />
<label>button one</label><br />
<input type="radio" name="button1" id="b2" value="b two" />
<label>button two</label><br />
<input type="radio" name="button1" id="b3" value="b three" />
<label>button three</label><br />
<input type="radio" name="button1" id="b4" value="b four" />
<label>button four</label><br />
<input type="radio" name="button1" id="b5" value="b five" />
<label>button five</label><br /><br />
<input type="submit" value="submit" />
</div>
</fieldset>
```

```
    </div>
    </form>
```

For each accordion `label`/`panel` pair, the `label` is displayed when the page is loaded, while the contents of the accordion panel are hidden. The `label` is given a role of `tab`, and the `panel` given a role of `tabpanel`. The `aria-expanded` attribute in the `label` is also set to `false`, to indicate to the AT devices that the panel is collapsed, and the `aria-hidden` is set to `true` on the `panel`, to indicate that the contents are not displayed:

```
// process tab panel elements
var elements = document.querySelectorAll(".elements");
for (var i = 0; i < elements.length; i++) {
    elements[i].style.display="none";
    elements[i].setAttribute("aria-hidden","true");
}

// process tab elements
var labels = document.querySelectorAll(".label");
for (var j = 0; j < labels.length; j++) {
    labels[j].onclick=switchDisplay;
    labels[j].style.display="block";
    labels[j].setAttribute("aria-expanded","false");
}
```

When the label is clicked, if the `aria-expanded` attribute is set to `false`, the panel is displayed, its `aria-hidden` attribute is set to `false`, and the `label`'s `aria-expanded` attribute is set to `true`. The opposite occurs if the `aria-expanded` attribute is set to `true`:

```
// when tab is clicked or enter key clicked
function switchDisplay() {

    var parent = this.parentNode;
    var targetid = "panel_" + this.id.split("_")[1];
    var target = document.getElementById(targetid);

    if (this.getAttribute("aria-expanded") == "true") {
      this.setAttribute("aria-expanded","false");
      target.style.display="none";
      target.setAttribute("aria-hidden","true");
    } else {
      this.setAttribute("aria-expanded","true");
      target.style.display="block";
      target.setAttribute("aria-hidden","false");
    }
    return false;
}
</script>
```

Discussion

The solution is a modification of the accordion solution in Recipe 13.5. The major structural differences are that one container element is used to wrap all of the accordion `label`/`panel` pairs, to indicate a grouping, each `tab`/`panel` pair is surrounded by a `field set` element, and the `div` element that acted as a label was replaced by a `legend` element.

One aspect of working with ARIA that I wasn't expecting is that it led me to reexamine how I create my widget-like applications, such as an accordion. In Recipe 13.4, I didn't group the individual accordion pairs into one cohesive whole because I didn't need to for the solution I created, and I wanted to keep my element use to a minimum.

The ARIA attributes reminded me that there are semantics to the structure of an accordion—semantics I wasn't capturing. For instance, I was working with a form but wasn't using form-specific elements. In the new version, instead of using `div` elements for all aspects of the form element accordion, I used actual form elements: `fieldset` and `legend`.

Another structural change is that a link is used to wrap the text in the label so that the element can receive keyboard focus. Hitting the Enter key in the label triggers a click event, since a link is a focusable element. Since I'm not capturing the click event in the link, it bubbles up to the parent element—the label.

I also added an additional visual element—a background image with an arrow, to indicate the direction the panel will open, as shown in Figure 14-3.

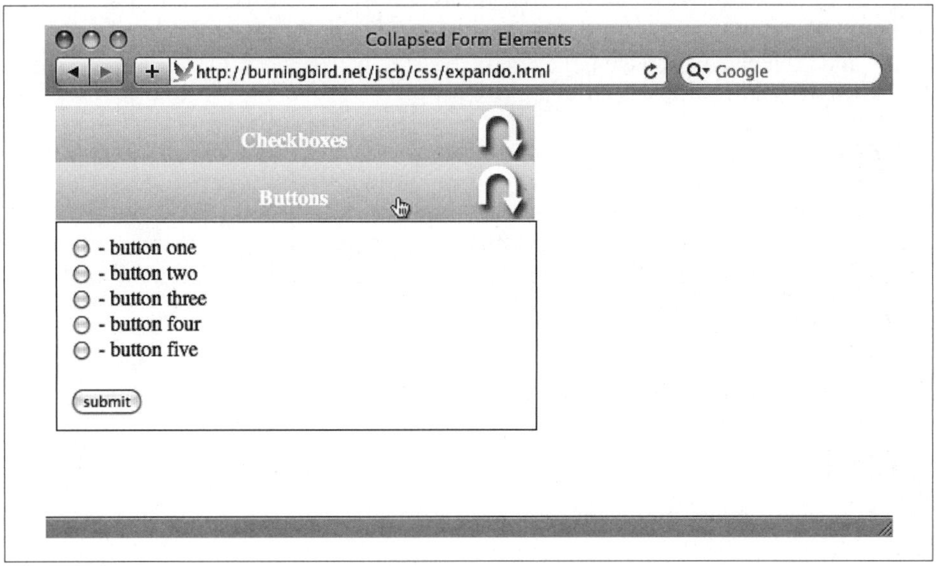

Figure 14-3. An accessible accordion

The reason for the addition of the arrows is to ensure clarity of purpose for the grouping of elements. Those users unfamiliar with accordion applications, or who may have cognitive disabilities, can see there is an action associated with the label. I'm not sure about the type of arrow I used—a better approach might be a simple triangle.

The other change to the example was the addition of ARIA roles and states. At first, the accessibility additions may seem to be rather numerous, but each provides a specific piece of information necessary to understand what's happening with the accordion widget. Consider how you would describe an accordion if you were describing it over the phone to a friend: "The accordion is a group of label elements, each of which has text. Each label also has an arrow, and I know from prior experience with similarly structured web page objects that clicking each label opens a panel underneath. When I do click each label, a section of previously hidden web page is displayed directly beneath the label, and I'm able to see its contents. When I click other labels, their associated panels also display. However, when I click the label for an already open label, the panel it is associated with is removed from view."

In ARIA, these visual impressions are conveyed by the use of the `tablist` role on the outer container, and the role of `tab` on the label. In addition, the use of `aria-multiselect` also indicates that more than one panel can be expanded at the same time.

The fact that the panels are collapsed is indicated by the `aria-expanded` attribute, and that the panels aren't displayed is indicated by the `aria-hidden` on each. When you open the application with a screen reader, such as NVDA in Firefox, and close your eyes, what I described is more or less what the device states.

The application works with all the book's target browsers. However, the use of `query SelectorAll` doesn't work with IE7. An alternative would be to access elements by tag name, and then check each element's class to see how to handle it. You'll also want to avoid using CSS attribute selector syntax with IE7.

See Also

See Recipe 13.4 for another implementation of the accordion. For an excellent demonstration of the use of the ARIA attributes with an accordion, see the accordion example at the Illinois Center for Information Technology and Web Accessibility (*http://test.cita.illinois.edu/aria/tabpanel/tabpanel2.php*).

14.6 Displaying a Flash of Color to Signal an Action

Problem

Based on some action, you want to display a visual cue to signify the success of the action.

Solution

Use a flash to signal the success or failure of an action. The use of a red flash is standard to signal either a successful deletion, or an error; the use of a yellow flash is typically used to signal a successful update, or action:

```
var fadingObject = {
    yellowColor : function (val) {
        var r="ff";    var g="ff";
        var b=val.toString(16);
```

```
      var newval = "#"+r+g+b;
      return newval;
   },

    fade : function (id,start,finish) {
    this.count = this.start = start;
    this.finish = finish;
    this.id = id;
    this.countDown = function() {
       this.count+=30;
       if (this.count >= this.finish) {
          document.getElementById(this.id).style.background=
                                             "transparent";
          this.countDown=null;
          return;
       }
       document.getElementById(this.id).style.backgroundColor=
          this.yellowColor(this.count);
       setTimeout(this.countDown.bind(this),100);
    }
  }
};
...
// fade page element identified as "one"
fadingObject.fade("one", 0, 300);
fadingObject.countDown();
```

Discussion

A flash, or *fade* as it is frequently called, is a quick flash of color. It's created using a recurring timer, which changes the background color of the object being flashed. The color is varied by successively changing the values of the nondominant RGB colors, or colors from a variation of 0 to 255, while holding the dominant color or colors at FF. Figure 14-4 shows how this color variation works with the color green. If for some reason the green color can't be perceived (such as this figure being in a paper copy of this book, or because of color blindness), the color shows as successions of gray. As you progress down the figure, the color gets progressively paler, as the nondominant red and blue values are increased, from initial hexadecimal values of 00, to FF(255).

The color yellow used in the solution kept the red and green values static, while changing the blue. A red flash would keep the red color static, while adjusting both the green and blue.

In the solution, I'm setting the beginning and ending colors for the flash when I call the fade method on the object, fadingObject. Thus, if I don't want to start at pure yellow or end at white, I can begin with a paler color, or end with a paler color.

A color flash is used to highlight an action. When used with Ajax, a red flash can single the deletion of a table row just before the row is removed from the table. The flash is an additional visual cue, as the table row being deleted helps set the context for the flash. A yellow flash can do the same when a table row is updated.

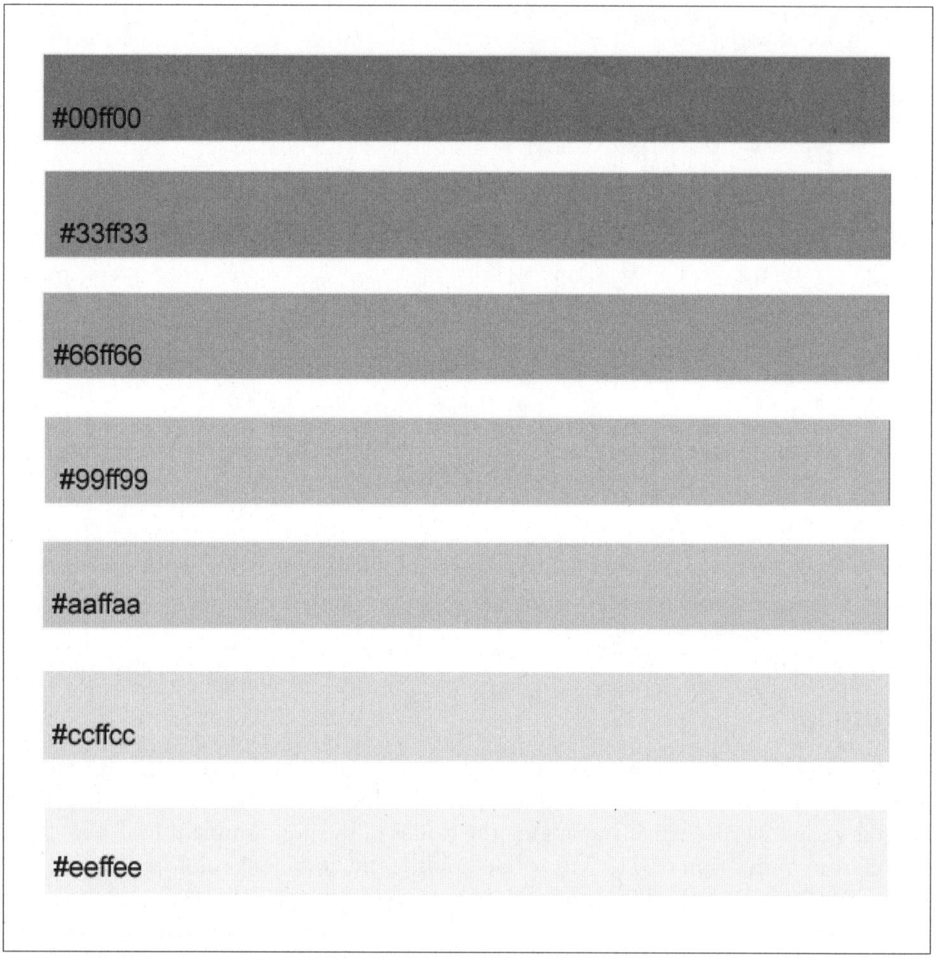

#00ff00	
#33ff33	
#66ff66	
#99ff99	
#aaffaa	
#ccffcc	
#eeffee	

Figure 14-4. Demonstrating how a color flash effect changes

A flash can also be used with an alert message. In Recipe 14.2, I created an alert that displayed a solid color until removed from the page. I could also have used a red flash to highlight the message, and left the background a pale pink at the end:

```
function generateAlert(txt) {

    // create new text and div elements and set
    // Aria and class values and id
    var txtNd = document.createTextNode(txt);
    msg = document.createElement("div");
    msg.setAttribute("role","alert");
    msg.setAttribute("id","msg");
    obj.fade("msg", 0, 127);
    obj.redFlash();
    msg.setAttribute("class","alert");
```

```
        // append text to div, div to document
        msg.appendChild(txtNd);
        document.body.appendChild(msg);
    }
```

The only requirement for the solution would be to either make the color-fade effect more generic, for any color, or add a new, specialized `redFlash` method that does the same as the yellow.

Previously, if the color flash hasn't been considered an accessibility aid, it's also not considered an accessibility hindrance, either. As I mentioned earlier, it should be paired with some other event or response that provides information about what's happening. In the code snippet, when the alert message is displayed, it's done with a flash, but the ARIA alert `role` is also assigned so that those using a screen reader get notified.

How about other accessibility concerns, though, such as photosensitive epilepsy? Or those with cognitive impairments where page movement or light flickering can disrupt the ability to absorb the page content?

A simple color flash as demonstrated should not result in any negative reaction. It's a single progressive movement, rather than a recurring flicker, and over quickly. In fact, the WebAIM website—which is focused on accessibility—makes use of a yellow flash in an exceedingly clever and accessible way.

If you access one of the WebAIM articles, such as the one on keyboard accessibility (*http://www.webaim.org/techniques/keyboard/tabindex.php*), and click one of the links that takes you to an in-page anchor, the page (once it has scrolled to the anchor location) gives material associated with the anchor a subtle and quick yellow flash to highlight its location.

In the site's JavaScript, the author of the JavaScript writes:

```
// This technique is a combination of a technique I used for
// highlighting FAQ's using anchors
// and the ever popular yellow-fade technique used by
// 37 Signals in Basecamp.

// Including this script in a page will automatically do two
// things when the page loads...
// 1. Highlight a target item from the URL (browser address bar)
// if one is present.
// 2. Set up all anchor tags with targets pointing to the current
// page to cause a fade on the target element when clicked.
```

In other words, when the page is loaded, the author accesses all anchors in the page:

```
var anchors = document.getElementsByTagName("a");
```

The author then traverses this array, checking to see if the anchor has a fragment identifier (#):

```
if (anchors[i].href.indexOf('#')>-1)
```

If so, then clicking that link also causes the section to highlight:

```
anchors[i].onclick = function(){Highlight(this.href);return true};
```

I haven't seen a flash used for this effect before, and it demonstrates how accessible a flash can be when used for good effect. If you've ever clicked an in-page link that goes to a page fragment located toward the bottom of the page, you know how frustrating it can be to find exactly which section is referenced by the link when there is not enough page left to scroll the item to the top.

Now, with the use of page-fragment link highlighting, you can immediately locate the linked section. And since the highlight fades, once the section is located, you don't have to put up with the colored background, which can impact on the amount of contrast between color of text and color of background.

See Also

Gez Lemon has an excellent article on photosensitive epilepsy at *http://juicystudio.com/ article/photosensitive-epilepsy.php.*

14.7 Adding ARIA Attributes to a Tabbed Page Application

Problem

You want to split the page contents into separate panels, and only display one at a time. You also want the application to be accessible.

Solution

Use a tabbed page application and include the ARIA roles `tablist`, `tabpanel`, and `tab`, as well as the `aria-hidden` state.

The tabbed page is a `div` element, as is the container, with the tabs as list items (`li`) within a single unordered list (`ul`) at the top. The container `div` is given a role of `tablist`, and each of the `li` elements given a role of `tab`. The tabbed panels are `div` elements containing whatever type of contents, and each is given a role of `tabpanel`. The relationship between panel and tab is made with the `aria-labeledby` attribute:

```
<div class="tabcontainer" role="tablist">
  <div class="tabnavigation" role="tab">
    <ul>
      <li id="tabnav_1" role="tab"><a href="">Page One</a></li>
      <li id="tabnav_2" role="tab"><a href="">Page Two</a></li>
      <li id="tabnav_3" role="tab"><a href="">Page Three</a></li>
    </ul>
  </div>

  <div class="tabpages">
    <div class="tabpage" role="tabpanel" aria-labeledby="tabnav_1"
aria-hidden="false" id="tabpage_1">
```

```
        <p>page 1</p>
      </div>
      <div class="tabpage" role="tabpanel" aria-labeledby="tabnav_2"
aria-hidden="true" id="tabpage_2">
          <p>page 2</p>
      </div>
      <div class="tabpage" role="tabpanel" aria-labeledby="tabnav_3"
aria-hidden="true" id="tabpage_3">
          <p>page 3</p>
      </div>
    </div>
  </div>
```

When the page loads, the tabs are displayed and all but the first of the panels are hidden. The hidden panels are assigned an `aria-hidden` attribute value of `true`. The click event handler for all of the tab elements is assigned a function, `displayPage`, to control the tab page display. A custom data attribute, `data-current`, on the tabbed page container is used to store which tab is currently selected:

```
// set up display
// for each container display navigation
// hide all but first page, highlight first tab
window.onload=function() {

  // for each container
  var containers = document.querySelectorAll(".tabcontainer");
  for (var j = 0; j < containers.length; j++) {

    // display and hide elements
    var nav = containers[j].querySelector(".tabnavigation ul");
    nav.style.display="block";

    // set current tab
    var navitem = containers[j].querySelector(".tabnavigation ul li");
    var ident = navitem.id.split("_")[1];
    navitem.parentNode.setAttribute("data-current",ident);
    navitem.setAttribute("style","background-color: #ccf");

    // set displayed tab panel
    var pages = containers[j].querySelectorAll(".tabpage");
    for (var i = 1; i < pages.length; i++) {
      pages[i].style.display="none";
      pages[i].setAttribute("aria-hidden","true");
    }

    // for each tab, attach event handler function
    var tabs = containers[j].querySelectorAll(".tabnavigation ul li");
    for (var i = 0; i < tabs.length; i++) {
      tabs[i].onclick=displayPage;
    }
  }
}
```

When a tab is clicked, the old tabbed entry is cleared by setting the background of the tab to white and hiding the panel. The new entry's tab is highlighted (background color is changed), and its associated panel is displayed. The hidden panel's `aria-hidden` attribute is set to `true`, while the displayed panel's `aria-hidden` attribute is set to `false`. The custom data attribute `data-current` is set to the new tab selection, and the clicked tab's `id` is used to derive the related panel's ID:

```
// click on tab
function displayPage() {

   // hide old selection
   var current = this.parentNode.getAttribute("data-current");
   var oldpanel = document.getElementById("tabpage_" + current);

   document.getElementById("tabnav_" + current).setAttribute("style",
   "background-color: #fff");
   oldpanel.style.display="none";
   oldpanel.setAttribute("aria-hidden","true");

   // display new selection
   var ident = this.id.split("_")[1];
   this.setAttribute("style","background-color: #ccf");
   var newpanel = document.getElementById("tabpage_" + ident);

   newpanel.style.display="block";
   newpanel.setAttribute("aria-hidden","false");
   this.parentNode.setAttribute("data-current",ident);

   return false;
}
```

Discussion

The code in the solution is very similar to that in Recipe 13.7; the only difference is the addition of the ARIA roles and attributes. The changes are minor—I highlighted the lines in the JavaScript that were added to enable ARIA support. As you can see, adding accessibility with ARIA is not an onerous task.

Another excellent demonstration of an ARIA-enabled tabbed page can be found at the Illinois Center for Information Technology and Web Accessibility (*http://test.cita.uiuc .edu/aria/tabpanel/tabpanel1.php*). Though the code to manage the tabbed page behavior differs significantly from mine, the relative structure and use of ARIA roles and attributes is identical. The main difference between the two implementations is that my example uses a link to make my tabs clickable, while the external example uses `tabindex`. The external application also makes more extensive use of the keyboard.

As mentioned in Recipe 14.5, working with the ARIA attributes provides a new way of looking at widget-like applications like tabbed pages and accordions. The Illinois Center I just mentioned actually lists both the accordion and tabbed page example in one section specific to tabbed pages, because they have very similar behavior. The only difference is one is multiselectable, the other not; one requires modification to the label to signify which label is associated with which panel, while the other does not need this information. By looking at both types of widgets with a fresh viewpoint, I've learned new ways to use both: instead of creating vertical accordion panels, I've also started using horizontal panels; rather than tabs being located at the top of a tabbed application, I've started placing them on the side. It taught me to appreciate how they are both semantically linked, and how to ensure this semantic similarity is preserved in both structure and code.

See Also

Recipe 14.4 covers some of the implementation details with using `tabindex`.

14.8 Live Region

Problem

You have a section of a web page that is updated periodically, such as a page section that lists recent updates to a file, or one that reflects recent Twitter activity on a subject. You want to ensure that when the page updates, those using a screen reader are updated with the new information.

Solution

Use ARIA region attributes on the element being updated:

```
<ul id="update" role="log" aria-alive="polite" aria-atomic="true"
aria-relevant="additions">
</ul>
```

Discussion

A section of the web page that can be updated after the page is loaded, and without direct user intervention, calls for the use of ARIA Live Regions. These are probably the simplest ARIA functionality to implement, and they provide immediate, positive results. And there's no code involved, other than the JavaScript you need to create the page updates.

I took the example application from Recipe 18.9, which updates the web page based on the contents of a text file on the server that the application retrieves using Ajax, and provided two minor updates.

First, I modified the code that polls for the updates to check how many items have been added to the unordered list after the update. If the number is over 10, the oldest is removed from the page:

```
// process return
function processResponse() {
    if(xmlhttp.readyState == 4 && xmlhttp.status == 200) {
        var li = document.createElement("li");
        var txt = document.createTextNode(xmlhttp.responseText);
        li.appendChild(txt);
```

```
            var ul = document.getElementById("update");
            ul.appendChild(li);

            // prune top of list
            if (ul.childNodes.length > 10) {
              ul.removeChild(ul.firstChild);
            }

        } else if (xmlhttp.readyState == 4 && xmlhttp.status != 200) {
            alert(xmlhttp.responseText);
        }
    }
```

With this change, the list doesn't grow overly long.

I made one more change, adding the ARIA roles and states to the unordered list that serves as the updatable live region:

```
<ul id="update" role="log" aria-live="polite" aria-atomic="true"
aria-relevant="additions s">
```

From left to right: the `role` is set to `log`, because I'm polling for log updates from a file, and only displaying the last 10 or so items. Other options include `status`, for a status update, and a more general `region` value, for an undetermined purpose.

The `aria-live` region attribute is set to `polite`, because the update isn't a critical update. The `polite` setting tells the screen reader to voice the update, but not interrupt a current task to do so. If I had used a value of `assertive`, the screen reader would interrupt whatever it is doing and voice the content. Always use `polite`, unless the information is critical.

The `aria-atomic` is set to `true`, so that the screen reader only voices new additions. It could get very annoying to have the screen reader voice the entire set with each new addition, as would happen if this value is set to `false`.

Lastly, the `aria-relevant` is set to `additions`, as we don't care about the entries being removed from the top. This is actually the default setting for this attribute, so in this case it wasn't needed. In addition, AT devices don't have to support this attribute. Still, I'd rather list it than not. Other values are `removals`, `text`, and `all` (for all events). You can specify more than one, separated by a space.

This ARIA-enabled functionality was probably the one that impressed me the most. One of my first uses for Ajax, years ago, was to update a web page with information. It was frustrating to test the page with a screen reader (JAWS, at the time) and hear nothing but silence every time the page was updated. I can't even imagine how frustrating it was for those who needed the functionality.

Now we have it, and it's so easy to use. It's a win-win.

See Also

See Recipe 18.9 for more of the code for the live update.

CHAPTER 15

Creating Media Rich and Interactive Applications

15.0 Introduction

Pretty pictures. Cool videos. Sound!

The Web of the future will be a richer place, indeed, with the new and improved innovations ready to use. Our old friends SVG and Canvas are getting new life and generating new interest. Added to them are the new video and audio elements included in HTML5, and the near-future potential of 3D graphics.

JavaScript and CSS provide a malleable palette in which to paint web pages, but SVG and the `canvas` element provide the capability to take those pages into new and exciting territory.

SVG, or Scalable Vector Graphics, is an XML-based vector graphics language that can be used to create scalable vector graphics within web pages. You can insert the SVG into object elements, or in certain circumstances embed the SVG directly in the web page. New advances also allow you to include SVG using the `img` element, and CSS.

SVG is normally a static XML markup, and not dependent on JavaScript. However, as will be demonstrated later in the chapter, SVG and JavaScript can be used to create any number of dynamic graphics.

The `canvas` element originated with Apple, and is now becoming standardized as part of the HTML5/Web Applications 1.0 effort. Unlike SVG, the `canvas` element is totally dependent on JavaScript. We add `canvas` elements into our page and then use a 2D context API in order to draw into these elements.

SVG and Canvas are implemented in varying degrees in all of this book's target browsers, except for Internet Explorer (though recently we learned that IE9 will support SVG, at least). However, recipes in this chapter provide how-tos for enabling support for both, in all browsers and in most environments.

Newcomers joining the media environment are the `audio` and `video` elements included in HTML5, and already implemented, albeit with some differences, in our target browsers. Where before we depended on Flash to play video, now we can embed videos natively and manipulate the videos using JavaScript.

The last newcomer introduced in this chapter isn't really a newcomer, but an old friend with a new face: WebGL (Web Graphics Library), and via plug-ins, the newer X3D. Years ago, I used to work with VRML (Virtual Reality Modeling Language), which was the earliest version of 3D on the Web. These 3D technologies pick up where VRML left off, providing a new three-dimensional world to explore.

Since this is only one chapter, and I'm not the most artistic person in the world, I'm focusing primarily on introducing all of these wonderful new tools and providing some basic how-tos, such as how can you get SVG to work in IE. Once you have a good idea of how these media technologies work, you can explore the Web and examine the already rich set of demos and uses in order to find inspiration for your own adventures.

See Also

See the current working draft for the Canvas 2D API at *http://dev.w3.org/html5/canvas -api/canvas-2d-api.html*, though note that this URL is likely to change. Keep up with current work on SVG at *http://www.w3.org/Graphics/SVG/*.

15.1 Creating Basic Shapes in Canvas (Using the canvas Element)

Problem

You want to create multiple shapes, such as overlapping squares, in the `canvas` element.

Solution

Insert a `canvas` element into the web page:

```
<canvas width="600" height="500">
<p>Two overlapping squares</p>
</canvas>
```

Then use the Canvas 2D API to create the shapes. The following creates three over-lapping rectangles:

```
var imgcanvas = document.getElementById("imgcanvas");
if (imgcanvas.getContext) {
   var ctx = imgcanvas.getContext('2d');
   ctx.fillStyle="rgba(255,0,0,.1)";
   ctx.strokeStyle="#000000";

   // rect one
   ctx.fillRect(0,0,100,100);
```

```
    ctx.strokeRect(0,0,100,100);

    // rect two
    ctx.fillRect(50,50,100,200);

    // rect three
    ctx.strokeRect(80,130,200,100);

}
```

Discussion

The canvas element is inserted into the web page in the location you want the canvas drawing to exist. You can provide a styling for the element, but it's not going to impact on the actual canvas drawing, which is managed via the Canvas 2D API.

You can set the width and height of the canvas element using the width and height attributes. You can also, as shown in the solution, provide fallback content—in this case, a paragraph describing what's being drawn within the canvas element.

In JavaScript, you have to get the canvas element's context first. Though most implementations of the canvas element only support a 2D context, you'll still need to specify 2d when accessing the context. When support for 3D is added, you'd pass in a value of 3d.

Before you begin drawing, test to see if the canvas element is supported:

```
if (imgcanvas.getContent) {
    var ctx = imgcanvas.getContext('2d');
    ...
}
```

Once you have the canvas context, all the API calls from that point go to that specific canvas element. The solution demonstrates creating three rectangles, as shown in Figure 15-1. There are three different rectangle methods:

fillRect
  Uses the currently set fillStyle value to fill the rectangle

strokeRect
  Uses the currently set strokeStyle value to outline the rectangle

clearRect
  Clears whatever is drawn within the rectangle area

The last method, clearRect, wasn't demonstrated in the solution; it actually removes the pixels within the rectangle area. Since the canvas element is transparent by default, this would expose the document content underneath the canvas element.

All three methods take an origin, a width, and a height, in the following order: x, y, width, height. The origin increases from top to bottom, and from left to right, so an x,y value of 0,0 would place the upper-left corner of the rectangle at the upper-left corner of the canvas.

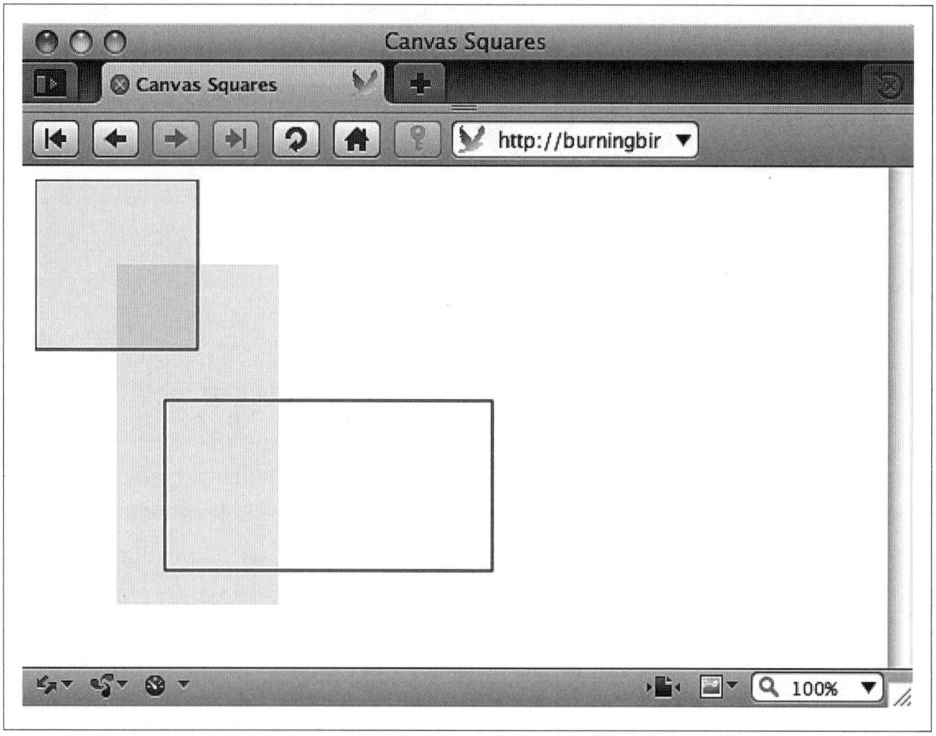

Figure 15-1. Three rectangles drawn in the canvas area

The canvas element is supported in all major browsers except Internet Explorer. Recipe 15.2 provides a solution that allows the canvas element to work with IE.

See Also

It's important to provide fallback content not only for accessibility purposes, but in those cases where JavaScript is not enabled.

Current work is underway with the W3C to provide more in-depth accessibility information with the canvas element. Until implemented, though, you shouldn't use the canvas element for important information (unless you provide a fallback), or for site navigation or other critical site use.

15.2 Implementing Canvas Applications in IE

Problem

You want to ensure your Canvas application works in IE.

Solution

Use a Canvas emulation library, such as *explorercanvas*, created by Erik Arvidsson:

```
<!--[if IE]><script src="excanvas.js"></script><![endif]-->
```

Discussion

The *explorercanvas* library works by emulating the **canvas** element using Microsoft's Virtual Markup Language (VML)—the company's own version of a vector graphics language.

Example 15-1 is a web page that contains a link to the *explorercanvas* library, and the canvas example from Recipe 15.1. The example creates three rectangles in a **canvas** element. The difference between the two applications is that this version works with IE.

Example 15-1. Cross-browser application creating three rectangles in a canvas element

```
<!DOCTYPE html>
<head>
<title>Canvas Squares</title>
<meta charset="utf-8" />
<!--[if IE]><script src="excanvas.js"></script><![endif]-->

<script type="text/javascript">
//<![CDATA[

window.onload=function() {

  var imgcanvas = document.getElementById("imgcanvas");
  if (imgcanvas.getContext) {
    var ctx = imgcanvas.getContext('2d');
    ctx.fillStyle="rgba(255,0,0,.1)";
    ctx.strokeStyle="#000000";

    // rect one
    ctx.fillRect(0,0,100,100);
    ctx.strokeRect(0,0,100,100);

    // rect two
    ctx.fillRect(50,50,100,200);

    // rect three
    ctx.strokeRect(80,130,200,100);

  }
}

//]]>
</script>
</head>
<body>
<canvas id="imgcanvas" width="400" height="250">
<p>Three rectangles, overlapping</p>
```

```
</canvas>
</body>
```

There is an additional constraint to using *explorercanvas*: if you create the canvas element dynamically using the `document.createElement` method, you need to include the
following code so that the library can map the `getContext` method to the new `canvas`
element:

```
var newcanvas = document.createElement("canvas");
G_vmlCanvasManager.initElement(newcanvas);
var ctx = newcanvas.getContext('2d');
```

Download *explorercanvas* from *http://code.google.com/p/explorercanvas/*.

15.3 Creating a Dynamic Line Chart in Canvas

Problem

You want to display a line chart in your web page, but the data changes over time, and
you want to dynamically update it.

Solution

Use the `canvas` element and the `path` method to create the chart. When the data changes,
update the chart:

```
var array1 = [[100,100], [150, 50], [200,185],
              [250, 185], [300,250], [350,100], [400,250],
              [450, 100], [500,20], [550,80], [600, 120]];

var imgcanvas = document.getElementById("imgcanvas");

if (imgcanvas.getContext) {
  var ctx = imgcanvas.getContext('2d');


  // rect one
  ctx.strokeRect(0,0,600,300);

  // line path
  ctx.beginPath();
  ctx.moveTo(0,100);
  for (var i = 0; i < array1.length; i++) {
    ctx.lineTo(array1[i][0], array1[i][1]);
  }
  ctx.stroke();
}
```

Discussion

Canvas paths are the way to create arbitrary shapes in Canvas. After getting the canvas
context, `ctx`, the path is begun with a call to `ctx.beginPath()`. This marks the beginning

of the path, and calling the method again starts a new path. The next line of code is `ctx.moveTo`, which moves the drawing "pen" to a beginning location without drawing. From that point, several calls are made to `lineTo`, using an array of paired values representing the x,y location for each line endpoint.

After all of the line points have been defined, the path is drawn. We're not creating a closed path, so I'm not using `ctx.closePath()`, which would attempt to draw a line from the ending point to the beginning point. Instead, I'm drawing the line given the points that have been defined, using `ctx.stroke()`.

This creates a single path. To dynamically update the chart, you can incorporate timers, and either replace the path (by creating an entirely new context, which would erase the old), or add the new line chart to the same chart. Example 15-2 shows a web page that creates the line in the solution and then creates two others, each drawn after a short period of time using timers. The colors for the stroke path are changed between lines.

Example 15-2. Using timers to dynamically update a line chart

```
<!DOCTYPE html>
<head>
<title>Canvas Chart</title>
<meta charset="utf-8" />
<!--[if IE]><script src="excanvas.js"></script><![endif]-->

<script type="text/javascript">

window.onload=function() {

 var array1 = [[100,100], [150, 50], [200,185],
               [250, 185], [300,250], [350,100], [400,250],
               [450, 100], [500,20], [550,80], [600, 120]];

 var array2 = [[100,100], [150, 150], [200,135],
               [250, 285], [300,150], [350,150], [400,280],
               [450, 100], [500,120], [550,80], [600, 190]];

 var array3 = [[100,200], [150, 100], [200,35],
               [250, 185], [300,10], [350,15], [400,80],
               [450, 100], [500,120], [550,80], [600, 120]];

 var imgcanvas = document.getElementById("imgcanvas");

 if (imgcanvas.getContext) {
   var ctx = imgcanvas.getContext('2d');


   // rectangle wrapping line chart
   ctx.strokeRect(0,0,600,300);

   // first line
   ctx.beginPath();
   ctx.moveTo(0,100);
   for (var i = 0; i < array1.length; i++) {
```

```
        ctx.lineTo(array1[i][0], array1[i][1]);
    }
    ctx.stroke();

    setTimeout(function() {

        ctx.strokeStyle="#ff0000";

        // second line
        ctx.beginPath();
        ctx.moveTo(0,100);
        for (var i = 0; i < array2.length; i++) {
          ctx.lineTo(array2[i][0], array2[i][1]);
        }

        ctx.stroke();

        // second time out
        setTimeout(function() {
            ctx.strokeStyle="#00ff00";
            ctx.fillStyle="rgba(255,255,0,.1)";

            // third line
            ctx.beginPath();
            ctx.moveTo(0,100);
            for (var i = 0; i < array3.length; i++) {
                ctx.lineTo(array3[i][0],array3[i][1]);
            }

            ctx.stroke();
        }, 5000);
    }, 5000);

  }
}

</script>
</head>
<body>
<canvas id="imgcanvas" width="650" height="350">
<p>Include an image that has a static representation of the chart</p>
</canvas>
</body>
```

Figure 15-2 shows the line chart after all three lines have been drawn. Notice that the web page makes use of the *explorercanvas* library, *excanvas.js*, to ensure the chart also draws in Internet Explorer.

There are other path methods: `arc`, to draw curves, and `quadraticCurveTo` and `bezier CurveTo`, to draw quadratic and bezier curves. All of these methods can be combined in one path to create complex images.

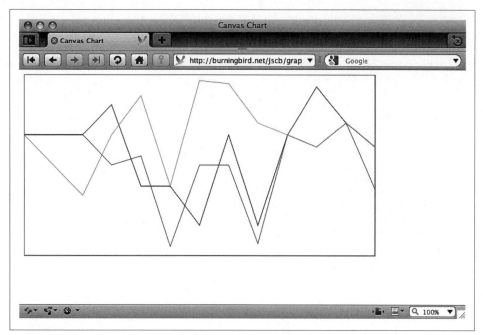

Figure 15-2. Canvas drawing from Example 15-2 using the path method

See Also

See Recipe 15.2 for how to incorporate *explorercanvas* into your applications. A good Canvas tutorial (*https://developer.mozilla.org/en/Canvas_tutorial*) can be found at Mozilla.

15.4 Adding JavaScript to an SVG File

Problem

You want to add JavaScript to an SVG file or element.

Solution

JavaScript in SVG is included in `script` elements, just as with XHTML. The DOM methods are also available for working with the SVG elements. One restriction for SVG that you don't have with HTML is that SVG is XML, so script blocks in an SVG file or element must have CDATA sections surrounding the actual script, as shown in the SVG file in Example 15-3.

Example 15-3. Demonstration of JavaScript within an SVG file

```
<?xml version="1.0" encoding="UTF-8" standalone="no"?>
<svg xmlns="http://www.w3.org/2000/svg"
xmlns:xlink="http://www.w3.org/1999/xlink" width="600" height="600">
  <script type="text/ecmascript">
    <![CDATA[

      // set element onclick event handler
      window.onload=function () {

        var square = document.getElementById("square");

        // onclick event handler, change circle radius
        square.onclick = function() {
          var color = this.getAttribute("fill");
          if (color == "#ff0000") {
            this.setAttribute("fill", "#0000ff");
          } else {
            this.setAttribute("fill","#ff0000");
          }
        }
      }
    ]]>
  </script>
  <rect id="square" width="400" height="400" fill="#ff0000"
   x="10" y="10" />
</svg>
```

Discussion

As the solution demonstrates, SVG is XML, and the rules for embedding script into XML must be adhered to. This means providing the script `type` within the `script` tag, as well as wrapping the script contents in a CDATA block.

The DOM methods `document.getElementById`, `getAttribute`, and `setAttribute` are the methods we've come to know so well in the rest of the book. The DOM methods aren't just HTML-specific; they're usable with any XML document, including SVG. What's new is the SVG-specific `fill` attribute, which is one of the color attributes that are standard for the SVG shape elements such as `rect`.

The solution is a standalone SVG file, with a `.svg` extension. But if we were to embed the SVG within an XHTML file served as `application/xhtml+xml`, such as that shown in Example 15-4, the color-changing animation would work the same.

Example 15-4. SVG element from Example 15-1, embedded into an XHTML page

```
<!DOCTYPE html PUBLIC
    "-//W3C//DTD XHTML 1.1 plus MathML 2.0 plus SVG 1.1//EN"
    "http://www.w3.org/2002/04/xhtml-math-svg/xhtml-math-svg.dtd">
<html xmlns="http://www.w3.org/1999/xhtml"
    xmlns:svg="http://www.w3.org/2000/svg"
    xmlns:xlink="http://www.w3.org/1999/xlink" xml:lang="en">
<head>
```

```
<title>Accessing Inline SVG</title>
<meta http-equiv="Content-Type"
content="application/xhtml+xml; charset=utf-8" />
</head>
<body>
<svg:svg width="600" height="600">
  <script type="text/ecmascript">
    <![CDATA[

      // set element onclick event handler
      window.onload=function () {

        var square = document.getElementById("square");

        // onclick event handler, change circle radius
        square.onclick = function() {
           var color = this.getAttribute("fill");
           if (color == "#ff0000") {
              this.setAttribute("fill","#0000ff");
           } else {
              this.setAttribute("fill","#ff0000");
           }
        }
      }
    ]]>
  </script>
  <svg:rect id="square" width="400" height="400" fill="#ff0000"
 x="10" y="10" />
</svg:svg>
</body>
</html>
```

Chrome, Safari, Opera, and Firefox all support SVG. IE8 doesn't, but IE9 will. Recipe 15.6 covers how you can enable SVG graphics in IE8.

15.5 Accessing SVG from Web Page Script

Problem

You want to modify the contents of an SVG element from script within the web page.

Solution

If the SVG is embedded directly in the web page, access the element and its attributes using the same functionality you would use with any other web page element:

```
var square = document.getElementById("ssquare");
square.setAttributeNS(null, "width", "500");
```

However, if the SVG is in an external SVG file embedded into the page via an **object** element, you have to get the document for the external SVG file in order to access the

SVG elements. The technique requires object detection because the process differs by browser:

```
// set element onclick event handler
window.onload=function () {

    var object = document.getElementById("object");
    var svgdoc;

    try {

        svgdoc = object.contentDocument;
    } catch(e) {
        try {

            svgdoc = object.getSVGDocument();

        } catch (e) {
            alert("SVG in object not supported in your environment");
        }
    }

    if (!svgdoc) return;

    var square = svgdoc.getElementById('square');
    square.setAttributeNS(null, "width", "500");
```

Discussion

The first option listed in the solution accesses SVG embedded in an XHTML file. You can access SVG elements using the same methods you've used to access HTML elements. Because SVG in XHTML does incorporate support for namespaces, I use the namespace version of the DOM methods, even when no namespace is used (it's set to null).

The second option is a little more involved, and depends on retrieving the document object for the SVG document. The first approach tries to access the contentDocument property on the object. If this fails, the application then tries to access the SVG document using the getSVGDocument object method. Once you have access to the SVG document object, you can use the same DOM methods you would use with elements native to the web page. The code works with all the browsers supported in this book except IE, which I'll cover in a later recipe.

Example 15-4 in Recipe 15.4, showed one way to embed SVG into the web page. This approach currently only works with XHTML pages, served as application/xml +xhtml. HTML5 adds native support to SVG in HTML, so in the future you'll also be able to embed SVG directly into HTML files, though currently only Firefox 3.6 supports this, and only with HTML5 enabled.

You can enable HTML5 support in Firefox 3.6 (and up, until it's the default) by typing about:config into the address bar, and setting the html5.enable preference to true. Note, though, that this is very cutting-edge and unstable.

Example 15-5 shows a second way to add SVG to a web page, and how to access the SVG element(s) from script in HTML.

Example 15-5. Accessing SVG in an object element from script

```
<!DOCTYPE html>
<head>
<title>SVG in Object</title>
<meta charset="utf-8" />
</head>
<body>
<object id="object" data="rect.svg"
style="padding: 20px; width: 600px; height: 600px">
<p>No SVG support</p>
</object>
<script type="text/javascript">

  var object = document.getElementById("object");
  object.onload=function() {
      var svgdoc;

      // get access to the SVG document object
      try {

         svgdoc = object.contentDocument;
      } catch(e) {
         try {

            svgdoc = object.getSVGDocument();

         } catch (e) {
           alert("SVG in object not supported in your environment");
         }
      }

      if (!svgdoc) return;
      var r = svgdoc.rootElement;

      // get SVG element and modify
      var square = svgdoc.getElementById('square');
      square.onclick = function() {

         //SVG supports namespaces
         var width = parseFloat(square.getAttributeNS(null,"width"));
         width-=50;
         square.setAttributeNS(null,"width",width);
         var color = square.getAttributeNS(null,"fill");
         if (color == "blue") {
```

```
        square.setAttributeNS(null,"fill","yellow");
        square.setAttributeNS(null,"stroke","green");
    } else {
        square.setAttributeNS(null,"fill","blue");
        square.setAttributeNS(null,"stroke","red");
    }
  }
 }
}
</script>

</body>
```

In addition to the different approaches to get the SVG document, you also have to handle browser differences in how the onload event handler works. Firefox and Opera fire the onload event handler for the window after all the document contents have loaded, including the SVG in the object element. However, Safari and Chrome, probably because of the shared WebKit core, fire the window.onload event handler before the SVG has finished loading.

In the example code, the object is accessed in script after it has loaded, and the object.onload event handler is then accessed to get the SVG document and assigned the function to the onclick event handler.

15.6 Emulating SVG in Internet Explorer

Problem

You want the SVG in your object element, or embedded in the page, to be visible to Internet Explorer users.

Solution

Use a library, such as SVGWeb, to facilitate the display of SVG.

If the SVG is incorporated into the page via an object element, use the following syntax:

```
<!--[if IE]>
<object src="graphic.svg" classid="image/svg+xml"
width="200" height="200"
id="svgObject">
<![endif]-->
<!--[if !IE>-->
<object data="graphic.svg" type="image/svg+xml" width="200"
height="200"
id="svgObject">
<!--<![endif]-->
</object>
```

The conditional comments are necessary in order for SVGWeb to do its magic correctly. Embedded SVG is much simpler. Just add the SVGWeb library, and enclose the SVG within a `script` element:

```
<script type="image/svg+xml">
   <svg...>
      ...
   </svg>
</script>
```

Discussion

Currently, there is no support for SVG in Internet Explorer. Microsoft has committed to supporting SVG and XHTML in IE9, due out sometime in 2011. Until then, we can use a library such as SVGWeb.

SVGWeb works by emulating the SVG in Flash. Since Flash is more or less ubiquitous on most people's sites, most folks won't have to install any additional plug-in.

To incorporate SVGWeb into your web pages and applications, once you've down-loaded the source and unzipped it, load the *src* directory to your web, and include a link to the SVGWeb JavaScript in your web pages:

```
<script src="src/svg.js" data-path="src/"></script>
```

This tag assumes that the SVGWeb code is still in the *src* directory, and that the libraries are not in the same directory as your web pages. If the libraries are in a different location, you need to provide the `data-path` custom data attribute and point to the relative lo-cation of the libraries.

 Download SVGWeb and view manuals and other help at *http://code .google.com/p/svgweb/*. Ample SDK (*http://www.amplesdk.com/*) is an-other excellent library that provides SVG support for IE, originally cre-ated by Sergey Ilinsky.

See Also

Recipe 15.7 discusses how SVGWeb works across browsers and in HTML.

15.7 Enable Interactive SVG Embedded in HTML

Problem

You want to embed SVG directly into an HTML page without having to use XHTML.

Solution

You have two options: you can use HTML5 to create the web page and wait until SVG in HTML is supported in all of your targeted browsers. Or you can use a JavaScript library, such as SVGWeb, to wrap your SVG:

```
<script type="image/svg+xml">
   <svg...>
      ...
   </svg>
</script>
```

Discussion

Previously, to embed SVG directly into a web page, you had to use XHTML rather than HTML. With HTML5, SVG is now supported in HTML, but the support for this change is still limited.

I introduced SVGWeb in Recipe 15.6 to enable SVG support in Internet Explorer. The library also provides support for embedding SVG directly into HTML pages. Until there's more widespread support for SVG in HTML5 documents (currently only supported by Firefox 3.6 and up), you should use a library such as SVGWeb.

If you are embedding SVG directly in HTML5, there is one major difference you need to be aware of: there is no namespace support in HTML5. The SVG namespace is bound to the svg element, as the MathML namespace is bound to the math element, but support for these and other SVG and MathML elements is hardcoded into the HTML5 specification rather than gracefully integrated because of namespace support.

This can affect your JavaScript application. If the SVG you embed in the page contains other namespaced elements, you can't use namespace functions in order to access the elements. Example 15-6 more fully demonstrates these concerns.

Example 15-6. SVG embedded in HTML5 served as text/html

```
<!DOCTYPE html>
<head>
<title>SVG</title>
<meta charset="utf-8" />

<script>

     // set element onclick event handler
     window.onload=function () {
        var circle = document.getElementById('redcircle');

        // onclick event handler, change circle radius
        circle.onclick = function() {
           var r = parseInt(this.getAttributeNS(null,"r"));
           r-=10;
           circle.setAttributeNS("","r",r);
           var  dc =
```

```
            document.getElementsByTagNameNS("http://purl.org/dc/elements/1.1/",
                    "title");
                for (var i = 0; i < dc.length; i++) {
                    var str = dc.item(i).namespaceURI + " " +
                    dc.item(i).prefix + " " + dc.item(i).localName + " " +
                                dc.item(i).textContent;
                    alert(str);
                }
            }
        }
</script>
</head>
<body>
<h1>SVG</h1>
<p>This is <code>text/html</code>!</p>
<h2>SVG</h2>
<svg id="svgelem"
     height="800" xmlns="http://www.w3.org/2000/svg">
        <circle id="redcircle" cx="300" cy="300" r="300" fill="red" />
  <metadata>
    <rdf:RDF xmlns:cc="http://web.resource.org/cc/"
xmlns:dc="http://purl.org/dc/elements/1.1/"
xmlns:rdf="http://www.w3.org/1999/02/22-rdf-syntax-ns#
">
        <cc:Work rdf:about="">
          <dc:title>Sizing Red Circle</dc:title>
          <dc:description></dc:description>
          <dc:subject>
            <rdf:Bag>
              <rdf:li>circle</rdf:li>
              <rdf:li>red</rdf:li>
              <rdf:li>graphic</rdf:li>
            </rdf:Bag>
          </dc:subject>
          <dc:publisher>
            <cc:Agent rdf:about="http://www.openclipart.org">
              <dc:title>Testing RDF in SVG</dc:title>
            </cc:Agent>
          </dc:publisher>
          <dc:creator>
            <cc:Agent>
              <dc:title id="title">Testing</dc:title>
            </cc:Agent>
          </dc:creator>
          <dc:rights>
            <cc:Agent>
              <dc:title>testing</dc:title>
            </cc:Agent>
          </dc:rights>
          <dc:date></dc:date>
          <dc:format>image/svg+xml</dc:format>
        <dc:type rdf:resource="http://purl.org/dc/dcmitype/StillImage"/>
 <cc:license rdf:resource="http://web.resource.org/cc/PublicDomain"/>
          <dc:language>en</dc:language>
        </cc:Work>
```

```
    <cc:License rdf:about="http://web.resource.org/cc/PublicDomain">
 <cc:permits rdf:resource="http://web.resource.org/cc/Reproduction"/>
 <cc:permits rdf:resource="http://web.resource.org/cc/Distribution"/>
<cc:permits
rdf:resource="http://web.resource.org/cc/DerivativeWorks"/>
      </cc:License>
    </rdf:RDF>
  </metadata>
  </svg>
</body>
```

In the example, an SVG element is embedded into an HTML5 web page that is served as text/html. Clicking the red circle changes the circle dimensions, using the namespace versions of document.getElementsByTagName, passing in null as the namespace. The script also accesses all Dublin Core namespaced (dc) titles in the SVG, and displays them in alerts.

When the circle is clicked, it resizes, but nothing is printed out. How can this be? The JavaScript doesn't have any errors, and there's obviously Dublin Core namespaced titles in the page.

The big disconnect is the page is served as HTML, and the namespaces only work correctly in an XML-based format, like XHTML. If I were to make one seemingly small change in the code, from:

```
var  dc =
document.getElementsByTagNameNS("http://purl.org/dc/elements/1.1/",
"title");
```

to:

```
var  dc = document.getElementsByTagName("dc:title");
```

I would get a reference to all four dc:title elements in the SVG metadata section. However, there are still problems.

If I were to convert the example into XHTML by adding an html element with the default namespace before the head element:

```
<html xmlns="http://www.w3.org/1999/xhtml" lang="en" xml:lang="en">
```

Then add an ending HTML tag, and wrap the scripting block in a CDATA section:

```
<script>
//<![CDATA[
...
//]]>
</script>
```

And then run the application, I would get the dc:title values using the original document.getElementsByTagNS, but the alert message is different than for the HTML result. Here's an example, from the XHTML application:

```
http://purl.org/dc/elements/1.1/dc title Sizing Red Circle
```

The equivalent from the HTML application is:

```
http://www.w3.org/2000/svg null dc:title Sizing Red Circle
```

Returning to the code, these values are printed out via the following two lines of code:

```
var str = dc.item(i).namespaceURI + " " + dc.item(i).prefix + " " +
dc.item(i).localName + " " + dc.item(i).textContent;
alert(str);
```

Where the two environments differ, drastically, is that all of the elements within the SVG element are included within the SVG namespace when the page is loaded as HTML. In the XHTML version, they're included in the proper namespace. So, the very first property printed, the element's namespaceURI, contains different values because of the different namespace support.

The next property, the item's prefix, is null in the HTML version. That's expected, because if the application doesn't understand namespaces, it doesn't understand that dc:title is both prefix and element name. The localName property is also different. In the XHTML version, this is the element name minus the prefix, which is title. In the HTML version, the localName is dc:title—the prefix becomes just another part of the local name.

The only property where both applications return the same value is the textContent of the title.

For the most part, the namespace issue shouldn't be a problem if you're using pure SVG in your web page, without any elements from other namespaces. Of course, a lot of SVG we find "in the wild" have namespaced elements, including license information that we need to keep with the image. Still, we shouldn't have too many problems, because we're mainly going to want to access the SVG elements from client-side Java-Script, rather than the licenses or other namespaced elements.

There is another option, and this is where SVGWeb steps in and solves more than one problem. Not only does SVGWeb enable the support of embedded SVG within an HTML document (and not just HTML5 documents), but it corrects the namespace problems.

I added the SVGWeb library into Example 15-6, the HTML document, and wrapped the SVG element in a script tag, with the SVG MIME type:

```
<script src="svgweb/src/svg.js" data-path="svgweb/src/"></script>
...
<script type="image/svg+xml">
  <svg id="svgelem"
    height="800" xmlns="http://www.w3.org/2000/svg">
    ...
  </svg>
</script>
```

Now when I try the same application, the results I get from the SVGWeb-assisted HTML page are identical to the results I get for the XHTML page. I can use the namespace version of DOM methods, such as `document.getElementsByTagNameNS`, and get the same results.

However, the application doesn't work with IE8. The reason is that when using SVGWeb with an SVG-enabled browser, such as Safari or Opera, SVGWeb creates the SVG within a XML context, but it is still SVG. However, with IE8, SVGWeb creates the graphic as Flash, not SVG.

Because SVGWeb is creating the SVG as Flash, we also have to move the namespace definitions to the outer SVG element:

```
<svg id="svgelem"
     height="800"
     xmlns="http://www.w3.org/2000/svg"
     xmlns:cc="http://web.resource.org/cc/"
     xmlns:dc="http://purl.org/dc/elements/1.1/"
     xmlns:rdf="http://www.w3.org/1999/02/22-rdf-syntax-ns#">
  ...
</svg>
```

Event handling is also managed through SVGWeb, which means we're going to get unexpected results when using the older DOM Level 0 event handling:

```
circle.onclick=function() {
...
}
```

Instead, SVGWeb provides cross-browser `addEventListener` functionality, both for the `window` object and for all SVG elements. And, instead of capturing the load event for the window, you'll capture a specialized event, `SVGLoad`:

```
window.addEventListener("SVGLoad",functionName,false);
```

Because the SVGWeb-enabled `addEventListener` function is implemented using IE's `attachEvent` for IE8, the application also doesn't have access to `this`, for object context. The external element reference is used instead.

Here's the finished scripting block, which encompasses all of these changes and works in IE8 as well as Safari, Chrome, Opera, and Firefox:

```
<script>

  // set element onclick event handler
  window.addEventListener('SVGLoad', function () {
     var circle = document.getElementById("redcircle");

     // onclick event handler, change circle radius
     circle.addEventListener('click', function(evt) {

     // reference circle, rather than this
        var r = parseInt(circle.getAttribute("r"));
        r-=10;
        circle.setAttribute("r",r);

        var  dc = document.getElementsByTagNameNS("http://purl.org/dc/elements/1.1/",
```

```
                                                                "title");

        for (var i = 0; i < dc.length; i++) {
           var str = dc.item(i).namespaceURI + " " +
dc.item(i).prefix + " " +
                   dc.item(i).localName + " " + dc.item(i).textContent;
           alert(str);
        }
     }, false);
   }, false);
</script>
```

Now the application works in all target browsers, including correct handling of the namespaces.

See Also

See where to get SVGWeb and how to install it in Recipe 15.6. You'll want to read the Issues section of the documentation (*http://codinginparadise.org/projects/svgweb/docs/ UserManual.html#known_issues*) before beginning your project.

See Recipe 11.2 for more on using document.getElementsByTagNameNS() and namespaces. The issues associated with attachEvent and this are covered in Recipe 7.5.

15.8 Using the Math Functions to Create a Realistic, Ticking Analog Clock in SVG

Problem

You want to embed an animated analog clock into your site's sidebar.

Solution

Use SVG to create the clock, utilizing both the Date object and the Math objects, in addition to a timer to manage the clock hands. The JavaScript to manage the hands is a derivative of other applications that also implement analog clocks, such as Java applets from long ago:

```
<script>
  var seconds = document.getElementById("seconds");
  var minutes = document.getElementById("minutes");
  var hours   = document.getElementById("hours");

  function setClock(date) {
    var s = (date.getSeconds() + date.getMilliseconds() / 1000) *
    Math.PI / 30;
    var m = date.getMinutes() * Math.PI / 30 + s / 60;
    var h = date.getHours() * Math.PI / 6 + m / 12;

    seconds.setAttribute("x2", 0.90 * Math.cos(s));
```

```
      seconds.setAttribute("y2", 0.90 * Math.sin(s));
      minutes.setAttribute("x2", 0.65 * Math.cos(m));
      minutes.setAttribute("y2", 0.65 * Math.sin(m));
      hours  .setAttribute("x2", 0.40 * Math.cos(h));
      hours  .setAttribute("y2", 0.40 * Math.sin(h));
    }

    setInterval("setClock(new Date())", 1000);
  </script>
```

Discussion

The animated analog clock is my own version of "Hello, World" in SVG. (Mine and several other people, because if you search on "SVG analog clock," you'll find several very attractive and interesting variations.) I like that it makes use of many unique aspects of SVG, as well as other JavaScript objects, such as `Date` and `Math`. Depending on how fancy you make it, the amount of code is small enough to not strain bandwidth, and the animation is simple enough not to task the CPU.

You don't have to implement the second hand for the clock, though I think it adds more realism. The hands are straight lines that are the same length. With each iteration of the timer, the orientation of the lines changes, using the `Math.cos` and `Math.sin` methods. The values for these methods are derived from a formula that makes use of values accessed from the `Date` object, and modified using `Math.PI`.

Once you have the clock orientation and the hands, you can go to town on decorating the clock. Figure 15-3 shows one of my favorite clock designs. A basic clock can be found in Example 15-7. All it does is create a clock with tick marks and hands—consider it a drawing board.

Example 15-7. Very basic clock mechanism, just needing to be prettied up

```
<?xml version="1.0"?>
<svg version="1.1" xmlns="http://www.w3.org/2000/svg"
viewBox="0 0 3 3">
 <defs>
    <style type="text/css">
      path {
        stroke: black;
        stroke-width: 0.02;
        fill: none;
      }
      line {
        stroke-linecap: round;
      }

      #seconds {
        stroke: red;
        stroke-width: 0.01;
      }
      #minutes {
        stroke: black;
```

```
      stroke-width: 0.03;
    }
    #hours {
      stroke: black;
      stroke-width: 0.03;
    }
  </style>
</defs>
    <g transform="rotate(-90) translate(-1.3,1.3) ">

        <circle cx="0" cy="0" r="1.0" fill="white" />

        <!-- decorative border -->
        <circle cx="0" cy="0" r="1.0" fill-opacity="0"
        stroke-width="0.02" stroke="black" />


    <!-- clock hands -->
<line id="hours"   x1="0" y1="0" x2="0.70" y2="0" stroke-width="1"/>
 <line id="minutes" x1="0" y1="0" x2="0.85" y2="0"/>
 <line id="seconds" x1="0" y1="0" x2="0.90" y2="0"/>
 </g>
 <script>
   var seconds = document.getElementById("seconds");
   var minutes = document.getElementById("minutes");
   var hours   = document.getElementById("hours");

   function setClock(date) {
     var s = (date.getSeconds() + date.getMilliseconds() / 1000) *
     Math.PI / 30;
     var m = date.getMinutes() * Math.PI / 30 + s / 60;
     var h = date.getHours() * Math.PI / 6 + m / 12;

     seconds.setAttribute("x2", 0.90 * Math.cos(s));
     seconds.setAttribute("y2", 0.90 * Math.sin(s));
     minutes.setAttribute("x2", 0.65 * Math.cos(m));
     minutes.setAttribute("y2", 0.65 * Math.sin(m));
     hours  .setAttribute("x2", 0.40 * Math.cos(h));
     hours  .setAttribute("y2", 0.40 * Math.sin(h));
   }

   setInterval("setClock(new Date())", 1000);
  </script>
</svg>
```

15.9 Integrating SVG and the Canvas Element in HTML

Problem

You want to use the canvas element and SVG together within a web page.

Figure 15-3. Basic clock, decorated with eye candy and text

Solution

One option is to embed both the SVG and the **canvas** element directly into the X/HTML page (we'll stick with XHTML for now), and then access the **canvas** element from script within SVG:

```
<canvas id="myCanvas" width="400px" height="100px">
    <p>canvas item alternative content</p>
</canvas>

<svg id="svgelem"
    height="400" xmlns="http://www.w3.org/2000/svg">
    <title>SVG Circle</title>

        <script type="text/javascript">
          <![CDATA[
          window.onload = function () {
              var context =
document.getElementById("myCanvas").getContext('2d');

              context.fillStyle = 'rgba(0,200,0,0.7)';
              context.fillRect(0,0,100,100);

          };
          ]]>
        </script>
```

```
        <circle id="redcircle" cx="300" cy="100" r="100" fill="red" stroke="#000" />
    </svg>
```

Or you can embed the **canvas** element as a foreign object directly in the SVG:

```
    <svg id="svgelem"
        height="400" xmlns="http://www.w3.org/2000/svg"
    xmlns:xhtml="http://www.w3.org/1999/xhtml">
        <title>SVG Circle with metadata</title>

        <script type="text/javascript">
          <![CDATA[
          window.onload = function () {
             var context2 = document.getElementById("thisCanvas").getContext('2d');
             context2.fillStyle = "#ff0000";
             context2.fillRect(0,0,200,200);
          };
          ]]>
        </script>

        <foreignObject width="300" height="150">
           <xhtml:canvas width="300" height="150" id="thisCanvas">
            alternate content for browsers that do not support Canvas
           </xhtml:canvas>
        </foreignObject>
        <circle id="redcircle" cx="300" cy="100" r="100" fill="red" stroke="#000" />
    </svg>
```

Discussion

When the SVG element is embedded into the current web page, you can access HTML elements from within the SVG. However, you can also embed elements directly in SVG, using the SVG `foreignObject` element. This element allows us to embed XHTML, MathML, RDF, or any other XML-based syntax.

In both solutions, I was able to use `document.getElementById`. However, if I wanted to manipulate the elements using other methods, such as `document.getElementsByTag Name`, I had to be careful about which version of the method I use. For instance, I can use `getElementsByTagName` for the outer **canvas** element, but I would need to use the namespace version of the method, `getElementsByTagNameNS`, for the contained **canvas** element, passing in the XHTML namespace included in the SVG element:

```
    var xhtmlnx = "http://www.w3.org/1999/xhtml";
    var context = document.getElementsByTagNameNS( xhtmlns,
                        'canvas')[0].getContext('2d');
    context.fillStyle = '#0f0';
    context.fillRect(0,0,100,100);
```

Once you have the canvas context, you use the element like you would from script within HTML: add rectangles, draw paths, create arcs, and so on.

Why would you use both at the same time? Each has its own advantages. One use of SVG and Canvas together is to provide a fallback for the canvas element, since the SVG writes to the DOM and persists even if JavaScript is turned off, while the canvas element does not.

The canvas element is also faster in frame-type animations. However, the performance advantages you get with the canvas element lessen as you increase the size of the display. SVG scales beautifully.

15.10 Turning on WebGL Support in Firefox and WebKit/Safari

Problem

You want to jump into the world of 3D.

Solution

Both Firefox nightly (Minefield) and the WebKit nightly have support for WebGL, a cross-platform 3D graphics system derived from the OpenGL effort, and making use of the canvas element. You will have to turn on support for both.

For Firefox, access the configuration options page by typing about:config into the address bar. Once past the warning page, find the webgl.enabled_for_all_sites option, and change the value to true.

For WebKit, open a Terminal window and type this at the command line:

```
defaults write com.apple.Safari WebKitWebGLEnabled -bool YES
```

Discussion

The world of 3D development in browsers is both old and new. Years ago, we had support for various forms of 3D development, such as VRML. However, most implementations required a plug-in, and they weren't the best-performing functionalities.

Today, there's two different 3D approaches: WebGL, which is an effort being developed and promoted by the Khronos Group, a consortium of media companies; X3D, developed by the Web3D group, which is a descendant of the older VRML effort.

The differences between the two is that WebGL is JavaScript-based, with the image developed on the canvas element, while X3D is based in XML:

```
<Transform>
  <Shape>
    <Appearance>
      <Material diffuseColor="0 1 0"/>
    </Appearance>
    <Cylinder height="0.1" radius="0.5"/>
  </Shape>
</Transform>
```

The Khronos Group is working on creating a browser-based runtime that will enable X3D to run on WebGL, and there is discussion ongoing about some form of integration between X3D and HTML5. However, from a scripter's point of view, we're primarily interested in WebGL.

See Also

Mozilla has a nice WebGL support page, with tutorials and demos at *https://developer .mozilla.org/en/WebGL*. The WebKit blog also has a nice introduction to WebGL in WebKit at *http://webkit.org/blog/603/webgl-now-available-in-webkit-nightlies/*. There's also a website devoted to WebGL at *http://learningwebgl.com/blog/*. The Khronos Group website is at *http://www.khronos.org/webgl/*. The X3D for Developers site is at *http://www.web3d.org/x3d/*.

15.11 Running a Routine When an Audio File Begins Playing

Problem

You want to provide an audio file and then pop up a question or other information when the audio file begins or ends playing.

Solution

Use the new HTML5 `audio` element:

```
<audio id="meadow" controls>
   <source src="meadow.mp3" type="audio/mpeg3"/>
   <source src="meadow.ogg" type="audio/ogg" />
   <source src="meadow.wav" type="audio/wav" />
<p><a href="meadow.wav">Meadow sounds</a></p>
</audio>
```

and capture its end or play event:

```
function manageEvent(eventObj, event, eventHandler) {
   if (eventObj.addEventListener) {
      eventObj.addEventListener(event, eventHandler,false);
   } else if (eventObj.attachEvent) {
      event = "on" + event;
      eventObj.attachEvent(event, eventHandler);
   }
}

window.onload=function() {
  var meadow = document.getElementById("meadow");
  manageEvent(meadow,"play",aboutAudio);
}
```

then display the information:

```
function aboutAudio() {
  var txt = document.createTextNode("This audio file was a recording
  from the Shaw Nature Reserve in Missouri");
  var div = document.createElement("div");
```

```
    div.appendChild(txt);
    div.setAttribute("role","alert");
    document.body.appendChild(div);
}
```

Discussion

HTML5 added two new media elements: `audio` and `video`. These simple-to-use controls provide a way to play audio and video files without having to use Flash.

In the solution, the `audio` element's `controls` Boolean attribute is provided, so the controls are displayed. The element has three `source` children elements, providing support for three different types of audio files: WAV, MP3, and Ogg Vorbis. The use of the `source` element allows different browsers to find the format (codec) that they support. For the `audio` element, the browser support is:

- Firefox (3.5 and up) only supports WAV and Ogg Vorbis
- Opera (10.5) only supports WAV (at this time)
- Chrome supports MP3 and Ogg Vorbis
- Safari supports MP3 and WAV

IE8 does not support the `audio` element, but IE9 will, and will most likely only support MP3 and WAV. However, a link to the WAV file is provided as a fallback, which means people using a browser that doesn't support `audio` can still access the sound file. I could have also provided an `object` element, or other fallback content.

The new media elements come with a set of methods to control the playback, as well as events that can be triggered when the event occurs. In the solution, the `ended` event is captured and assigned the event handler `aboutAudio`, which displays a message about the file after the playback is finished. Notice that though I'm using a DOM Level 0 event handler with the window load event, I'm using DOM Level 2 event handling with the `audio` element. The reason is that at the time I wrote this, making an assignment to the element's `onplay` (or `onended`) event did not work. However, I could use the DOM Level 2 event handler and the inline event handler without a problem:

```
<audio id="meadow" src="meadow.wav" controls
onended="alert('All done')">
<p><a href="meadow.wav">Meadow sounds</a></p>
</audio>
```

It's interesting seeing the appearance of the elements in all of the browsers that currently support them. There is no standard look, so each browser provides its own interpretation. You can control the appearance by providing your own playback controls and using your own elements/CSS/SVG/Canvas to supply the decoration.

See Also

See Recipe 15.12 for a demonstration of using the playback methods and providing alternative visual representations for the new media elements, as well as providing a different form of fallback.

15.12 Controlling Video from JavaScript with the video Element

Problem

You want to embed video in your web page, and not use Flash. You also want a consistent look for the video control, regardless of browser and operating system.

Solution

Use the new HTML5 video element:

```
<video id="meadow" poster="purples.jpg" >
   <source src="meadow.m4v" type="video/mp4"/>
   <source src="meadow.ogv" type="video/ogg" />
   <object width="425" height="344">
   <param name="movie"
value="http://www.youtube.com/v/CNRTeSoSbgg&hl=en_US&fs=1&"></param>
   <embed src="http://www.youtube.com/v/CNRTeSoSbgg&hl=en_US&fs=1&"
type="application/x-shockwave-flash"
   allowscriptaccess="always" allowfullscreen="true" width="425"
height="344">
   <p>Audio slideshow from Shaw Nature Center</embed></object>
</video>
```

And provide controls for it via JavaScript, as shown in Example 15-8. Buttons are used to provide the video control, and text in a div element is used to provide feedback on time during the playback.

Example 15-8. Providing a custom control for the HTML5 video element

```
<!DOCTYPE html>
<head>
<title>Meadow Video</title>
<script>

function manageEvent(eventObj, event, eventHandler) {
   if (eventObj.addEventListener) {
      eventObj.addEventListener(event, eventHandler,false);
   } else if (eventObj.attachEvent) {
      event = "on" + event;
      eventObj.attachEvent(event, eventHandler);
   }
}
```

```
window.onload=function() {

  // events for buttons
  manageEvent(document.getElementById("start"),"click",startPlayback);
  manageEvent(document.getElementById("stop"),"click",stopPlayback);
  manageEvent(document.getElementById("pause"),"click",pausePlayback);

  // setup for video playback
  var meadow = document.getElementById("meadow");
  manageEvent(meadow,"timeupdate",reportProgress);

  // video fallback
  var detect = document.createElement("video");
  if (!detect.canPlayType) {
    document.getElementById("controls").style.display="none";
  }
}

// start video, enable stop and pause
// disable play
function startPlayback() {
  var meadow = document.getElementById("meadow");
  meadow.play();
  document.getElementById("pause").disabled=false;
  document.getElementById("stop").disabled=false;
  this.disabled=true;
}

// pause video, enable start, disable stop
// disable pause
function pausePlayback() {
  document.getElementById("meadow").pause();
  this.disabled=true;
  document.getElementById("start").disabled=false;
  document.getElementById("stop").disabled=true;
}

// stop video, return to zero time
// enable play, disable pause and stop
function stopPlayback() {
  var meadow = document.getElementById("meadow");
  meadow.pause();
  meadow.currentTime=0;
  document.getElementById("start").disabled=false;
  document.getElementById("pause").disabled=true;
  this.disabled=true;
}

// for every time divisible by 5, output feedback
function reportProgress() {
  var time = Math.round(this.currentTime);
  var div = document.getElementById("feedback");
  div.innerHTML = time + " seconds";
}
```

```
</script>

</head>
<body>
<video id="meadow" poster="purples.jpg" >
    <source src="meadow.m4v" type="video/mp4"/>
    <source src="meadow.ogv" type="video/ogg" />
    <object width="425" height="344">
    <param name="movie"
value="http://www.youtube.com/v/CNRTeSoSbgg&hl=en_US&fs=1&"></param>
    <embed src="http://www.youtube.com/v/CNRTeSoSbgg&hl=en_US&fs=1&"
type="application/x-shockwave-flash"
    allowscriptaccess="always" allowfullscreen="true" width="425"
height="344">
    <p>Audio slideshow from Shaw Nature Center</embed></object>
</video>
<div id="feedback"></div>
<div id="controls">
<button id="start">Play</button>
<button id="stop">Stop</button>
<button id="pause">Pause</button>
</controls>
</body>
```

Discussion

The new HTML5 video element, as with the HTML5 audio element, can be controlled with its own built-in controls, or you can provide your own, as shown in Example 15-8. The media elements support the following methods:

play
> Starts playing the video

pause
> Pauses the video

load
> Preloads the video without starting play

canPlayType
> Tests if the user agent supports the video type

The media elements don't support a stop method, so I emulated one by pausing video play and then setting the video's currentTime attribute to 0, which basically resets the play start time. The only browser this didn't work in was Chrome. It worked in Opera 10.5, Firefox 3.5, and WebKit/Safari.

I also used currentTime to print out the video time, using Math.round to round the time to the nearest second, as shown in Figure 15-4.

Figure 15-4. Playing a video using the video control, displaying the number of seconds of video

The video control is providing two different video codecs: H.264 (*.mp4*), and Ogg Theora (*.ogv*). Firefox, Opera, and Chrome support Ogg Theora, but Safari/WebKit only supports the H.264 formatted video. However, by providing both types, the video works in all of the browsers that support the `video` element. For the browsers that currently don't support `video`, such as IE, the fallback YouTube video is provided, and if that doesn't work, then there's text. In addition, if the `video` element is not supported, the video controls are hidden.

The video and audio controls are inherently keyboard-accessible. If you do replace the controls, you'll want to provide accessibility information with your replacements. The video control doesn't have built-in captioning, but work is underway to provide the API for captioning.

Microsoft has stated it will support the `video` element in IE9, and the H.264 codec.

See Also

For more on the new `video`/`audio` elements, see Opera's introduction (*http://dev.opera .com/articles/view/introduction-html5-video/*), Safari/WebKit's (*http://webkit.org/blog/ 140/html5-media-support/*), and Mozilla's (*https://developer.mozilla.org/En/Using_au dio_and_video_in_Firefox*).

A good place for more information on Ogg Theora is the Theora Cookbook (*http://en .flossmanuals.net/TheoraCookbook/*).

At the time this book entered production, Google had released another video codec, WebM, for royalty free access. Several browsers have promised to support this codec. For more information, see the WebM Project site (*http://www.webmproject.org/*).

CHAPTER 16

JavaScript Objects

16.0 Introduction

Your JavaScript applications can consist entirely of functions and variables—both local and global—but if you want to ensure ease of reuse, compactness of code, and efficiency, as well as code that plays well with other libraries, you're going to need to consider opportunities to encapsulate your code into objects.

Luckily, working with objects in JavaScript isn't much more complicated than working with functions. After all, a JavaScript function is an object, and all objects are, technically, just functions.

Confused yet?

Unlike languages such as Java or C++, which are based on classes and class instances, JavaScript is based on *prototypal inheritance*. What prototypal inheritance means is that reuse occurs through creating new instances of existing objects, rather than instances of a class. Instead of extensibility occurring through class inheritance, prototypal extensibility happens by enhancing an existing object with new properties and methods.

Prototype-based languages have an advantage in that you don't have to worry about creating the classes first, and then the applications. You can focus on creating applications, and then deriving the object framework via the effort.

It sounds like a mishmash concept, but hopefully as you walk through the recipes you'll get a better feel for JavaScript's prototype-based, object-oriented capabilities.

ECMAScript and all its variations, including JavaScript, isn't the only prototype-based language. The Wikipedia page on prototype-based languages (*http://en.wikipedia.org/wiki/Prototype-based_programming*), lists several.

See Also

Several of the recipes in this book are based on new functionality that was introduced in ECMAScript 5. You can access the complete ECMAScript 5 specification (a PDF) at *http://www.ecmascript.org/docs/tc39-2009-043.pdf*.

Note that the implementation of the new functionality is sketchy. I'll point out browser support as I go.

16.1 Defining a Basic JavaScript Object

Problem

You want to create a custom, reusable JavaScript object.

Solution

Define a new object explicitly using functional syntax, and then create new instances, passing in the data the object *constructor* is expecting:

```
function Tune (song, artist) {
    this.title = song;
    this.artist = artist;
    this.concat=function() {
        return this.title + "-" + this.artist;
    }
}

window.onload=function() {
    var happySong = new Array();
    happySong[0] = new Tune("Putting on the Ritz", "Ella Fitzgerald");

    // print out title and artist
    alert(happySong[0].concat());
}
```

Discussion

As you can see from the solution, there is no class description, as you might expect if you've used other languages. A new object is created as a function, with three members: two properties, `title` and `artist`, and one method, `concat`. You could even use it like a function:

```
Tune("test","artist");
```

However, using the object like a function, as compared to using it as an object constructor, has an odd and definitely unexpected consequence.

The `new` keyword is used to create a new `Tune` instance. Values are passed into the object constructor, which are then assigned to the `Tune` properties, `title` and `artist`, via the `this` keyword. In the solution, `this` is a reference to the object instance. When you assign the property values to the object instance, you can then access them at a later time, using syntax like *happySong[0].title*. In addition, the Tune object's concat method also has access to these properties.

However, when you use Tune like a regular function, this doesn't represent an object instance, because there isn't any. Instead, this references the owner of the Tune function, which in this case, is the global window object:

```
// treating Tune like a function
Tune("the title", "the singer");
alert(window.concat()); // lo and behold,
                       // "the title the singer" prints out
```

Completely unexpected and unwelcome behavior.

To summarize: to create a new object type, you can create a function with both properties and methods. To ensure the properties are assigned to the correct object, treat the object like a constructor using the new operator, rather than as a function. The this keyword establishes ownership of the properties, which is the Tune object instance, if the function is used as an object constructor and not a regular function.

See Also

See Recipe 16.2 for more information about the role this plays with JavaScript objects.

16.2 Keeping Object Members Private

Problem

You want to keep one or more object properties private, so they can't be accessed outside the object instance.

Solution

When creating the private data members, do *not* use the this keyword with the member:

```
function Tune(song,artist) {
   var title = song;
   var artist = artist;
   this.concat = function() {
      return title + " " + artist;
   }
}

window.onload=function() {

   var happySongs = new Array();
   happySongs[0] = new Tune("Putting on the Ritz", "Ella Fitzgerald");

   try {
```

```
  // error
  alert(happySongs[0].title);
} catch(e) {
  alert(e);
}

// prints out correct title and artist
alert(happySongs[0].concat());
}
```

Discussion

Members in the object constructor (the function body), are not accessible outside the object unless they're assigned to that object using this. If they're attached to the object using the var keyword, only the Tune's *inner function*, the concat method, can access these now-private data members.

This type of method—one that can access the private data members, but is, itself, exposed to public access via this—has been termed a *privileged method* by Douglas Crockford, the father of JSON (JavaScript Object Notation). As he himself explains (at *http://www.crockford.com/javascript/private.html*):

> This pattern of public, private, and privileged members is possible because JavaScript has closures. What this means is that an inner function always has access to the vars and parameters of its outer function, even after the outer function has returned. This is an extremely powerful property of the language [. . . .] Private and privileged members can only be made when an object is constructed. Public members can be added at any time.

See Also

See Recipe 6.5 for more on function closures. See Recipe 16.3 for more on adding public members after the object has been defined.

16.3 Expanding Objects with prototype

You want to extend an existing object with a new method.

Solution

Use the Object prototype to extend the object:

```
Tune.prototype.addCategory = function(categoryName) {
    this.category = categoryName;
}
```

Discussion

Every object in JavaScript inherits from Object, and all methods and other properties are inherited via the prototype object. It's through the prototype object that we can extend any object, and that includes the built-in objects, such as String and Number. Once an object has been extended via the prototype property, all instances of the object within the scope of the application have this functionality.

In Example 16-1, the new object, Tune, is defined using function syntax. It has two private data members, a title and an artist. A publicly accessible method, concat, takes these two private data members, concatenates them, and returns the result.

After a new instance of the object is created, and the object is extended with a new method and data member, the new method is used to update the existing object instance.

Example 16-1. Instantiating a new object, adding values, and extending the object

```
<!DOCTYPE html>
<head>
<title>Tune Object</title>
<script>


  function Tune(song,artist) {
    var title = song;
    var artist = artist;
    this.concat = function() {
      return title + " " + artist;
    }
  }

window.onload=function() {
  // create instance, print out values
  var happySong = new Tune("Putting on the Ritz", "Ella Fitzgerald");

  // extend the object
  Tune.prototype.addCategory = function(categoryName) {
      this.category = categoryName;
  }

  // add category
  happySong.addCategory("Swing");

  // print song out to new paragraph
  var song = "Title and artist: " + happySong.concat() +
             " Category: " + happySong.category;
  var p = document.createElement("p");
  var txt = document.createTextNode(song);
  p.appendChild(txt);
  document.getElementById("song").appendChild(p);
}

</script>

</head>
<body>
<h1>Tune</h1>
```

```
<div id="song">
</div>
</body>
</html>
```

Figure 16-1 shows the page after the new element and data have been appended.

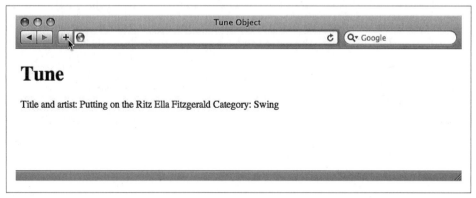

Figure 16-1. Demonstration of custom JavaScript object after values printed out

The **prototype** property can also be used to override or extend external or global objects. Before ECMAScript 5 added `trim` as a default method for the `String` object, applications used to extend the `String` object by adding a `trim` method through the **prototype** object:

```
String.prototype.trim = function() {
  return (this.replace(/^[\s\xA0]+/, "").replace(/[\s\xA0]+$/, ""));
}
```

Needless to say, you'd want to use extreme caution when using this functionality with global objects. Applications that have extended the `String` object with a homegrown `trim` method may end up behaving differently than applications using the new standard `trim` method.

Using **prototype** with your own objects is usually safe. The only time you may run into problems is if you provide your objects as an external library, and others build on them.

16.4 Adding Getter/Setter to Objects

Problem

You want to provide property access to protected data.

Solution

Use the getter/setter functionality introduced with ECMAScript 3.1 with your (or outside) objects:

```
function Tune() {
  var artist;
  var song;

  this.__defineGetter__("artist",function() {
      return artist});

  this.__defineSetter__("artist",function(val) {
      artist = "By: " + val});

  this.__defineGetter__("song",function() {
      return "Song: " + song});

  this.__defineSetter__("song",function(val) {
      song=val});
}

window.onload=function() {
  var happySong = new Tune();

  happySong.artist="Ella Fitzgerald";
  happySong.song="Putting on the Ritz";

  alert(happySong.song + " " + happySong.artist);
}
```

Discussion

We can add functions to our objects to get private data, as demonstrated in Recipe 16.2. However, when we use the functions, they are obvious functions. The getter/setter functionality is a special syntax that provides property-like access to private data members. The getter and setter functions provide an extra layer of protection for the private data members. The functions also allow us to prepare the data, as demonstrated with the solution, where the **song** and **artist** strings are concatenated to labels.

You can define the getter and setter functions within the object constructor, as shown in the solution:

```
this.__defineGetter__("song",function() {
    return "Song: " + song});

this.__defineSetter__("song",function(val) {
    song=val});
```

You can also add a getter/setter with other objects, including DOM objects. To add a getter/setter outside of the object constructor, you first need to access the object's **prototype** object, and then add the getter/setter functions to the **prototype**:

```
var p = Tune.prototype;

p.__defineGetter__("song",function() {
    return "Song: " + title});
```

```
p.__defineSetter__("song",function(val) {
    title=val});
```

You can also use getter/setters with "one-off" objects, used to provide JavaScript name-spacing (covered later in the chapter):

```
var Book = {
    title: "The JavaScript Cookbook",
    get booktitle() {
        return this.title;
    },
    set booktitle(val) {
        this.title = val;
    }
};

Book.booktitle = "Learning JavaScript";
```

This approach can't be used to hide the data, but can be used to control the display of the data, or to provide special processing of the incoming data before it's stored in the data member.

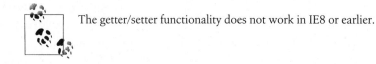 The getter/setter functionality does not work in IE8 or earlier.

See Also

See Recipe 16.6 for demonstrations of the new ECMAScript 5 property methods. Recipe 16.11 covers JavaScript namespacing.

16.5 Inheriting an Object's Functionality

Problem

When creating a new object type, you want to inherit the functionality of an existing JavaScript object.

Solution

Use the concept of constructor chaining and the `Function.apply` method to emulate traditional class inheritance behavior in JavaScript:

```
function oldObject(param1) {
    this.param1 = param1;
    this.getParam=function() {
        return this.param1;
    }
}
```

```
function newObject(param1,param2) {
   this.param2 = param2;
   this.getParam2 = function() {
      return this.param2;
   }
   oldObject.apply(this,arguments);
   this.getAllParameters=function() {
      return this.getParam() + " " + this.getParam2();
   }
}

window.onload=function() {
   newObject.prototype = new oldObject();
   var obj = new newObject("value1","value2");

   // prints out both parameters
   alert(obj.getAllParameters());
}
```

Discussion

In the solution, we have two objects: the original, `oldObject`, and `newObject` that inherits functionality from the older object. For this to work, a couple of things are happening.

First, in the constructor for `newObject`, an apply method is called on `oldObject`, passing in a reference to the new object, and the argument array. The `apply` method is inherited from the `Function` object, and takes a reference to the calling object, or the window object if the value is null, and an optional argument array.

The second part of the inheritance is the line:

```
newObject.prototype=new oldObject();
```

This is an example of constructor chaining in JavaScript. What happens is when you create a new instance of `newObject`, you're also creating a new instance of `oldObject`, in such a way that `newObject` inherits both the older object's methods and property.

It is this combination of constructor chaining, which chains the constructors of the new objects together, and the `apply` method, which passes both object context and data to the inherited object, that implements inheritance behavior in JavaScript. Because of this inheritance, the new object has access not only to its own property, `param2`, and method, `getParam2`, but also has access to the old object's `param1` and `getParam` property and method.

To see another example of JavaScript inheritance, Example 16-2 shows it working with another couple of objects: a `Book` object and a `TechBook` object, which inherits from `Book`. The lines that implement the inheritance are bolded.

Example 16-2. Demonstrating object inheritance in JavaScript

```html
<!DOCTYPE html>
<head>
<title>Constructor Chaining</title>
<script type="text/javascript">

function Book (title, author) {
  var title = title;
  var author = author;
  this.getTitle=function() {
     return "Title: " + title;
  }
  this.getAuthor=function() {
     return "Author: " + author;
  }
}

function TechBook (title, author, category) {

   var category = category;
   this.getCategory = function() {
     return "Technical Category: " + category;
   }

   Book.apply(this,arguments);
   this.getBook=function() {
    return this.getTitle() + " " + author + " " + this.getCategory();
   }
}

window.onload=function() {

  // chain the object constructors
  TechBook.prototype = new Book();

  // get all values
  var newBook = new TechBook("The JavaScript Cookbook",
  "Shelley Powers", "Programming");
  alert(newBook.getBook());

  // now, individually
  alert(newBook.getTitle());
  alert(newBook.getAuthor());
  alert(newBook.getCategory());
}

</script>
</head>
<body>
<p>some content</p>
</body>
```

Unlike the objects in the solution, all of the data members in both objects in Example 16-2 are protected, which means the data can't be directly accessed outside the objects. Yet notice when all three Book properties—title, author, and category—are printed out via the getBook method in the TechBook object, that TechBook has access to the Book author and title properties, in addition to its own category. That's because when the new TechBook object was created, a new Book object was also created and inherited by the new TechBook object. To complete the inheritance, the data used in the constructor for TechBook is passed through the Book object using the apply method.

Not only can the TechBook object directly access the Book instance data, you can access both of the Book object's methods, getAuthor and getCategory, directly on the instantiated TechBook object instance.

16.6 Extending an Object by Defining a New Property

Problem

You want to extend an existing object by adding a new property, but without changing the object's constructor function.

Solution

Use the new ECMAScript Object.defineProperty method to define one property:

```
Object.defineProperty(newBook, "publisher", {
        value: "O'Reilly",
        writable: false,
        enumerable: true,
        configurable: true});
```

Use the Object.defineProperties method to define more than one property:

```
Object.defineProperties(newBook, {
    "stock": {
        value: true,
        writable: true,
        enumerable: true,
    },
    "age": {
        value: "13 and up",
        writable: false
    }
});
```

Discussion

Properties are handled differently in ECMAScript 5. Where before all you could do was assign a value, now you have greater control over how an object's properties are managed. This greater control comes about through the provision for several new attributes that can be assigned to a property when it's created. These new attributes make up what is known as the *property descriptor* object, and include:

writable

   If true, property can be changed; otherwise, not.

configurable

   If true, property can be deleted, or changed; otherwise, not.

enumerable

   If true, property can be iterated.

The type of property descriptor can also vary. If the descriptor is a *data descriptor*, another attribute is value, demonstrated in the solution and equivalent to the following:

```
someObject.newProperty = "somevalue";
```

If the descriptor is an *accessor descriptor*, the property has a getter/setter, similar to what was covered in Recipe 16.4. A restriction when defining an accessor property is that you can't set the writable attribute:

```
Object.defineProperty(TechBook, "category", {
    get: function () { return category; },
    set: function (value) { category = value; },
    enumerable: true,
    configurable: true});
var newBook = new TechBook(...);
newBook.publisher="O'Reilly";
```

You can also discover information about the property descriptor for a property with the Object.getOwnPropertyDescription method. To use, pass in the object and the property name whose property descriptor you wish to review:

```
var propDesc = Object.getOwnPropertyDescriptor(newBook,"category");
alert(propDesc.writable); // true if writable, otherwise false
```

The property has to be publicly accessible (not a private member). Easily view all of the property attributes using the JSON object's stringify method:

```
var val = Object.getOwnPropertyDescriptor(TechBook,"category");
alert(JSON.stringify(val)); // {"enumerable":true,"configurable":true}
```

If the property descriptor configurable attribute is set to true, you can change descriptor attributes. For instance, to change the writable attribute from false to true, use the following:

```
Object.defineProperty(newBook, "publisher", {
    writable: true});
```

The previously set attributes retain their existing values.

Example 16-3 demonstrates the new property descriptors, first on a DOM object, then a custom object.

Example 16-3. Trying out new object property methods

```html
<!DOCTYPE html>
<head>
<title>Object Properties</title>
<script type="text/javascript">

// Book custom object
function Book (title, author) {
  var title = title;
  var author = author;
  this.getTitle=function() {
    return "Title: " + title;
  }
  this.getAuthor=function() {
    return "Author: " + author;
  }
}

// TechBook, inheriting from Book
function TechBook (title, author, category) {

  var category = category;
  this.getCategory = function() {
    return "Technical Category: " + category;
  }

  Book.apply(this,arguments);
  this.getBook=function() {
    return this.getTitle() + " " + author + " " + this.getCategory();
  }
}
window.onload=function() {

  try {

    // DOM test, WebKit bites the dust on this one
    var img = new Image();

    // add new property and descriptor
    Object.defineProperty(img, "geolatitude", {
      get: function() { return geolatitude; },
      set: function(val) { geolatitude = val;},
      enumerable: true,
      configurable: true});

    // test configurable and enumerable attrs
    var props = "Image has ";
    for (var prop in img) {
      props+=prop + " ";
    }
    alert(props);

  } catch(e) {
    alert(e);
  }
```

```
    try {
      // now we lose IE8

      // chain the object constructors
      TechBook.prototype = new Book();

      // add new property and property descriptor
      Object.defineProperty(TechBook, "experience", {
        get: function () { return category; },
        set: function (value) { category = value; },
        enumerable: false,
        configurable: true});

      // get property descriptor and print
      var val = Object.getOwnPropertyDescriptor(TechBook,"experience");
      alert(JSON.stringify(val));

      // test configurable and enumerable
      props = "TechBook has ";
      for (var prop in TechBook) {
        props+=prop + " ";
      }
      alert(props);

      Object.defineProperty(TechBook, "experience", {
        enumerable: true});

      props = "TechBook now has ";
      for (var prop in TechBook) {
        props+=prop + " ";
      }
      alert(props);

      // create TechBook instance
      var newBook = new TechBook("The JavaScript Cookbook",
"Shelley Powers", "Programming");

      // test new setter
      newBook.experience="intermediate";

      // test data descriptor
      Object.defineProperty(newBook, "publisher", {
          value: "O'Reilly",
          writable: false,
          enumerable: true,
          configurable: true});

      // test writable
      newBook.publisher="Some Other";
      alert(newBook.publisher);

    } catch(e) {
      alert(e);
    }
}
```

```
</script>
</head>
<body>
<p>some content</p>
</body>
```

These methods are very new. At the time I wrote this recipe, they only work in nightly builds for WebKit and Firefox (Minefield), and in a very limited sense with IE8.

The IE8 limitation is that the new property methods only work with DOM elements. The `Object.defineProperty` method works with the `Image` element, but not with the custom objects. However, using `defineProperty` on DOM elements causes an exception in WebKit. None of the new property methods work with Opera. The Firefox Minefield nightly and the Chrome beta were the only browsers that currently work with both types of objects, as shown in Figure 16-2, which displays the `Image` object properties in Firefox.

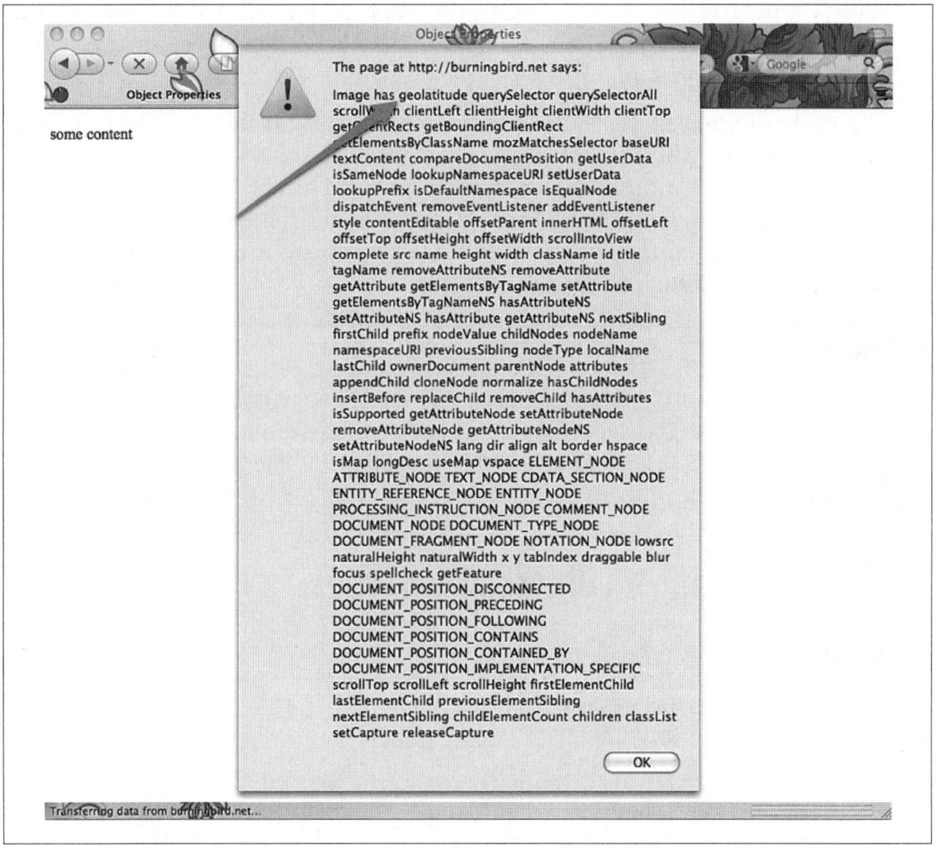

Figure 16-2. Displaying Image properties after adding a new property with defineProperty

After printing out the `Image` properties, a new property (`experience`) and property descriptor are added to the TechBook custom object. The `Object.getOwnPropertyDescrip tor` is called, passing in the TechBook object and the property name, `experience`. The property descriptor object is returned, and the `JSON.stringify` method is used on the object to print out the values:

```
{"enumerable":false,"configurable:true}
```

Next, the property descriptor values are tested. Currently, because the `experience` property is not enumerable, the use of the `for...in` loop can't enumerate through the properties, and the result is:

```
Techbook has prototype
```

The new `experience` property's `enumerable` attribute is then changed to `true`, because the property descriptor for `experience` allows modification on descriptor values. Enumerating over the `experience` property now yields the following string for Firefox:

```
Techbook has prototype experience
```

However, Chrome does not pick up the `prototype` property. The next two lines of code create a new instance of the `TechBook` object and adds an `experience`, which is then printed out to demonstrate the success of the property.

The last code in the example adds another new property (`publisher`) and property descriptor. This is a data property descriptor, which can also take a default value: "O'Reilly". The `writable` property descriptor is set to `false`, and configurable and enumerable descriptors are set to `true`. The code then tries to change the publisher value. However, the original publisher value of `O'Reilly` prints out because the `publisher` property `writable` attribute is set to `false`.

See Also

See Recipe 16.7 for more on property enumeration. Though not all browsers support `defineProperty` and `defineProperties` yet, there are workarounds, as detailed by John Resig in a nice article (*http://ejohn.org/blog/ecmascript-5-objects-and-properties/*) describing the new object property capabilities.

16.7 Enumerating an Object's Properties

Problem

You want to see what properties an object has.

Solution

Use a specialized variation of the `for` loop to iterate through the properties:

```
for (var prop in obj) {
    alert(prop); // prints out the property name
}
```

or use the new ECMAScript 5 `Object.keys` method to return the names for all properties that can be enumerated:

```
alert(Object.keys(obj).join(", "));
```

or use another new ECMAScript 5 method, `Object.getOwnPropertyNames(obj)`, to get the names of all properties, whether they can be enumerated or not:

```
var props = Object.getOwnPropertyNames(obj);
```

Discussion

For an object instance, `newBook`, based on the following object definitions:

```
function Book (title, author) {
  var title = title;
  this.author = author;
  this.getTitle=function() {
     return "Title: " + title;
  }
  this.getAuthor=function() {
     return "Author: " + author;
  }
}

function TechBook (title, author, category) {

  var category = category;
  this.getCategory = function() {
    return "Technical Category: " + category;
  }

  Book.apply(this,arguments);
  this.getBook=function() {
   return this.getTitle() + " " + author + " " + this.getCategory();
  }
}

  // chain the object constructors
  TechBook.prototype = new Book();

  // create new tech book
  var newBook = new TechBook("The JavaScript Cookbook",
"Shelley Powers", "Programming");
```

using the `for...in` loop:

```
var str = "";
for (var prop in newBook) {
   str = str + prop + " ";
}

alert(str);
```

a message pops up with the following values:

```
getCategory author getTitle getAuthor getBook
```

Neither the `category` property in `TechBook` nor the `title` property in `Book` are returned, as these are private data members. When using WebKit nightly or Firefox Minefield, the same result is returned when using the new `Object.keys` method:

```
alert(Object.keys(newBook).join(" "));
```

The same result is also returned, again with WebKit nightly or Firefox Minefield, when using the new `Object.getOwnPropertyNames` method:

```
var props = Object.getOwnPropertyNames(newBook);
alert(props.join(" "));
```

However, if I add a property descriptor for the `title` property, making it enumerable:

```
// test data descriptor
Object.defineProperty(newBook, "title", {
        writable: true,
        enumerable: true,
        configurable: true});
```

When I enumerate over the properties again, this time the `title` displays among the properties, even though it still can't be accessed or reset directly on the object.

We can also use these same property enumerators over the object constructors (`Book` or `TechBook`) or any of the built-in objects. However, the values we get back when we enumerate over `Book`, as compared to the instance, `newBook`, do vary among the methods. The `for...in` loop returns just one property, `prototype`, as does the `Object.keys` method. That's because `prototype` is the only enumerable property for the `Function` object. While `newBook` is an instance of `Book`, `Book`, itself is an instance of the `Function` object.

The `Object.getOwnPropertyNames`, however, returns the following set of properties for `Book`:

```
arguments callee caller length name prototype
```

Unlike `Object.keys` and the `for...in` loop, `Object.getOwnPropertyNames` returns a list of all properties, not just those that are enumerable. This leads to a new question: why did `Object.getOwnPropertyNames` not return all of the properties for the `newBook` instance? It should have picked up `title` before it was made enumerable, as well as `TechBook`'s private member, `category`.

I added another property descriptor to `newBook`, this time for `category`, and this time with `enumerable` set to `false`:

```
Object.defineProperty(newBook,"category", {
        writable: true,
        enumerable: false,
        configurable: true});
```

The `category` property isn't listed when I use `for...in` or `Object.keys`, but this time it is picked up by `Object.getOwnPropertyNames`.

It would seem that a property must either be publicly accessible, or have a property descriptor for it to be picked up by Object.getOwnPropertyNames, at least for these earlier implementations of these new Object methods. I imagine the reason is to ensure consistent results between older ECMAScript implementations and newer ones: defining a property in older versions of ECMAScript is not the same as defining a property in the newer version.

Speaking of ECMAScript 5 and new Object methods, support for the older for...in loop is broad, but support for Object.keys and Object.getOwnPropertyNames, in addition to support for property descriptors, is sparse at this time. Opera does not support defineProperty and the associated new ECMAScript 5 functionality. WebKit nightly and the Chrome beta support all of the new functionality, while the Firefox nightly (Minefield), supports Object.keys, but not getOwnPropertyNames. IE8's coverage is limited because it only supports the new methods on DOM elements, such as Image, and not on custom objects.

See Also

For more on property descriptors, see Recipe 16.6.

16.8 Preventing Object Extensibility

Problem

You want to prevent others from extending an object.

Solution

Use the new ECMAScript 5 Object.preventExtensions method to lock an object against future property additions:

```
"use strict";

var Test = {
    value1 : "one",
    value2 : function() {
      return this.value1;
    }
};

try {
   Object.preventExtensions(Test);

    // the following fails, and throws an exception in Strict mode
   Test.value3 = "test";

} catch(e) {
   alert(e);
}
```

Discussion

Covering `Object.preventExtensions` is a leap of faith on my part, as no browser has implemented this new ECMAScript 5 functionality. However, by the time this book hits the streets, I expect (hope) at least a couple of browsers will have implemented this new feature.

The `Object.preventExtensions` method prevents developers from extending the object with new properties, though property values themselves are still writable. It sets an internal property, `Extensible`, to `false`. You can check to see if an object is extensible using `Object.isExtensible`:

```
if (Object.isExtensible(obj)) {
    // extend the object
}
```

Though you can't extend the object, you can edit existing property values, as well as modify the object's property descriptor.

See Also

Recipe 16.6 covers property descriptors.

Strict Mode

Another new ECMAScript 5 addition is demonstrated in the solution for Recipe 16.8: the new `Strict` mode. You can now put an application within a strict operating mode, which means that older, deprecated features are disabled or generate errors, and actions that may not throw errors but are not advisable will throw errors. It's a way of inherently ensuring production-quality code.

The ECMAScript 5 specification details what happens in `Strict` mode throughout the document. For instance, if you use the deprecated `with` statement, the application will throw an error; the use of the `delete` operator with a variable, function argument, or function will also generate an error; most uses of `eval` will generate errors, and so on. Annex C of the ECMAScript 5 specification lists all of the `Strict` mode restrictions and exceptions.

To turn `Strict` mode on, use the following at the top level of your code:

```
"use strict";
```

This includes quotes. Or, you can turn on `Strict` mode only within a function:

```
function somename() {
    "use strict";
};
```

When creating custom JavaScript objects, you can ensure their quality by using `Strict` mode. Currently, no browsers support `Strict` mode, but all plan to eventually.

16.9 Preventing Object Additions and Changes to Property Descriptors

Problem

You want to prevent extensions to an object, but you also want to disallow someone from changing the property descriptor for an object.

Solution

Use the new ECMAScript `Object.seal` method to seal the object against additions and modification of its property descriptor:

```
"use strict";

var Test = {
   value1 : "one",
   value2 : function() {
     return this.value1;
   }
}

try {
   // freeze the object
   Object.seal(Test);

   // the following would succeed
   Test.value2 = "two";

   // the following would fail, throw an error in Strict Mode
   Test.newProp = "value3";

   // so would the following
   Object.defineProperty(Title, "category", {
      get: function () { return category; },
      set: function (value) { category = value; },
      enumerable: true,
      configurable: true});
} catch(e) {
   alert(e);
}
```

Discussion

Like `Object.preventExtension`, covered in Recipe 16.8, the `Object.seal` method is another new ECMAScript 5 method that has no browser implementation yet, but should, knock on wood, by the time you read this book. Look for a first implementation in a Safari nightly build or a Firefox Minefield build.

The `Object.seal` method prevents extensions to an object, like `Object.preventExten`sions, but also prevents any changes to the object's property descriptor. To check if an object is sealed, you would use the `Object.isSealed` method:

```
if (Object.isSealed(obj)) ...
```

See Also

Property descriptors are described in Recipe 16.6, and `Object.preventExtensions` is covered in Recipe 16.8.

16.10 Preventing Any Changes to an Object

Problem

You've defined your object, and now you want to make sure that its properties aren't redefined or edited by other applications using the object.

Solution

Use the new ECMAScript 5 `Object.freeze` method to freeze the object against any and all changes:

```
"use strict";
  var Test = {
    value1 : "one",
    value2 : function() {
      return this.value1;
    }
  }

try {
  // freeze the object
  Object.freeze(Test);

  // the following would throw an error in Strict Mode
  Test.value2 = "two";

  // so would the following
  Test.newProperty = "value";

  // and so would the following
  Object.defineProperty(Title, "category", {
    get: function () { return category; },
    set: function (value) { category = value; },
    enumerable: true,
    configurable: true});
} catch(e) {
  alert(e);
}
```

Discussion

There are several new `Object` methods defined in ECMAScript 5 to provide better object management in JavaScript. The least restrictive is `Object.preventExtensions(obj)`, covered in Recipe 16.6, which disallows adding new properties to an object, but you can change the object's property descriptor, or modify an existing property value.

The next more restrictive method is `Object.seal`. The `Object.seal(obj)` method prevents any modifications or new properties from being added to the property descriptor, but you can modify an existing property value.

The most restrictive new ECMAScript 5 `Object` method is `Object.freeze`. The `Object.freeze(obj)` method disallows extensions to the object, and restricts changes to the property descriptor. However, `Object.freeze` also prevents any and all edits to existing object properties. Literally, once the object is frozen, that's it—no additions, no changes to existing properties.

You can check to see if an object is frozen using the companion method, `Object.isFrozen`:

```
if (Object.isFrozen(obj)) ...
```

No browser currently implements `Object.freeze` or `Object.isFrozen`, but this state should change relatively soon.

See Also

Recipe 16.6 covers property descriptors, Recipe 16.8 covers `Object.preventExtensions`, and Recipe 16.9 covers `Object.seal`.

16.11 One-Off Objects and Namespacing Your JavaScript

Problem

You want to encapsulate your library functionality in such a way as to prevent clashes with other libraries.

Solution

Use an object *literal*, what I call a *one-off object*, to implement the JavaScript version of namespacing. An example is the following:

```
var jscbObject = {

   // return element
   getElem : function (identifier) {
      return document.getElementById(identifier);
   },

   stripslashes : function(str) {
```

```
        return str.replace(/\\/g, '');
    },

    removeAngleBrackets: function(str) {
        return str.replace(/</g,'&lt;').replace(/>/g,'&gt;');
    }
};

var incoming = jscbObject.getElem("incoming");
var content = incoming.innerHTML;

var result = jscbObject.stripslashes(content);
result = jscbObject.removeAngleBrackets(result);

jscbObject.getElem("result").innerHTML=result;
```

Discussion

As mentioned elsewhere in this book, all built-in objects in JavaScript have a literal representation in addition to their more formal object representation. For instance, an `Array` can be created as follows:

```
var newArray = new Array('one','two','three');
```

or using the array literal notation:

```
var newArray = ['one','two','three'];
```

The same is true for objects. The notation for object literals is pairs of property names and associated values, separated by commas, and wrapped in curly brackets:

```
var newObj = {
    prop1 : "value",
    prop2 : function() { ... },
    ...
};
```

The property/value pairs are separated by colons. The properties can be scalar data values, or they can be functions. The object members can then be accessed using the object dot-notation:

```
var tmp = newObj.prop2();
```

Or:

```
var val = newObj.prop1 * 20;
```

Or:

```
getElem("result").innerHTML=result;
```

Using an object literal, we can wrap all of our library's functionality in such a way that the functions and variables we need aren't in the global space. The only global object is the actual object literal, and if we use a name that incorporates functionality, group, purpose, author, and so on, in a unique manner, we effectively namespace the functionality, preventing name clashes with other libraries.

This is the approach I use for every library, whether I create the library or use another, such as jQuery, Dojo, Prototype, and so on. As we'll see later in the book, object literal notation is also the notation used by JSON, which is now formally a part of the ECMAScript 5 specification.

See Also

See Recipe 17.1 for a discussion related to packaging your code into a library for external distribution. Also check out Chapter 19 for recipes related to JSON.

16.12 Rediscovering "this" with Prototype.bind

Problem

You want to control the scope assigned a given function.

Solution

Use the new ECMAScript 5 function `bind` method:

```
window.onload=function() {

    window.name = "window";

    var newObject = {
        name: "object",

        sayGreeting: function() {
            alert("Now this is easy, " + this.name);
            nestedGreeting = function(greeting) {
              alert(greeting + " " + this.name);
            }.bind(this);

            nestedGreeting("hello");
        }
    }

    newObject.sayGreeting("hello");
}
```

If the method isn't supported in your target browser(s), extend the `Function` object with the code popularized by the *Prototype.js* JavaScript library:

```
Function.prototype.bind = function(scope) {
  var _function = this;

  return function() {
    return _function.apply(scope, arguments);
  }
}
```

Discussion

The this keyword represents the owner or scope of the function. The challenge associated with this in current JavaScript libraries is that we can't guarantee which scope applies to a function.

In the solution, the literal object has a method, sayGreeting, which prints a message out using an alert, and then maps another nested function to its property, nestedGreeting.

Without the Function.bind method, the first message printed out would say, "Now this is easy object", but the second would say, "hello window". The reason the second printout references a different name is that the nesting of the function disassociates the inner function from the surrounding object, and all *unscoped* functions automatically become the property of the window object.

What the bind method does is use the apply method to bind the function to the object passed to the object. In the example, the bind method is invoked on the nested function, binding it with the parent object using the apply method.

bind is particularly useful for timers, such as setInterval. Example 16-4 is a web page with script that uses setTimeout to perform a countdown operation, from 10 to 0. As the numbers are counted down, they're inserted into the web page using the element's innerHTML property. Since most browsers have not implemented Function.bind as a standard method yet, I added the Function.prototype.bind functional code.

Example 16-4. Demonstration of the utility of Function.bind for timers

```
<!DOCTYPE html>
<head>
<title>Using bind with timers</title>
<meta http-equiv="Content-Type" content="text/html; charset=utf-8" />
<style type="text/css">
#item { font-size: 72pt; margin: 70px auto;
        width: 100px;}
</style>

<script>

if (!Function.bind) {
   Function.prototype.bind = function(scope) {
      var _function = this;

      return function() {
        return _function.apply(scope, arguments);
      }
   }
}

window.onload=function() {
   var theCounter = new Counter('item',10,0);
   theCounter.countDown();
```

```
}

function Counter(id,start,finish) {
    this.count = this.start = start;
    this.finish = finish;
    this.id = id;
    this.countDown = function() {
        if (this.count == this.finish) {
            this.countDown=null;
            return;
        }
        document.getElementById(this.id).innerHTML=this.count--;
        setTimeout(this.countDown.bind(this),1000);
    };

}
</script>
</head>
<body>
<div id="item">
10
</div>
</body>
```

If the line in bold text in the code sample had been the following:

```
setTimeout(this.countDown, 1000);
```

The application wouldn't have worked, because the object scope and counter would have been lost when the method was invoked in the timer.

16.13 Chaining Your Object's Methods

Problem

You wish to define your object's methods in such a way that more than one can be used at the same time, like the following, which retrieves a reference to a page element *and* sets the element's `style` property:

```
document.getElementById("elem").setAttribute("class","buttondiv");
```

Solution

The ability to directly call one function on the result of another in the same line of code is known as *method chaining*. It requires specialized code in whatever method you want to chain.

For instance, if you want to be able to chain the changeAuthor method in the following object, you must also return the object after you perform whatever other functionality you need:

```
function Book (title, author) {
  var title = title;
  var author = author;
  this.getTitle=function() {
    return "Title: " + title;
  }

  this.getAuthor=function() {
    return "Author: " + author;
  }

  this.replaceTitle = function (newTitle) {
    var oldTitle = title;
    title = newTitle;
  }

  this.replaceAuthor = function(newAuthor) {
    var oldAuthor = author;
    author = newAuthor;
  }
}

function TechBook (title, author, category) {

  var category = category;
  this.getCategory = function() {
    return "Technical Category: " + category;
  }

  Book.apply(this,arguments);
  this.changeAuthor = function(newAuthor) {
    this.replaceAuthor(newAuthor);
    return this;
  }
}

window.onload=function() {

try {

 var newBook = new TechBook("I Know Things", "Shelley Powers", "tech");
 alert(newBook.changeAuthor("Book K. Reader").getAuthor());

} catch(e) {
  alert(e.message);
}

}
```

Discussion

The key to making method chaining work is to return a reference to the object at the end of the method, as shown in the `replaceAuthor` method in the solution:

```
this.changeAuthor = function(newAuthor) {
  this.replaceAuthor(newAuthor);
  return this;
}
```

In this example, the line `return this` returns the object reference.

Chaining is extensively used within the DOM methods, as shown throughout this book, when we see functionality such as:

```
var result = str.replace(/</g,'&lt;').replace(/>/g,'&gt;');
```

Libraries such as jQuery also make extensive use of method chaining:

```
$(document).ready(function() {
  $("#orderedlist").find("li").each(function(i) {
    $(this).append( " BAM! " + i );
  });
});
```

If you examine the development version of jQuery (which is uncompressed and very readable), you'll see `return this` sprinkled all throughout the library's methods:

```
// Force the current matched set of elements to become
// the specified array of elements
// (destroying the stack in the process)
// You should use pushStack() in order to do this,
// but maintain the stack

setArray: function( elems ) {
  // Resetting the length to 0, then using the native Array push
  // is a super-fast way to populate an object with
  // array-like properties
  this.length = 0;
  push.apply( this, elems );

  return this;
},
```

See Also

Chapter 17 provides an introduction to using jQuery in your JavaScript applications.

JavaScript Libraries

17.0 Introduction

JavaScript developers have never been luckier. Today, there are several very fine Java-Script framework libraries we can use for our applications that take care of many of the more tedious aspects of JavaScript development. In fact, you might be thinking about why you would even need a book on just plain JavaScript, when you can use framework libraries like Dojo, Ample SDK, Prototype, or jQuery (which I'm featuring later in this chapter). Why put up with the hassle of cross-browser issues, or the minutiae of creating and instantiating `XMLHttpRequest` object directly just to make a simple Ajax call?

I could reply that in order to use a framework library like jQuery to its best ability, you need to understand what's happening under the hood. This is a valid answer, because if you don't know what you can do with JavaScript, you won't know what you can do with a JavaScript framework library.

However, I have another, more philosophical reason why you need to understand the basics of JavaScript, inspired in part by a short story by one of my favorite science fiction writers, Isaac Asimov.

Isaac Asimov wrote a story, "The Feeling of Power," in the 1950s. In the story, a simple technician named Myron Aub astounds military, political, and scientific leaders with his astonishing discovery: the ability to perform mathematical calculations using only a person's own mental ability, and a piece of paper and pencil.

In the future time in which Aub lives, people had become dependent on machines to do all of their calculations; they had forgotten how to perform even the most basic math. Asimov was inspired to write the story out of his growing concern about our increasing mechanistic dependencies. When you consider that high schools no longer teach basic mathematical procedures, such as how to compute a logarithm manually, because of our use of calculators and computers, Asimov demonstrated remarkable prescience with his story.

Now, I don't think we're in danger of forgetting how to code JavaScript from scratch, or how to build our own libraries—at least, not in the near future. But why let the framework library builders have all the fun with the language?

See Also

Directions for downloading jQuery are covered in a later section, but you can access Ample SDK at *http://www.amplesdk.com/*, find Prototype.js at *http://www.prototypejs .org/*, and check out Dojo Toolkit at *http://www.dojotoolkit.org/*. Another lightweight framework is MooTools (*http://mootools.net/*).

17.1 Packaging Your Code

Problem

You want to package your code into one or more JavaScript files.

Solution

If your code is in one big file, look for opportunities to extract reusable functionality into self-contained objects in a separate library.

If you find you have a set of functions you repeat in all of your applications, consider packaging them for reuse via an object literal. Transform the following:

```
function getElem(identifier) {
   return document.getElementById(identifier);
}

function stripslashes (str) {
     return str.replace(/\\/g, '');
}

function removeAngleBrackets(str) {
     return str.replace(/</g,'&lt;').replace(/>/g,'&gt;');
}
```

to:

```
var jscbObject = {

   // return element
   getElem : function (identifier) {
      return document.getElementById(identifier);
   },

   stripslashes : function(str) {
      return str.replace(/\\/g, '');
   },

   removeAngleBrackets: function(str) {
```

```
        return str.replace(/</g,'&lt;').replace(/>/g,'&gt;');
    }
};
```

Discussion

In the solution, I've taken three functions in the global space and converted them into three methods on one object. Not only does this reduce the clutter in the global space, but it helps prevent clashes with similar-sounding function names in other libraries.

Even as functions, though, they're a step up from code that's hardcoded to a specific use. For instance, if your code has the following to access a `style` property from an element:

```
// get width
var style;
var elem = div.getElementById("elem");
if (elem.currentStyle) {
    style = elem.currentStyle["width"];
} else if (document.defaultView &&
document.defaultView.getComputedStyle) {
    style = document.defaultView.getComputedStyle(elem,null).
getPropertyValue("width");
}
```

Repeating this code in more than one function in your application can quickly bloat the size of the JavaScript, as well as make it harder to read. *Modularize* the code by extracting it into a reusable function, and eventually into a new member of your library object literal:

```
var BBObjLibrary = {

    // get stylesheet style
    getStyle : function (obj, styleName) {
        if (obj.currentStyle)
            return obj.currentStyle[styleName];
        else if (document.defaultView &&
document.defaultView.getComputedStyle)
            return document.defaultView.getComputedStyle(obj,null).
getPropertyValue(styleName);
        return undefined;
    },
    ...
}
```

Even when you split your code into libraries of reusable objects, look for an opportunity to modularize your code into layers of functionality.

I have one library, *bb.js*, that provides basic functionality such as event handling, accessing generic style elements, processing keyboard events, and so on. I have another library, *mtwimg.js*, I use to provide image handling in a web page, similar to what the popular library Lightbox 2 provides. The latter is built up on top of the former, so that

I don't have to repeat the functionality in both libraries, but I also keep my *bb.js* library small, and focused.

When I created a third library, *accordion.js*, which creates automatic accordion widgets (also sometimes called collapsible sections), it was also built on the *bb.js* generic library, considerably reducing the development time. More importantly, if I eventually decide to drop support for my generic library in favor of another externally developed library, such as Dojo, Prototype, or jQuery, though the internal functionality in *accordion.js* and *mtwimg.js* has to change, the web pages that use both don't, because the latter two libraries' outward-facing functionality isn't affected. This is a concept known as *refactoring*: improving the efficiency of your code without affecting the external functionality.

Oh, and while you're at it: document your code. Though you may provide a minified version of your code for production use, consider providing a *nonminified*, well-documented version of your JavaScript libraries so that others can learn from your code, the same as you're able to learn from theirs.

See Also

Recipe 17.3 covers how to *minify* your JavaScript. Object literals are covered in Recipe 16.11. You can download Lightbox 2 at *http://www.huddletogether.com/projects/lightbox2/*. Creating accordion sections is covered in Recipe 13.6.

17.2 Testing Your Code with JsUnit

Problem

You followed the good structuring practices outlined in Recipe 17.1 to create your JavaScript objects. Now you want to thoroughly test your code before packaging it into a library for distribution.

Solution

Use a tool like JsUnit to create test cases to formally test your library. If your library contains an object method like the following:

```
function addAndRound(value1,value2) {
    return Math.round(value1 + value2);
}
```

JsUnit test cases could look like the following:

```
function testAddAndRound() {
    assertEquals("checking valid", 6, addAndRound(3.55, 2.33));
    assertNaN("checking NaN",addAndRound("three",
"Four and a quarter"));
}
```

Both tests would be successful: the first because the result of the function is equal to the value 6, and both results are numbers; the second because the result of the function call is NaN, which is what the test checks.

Discussion

Chapter 10 covered error handling and debugging using a variety of tools, depending on your preferred development browser. Now, you're ready to create more formal tests, not only for your own use, but for others. These types of tests are called *unit tests*.

A good rule of thumb when it comes to unit testing is that every requirement or use case for a library function (or object method) should have an associated test case (or cases). The unit test checks that the requirement is met, and the library function performs as expected. You can develop your own tests, but using something like JsUnit simplifies the test writing.

 The version of JsUnit I use is a JavaScript implementation of the well-known JUnit testing software, and was developed by Edward Hieatt. JsUnit can be downloaded at *http://www.jsunit.net/*, which also includes links for documentation and examples.

Once you've downloaded, unzipped, and installed the JsUnit folder, preferably in a test folder for your own application, create several test application pages to test your library's functionality. Each page will contain a link to the JsUnit engine and your library. If the JsUnit library is located in its folder direction in your development subdirectory, link it as follows:

```
<script type="text/javascript" src="app/jsUnitCore.js"></script>
<script type="text/javascript" src="lib/myLibrary.js"></script>
```

Use the JsUnit methods in script in the page to perform the tests, and the JsUnit web page, testRunner.html, to actually run the test. How the test functions are written are based on JUnit testing methodology: the function names begin with test and can have no parameters.

The JsUnit assertions used to write tests are:

assert ([comment],booleanValue)
Tests that a function returns a Boolean value.

assertTrue([comment],booleanValue)
Tests for true return.

assertFalse([comment], booleanValue)
Tests for false return.

assertEquals([comment], value1, value2)
Tests return result or variable for equality.

assertsNotEquals ([comment],value1,value2)
> Tests return result or variable against another value for nonequality.

assertNull([comment],value)
> Tests for null value or return.

assertNotNull([comment],value)
> Tests for nonnull value or return.

The first parameter in the functions—the comment—is optional. However, it does make it much easier to determine which test fails if you can see a unique comment for the test.

JsUnit supports other functions, such as setUp and tearDown, called before the tests are started and after they have finished, respectively. There are also three functions, which provide trace messages:

warn(message,[value])
> Warning message, with optional value

inform(message,[value])
> Information message, with optional value

debug(message,[value])
> Debugging information, with optional value

Once you've created your test page, you run the tests within the testRunner.html page. If some of the tests fail, errors will display under the test progress bar. If you double-click the test, you can get the test fail information, as shown in Figure 17-1.

To see the JsUnit functionality in action, Example 17-1 contains a simple object with three methods.

Example 17-1. Simple JavaScript object with methods

```
var BBTest = {
  concatWithSpace : function(string1, string2) {
    return string1 + " " + string2;
  },
  discoverNumber : function(string, number) {
    return string.indexOf(number);
  },
  divideNumbers : function (value1, value2) {
    return value1 / value2;
  },
  addAndRound : function(value1, value2) {
    return Math.round(value1 + value2);
  }
}
```

Example 17-2 is a JsUnit test page that tests the object methods.

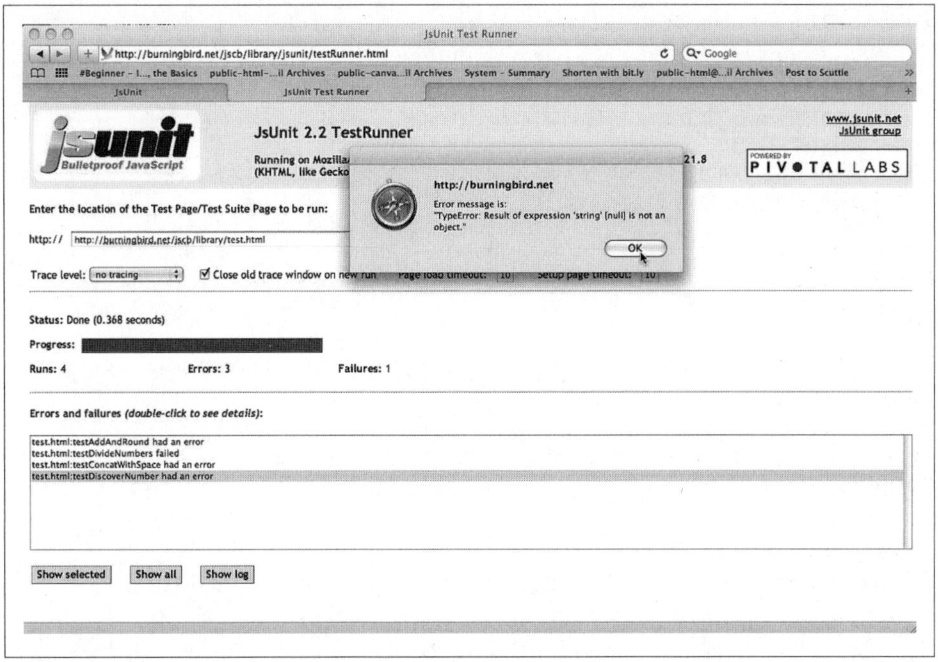

Figure 17-1. A JsUnit test run with some failed tests

Example 17-2. JsUnit Test page to test methods for object in Example 17-1

```
<!DOCTYPE html>
<head>
<title>Testing Library</title>
<script src="jsunit/app/jsUnitCore.js"></script>
<script src="test.js"></script>
<script>

function testConcatWithSpace() {
  inform("Testing concatWithSpace");
  assertEquals("Checking equality", "Shelley
Powers",BBTest.concatWithSpace("Shelley","Powers"));
}

function testDiscoverNumber() {
  inform("Testing discoverNumber");
  assertEquals("Checking valid params",5,
BBTest.discoverNumber("found5value",5));
}

function testDivideNumbers() {
  inform("Testing divideNumbers");
  assertNaN("Checking numeric ops with no numbers",
BBTest.divideNumbers("five","2"));
  assertNotEquals("Checking not equals","5",
BBTest.divideNumbers(10,2));
```

```
}

function testAddAndRound() {
  inform("Testing addAndRound");
  assertNaN("Checking NaN",BBTest.addAndRound("four",
"Three Quarter"));
  assertEquals("Checking correct values",6,
BBTest.addAndRound(2.33,3.45));
}

</script>

</head>
<body>
<p>Running tests of test.js. View source to see tests.</p>
</body>
```

Load the test page into the *testRunner.html* page, located within the *jsUnit* subdirectory.
All of the tests are successful, as shown in Figure 17-2.

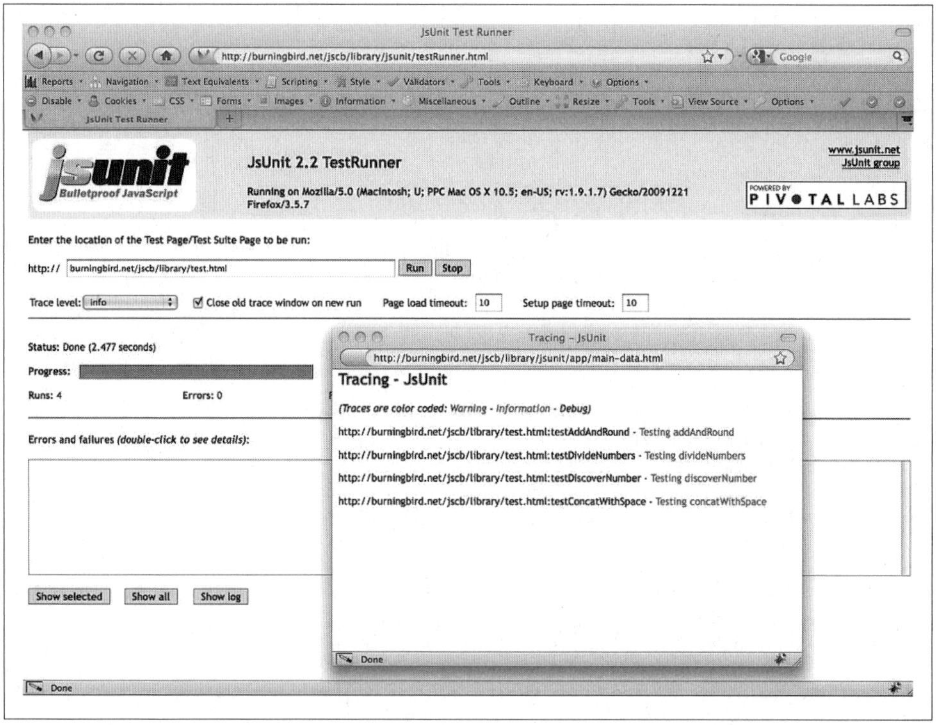

Figure 17-2. Successful run of test page in Example 17-2

JsUnit can be managed manually, or can be integrated into an automated testing environment, including integration with Apache Ant.

17.3 Minify Your Library

Problem

You want to compactly package your code for wider distribution.

Solution

After you've optimized your library code and tested it thoroughly through unit testing, compress it with a JavaScript optimizer.

Discussion

Once you've created your library, optimized it for efficiency, and run it through your unit testing, you're ready to prep your code for production use.

One preparation to make is to compress the JavaScript as much as possible, so the file is small and loads quickly. JavaScript compression is handled through *minify* applications you can find online, such as the well-known JavaScript Compressor, created by Dean Edwards, shown in Figure 17-3.

See Also

You can find JavaScript minifiers and compressors all over the Web by searching for "compress JavaScript" or "JavaScript minify". Dean Edwards's JavaScript compression tool can be found at *http://javascriptcompressor.com/*.

17.4 Hosting Your Library

Problem

You want to *open source* your code, but you don't want to have to maintain the libraries on your own server.

Solution

Use one of the source code hosts to host your code, and provide the tools to manage collaboration with other developers.

Discussion

One of the beautiful things about JavaScript is that many of the libraries and applications are open source, which means that not only are they typically free to use, but you can also adapt the library with your innovations, or even collaborate on the original. I strongly encourage open sourcing your libraries as much as possible. However, unless

Online Javascript compressor

Compress and obfuscate Javascript code online completely free using this compressor.

Paste your code: How to use?

```
   inform("Testing addAndRound");
   assertNaN("Checking NaN",BBTest.addAndRound("four","Three Quarter"));
   assertEquals("Checking correct values",6,BBTest.addAndRound(2.33,3.45));
}

//]]>
</script>

</head>
<body>
<p>Running tests of test.js. View source to see tests.</p>
</body>
```

(Compress) (Clear)   Base62 encode ☑ Shrink variables ☐

Copy:

```
eval(function(p,a,c,k,e,r){e=function(c){return(c<a?"":e(parseInt(c/a)))+
((c=c%a)>35?String.fromCharCode(c+29):c.toString(36))};if(!''.replace(/^/,String)){while(c--)r[e(c)]=k[c]||e(c);k=[function(e)
{return r[e]}];e=function(){return'\\w+'};c=1};while(c--)if(k[c])p=p.replace(new RegExp('\\b'+e(c)+'\\b','g'),k[c]);return p}('<!q
r><e><f>7 s</f><0 g="t/u/v.a"></0><0 g="h.a"></0><0>8 w(){9("7 i");b("1 x","j k",4.i("j","k"))}8 y(){9("7 l");b("1 z
A",5,4.l("B",5))}8 C(){9("7 c");m("1 D E F G H",4.c("I","2"));J("1 K L","5",4.c(10,2))}8 M(){9("7 d");m("1 N",4.d("O","P Q"));b("1
R S",6,4.d(2.T,3.U))}</0></e><n><p>V o W h.a.X Y Z 11 o.</p>
</n>',62,64,'script|Checking|||BBTest|||Testing|function|inform|js|assertEquals|divideNumbers|addAndRound|head|title|src|test
|concatWithSpace|Shelley|Powers|discoverNumber|assertNaN|body|tests||DOCTYPE|html|Library|jsunit|app|jsUnitCore|testC
oncatWithSpace|equality|testDiscoverNumber|valid|params|found5value|testDivideNumbers|numeric|ops|with|no|numbers|fiv
e|assertNotEquals|not|equals|testAddAndRound|NaN|four|Three|Quarter|correct|values|33|45|Running|of|View|source|to||see
'.split('|'),0,{}))
```

compression ratio: 1135/1058=1.073

(Decode)

Figure 17-3. Result of compressing the code from Example 17-1

you have the resources to mount a public-facing source code control system, you'll want to use one of the sites that provide support for open source applications.

One source code host is Google Code (*http://code.google.com/hosting/*), which contains a simple user interface to start a new project and upload code. You can choose between two version control software systems (Subversion and Mercurial), as well as one of a host of open source licenses.

There is a wiki component to each project where you can provide documentation, and a way to provide updates for those interested in the project. The site also provides issue-tracking software for people to file bugs, in addition to a Downloads link and a separate link for source code.

The SVG-enabling software SVGWeb, mentioned in Chapter 15, is hosted in Google Code. Figure 17-4 shows the front page for the project and the links to all of the secondary support pages, including the Wiki, Downloads, Issues, Source, and so on. There is no charge for hosting an application on Google Code.

Another increasingly popular host for open source projects is *github (http://github .com)*. Unlike Google Code, there are limits to what is supported for a free account on the service, but JavaScript libraries should not tax these limits. You shouldn't be faced with costs, as long as your projects are open source and publicly available. However, if you want to use the service for a private collaboration with several others, this service is available at a cost.

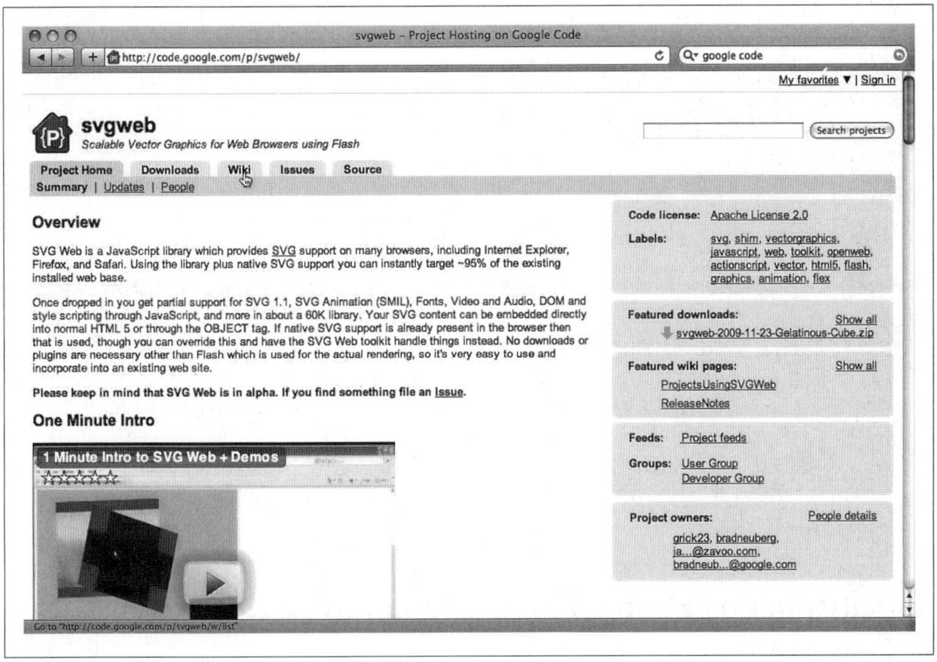

Figure 17-4. SVGWeb hosted at Google Code

As with Google Code, github supports source code control and collaboration from several people, including records of issues, downloads, a wiki support page, and a nice graphs page that provides graphics of language support, usage, and other interesting indicators.

The very popular jQuery library is hosted on github, as shown in Figure 17-5, though you download jQuery from its own domain.

Figure 17-5. The github page for the jQuery library

> Source Forge (*http://sourceforge.net/*) used to be the place to host your open source software in the past. However, the site blocks access to certain countries listed in the United States Office of Foreign Assets Control sanction list, and has fallen out of favor with many open source developers.

17.5 Using an External Library: Building on the jQuery Framework

Problem

You want to create application-specific libraries without having to create your own library of reusable routines.

Solution

Use one of the framework JavaScript libraries, such as Prototype, Dojo, or jQuery, in order to provide the basic functionality you need, but isolate the use so that you can swap frameworks if needed.

Discussion

There are good reasons—aside from the time saved—for using an existing JavaScript framework library such as jQuery. One is that the code is more robustly tested by several people. Another is that you can tap into a community of support when you run into problems in your applications.

I'm focusing primarily on jQuery because it is the library incorporated into most of the applications I use, including Drupal, the Content Management System (CMS) I use at my site. It's also small, specific, modular, and relatively uncomplicated. However, libraries such as Prototype, Dojo, Mootools, and others are also good, and you should examine each before making a decision.

 Download jQuery from *http://jquery.com/*. You can access both a minified version of the library and an uncompressed developer version.

To use jQuery, include a link to the library before providing links to your own or other, secondary libraries:

```
<script type="text/javascript" src="jquery.js"></script>
```

There are several application-specific libraries that are dependent on jQuery, so you may want to check if they provide jQuery as part of their own installation.

One aspect of jQuery that differs from most of the examples in this book is that jQuery's "starting" point for script is not `window.onload`, as I've used with most of the code samples. Instead, the jQuery library provides a page start routine that waits for DOM elements to be loaded, but does not wait for images or other media to finish loading. This beginning point is called the *ready event*, and looks like the following:

```
$(document).ready(function() {
    ...
});
```

The code snippet demonstrates a couple of other things about jQuery. First, notice the dollar sign element reference: `$(document)`. In jQuery, the dollar sign (`$`) is a reference to the main jQuery class, and acts as a selector for all element access in the application. If you're working with jQuery, use the jQuery selector rather than code your own element access, because the jQuery selector comes with prepackaged functionality essential for jQuery to operate successfully.

The syntax you use when querying for page elements is the same as the syntax for the `querySelector` and `querySelectorAll` methods, described in Chapter 11. It's based on CSS selector syntax for accessing a named element, such as the following:

```
#divOne{
    color: red;
}
```

Using jQuery to access this element looks like this:

```
$("#divOne").click(function() {
    alert("Well Hi World!");
});
```

This code snippet returns a reference to the `div` element identified by `divOne`, and then attaches a function to the element's `onclick` event handler that prints out a message.

The code also demonstrates another fundamental aspect of jQuery—it makes heavy use of *method chaining*. Method chaining is a way of appending methods one to another. In the code, rather than return a reference to the `div` element and then attach the event handler function to it, you attach the event handler directly to the element request.

There is extensive documentation and tutorials on using jQuery, so I'll leave an in-depth overview of jQuery for an off-book exercise. However, I did want to cover one important aspect of using jQuery—or any framework library with your own applications.

The key to making these work now and in the future is to wrap the library use in such a way that you can swap one library out for another, without having to recode your applications—or, at least, minimize the amount of recoding you would have to do.

Rather than use the jQuery ready event, create your own so you don't build a higher-level dependency on jQuery. Rather than use jQuery methods directly in your business logic, use your own objects and methods, and call the jQuery methods within these. By providing a layer of abstraction between the implementation of your application's business logic and the external framework library, if someday you stumble upon Frew, the Wonder Library, you can swap out jQuery (or Prototype, or Dojo) and build on Frew.

See Also

jQuery Cookbook (*http://oreilly.com/catalog/9780596159788/*) by Cody Lindley (O'Reilly) is an excellent book providing a comprehensive overview and detailed how-tos for jQuery. It's what I'm using to come up to speed on this powerful little library, and provides the best coverage on writing jQuery plug-ins (see Recipe 17.7).

See Recipe 11.4 for the use of the Selectors API and selector syntax. And see Recipe 16.13 for more on object method chaining.

17.6 Using Existing jQuery Plug-ins

Problem

You've made the decision to use jQuery as a framework. Now you want to incorporate some jQuery plug-ins and ensure they don't clash with your object libraries.

Solution

When you've found the plug-in(s) you want to use, check the documentation for all methods and properties, not just those you're interested in. Make sure that there isn't anything in the plug-in that can generate unwanted side effects when used in conjunction with your own application. Focus on using plug-ins that provide exactly what you need, and only what you need. Try to avoid over-generic plug-ins. Also make sure there aren't name clashes between the external plug-in and any you've created yourself.

As an example of a single-purpose, tightly focused plug-in, the jQuery Validation plug-in's only purpose is to validate form field data. It can validate for Zip code, email address, even credit card format. To use, annotate your form fields with specific classes, such as `required` for required fields, or `email` to validate the field as email. An example is the following, from the jQuery plug-in site:

```
<form class="cmxform" id="commentForm" method="get" action="">
 <fieldset>
   <legend>A simple comment form with submit validation and default
messages</legend>
   <p>
     <label for="cname">Name</label>
     <em>*</em><input id="cname" name="name" size="25"
class="required" minlength="2" />
   </p>
   <p>
     <label for="cemail">E-Mail</label>
     <em>*</em><input id="cemail" name="email" size="25"
class="required email" />
   </p>
   <p>
     <label for="curl">URL</label>
     <em>  </em><input id="curl" name="url" size="25"  class="url"
value="" />
   </p>
   <p>
     <label for="ccomment">Your comment</label>
     <em>*</em><textarea id="ccomment" name="comment" cols="22"
class="required"></textarea>
   </p>
   <p>
     <input class="submit" type="submit" value="Submit"/>
   </p>
 </fieldset>
 </form>
```

Then, in your script, make one function call:

```
j$("#commentForm").validate();
```

It doesn't get simpler than that.

Discussion

The plug-in in the solution, jQuery Validation, provides a small set of methods and several events that you can capture in order to perform any additional validation. You can also provide custom configuration for all displayed messages. Single-purpose, tightly focused plug-ins with few methods that provide events that you can intercept and customize for appearance should integrate well with your application.

Once integrated, though, you'll also need to incorporate unit tests for the plug-in, in addition to your own functions. You'll also have to check for updates to the plug-ins, and be aware of any issues and bugs. In particular, look for updates or potential problems with new releases of jQuery.

 The Validation plug-in can be downloaded at *http://docs.jquery.com/ Plugins/Validation*. Look for jQuery plug-ins at *http://plugins.jquery .com/*.

17.7 Convert Your Library to a jQuery Plug-in

Problem

You want to convert your library methods and functions into a jQuery plug-in for use by others.

Solution

If you want your method to participate in the jQuery chain and be used with selectors, assign your method to the `jQuery.fn` property:

```
jQuery.fn.increaseWidth = function() {
   return this.each(function() {
      var width = $(this).width() + 10;
      $(this).width(width);
   });
};
```

If your plug-in has one or more separate functions that do not need to participate in the jQuery chain, or be attached to a selector, create a `jQuery` function directly on the `jQuery` object:

```
jQuery.bbHelloWorld = function(who) {
   alert ("Hello " + who + "!");
};
```

If your function uses the jQuery dollar sign function ($) and you're concerned that the library could be used with other libraries that make use of $, wrap your function in an anonymous function. Instead of using the following jQuery method approach:

```
jQuery.fn.flashBlueRed = function() {
    return this.each(function() {
      var hex = rgb2hex($(this).css("background-color"));
      if (hex == "#0000ff") {
        $(this).css("background-color", "#ff0000");
      } else {
        $(this).css("background-color", "#0000ff");
      }
    });
};
```

use the following anonymous function syntax:

```
;(function($) {
    $.fn.flashBlueRed = function() {
      return this.each(function() {
        var hex = rgb2hex($(this).css("background-color"));
        if (hex == "#0000ff") {
          $(this).css("background-color", "#ff0000");
        } else {
          $(this).css("background-color", "#0000ff");
        }
      });
    };
})(jQuery);
```

Discussion

It's relatively simple to create a jQuery plug-in once you understand the nuances of the jQuery plug-in infrastructure.

If you're interested in creating a jQuery method that can be used with a jQuery selector and participate in the jQuery chain, you'll use the first syntax shown in the solution:

```
jQuery.fn.increaseWidth = function() {
    return this.each(function() {
      var width = $(this).width() + 10;
      $(this).width(width);
    });
};
```

However, if you want to make use of the dollar sign function ($) within the code, but still have the plug-in work within a multiple library setting, wrap the method in an anonymous function:

```
;(function($) {
    $.fn.flashBlueRed = function() {
      return this.each(function() {
        var hex = rgb2hex($(this).css("background-color"));
        if (hex == "#0000ff") {
          $(this).css("background-color", "#ff0000");
        } else {
          $(this).css("background-color", "#0000ff");
        }
      });
```

```
    };
})(jQuery);
```

Notice the following line in both examples:

```
return this.each(function () {
```

This code is necessary to allow the method to work on whatever is returned by the selector, regardless of whether it's a single item or a group of items. The line begins the code block that includes your actual method code.

Check out the semi-colon (;) just before the anonymous function. I picked this trick up from Cody Lindley in *jQuery Cookbook (http://oreilly.com/catalog/9780596159788/)* (O'Reilly). Putting the semicolon before the anonymous function ensures that the function won't break if another plug-in forgets to terminate a method or function with a semi-colon.

If you're only interested in adding a `jQuery` function that isn't part of the jQuery chain or which makes use of a selector, use the jQuery function syntax:

```
jQuery.bbHelloWorld = function(who) {
    alert ("Hello " + who + "!");
};
```

Once you have created your plug-in code, package it in a separate file; to use the code, all someone has to do is include the script, following the jQuery script.

An example of a plug-in file is shown in Example 17-3. This file has a couple of functions, specific to converting an RGB value to a hexadecimal. All of the functions are added to the `jQuery` object, and each is preceded by "bb", to act as namespace for the function.

The `bbGetRGB` function in the library is actually a function that exists as an internal (not publicly exposed) function within the jQuery User Interface (UI) library. It was originally created by Blair Mitchelmore for the `highlightFade` jQuery plug-in. However, I didn't want to include the jQuery UI, so I just borrowed the function for the example.

Example 17-3. A jQuery plug-in

```
// Parse strings looking for color tuples [255,255,255]
// pulled from internal jQuery function
jQuery.bbGetRGB = function(color) {
    var result;

    // Check if we're already dealing with an array of colors
    if ( color && color.constructor == Array && color.length == 3 )
        return color;

    // Look for rgb(num,num,num)
    if (result = /rgb\(\s*([0-9]{1,3})\s*,\s*([0-9]{1,3})\s*,\s*([0-
9]{1,3})\s*\)/.exec(color))
        return [parseInt(result[1],10), parseInt(result[2],10),
parseInt(result[3],10)];
```

```
    // Look for rgb(num%,num%,num%)
    if (result = /rgb\(\s*([0-9]+(?:\.[0-9]+)?)\%\s*,\s*([0-9]+(?:\.
[0-9]+)?)\%\s*,\s*([0-9]+(?:\.[0-9]+)?)\%\s*\)/.exec(color))
        return [parseFloat(result[1])*2.55, parseFloat(result[2])*
2.55, parseFloat(result[3])*2.55];

    // Look for #a0b1c2
    if (result = /#([a-fA-F0-9]{2})([a-fA-F0-9]{2})([a-fA-F0-9]{2})/.
exec(color))
        return [parseInt(result[1],16), parseInt(result[2],16),
parseInt(result[3],16)];

    // Look for #fff
    if (result = /#([a-fA-F0-9])([a-fA-F0-9])([a-fA-F0-9])/.
exec(color))
        return [parseInt(result[1]+result[1],16), parseInt(result[2]+result[2],16),
parseInt(result[3]+result[3],16)];

    // Look for rgba(0, 0, 0, 0) == transparent in Safari 3
    if (result = /rgba\(0, 0, 0, 0\)/.exec(color))
        return colors['transparent'];

    // Otherwise, we're most likely dealing with a named color
        return colors[$.trim(color).toLowerCase()];
};

jQuery.bbPadHex = function (value) {
    if (value.toString().length == 1) {
        value = "0" + value;
    }
    return value;
};

jQuery.bbConvertRGBtoHex = function(rgbString) {
    var colors = $.bbGetRGB(rgbString);
    var red = $.bbPadHex(parseInt(colors[0]).toString(16));
    var green = $.bbPadHex(parseInt(colors[1]).toString(16));
    var blue = $.bbPadHex(parseInt(colors[2]).toString(16));

    return "#" + red + green + blue;
};
```

bbPadHex, bbConvertRGBtoHex, and bbGetRGB are added as jQuery functions, the
flashBlueRed method is wrapped in an anonymous function, and the increaseWidth
method is a straight jQuery method. Example 17-4 shows the two methods in action.
Notice how the increaseWidth method is chained to the flashBlueRed method, and both
work on the element returned with the jQuery selector.

Example 17-4. Web page and application that use the new plug-in

```html
<!doctype html>
<html>
  <head>
  <style>
  #test
  {
    background-color: #0000ff;
    width: 500px;
    padding: 10px;
    color: #ffffff;
    font-weight: bold;
    font-size: larger;
  }
  </style>
    <script type="text/javascript" src="jquery.js"></script>
    <script type="text/javascript" src="basic.js"></script>

    <script type="text/javascript">

      $(document).ready(function() {
        $("#test").click(function() {
          $(this).flashBlueRed().increaseWidth();
        });
      });
    </script>
  </head>
  <body>
  <div id="test">
    hi, click me to change color
  </div>
  </body>
</html>
```

17.8 Safely Combining Several Libraries in Your Applications

Problem

You want to incorporate more than one external library, as well as your own, into one application without each stepping all over the others.

Solution

The safest approach for using multiple libraries is to pick ones that are all based on the same framework, such as using only libraries based on Dojo, Prototype, or jQuery, the framework used in earlier recipes.

If that strategy doesn't work, make sure the libraries all use good programming practices, and none are overriding functionality or event handling provided by the others.

Discussion

Regardless of library purpose, there are fundamental rules governing the behavior of libraries that must be followed. Well-designed libraries do not do things like this:

```
window.onload=function() {...}
```

I use the DOM Level 0 `window.onload` event handler with the examples in the book because it's quick, simple, and doesn't add a lot of code to the sample. However, if you have one library that uses the old DOM Level 0 event handling, it will overwrite the event capturing utilized by the other libraries and your own application. Well-designed libraries don't use DOM Level 0 event handling. Well-designed libraries also namespace all of their functionality. You won't find the following in a well-defined library:

```
function foo() { ... }
function bar() { ... }
```

Each function like this ends up in the global space, which increases the likelihood of clashes with other libraries, and your own applications. Well-designed libraries use object literals to namespace their functionality:

```
var BigObject = {
    foo : function () { },
    bar : function () { }
}
```

A library that plays well with other libraries and applications will not extend existing objects via the `prototype` object. Yes, I know it's a wonderful way of extending objects, and fundamental to JavaScript, but you can't control one library from overriding another if both are extending the `prototype` property for the same object. Besides, if the framework and external libraries you use don't extend existing objects via the object's `prototype`, this leaves you free to play in your application.

Come to that, library builders should never assume that their library is the only one used in a project.

Well-designed libraries provide event hooks so that you can hook into the library at the points where it performs a major action. In Recipe 17.7, the jQuery plug-in described in the solution provided event handler hooks you can use to provide your own functionality before or after the plug-in's validation routine.

Well-designed libraries provide good documentation of all of the publicly exposed bits, including methods, properties, and events. You shouldn't have to guess how to use the library, or examine minute portions of the code, in order to figure out what you need to do.

Well-designed libraries are well-tested, and provide a way to report bugs and view existing bugs. If there's a major security problem with an existing library, you need to know about it. If there are minor bugs, you need to know about these, too. Libraries that provide a subdirectory with self-tests rate high in my book.

Well-designed libraries provide nonminified, original source code. This isn't essential—just helpful, and something I look for in a library.

It goes without saying that a good library is one actively maintained, but it can't hurt to repeat this assertion. An even better library is one that's open sourced, and maintained by a community of users—or is one you can maintain on your own, if the original maintainer can no longer perform this action.

To summarize:

- A good library does not use DOM Level 0 event handling.
- A well-defined library uses object literals to namespace its functionality.
- A well-defined library introduces few global objects.
- Libraries that play well with others provide event hooks. Well-behaved libraries also don't extend existing objects via the `prototype` property.
- Solid libraries are well-tested, and hopefully provide these self-tests as deliverables.
- Stable libraries are actively maintained and, preferably, open sourced.
- Secure libraries provide documentation of known bugs and problems, and a way to report on any bugs and problems you find.
- Usable libraries are well-documented. Bandwidth-friendly libraries are optimized and compressed, though you can always compress the library yourself
- Confident libraries aren't built on the assumption that no other library will be used.

For the most part, you should be able to find what you need and have it work with your preferred framework. Be cautious when it comes to using a library that requires you add a new framework, which then needs to coexist with another framework. However, most well-built framework libraries *could* work with others.

As an example of framework coexistence, and since I'm focusing on jQuery in this chapter, if you use jQuery, you can use another framework library, such as Prototype, MooTools, or Dojo. The use of global namespaces should prevent name clashes. The only exception to the namespace rule is the dollar sign ($), function, which is also used by Prototype. You can override the use of the $ by adding the following, after all the libraries have been loaded:

```
jQuery.noConflict();
```

Once you add this code, instead of:

```
$("#elem").fadeOut('slow');
```

use:

```
jQuery("#elem").fadeOut('slow');
```

There are other approaches, too, including assigning a new short character replacement, but these are detailed in the jQuery documentation.

You can use most well-made framework libraries together, but there is tremendous overlap in functionality between the libraries, and this overlap in functionality comes with a cost: bandwidth to download the libraries. Try to avoid using more than one framework library at a time. Find the one you like, and be prepared to commit to it for some time to come.

See Also

The jQuery web page documenting how to use the framework with other libraries is at *http://docs.jquery.com/Using_jQuery_with_Other_Libraries*.

CHAPTER 18

Communication

18.0 Introduction

This book has explored a lot of subjects, but the functionality that revolutionized web client development is (arguably) Ajax. With Ajax, we're no longer dependent on the slow, cumbersome round-trips and associated page load times that plagued early websites. Now we can make an Ajax call, get some data, update the page—sometimes without the user even being aware that the activity is happening.

Ajax is also a relatively uncomplicated functionality, at least compared to other JavaScript functionality I've covered in the book. The main steps to an Ajax application are:

- Prepare the server-side API call.
- Make the call.
- Process the result.

Of course, there are interesting challenges that can occur at any time during these three steps, but for a basic application, it really is just that simple.

Ajax is now joined by a new communication kid: the `postMessage`. This new functionality originated with HTML5, though it has since split off to its own specification. It's an uncomplicated functionality that allows for easy communication between a parent and child window, even if the child window is located in another domain.

 There are two other new communication APIs in work: Cross Origin Resource Sharing (CORS) and the Web Sockets API. Both are being developed in the W3C, and both are currently in Working Draft state: CORS at *http://www.w3.org/TR/access-control/* and Web Sockets at *http://dev.w3.org/html5/websockets/*.

CORS is a way of doing cross-domain Ajax calls, and is currently implemented in Firefox 3.5 and up, and Safari 4.x and up. The Web Sockets API is a bidirectional communication mechanism, implemented only in Chrome at this time.

18.1 Accessing the XMLHttpRequest Object

Problem

You want to access an instance of the XMLHttpRequest object.

Solution

If you're not concerned about support for IE6, you can use the following:

```
var xmlHttp = new XMLHttpRequest();
```

This works with all of the target browsers for this book, and is the only method I used in examples in the book. However, if you must still support IE6 and you're not using one of the JavaScript libraries, you'll need to use the following cross-browser code:

```
if (window.XMLHttpRequest) {
    xmlHttp = new XMLHttpRequest();
} else if (window.ActiveXObject) {
    xmlHttp = new ActiveXObject("Microsoft.XMLHTTP");
}
```

Discussion

Microsoft invented the XMLHttpRequest object as an ActiveX object. However, the XMLHttpRequest object that we know and primarily use today, even in newer versions of IE, evolved independently. There's now an effort underway to standardize the object within the W3C.

The XMLHttpRequest object isn't very complicated. Here are the supported client application methods, which are explored in more depth in the other recipes in this chapter:

open
: Initializes a request. Parameters include the method (GET or POST), the request URL, whether the request is asynchronous, and a possible username and password. By default, all requests are sent asynchronously.

setRequestHeader
: Sets the MIME type of the request.

send
: Sends the request.

sendAsBinary
: Sends binary data.

abort
: Aborts an already sent request.

getResponseHeader
: Retrieves the header text, or null if the response hasn't been returned yet or there is no header.

getAllResponseHeaders
> Retrieves the header text for a multipart request.

All of our target browsers support the methods just listed. There's also an additional, frequently used method, overrideMimeType, not included in the list. I didn't include it because it's not part of the XMLHttpRequest standardization process, and one browser company doesn't support it (Microsoft).

The overrideMimeType method is normally used to override the MIME type of the server response., As an example, the following overrides whatever the server's response is, and the returned resource is treated as XML:

```
xmlhttp.overrideMimeType('text/xml');
```

Lack of support for overrideMimeType is an inconvenience but not a showstopper. Either we'll need to process the data according to MIME type or ensure that our server applications set the proper content header for the data. For instance, if we want to ensure that our client application receives data as XML, we can use the following in a PHP application:

```
header("Content-Type: text/xml; charset=utf-8");
```

There are also a number of properties supported by all browsers:

status
> The HTTP result status of the request response.

statusText
> The response text returned from the server.

readyState
> The state of the request.

responseText
> The text-based response to the request.

responseXML
> The response to the request as an XML-based DOM object.

There are other properties, some proprietary and some not, but these are the ones we're concerned with in this book.

A major restriction associated with the XMLHttpRequest object is the *same-origin security restriction*. This means that you can't use XMLHttpRequest to make a service request to an API in another domain.

See Also

Recipe 18.7 provides a solution and a discussion related to the same-origin restriction with XMLHttpRequest. The W3C XMLHttpRequest draft specification can be found at *http://www.w3.org/TR/XMLHttpRequest/*.

18.2 Preparing the Data for Transmission

Problem

You want to process form data for an Ajax call rather than send the data via the usual form submit process.

Solution

Access the data from form fields or other page elements:

```
var state = document.getElementById("state").value;
```

If the data is user-supplied, such as the data from a text field, encode the result using the encodeURIComponent function, so any characters in the text that could impact on the Ajax call are escaped:

```
var state = encodeURIComponent(document.getElementById("state").value);
```

You shouldn't need to escape data from radio buttons, checkboxes, selections, or any other form element in which your application controls the data, as you can make sure those values are in the proper format.

Discussion

Depending on the type of action, data for an Ajax call can come from user-supplied text, such as that typed into a text field. When it is, you'll need to ensure that the data can be used in the Ajax request by escaping certain characters, such as an ampersand (&), plus sign (+), and equal sign (=).

The following string:

```
This is $value3 @value &and ** ++ another
```

Is encoded as:

```
This%20is%20%24value3%20%40value%20%26and%20**%20%2B%2B%20another
```

The spaces are escaped as %20, the dollar sign as %24, the ampersand as %26, and the plus sign as %2B, but the alphanumeric characters and the reserved asterisk characters are left alone.

Once escaped, the data can be attached as part of an Ajax request. If the Ajax request is going to be a POST rather than a GET request, further encoding is needed—the spaces should be encoded as pluses. Replace the %20 with +, following the call to encodeURIComponent. You can package this functionality for reuse:

```
function postEncodeURIComponent(str) {
    str=encodeURIComponent(str);
    return str.replace(/%20/g,"+");
}
```

The escaping ensures that the Ajax request will be successfully communicated, but it doesn't ensure that the Ajax request is safe. All data input by unknown persons should always be scrubbed to prevent SQL injection or cross-site scripting (XSS) attacks. However, this type of security should be implemented in the server-side application, because if people can put together a GET request in JavaScript, they can put together a GET request directly in a browser's location bar and bypass the script altogether. The only time you need to scrub the input in JavaScript is if you're planning on embedding a user's data directly back into the page.

18.3 Determining the Type of Query Call

Problem

You're not sure whether to send your Ajax call as a GET or a POST.

Solution

For an update, send a POST request. Set the first parameter in the XMLHttpRequest open method to POST, call the setRequestHeader to set the content-type, and send the request parameters in the send method:

```
xmlhttp.open('POST',url,true);
xmlhttp.setRequestHeader("Content-Type",
"application/x-www-form-urlencoded");
xmlhttp.send(param);
```

For a query, send a GET request. The first parameter in the XMLHttpRequest open method is set to GET, the parameters are appended on to the URL for the request, and null is passed as parameter in the send method:

```
url = url + "?" + param;
xmlhttp.open('GET',url,true);
xmlhttp.send(null);
```

Discussion

What the server component of the application is expecting has the most impact on your request type decision. However, accepted practice is that a request for data should be made with a GET, while an update should occur through a POST.

The request type practice used in Ajax is derived from RESTful guidelines (REST translates as REpresentational State Transfer). According to the guidelines, there are four types of HTTP requests:

GET
    Used for retrieving information, with parameters attached to the URL.
POST
    Used for creating new data, and parameters are sent via function parameter.

DELETE
   Used for deleting data records, and parameters are sent via function parameter.

PUT
   Used to send an update, and parameters are sent via function parameter.

There is broad support only for the GET and POST requests at this time, so I'll focus on these two.

A GET HTTP request is used to retrieve information, and the parameters are attached to the URL in the request. A function that processes a GET request could look like the following, which passes two parameters with the request:

```
function sendData(evt) {

    // cancel default form submittal
    evt = evt || window.event;
    evt.preventDefault();
    evt.returnValue = false;

    // get input data
    var one = encodeURIComponent(document.getElementById("one").value);
    var two = encodeURIComponent(document.getElementById("two").value);
    var params = "one=" + one + "&two=" + two;

    // prep request
    if (!http) {
        http = new XMLHttpRequest();
    }
    var url = "ajaxserver.php?" + params;
    http.open("GET", url, true)

    // callback function
    http.onreadystatechange=processResult;

    // make Ajax call with params
    http.send(null);
}
```

In the code snippet, two parameters are passed with the request. First, they're escaped, using `encodeURIComponent`. Next, they're attached to the URL using RESTful GET notation:

```
http://somecompany.com?param=value&param2=value2
```

The parameters for the `XMLHttpRequest` open method are:

GET
   A GET request

url
   The URL for the service

`true`
   Whether the operation is performed asynchronously

The optional third asynchronous parameter should always be set to true, or the page blocks until the server request returns. This is not a cool thing to do to your page readers.

There are two other optional parameters not shown: username and password. If the application is protected on the server side, the username and password can be used for authentication.

A POST request with two parameters would look like the following:

```
function sendData(evt) {

    // cancel default form submittal
    evt = evt || window.event;
    evt.preventDefault();
    evt.returnValue = false;

    // get input data
    var one = encodeURIComponent(document.getElementById("one").value).
    replace(/%20/g,'+');
    var two = encodeURIComponent(document.getElementById("two").value).
    replace(/%20/g,'+');
    var params = "one=" + one + "&two=" + two;

    // prep request
    if (!http) {
        http = new XMLHttpRequest();
    }
    var url = "ajaxserver.php";
    http.open("POST", url, true)

    // set up Ajax headers
    http.setRequestHeader("Content-Type",
    "application/x-www-form-urlencoded");
    http.setRequestHeader("Content-length", params.length);
    http.setRequestHeader("Connection", "close");

    // callback function
    http.onreadystatechange=processResult;

    // make Ajax call with params
    http.send(params);
}
```

This code differs from the code for the GET request in several ways. The first is that after encoding, the spaces in the parameters are converted from %20 to +. The second is they're concatenated into a parameter-formatted string, which is sent within the send method.

The first parameter of the open method is set to POST, but the other two parameters are the same as those sent with the GET request: the application URL and the asynchronous flag.

Additional calls are made to the setRequestHeader method, to set Connection and Content-length request headers. You can use it to send any HTTP request header, but you must provide the Content-Type for the POST—in this case, a multipart form request.

Both of the request approaches set the callback function for the Ajax object call's onreadystatechange event handler.

See Also

Recipe 18.1 covers how to get the XMLHttpRequest object, and Recipe 18.2 covers how to encode parameters.

18.4 Adding a Callback Function to an Ajax Request

Problem

You want to process the result of an Ajax request, even if the result does an update rather than a query.

Solution

When processing the Ajax request, before calling the XMLHttpRequest object's send method, assign the object's onreadystatechange property to the callback function's name:

```
xmlhttp.open("GET", url, true);
xmlhttp.onreadystatechange=callbackFunction;
xmlhttp.send(null);
```

Discussion

The readyState attribute for the XMLHttpRequest object is updated based on the state of the request. In order to check the state of the request, you need to assign the onreadystatechange event handler to a callback function that is called every time the ready state changes.

You should use onreadystatechange with every Ajax call, even one in which you're doing an update rather than processing a request. Without the callback function, you have no way of knowing if the update operation was successful, and if not, what kind of error occurred.

The readyState property has the values shown in Table 18-1 during the Ajax request.

Table 18-1. Values of XMLHttpRequest readyState property

Value	STATE	Purpose
0	UNINITIALIZED	open has not been called yet
1	LOADING	send has not been called yet
2	LOADED	send has been called

Value	STATE	Purpose
3	INTERACTIVE	Downloading response is not completed
4	COMPLETED	Request is complete

You should not set onreadystatechange if your request is synchronous, because the code won't continue until the request returns anyway—you can check the result of the operation in the very next line of the code, if you're so inclined.

 I can't stress strongly enough: please avoid synchronous Ajax calls. Locking the page up until the request finishes is just not a good thing.

See Also

Recipe 18.5 covers how to check the status and results of an Ajax request.

18.5 Checking for an Error Condition

Problem

You want to check the status of the Ajax request.

Solution

In addition to checking the readyState property in the onreadystatechange event handler, you can also check the XMLHttpRequest's status:

```
function processResult() {
    if (http.readyState == 4 && http.status == 200) {
        document.getElementById("result").innerHTML=http.responseText;
    }
}
```

Discussion

The XMLHttpRequest's status property is where the response to the request is returned. You hope for a value of 200, which means the request is successful. If the request is something else, such as 403 (forbidden) or 500 (server error), you can access the XMLHttpRequest's statusText property to get more detailed information:

```
function processResult() {
    if (http.readyState == 4 && http.status == 200) {
        document.getElementById("result").innerHTML=http.responseText;
    } else {
        alert(http.statusText);
```

```
        }
    }
```

18.6 Processing a Text Result

Problem

You want to process HTML returned as text.

Solution

If you trust the server application, and the text is formatted to use immediately in the page, the simplest approach is to assign the text to the `innerHTML` property of the element where it should be placed:

```
function processResult() {
    if (http.readyState == 4 && http.status == 200) {
        document.getElementById("result").innerHTML=http.responseText;
    }
}
```

Discussion

If you're writing both the server and client sides of the application, why make it hard on yourself? Format the response in the server application in such a way that it can be added into the web page using the easiest possible approach, and nothing is easier than `innerHTML`.

However, if the response text isn't formatted for immediate publication, you'll have to use `String` functions, possibly in combination with regular expressions, to extract the data you need. If HTML formatting isn't possible or desirable, and you have any control of the server application, try to format it either as XML or JSON, both of which can be more easily supported in the JavaScript environment.

See Also

See Recipe 19.1 for extracting information from an XML response. See Recipe 19.4 and Recipe 19.5 for converting JSON formatted text into a JavaScript object. See Recipe 12.1 for an introduction to `innerHTML`.

18.7 Making an Ajax Request to Another Domain (Using JSONP)

Problem

You want to query for data using a web service API, such as the Netflix API or Twitter's API. However, the Ajax same-origin policy prevents cross-domain communication.

Solution

The most commonly used technique to solve the cross-domain problem, and the approach I recommend, is to create a server-side proxy application that is called in the Ajax application. The proxy then makes the call to the other service's API, returning the result to the client application. This is safe, secure, and very efficient, because we can clean the data before returning it to the Ajax application.

There is another approach: use JSONP (JSON, or JavaScript Object Notation, with Padding) to workaround the security issues. I once used this approach to create a mashup between Google Maps and a Flickr query result:

```
function addScript( url) {
    var script = document.createElement('script');
    script.type="text/javascript";
    script.src = url;
    document.getElementsByTagName('head')[0].appendChild(script);
```

The URL looked like the following, including a request to return the data formatted as JSON, and providing a callback function name:

```
http://api.flickr.com/services/rest/?method=flickr.photos.search&user_id=xxx&api_ke
y=xxx&format=json&
jsoncallback=processPhotos
```

When the `script` tag is created, the request to Flickr is made, and since I passed in the request for a JSON formatted result and provided a callback function name, that's how the return was provided. The callback string is similar to the following:

```
// assign photos globally, call first to load
function processPhotos(obj) {
  photos = obj.photos.photo;
  ...
}
```

The callback function would pass the data formatted as a JSON object in the function argument.

Discussion

Ajax works within a protected environment that ensures we don't end up embedding dangerous text or code into a web page because of a call to an external application (which may or may not be secure).

The downside to this security is that we can't directly access services to external APIs, such Flickr, Twitter, and Google. Instead, we need to create a server-side proxy application, because server applications don't face the cross-domain restriction.

The workaround is to use something like JSONP, demonstrated in the solution. Instead of using `XMLHttpRequest`, we convert the request URL into one that we can attach to a script's `src` attribute, because the `script` element does not follow the same-origin policy. It couldn't, or we wouldn't be able to embed applications such as Google Maps into the application.

If the service is amenable, it returns the data formatted as JSON, even wrapping it in a callback function. When the script is created, it's no different than if the function call is made directly in our code, and we've passed an object as a parameter. We don't even have to worry about converting the string to a JavaScript object.

It's a clever trick, but I don't recommend it. Even with secure services such as Flickr and Twitter, there is the remote possibility that someone could find a way to inject JavaScript into the data via the client-side application for the service, which can cause havoc in our own applications.

It's better to be smart then clever. Use a proxy application, scrub the result, and then pass it on to your client application.

See Also

Chapter 19 covers JSON in more detail.

18.8 Populating a Selection List from the Server

Problem

Based on a user's actions with another form element, you want to populate a selection list with values.

Solution

Capture the change event for the trigger form element:

```
document.getElementById("nicething").onchange=populateSelect;
```

In the event handler function, make an Ajax call with the form data:

```
var url = "nicething.php?nicething=" + value;
xmlhttp.open('GET', url, true);
xmlhttp.onreadystatechange = getThings;
xmlhttp.send(null);
```

In the Ajax result function, populate the selection list:

```
    if(xmlhttp.readyState == 4 && xmlhttp.status == 200) {
      var select = document.getElementById("nicestuff");
      select.length=0;
      var nicethings = xmlhttp.responseText.split(",");
      for (var i = 0; i < nicethings.length; i++) {
        select.options[select.length] =
new Option(nicethings[i],nicethings[i]);
      }
      select.style.display="block";
    } else if (xmlhttp.readyState == 4 && xmlhttp.status != 200) {
```

```
                    document.getElementById('nicestuff').innerHTML =
              'Error: Search Failed!';
                  }
```

Discussion

One of the more common forms of Ajax is to populate a **select** or other form element based on a choice made by the user. Rather than have to populate a **select** element with many options, or build a set of 10 or 20 radio buttons, you can capture the user's choice in another form element, query a server application based on the value, and then build the other form elements based on the value—all without leaving the page.

Example 18-1 demonstrates a simple page that captures the change event for radio buttons within a **fieldset** element, makes an Ajax query with the value of the selected radio button, and populates a selection list by parsing the returned option list. A comma separates each of the option items, and new options are created with the returned text having both an option label and option value. Before populating the **select** element, its length is set to 0. This is a quick and easy way to truncate the **select** element— removing all existing options, and starting fresh.

Example 18-1. Creating an on-demand select Ajax application

```html
<!DOCTYPE html>
<head>
<title>On Demand Select</title>
<style>
#nicestuff
{
  display: none;
  margin: 10px 0;
}
#nicething
{
  width: 400px;
}
</style>
<script>

var xmlhttp;

function populateSelect() {

  var value;

  var inputs = this.getElementsByTagName('input');
  for (var i = 0; i < inputs.length; i++) {
    if (inputs[i].checked) {
      value = inputs[i].value;
      break;
    }
  }

  // prepare request
```

```
  if (!xmlhttp) {
    xmlhttp = new XMLHttpRequest();
  }
  var url = "nicething.php?nicething=" + value;
  xmlhttp.open('GET', url, true);
  xmlhttp.onreadystatechange = getThings;
  xmlhttp.send(null);
}
// process return
function getThings() {
   if(xmlhttp.readyState == 4 && xmlhttp.status == 200) {
     var select = document.getElementById("nicestuff");
     select.length=0;
     var nicethings = xmlhttp.responseText.split(",");
     for (var i = 0; i < nicethings.length; i++) {
        select.options[select.length] = new Option(nicethings[i],
nicethings[i]);
     }
     select.style.display="block";
   } else if (xmlhttp.readyState == 4 && xmlhttp.status != 200) {
     alert("No items returned for request");
   }
}

window.onload=function() {

   document.getElementById("submitbutton").style.display="none";
   document.getElementById("nicething").onclick=populateSelect;
}

</script>

</head>
<body>
<form action="backupprogram.php" method="get">
<p>Select one:</p>
<fieldset id="nicething">
<input type="radio" name="nicethings" value="bird" /><label
for="bird">Birds</label><br />
<input type="radio" name="nicethings" value="flower" /><label
for="flower">Flowers</label><br />
<input type="radio" name="nicethings" value="sweets" /><label
for="sweets">Sweets</label><br />
<input type="radio" name="nicethings" value="cuddles" />
<label for="cuddles">Cute Critters</label>
</fieldset>
<input type="submit" id="submitbutton" value="get nice things" />
<select id="nicestuff"></select>
</body>
```

The form does have an assigned **action** page, and a submit button that's hidden when the script is first run. These are the backup if scripting is turned off.

18.9 Using a Timer to Automatically Update the Page with Fresh Data

Problem

You want to display entries from a file, but the file is updated frequently.

Solution

Use Ajax and a timer to periodically check the file for new values and update the display accordingly.

The Ajax we use is no different than any other Ajax request. We'll use a GET, because we're retrieving data. We put together the request, attach a function to the onreadystatechange event handler, and send the request:

```
var url = "updatedtextfile.txt";
xmlhttp.open("GET", url, true);
xmlhttp.onreadystatechange=updateList;
xmlhttp.send(null);
```

The fact that we're doing a direct request on a static text file might be new, but remember that a GET request is more or less the same as the requests we put into the location bar of our browsers. If something works in the browser, it should successfully return in an Ajax GET request...within reason.

In the code that processes the response, we just place the new text into a new unordered list item and append it to an existing ul element:

```
// process return
function processResponse() {
   if(xmlhttp.readyState == 4 && xmlhttp.status == 200) {
     var li = document.createElement("li");
     var txt = document.createTextNode(xmlhttp.responseText);
     li.appendChild(txt);
     document.getElementById("update").appendChild(li);
   } else if (xmlhttp.readyState == 4 && xmlhttp.status != 200) {
     alert(xmlhttp.responseText);
   }
}
```

The new part is the timer. The timer is controlled with start and stop buttons. When the start button is clicked the first time, the code disables the start button first, initiates the first Ajax call, and then starts a timer. There's a reason for this, as we'll see in a second:

```
// timer
function startTimer() {
  populateList();
  timer=setTimeout(timerEvent,15000);
}
```

The reason we want to make the Ajax call first is that the timer function `timerEvent` checks the `readyState` of the `XMLHttpRequest` object when it's invoked. If the value is not 4, which means the last request was completed, it doesn't make another Ajax call. We don't want to have multiple requests out at the same time:

```
function timerEvent() {
  if (xmlhttp.readyState == 4) {
    populateList();
  }
  timer=setTimeout(timerEvent, 15000);
}
```

Lastly, we'll add a cancel timer event. In this case we're using a global timer variable, but in a production application we want to use either an anonymous function to wrap everything, or create an object literal to maintain both data and methods:

```
function stopTimer() {
  clearTimeout(timer);
}
```

Discussion

The key to using timers with Ajax calls is to make sure that the last call is completed before making the next. By including a check on the `XMLHttpRequest` object's `readyState` property, if the value isn't 4, we know to skip this Ajax call and just reset the timer for the next go round. We can also put in a check for the request status, and cancel the timer event altogether if we're concerned about hitting a failing service, over and over again.

When I ran the application that included the solution code, I changed the text file by using the Unix `echo` command:

```
$ echo "This is working" > text.txt
```

And then watched as the text showed up on the page, as shown in Figure 18-1.

If you're planning on using this form of polling with another service, such as against the Twitter API, be aware that if you're considered abusive of the service, you may get kicked off. Check to see if there are restrictions for how often you can access a service using the API.

 Depending on the browser, you may run into caching issues if you access the *text.txt* file locally. Providing a full URL should prevent this from occurring.

A few years ago, there was interest in a push rather than pull type of Ajax communication. Encompassed under the coined term of *Comet*, the concept was that the server would initiate the communication and push the data to the client, rather than the client pulling the data from the server. Eventually, the concept led to work in the W3C on a

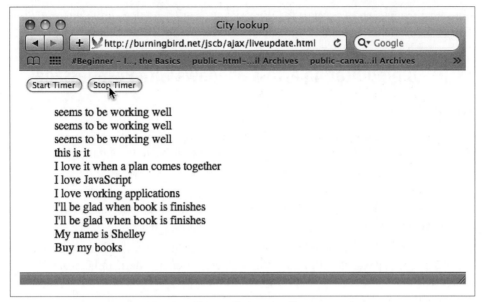

Figure 18-1. Demonstration of updates from polled Ajax calls

new JavaScript API called WebSockets. Currently only implemented in Chrome, Web-Sockets enables bidirectional communication between server and client by using the `send` method on the WebSocket object for communicating to the server, and then attaching a function to WebSocket's `onmessage` event handler to get messages back from the server, as demonstrated in the following code from the Chromium Blog:

```
if ("WebSocket" in window) {
  var ws = new WebSocket("ws://example.com/service");
  ws.onopen = function() {
    // Web Socket is connected. You can send data by send() method.
    ws.send("message to send"); ....
  };
  ws.onmessage = function (evt) { var received_msg = evt.data; ... };
  ws.onclose = function() { // websocket is closed. };
} else {
  // the browser doesn't support WebSocket.
}
```

Another approach is a concept known as *long polling*. In long polling, we initiate an Ajax request as we do now, but the server doesn't respond right away. Instead, it holds the connection open and does not respond until it has the requested data, or until a waiting time is exceeded.

See Also

See Recipe 14.8 for a demonstration of using this same functionality with an ARIA *live region* to ensure the application is accessible for those using screen readers. The W3C WebSockets API specification is located at *http://dev.w3.org/html5/websockets/*, and the

Chrome introduction of support for WebSockets is at *http://blog.chromium.org/2009/12/web-sockets-now-available-in-google.html*.

18.10 Communicating Across Windows with PostMessage

Problem

Your application needs to communicate with a widget that's located in an iFrame. However, you don't want to have to send the communication through the network.

Solution

Use the new HTML5 `postMessage` to enable back-and-forth communication with the iFrame widget, bypassing network communication altogether.

One or both windows can add an event listener for the new message event. To ensure the event handling works with IE as well as Opera, Firefox, Safari, and Chrome, using object detection:

```
function manageEvent(eventObj, event, eventHandler) {
   if (eventObj.addEventListener) {
      eventObj.addEventListener(event, eventHandler,false);
   } else if (eventObj.attachEvent) {
      event = "on" + event;
      eventObj.attachEvent(event, eventHandler);
   }
}
```

The sender window that has the iFrame prepares and posts the message to the widget window:

```
function sendMessage() {
  try {
    var farAwayWindow =
document.getElementById("widgetId").contentWindow;
    farAwayWindow.postMessage(
"dragonfly6.thumbnail.jpg,Dragonfly on flower",
                         'http://burningbird.net');
  } catch (e) {
    alert(e);
  }
};
```

Two parameters are required for the HTML5 implementation of `postMessage`: the first is the message string; the second is the target window's *origin*. If the iFrame window's source is something like *http://somecompany.com/test/testwindow.html*, then the target origin would be *http://somecompany.com*. You could also use "*" for the target origin. This is a wildcard, which means the value will match to any origin.

In the receiving window, an event listener picks up the message and responds accordingly. In this example, the string is split on the comma (,); the first part of the string is assigned the image element's `src` property, and the second is assigned the image element's `alt` property:

```
function receive(e) {

    var img = document.getElementById("image");
    img.src = e.data.split(",")[0];
    img.alt = e.data.split(",")[1];

    e.source.postMessage("Received " + e.data, "*");
}
```

In the code, the widget window responds with a `postMessage` of its own, but uses the wildcard origin. The widget window also doesn't check to see what domain sent the message. But when it responds, the host window checks `origin`:

```
function receive(e) {
  if (e.origin == "http://burningbird.net")
    ... does something with response message
}
```

Discussion

The `postMessage` functionality is based on listener/sender functionality. Example 18-2 contains an example sender page. It contains an iFrame in which a requested image is displayed when the cross-document communication finishes. When you click on the web page, a message is posted to the listener to parse the message, find the name for a photograph, and add the photograph to an `img` element in the page.

Example 18-2. Sender page

```
<!DOCTYPE html>
<head>
<title>Sender</title>
<script>

function manageEvent(eventObj, event, eventHandler) {
    if (eventObj.addEventListener) {
        eventObj.addEventListener(event, eventHandler,false);
    } else if (eventObj.attachEvent) {
        event = "on" + event;
        eventObj.attachEvent(event, eventHandler);
    }
}

window.onload=function() {

  manageEvent(document.getElementById("button1"),"click",sendMessage);
  manageEvent(window,"message",receive);

}

// make sure to change URL to your location
function sendMessage() {
```

```
    try {
        var farAwayWindow =
document.getElementById("widgetId").contentWindow;
        farAwayWindow.postMessage(
"dragonfly6.thumbnail.jpg,Dragonfly on flower",
                                'http://jscb.burningbird.net');
    } catch (e) {
        alert(e);
    }
};

// change URL to your location
function receive(e) {
    if (e.origin == "http://jscb.burningbird.net")
        alert(e.data);
}
</script>

</head>
<body>
<div><button id="button1">Load the photo</button></div>
<iframe src="example18-3.html" id="widgetId"></iframe>
</body>
```

Example 18-3 contains the listener page.

Example 18-3. Listener page

```
<!DOCTYPE html>
<head>
<title>Listener</title>
<script>

function manageEvent(eventObj, event, eventHandler) {
    if (eventObj.addEventListener) {
        eventObj.addEventListener(event, eventHandler,false);
    } else if (eventObj.attachEvent) {
        event = "on" + event;
        eventObj.attachEvent(event, eventHandler);
    }
}

window.onload=function() {

    manageEvent(window,"message",receive);

}

function receive(e) {

    var img = document.getElementById("image");
    img.src = e.data.split(",")[0];
    img.alt = e.data.split(",")[1];

    e.source.postMessage("Received " + e.data,
```

```
"http://burningbird.net");
}
</script>

</head>
<body>
<img src="" id="image" alt="" />
</body>
```

Figure 18-2 shows the page after the successful communication.

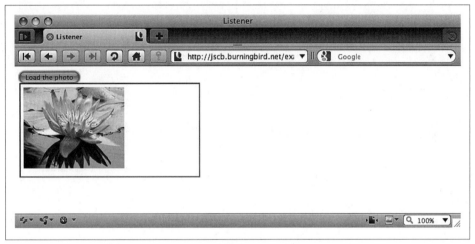

Figure 18-2. Result of postMessage communication and loading an image

The new `postMessage` will soon be joined by a message channel capability, and both are attuned to use with widgets. This capability enables a higher level of interactivity between the hosting window and the widget that wasn't possible before, either because of network activity or because of same-origin security restrictions.

The loosening of security restrictions is also a risk associated with `postMessage`. We can help mitigate the risk by following some simple rules:

- Use the `targetOrigin` rather than the wildcard (*) when posting a message.
- Use the `origin` value in the return message object to ensure the sender is the expected agent.
- Check and double-check message data received. Needless to say, don't pass it to `eval`, and avoid plunking the data directly into a page using `innerHTML`.

Companies providing widgets can also add a layer of security. For instance, when a person downloads a widget, he also registers the domain where the widget is used. This is the same functionality that Google uses when you use the Google Maps API: you register the domain where the map API is used, and if the domain differs, the API doesn't work.

The widget company can use this to check the message's origin, and also use this information when sending any `postMessage` response. In addition, the widget company can use whatever precaution necessary with the sent data and respond in kind.

Working with Structured Data

19.0 Introduction

Even though it's primarily a client-side development tool, JavaScript has access to several very sophisticated techniques and mechanisms for working with structured data.

Originally, most complex data management, particularly in relation to Ajax calls, was based either in HTML fragments or XML. HTML fragments are still popular. When returned from an Ajax request, the HTML formatted string can be used with `innerHTML` in order to easily append the HTML into the page. Of course, you have to trust the data you receive, and you can't manipulate it until you actually insert the data into the page. Either that, or use various `String` functions to parse pieces out of the HTML string.

Data returned as XML is a richer option, because you can use the string to create a separate document object, from which you can access individual elements, just like you query the web page document now.

XML data is still widely supported, but another structure has gained a great deal of popularity: JavaScript Object Notation, or JSON. It's so popular that JSON has been added to the most recent version of JavaScript, ECMAScript 5. JSON provides the richness of XML but without the performance hit client-side processing of XML can add.

JSON is basically the string serialization of JavaScript objects. Before ECMAScript 5, you had to use the `eval` function to convert the string to an object . Unfortunately, using the `eval` function on an unknown string is an application-security vulnerability. To ensure the string was safe, the originator of JSON, Douglas Crockford, created a library to process the JSON safely. The same functionality is now built into JavaScript.

Support for complex data extends beyond what is built into JavaScript. There are multiple approaches for annotating the web page elements with metadata that can be accessed within the page and without. Two metadata approaches, RDFa and

Microformats, have widespread support, including specialized JavaScript libraries. I'll be touching on these later in the chapter.

19.1 Process an XML Document Returned from an Ajax Call

Problem

You need to prepare your Ajax application to deal with data returned formatted as XML.

Solution

Access the returned XML via the `responseXML` property on the `XMLHttpRequest` object:

```
if (xmlHttpObj.readyState == 4 && xmlHttpObj.status == 200) {
    var citynodes = xmlHttpObj.responseXML.getElementsByTagName("city");
    ...
}
```

Discussion

When an Ajax request returns XML, it can be accessed as a document object via the `XMLHttpRequest` object's `responseXML` property. You can then use the query techniques covered in earlier chapters, such as Chapter 11, to access any of the data in the returned XML.

If the server-side application is returning XML, it's important that it return a MIME type of `text/xml`, or the `responseXML` property will be `null`. If you're unsure whether the API returns the proper MIME type, or if you have no control over the API, you can override the MIME type when you access the `XMLHttpRequest` object:

```
if (window.XMLHttpRequest) {
    xmlHttpObj = new XMLHttpRequest();
    if (xmlHttpObj.overrideMimeType) {
        xmlHttpObj.overrideMimeType('text/xml');
    }
}
```

The `overrideMimeType` is not supported with IE, nor is it supported in the first draft for the W3C `XMLHttpRequest` specification. If you want to use `responseXML`, either change the server-side application so that it supports the `text/xml` MIME type, or convert the text into XML using the following cross-browser technique:

```
if (window.DOMParser) {
    parser=new DOMParser();
    xmlResult = parser.parserFromString(xmlHttpObj.responseText,
    "text/xml");
} else {
    xmlResult = new ActiveXObject("Microsoft.XMLDOM");
    xmlResult.async = "false"
    xmlResult.loadXML(xmlHttpObj.responseText);
```

```
    }
    var stories = xmlResult.getElementsByTagName("story");
```

Parsing XML in this way adds another level of processing. It's better, if possible, to return the data formatted as XML from the service.

See Also

The W3C specification for `XMLHttpRequest` can be found at *http://www.w3.org/TR/ XMLHttpRequest/*.

19.2 Extracting Pertinent Information from an XML Tree

Problem

You want to access individual pieces of data from an XML document.

Solution

Use the same DOM methods you use to query your web page elements to query the XML document. As an example, the following will get all elements that have a tag name of `"story"`:

```
    var stories = xmlHttpObj.responseXML.getElementsByTagName("story");
```

Discussion

Once you have the XML document, you can use the DOM methods covered in Chapter 11 to query any of the data in the document via the Ajax `responseXML` property, or even one that you've created yourself from scratch.

To demonstrate, Example 19-1 shows a PHP application that returns an XML result when passed a category value. The application returns a list of stories by category, and their associated URL. If the category string isn't passed or the category isn't found, the application returns an error message that's formatted in the same formatting as the other values, except that the URL value is set to "none". This ensures a consistent result from the application.

It's not a complicated application or a complex XML result, but it's sufficient to demonstrate how XML querying works. Notice that the header is instructed to return the content with a MIME type of `text/xml`.

Example 19-1. PHP application that returns an XML result

```php
<?php

  //If no search string is passed, then we can't search
  if(empty($_GET['category'])) {
    $result =
"<story><url>none</url><title>No Category Sent</title></story>";
```

```php
  } else {
    //Remove whitespace from beginning & end of passed search.
    $search = trim($_GET['category']);
    switch($search) {
      case "CSS" :
        $result = "<story><url>
http://realtech.burningbird.net/graphics/css/opacity-returns-ie8
</url>" .
                  "<title>Opacity returns to IE8</title></story>" .
                  "<story>
<url>
http://realtech.burningbird.net/graphics/css/embedded-fonts-font-face
</url>" .
                  "<title>Embedded Fonts with Font Face</title>
</story>";
        break;
      case "ebooks" :
        $result = "<story><url>
http://realtech.burningbird.net/web/ebooks/kindle-clipping-limits
</url>" .
                  "<title>Kindle Clipping Limits</title></story>" .
                  "<story><url>
http://realtech.burningbird.net/web/ebooks/kindle-and-book-freebies
</url>" .
                  "<title>Kindle and Book Freebies</title></story>";
        break;
      case "video" :
        $result = "<story><url>
http://secretofsignals.burningbird.net/science/how-things-work/
video-online-crap-shoot</url>" .
                  "<title>The Video Online Crap Shoot</title>
</story>" .
                  "<story>
<url>http://secretofsignals.burningbird.net/toys-and-technologies/
gadgets/review-flip-ultra-camcorder</url>" .
                  "<title>Review of the Flip Ultra Camcorder</title>
</story>" .
                  "<story><url>
http://secretofsignals.burningbird.net/reviews/movies-disc/gojira

</url>" .
                  "<title>Gojira</title></story>" .
                  "<story><url>
http://secretofsignals.burningbird.net/reviews/movies-disc/
its-raging-squid</url>" .
                  "<title>It's a Raging Squid</title></story>";
        break;
      case "missouri" :
        $result =
"<story><url>http://missourigreen.burningbird.net/times-past/
missouri/tyson-valley-lone-elk-and-bomb</url>" .
        "<title>Tyson Valley, a Lone Elk, and a Bomb</title>
</story>";
        break;
      default :
```

```
        $result = "<story><url>none</url><title>No Stories Found</title></story>";
        break;
    }
}

$result ='<?xml version="1.0" encoding="UTF-8" ?>' .
          "<stories>" . $result . "</stories>";
header("Content-Type: text/xml; charset=utf-8");
echo $result;
?>
```

Example 19-2 shows a web page with a JavaScript application that processes a radio button selection for a **story** category. The application forms an Ajax request based on the category, and then processes the returned XML in order to output a list of stories, linked with their URLs.

Example 19-2. JavaScript application to process story information from returned XML

```
<!DOCTYPE html>
<html xmlns="http://www.w3.org/1999/xhtml" xml:lang="en" lang="en">
<head>
<title>Stories</title>
<meta charset="utf-8" />
<script type="text/javascript">
//<![CDATA[

var xmlHttpObj;

window.onload=function() {
  var radios = document.forms[0].elements["category"];
  for (var i = 0; i < radios.length; i++) {
    radios[i].onclick=getStories;
  }
}

function getStories() {
   // category
   var category = encodeURIComponent(this.value);

   // ajax object
   if (window.XMLHttpRequest) {
      xmlHttpObj = new XMLHttpRequest();
   }

   // build request
   var url = "stories.php?category=" + category;
   xmlHttpObj.open('GET', url, true);
   xmlHttpObj.onreadystatechange = getData;
   xmlHttpObj.send(null);

}
function getData() {
  if (xmlHttpObj.readyState == 4 && xmlHttpObj.status == 200) {
    try {
```

```
        var result = document.getElementById("result");
        var str = "<p>";

        var stories =
xmlHttpObj.responseXML.getElementsByTagName("story");
        for (var i = 0; i < stories.length; i++) {
          var story = stories[i];
          var url = story.childNodes[0].firstChild.nodeValue;
          var title = story.childNodes[1].firstChild.nodeValue;
          if (url === "none")
              str += title + "<br />";
          else
              str += "<a href='" + url + "'>" + title + "</a><br />";
        }

        // finish HTML and insert
        str+="</p>";
        result.innerHTML=str;
    } catch (e) {
      alert(e.message);
    }
  }
}
//]]>
</script>
</head>
<body>
<form id="categoryform">
CSS: <input type="radio" name="category" value="CSS" /><br />
eBooks: <input type="radio" name="category" value="ebooks" /><br />
Missouri: <input type="radio" name="category" value="missouri" />
<br />
Video: <input type="radio" name="category" value="video" /><br />
</form>
<div id="result">
</div>
</body>
</html>
```

When processing the XML code, the application first queries for all **story** elements, which returns a **nodeList**. The application cycles through the collection, accessing each **story** element in order to access the story URL and the title, both of which are child nodes. Each is accessed via the **childNodes** collection, and their data, contained in the **nodeValue** attribute, is extracted.

The story data is used to build a string of linked story titles, which is output to the page, as shown in Figure 19-1. Note that rather than use a succession of **childNodes** element collections to walk the trees, I could have used the Selectors API to access all URLs and titles, and then traversed both collections at one time, pulling the paired values from each, in sequence:

```
var urls = xmlHttpObj.responseXML.querySelectorAll("story url");
var titles = xmlHttpObj.responseXML.querySelectorAll("story title");
```

```
for (var i = 0; i < urls.length; i++) {
    var url = urls[i].firstChild.nodeValue;
    var title = titles[i].firstChild.nodeValue;
    if (url === "none")
        str += title + "<br />";
    else
        str += "<a href='" + url + "'>" + title + "</a><br />";
}
}
```

I could have also used getElementsByTagName against each returned story element—
anything that works with the web page works with the returned XML.

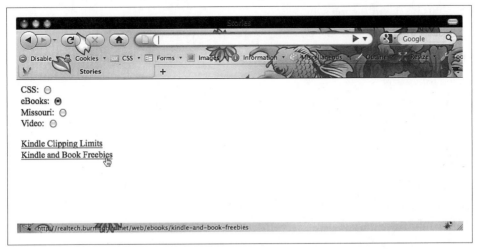

Figure 19-1. Processing XML: returning story titles and URLs from a server-side application

The try...catch error handling should catch any query that fails because the XML is
incomplete. In the example, the error is printed out in an alert—but you'll want to use
friendlier and more helpful error handling.

 The document returned in responseXML, or created using DOMParser, has
access to the XML DOM APIs, but not the HTML DOM APIs. For the
most part, this shouldn't be a problem, as most of the functionality
you'll use is based on the more generic XML DOM APIs.

See Also

Chapter 11 covers most of the DOM query techniques that work with the XML returned
via responseXML, as well as accessing the web page elements. Recipe 9.4 demonstrates
how to process radio button events, and Recipe 12.1 demonstrates how to use
innerHTML to update the web page contents.

Recipe 19.1 provides a way to process XML when it's returned as text, via `responseText`.

19.3 Generate a JavaScript Object with JSON, Old-School Style

Problem

You need to convert the JSON text from an Ajax call into a JavaScript object.

Solution

Use the `eval` function to evaluate the string formatted as JSON, creating a JavaScript object using the following syntax:

```
var jsonobj = '{"test" : "value1", "test2" : 3.44, "test3" : true}';
var obj = eval("(" + jsonobj + ")");
alert(obj.test2); // prints out 3.44
```

or the following:

```
var jsonobj = '{"test" : "value1", "test2" : 3.44, "test3" : true}';
eval("var obj="+jsonobj);
alert(obj.test);
```

Discussion

The solution presents a simple, three-property object created in JSON. To figure out how to create JSON, think about how you create an object literal and just translate it into a string.

If the object is an array:

```
var arr = new Array("one","two","three");
```

the JSON notation would be equivalent to the literal notation for the array:

```
"['one','two','three'];
```

If an object:

```
var obj3 = {
    prop1 : "test",
    result : true,
    num : 5.44,
    name : "Joe",
    cts : [45,62,13]};
```

the JSON notation would be:

```
{"prop1":"test","result":true,"num":5.44,"name":"Joe","cts":[45,62,13]}
```

Notice in JSON how the property names are in quotes, but the values are only quoted when they're strings. In addition, if the object contains other objects, such as an array, it's also transformed into its JSON equivalent. However, the object *cannot* contain methods. If it does, an error is thrown. JSON works with data objects only.

The two "old-school" techniques to generate objects from the JSON formatted string use the eval method. The first assigns the object to a variable and requires that you surround the JSON with parentheses:

```
var obj = eval ("(" + objJSON + ")");
```

The reason for the parentheses is so the eval statement treats the text as an object initializer, rather than some other type of code.

The second approach is to include the variable assignment as the left side of the expression and the JSON as the right, within the eval method:

```
eval("obj=" + objJSON);
```

The result of the eval function is a JavaScript object, in which you can access values directly:

```
alert(obj3.prop1); // prints out test
```

The use of JSON exploded with the growing popularity of Ajax. Rather than returning plain text, HTML, or XML, applications could return a text string formatted as JSON, and the text could be converted to a JavaScript object with one function call.

Of course, this meant that the JSON was inherently insecure. If you couldn't trust in the source of the string, you certainly couldn't trust it to the eval method, which processes whatever string is passed to it. To work around the insecurities of JSON, Douglas Crockford, the father of JSON, created *json2.js*, a small library that provides a safe version of eval. Once you include the library, you process the JSON using the following syntax:

```
var obj = JSON.parse(objJSON);
```

> Discover more variations of JSON syntax at *http://www.json.org*. The site also includes a link to *json2.js*.

See Also

Until the built-in JSON capability is supported in all your site's target browsers, you'll still need the old-school JSON techniques. However, using the *json2.js* library can emulate a built-in JSON object, introduced in Recipe 19.5.

19.4 Parse a JSON Formatted String

Problem

You want to safely create a JavaScript object from JSON. You also want to replace the numeric representation of true and false (0 and 1, respectively) with their Boolean counterparts (false and true).

Solution

Parse the object with the new JSON built-in capability, added to browsers in ECMA-Script 5. To transform the numeric values to their Boolean counterparts, create a replacer function:

```
var jsonobj = '{"test" : "value1", "test2" : 3.44, "test3" : 0}';
var obj = JSON.parse(jsonobj, function (key, value) {
   if (typeof value == 'number') {
      if (value == 0)
         value = false;
      else if (value == 1) {
         value = true;
      }
   }
   return value;
   });

alert(obj.test3); // prints false
```

Discussion

ECMAScript 5 added native support for JSON with the JSON object. It's not a complex object, as it only provides two methods: stringify and parse. Like Math, it's a static object that you use directly.

The parse method takes two arguments: a JSON formatted string and an optional replacer function. This function takes a key/value pair as parameters, and returns either the original value or a modified result.

In the solution, the JSON formatted string is an object with three properties: a string, a numeric, and a third property, which has a numeric value but is really a Boolean with a numeric representation: 0 is false, 1 is true.

To transform all 0, 1 values into false, true, a function is provided as the second argument to JSON.parse. It checks each property of the object to see if it is a numeric. If it is, the function checks to see if the value is 0 or 1. If the value is 0, the return value is set to false; if 1, the return value is set to true; otherwise, the original value is returned.

The ability to transform incoming JSON formatted data is essential, especially if you're processing the result of an Ajax request or JSONP response. You can't always control the structure of the data you get from a service.

 IE8 does not support the JSON object. Opera has placed some restrictions on what can be supported in JSON: strings must be double quoted, and there are no hexadecimal values and no tabs in strings.

See Also

See Recipe 19.5 for a demonstration of JSON.stringify.

19.5 Convert an Object to a Filtered/Transformed String with JSON

Problem

You need to convert a JavaScript object to a JSON formatted string for posting to a web application. However, the web application has data requirements that differ from your client application.

Solution

Use the JSON.stringify method, passing in the object as first parameter and providing a transforming function as the second parameter:

```
function convertBoolToNums(key, value) {
    if (typeof value == 'boolean') {
        if (value)
            value = 1;
        else
            value = 0;
    }
    return value;
};

window.onload=function() {

  var obj = {"test" : "value1", "test2" : 3.44, "test3" : false};
  var jsonobj = JSON.stringify(obj, convertBoolToNums, 3);

  alert(jsonobj); // test3 should be 0
}
```

Discussion

The `JSON.stringify` method takes three parameters: the object to be transformed into JSON, an optional function or array used either to transform or filter one or more object values, and an optional third parameter that defines how much and what kind of whitespace is used in the generated result.

In the solution, a function is used to check property values, and if the value is a Boolean, convert `false` to 0, and `true` to 1. The function results are transformed into a string if the return value is a number or Boolean. The function can also act as a filter: if the returned value from the function is `null`, the property/value pair are removed from the JSON.

You can also use an array rather than a function. The array can contain strings or numbers, but is a *whitelist* of properties that are allowed in the result. The following code:

```
var whitelist = ["test","test2"];

var obj = {"test" : "value1", "test2" : 3.44, "test3" : false};
var jsonobj = JSON.stringify(obj, whitelist, 3);
```

would result in a JSON string including the object's **test** and **test2** properties, but not the third property (**test3**):

```
{
   "test": "value1",
   "test2": 3.44
}
```

The last parameter controls how much whitespace is used in the result. It can be a number representing the number of spaces or a string. If it is a string, the first 10 characters are used as whitespace. If I use the following:

```
var jsonobj = JSON.stringify(obj, whitelist, "***");
```

the result is:

```
{
***"test": "value1",
***"test2": 3.44
}
```

The use of `stringify` with a replacer function worked with Safari 4, but did not successfully transform the Boolean value with Firefox. At the time this was written, there is an active bug for Firefox because the replacer function only works with arrays.

See Also

See Recipe 19.4 for a discussion on `JSON.parse`.

19.6 Convert hCalendar Microformat Annotations into a Canvas Timeline

Problem

You want to plot the events annotated with the hCalendar Microformat on a Canvas-based graph. The hCalendar event syntax can differ, as the following two legitimate variations demonstrate:

```
<p><span class="vevent">
 <span class="summary">Monkey Play Time</span>
 on <span class="dtstart">2010-02-05</span>
 at <span class="location">St. Louis Zoo</span>.
</span></p>

<div class="vevent" id="hcalendar-Event">
  <abbr class="dtstart" title="2010-02-25">February 25th</abbr>,
   <abbr class="dtend" title="2010-02-26"> 2010</abbr>
  <span class="summary">Event</span></div>
```

With one format, the dtstart class is on a span element; with the other format, the dtstart class is on an abbr element.

Solution

Find all elements with a class of vevent:

```
var events = document.querySelectorAll("[class='vevent']");
var v = events;
```

Within each, find the element with a class of dtstart. There should only be one, and there should always be one. By Microformat convention, if the dtstart element is an abbr, the start date is found in a title attribute on the element. If the dtstart element is a span, the start date is found in the element's textContent, and is then split out of the date string to find the actual day:

```
var days = new Array();
for (var i = 0; i < events.length; i++) {
   var dstart = events[i].querySelectorAll("[class='dtstart']");
   var dt;
   if (dstart[0].tagName == "SPAN") {
      dt = dstart[0].textContent;      }
   else if (dstart[0].tagName == "ABBR") {
      dt = dstart[0].title;
   }
   var day = parseInt(dt.split("-")[2]);
   days.push(day);
}
```

The value is then used to graph the line in a canvas element.

Discussion

Microformats are both simple and complicated. They're simple in that it's easy to find the data, but they're complicated because the rules surrounding the data are very loose. As the solution demonstrates, an hCalendar event start date can be recorded in span elements or abbr elements; the dates are ISO 8601, but could be just dates, or datetime.

The advantage to working with Microformats using client-side JavaScript is that we usually have some control over the format of the Microformats. For instance, if we have a social-networking site where people are entering events, we have no control over what events are created, but we do have control over the format and can ensure that it's consistent.

Once we know the form of the Microdata used in the page, it isn't complicated to get the data. For the most part, we're retrieving elements based on class name, and making queries on these elements' subtrees for elements with different class names. Though there are few rules to Microformats, there *are* rules. For instance, the hCalendar data used in the solution has at least three rules: the outer element has a vevent class, there must be a summary and a dtstart element, and if the dtstart element is a span, the data is the textContent; if it is an abbr, the data is the title.

Since IE8 does not support textContent, the code performs a test for textContent. If it isn't found, then IE8 gets the text from the (IE-originated) innerText or innerHTML property:

```
for (var i = 0; i < events.length; i++) {
    var dstart = events[i].querySelectorAll("[class='dtstart']");
    var dt;
    if (dstart[0].tagName == "SPAN") {
        if (dstart[0].textContent)
            dt = dstart[0].textContent;
        else
            dt = dstart[0].innerText;
    } else if (dstart[0].tagName == "ABBR") {
        dt = dstart[0].title;
    }
    var day = parseInt(dt.split("-")[2]);
    days.push(day);
}
```

Make sure to include the ExplorerCanvas *excanvas.js* library before your script, in order to ensure the canvas element and commands work with IE:

```
<!--[if IE]><script src="excanvas.js"></script><![endif]-->
```

Example 19-3 pulls all of the components together into a full-page application, including the Canvas drawing. The tick marks in the Canvas element are expanded to 10 times their size to make them easier to see on the line. The page is an event calendar for a month at the zoo.

Example 19-3. Extracting Microformat events from page and charting them on a Canvas line graph

```
<!DOCTYPE html>
<head>
<title>Microformats</title>
<!--[if IE]><script src="excanvas.js"></script><![endif]-->
<script>

window.onload=function() {

    var events = document.querySelectorAll("[class='vevent']");
    var v = events;
    var days = new Array();
    for (var i = 0; i < events.length; i++) {
        var dstart = events[i].querySelectorAll("[class='dtstart']");
        var dt;
        if (dstart[0].tagName == "SPAN") {
            if (dstart[0].textContent)
                dt = dstart[0].textContent;
            else
               dt = dstart[0].innerText;
        } else if (dstart[0].tagName == "ABBR") {
            dt = dstart[0].title;
        }
        var day = parseInt(dt.split("-")[2]);
        days.push(day);
    }

    var ctx = document.getElementById("calendar").getContext('2d');

    // draw out
    days.sort(function(a,b) { return a - b});

    ctx.fillStyle="red";
    ctx.strokeStyle="black";

    ctx.beginPath();
    ctx.moveTo(0,100);
    ctx.lineTo(280,100);
    ctx.stroke();

    for (var i = 0; i < days.length; i++) {
      var x1 = days[i] * 10;
      var t1 = 70;
      var x2 = 5;
      var t2 = 30;
      ctx.fillRect(x1,t1,x2,t2);
    }
}

</script>
</head>
<body>
<div>
  <p><span class="vevent">
    <span class="summary">Monkey Play Time</span>
```

```
       on <span class="dtstart">2010-02-05</span>
       at <span class="location">St. Louis Zoo</span>.
       </span>
       </p>
</div>
<div class="vevent">
  <abbr class="dtstart" title="2010-02-25">February 25th</abbr>,
  <abbr class="dtend" title="2010-02-26"> 2010</abbr>
  <span class="summary">Event</span>
</div>
<p>
    <span class="vevent">
    <span class="summary">Tiger Feeding</span>
    on <span class="dtstart">2010-02-10</span>
    at <span class="location">St. Louis Zoo</span>.
    </span>
</p>
<p><span class="vevent">
    <span class="summary">Penguin Swimming</span>
    on <span class="dtstart">2010-02-20</span>
    at <span class="location">St. Louis Zoo</span>.
    </span>
</p>
<div class="vevent">
    <abbr class="dtstart" title="2010-02-19">February 19th</abbr>,
    <abbr class="dtend" title="2010-02-26"> 2010</abbr>
    <span class="summary">Sea Lion Show</span>
</div>
<canvas id="calendar" style="width: 600px; height: 100px; margin: 10px; ">
    <p>Dates</p>
</canvas>
</body>
```

The application works in all of our target browsers, including IE8, as shown in Figure 19-2. IE7 does not support the `querySelectorAll` method.

See Also

For more on Microformats, see the Microformats website (*http://microformats.org/*).
See more on the `canvas` element in Chapter 15, and more on ExplorerCanvas in Recipe 15.2.

19.7 Glean Page RDFa and Convert It into JSON Using rdfQuery and the jQuery RDF Plug-in

Problem

You're using Drupal 7, a Content Management System (CMS) that annotates the page metadata with RDFa—Resource Description Framework (RDF) embedded into X/HTML. Here's an example of the type of data in the page (from the RDFa specification):

```
<h1>Biblio description</h1>
<dl about="http://www.w3.org/TR/2004/REC-rdf-mt-20040210/"
id="biblio">
  <dt>Title</dt>
   <dd property="dc:title">
RDF Semantics - W3C Recommendation 10 February 2004</dd>
  <dt>Author</dt>
   <dd rel="dc:creator" href="#a1">
    <span id="a1">
      <link rel="rdf:type" href="[foaf:Person]" />
      <span property="foaf:name">Patrick Hayes</span>
      see <a rel="foaf:homepage"
href="http://www.ihmc.us/users/user.php?UserID=42">homepage</a>
    </span>
   </dd>
</dl>
```

You want to convert that RDFa formatted data into a JavaScript object, and eventually into JSON for an Ajax call.

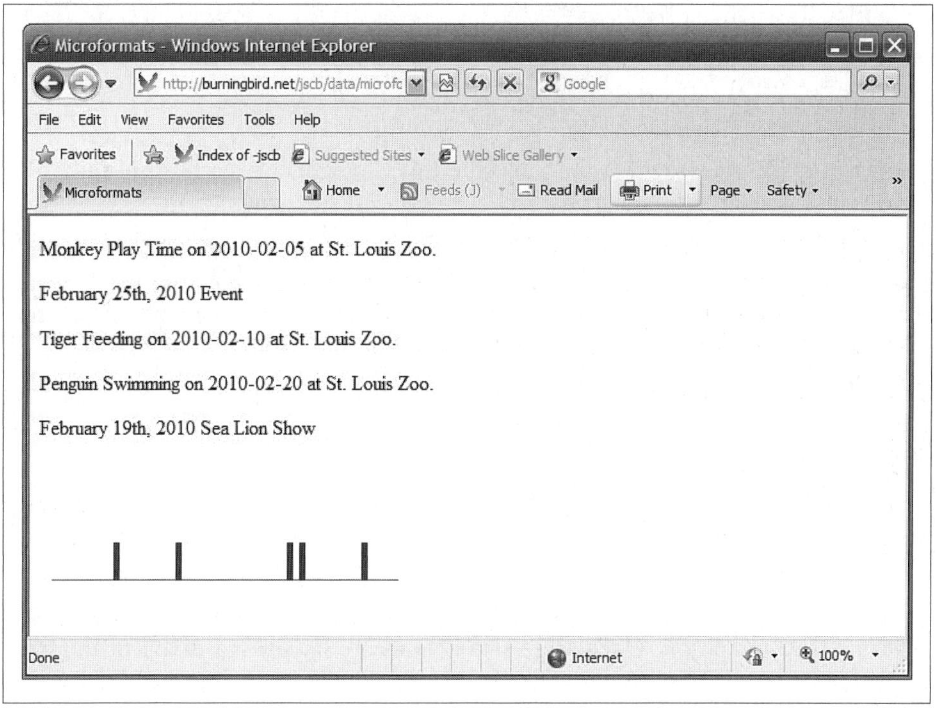

Figure 19-2. Microformat hCalendar application in IE

Solution

Use one of the RDFa JavaScript libraries, such as rdfQuery, which has the added advantage of being built on jQuery (the default JavaScript library used with Drupal). The rdfQuery library also implements an RDFa gleaner, which is functionality that can take a jQuery object and glean all of the RDFa from it and its subtree, automatically converting the data into RDF triples and storing them into an in-memory database:

```
var triplestore = $('#biblio').rdf()
  .base('http://burningbird.net')
  .prefix('rdf','http://www.w3.org/1999/02/22-rdf-synax-ns#')
  .prefix('dc','http://purl.org/dc/elements/1.1/')
  .prefix('foaf','http://xmlns.com/foaf/0.1/');
```

Once you have the data, you can export a JavaScript object of the triples:

```
var data = triplestore.databank.dump();
And then you can convert that into JSON:
var jsonStr = JSON.stringify(d);
```

Discussion

RDF is a way of recording metadata in such a way that data from one site can be safely combined with data from many others, and queried for specific information or used in rules-based derivations. The data is stored in a format known as a *triple*, which is nothing more than a simple subject-predicate-object set usually displayed as:

```
<http://www.example.org/jo/blog> foaf:primaryTopic <#bbq> .
<http://www.example.org/jo/blog> dc:creator "Jo" .
```

These triples basically say that the subject in this, a blog identified by a specific URL, has a primary topic of "bbq," or barbecue, and the creator is named Jo.

This is a book on JavaScript, so I don't want to spend more time on RDFa or RDF. I'll provide links later where you can get more information on both. For now, just be aware that we're going to take that RDFa annotation in the page, convert it into a triple store using rdfQuery, and then export it as a JavaScript object, and eventually JSON.

The RDFa, embedded into X/HTML, has the opposite challenges from Microformats: the syntax is very regular and well-defined, but accessing the data can be quite challenging. That's the primary reason to use a library such as rdfQuery.

In the solution, what the code does is use jQuery selector notation to access an element identified by "biblio", and then use the `.rdf()` gleaner to extract all of the RDFa out of the object and its subtree and store it in an in-memory data store.

The solution then maps the prefixes for the RDFa: dc is mapped to *http://purl.org/dc/elements/1.1/*, and so on. Once these two actions are finished, a dump of the store creates a JavaScript object containing the triple objects extracted from the RDFa, which are then converted into JSON using the `JSON.stringify` method. The resulting string with the five derived triples looks like this:

```
{"http://www.w3.org/TR/2004/REC-rdf-mt-
20040210/":{"http://purl.org/dc/elements/1.1/title":[{"type":"literal",
"value":"RDF Semantics - W3C Recommendation 10 February
2004"}],"http://purl.org/dc/elements/1.1/creator":[{"type":"uri",
"value":
```

```
"http://burningbird.net/jscb/data/rdfa.xhtml#a1"}]},
"http://burningbird.net/jscb/data/rdfa.xhtml#a1":
{"http://www.w3.org/1999/02/22-rdf-syntax-
ns#type":[{"type":"uri","value":"http://xmlns.com/foaf/0.1/Person"}],
"http://xmlns.com/foaf/0.1/name":[{"type":"literal","value":"Patrick
Hayes"}],"http://xmlns.com/foaf/0.1/homepage":[{"type":"uri",
"value":"http://www.ihmc.us/users/user.php?UserID=42"}]}}
```

Which converts into Turtle notation as:

```
<http://www.w3.org/TR/2004/REC-rdf-mt-20040210/> <http://purl.org/dc/elements/1.1/title>
  "RDF Semantics - W3C Recommendation 10 February 2004" .
<http://www.w3.org/TR/2004/REC-rdf-mt-20040210/>
<http://purl.org/dc/elements/1.1/creator>
<http://burningbird.net/jscb/data/rdfa.xhtml#a1> .
<http://burningbird.net/jscb/data/rdfa.xhtml#a1>
  <http://www.w3.org/1999/02/22-rdf-syntax-ns#type>
<http://xmlns.com/foaf/0.1/Person> .
<http://burningbird.net/jscb/data/rdfa.xhtml#a1>
<http://xmlns.com/foaf/0.1/name> "Patrick Hayes" .
<http://burningbird.net/jscb/data/rdfa.xhtml#a1>
<http://xmlns.com/foaf/0.1/homepage>
<http://www.ihmc.us/users/user.php?UserID=42> .
```

Once you have the string, you can use it in an Ajax call to a web service that makes use of RDF or JSON, or both.

Example 19-4 combines the pieces of the solution into a full-page application in order to more fully demonstrate how each of the components works together. The application prints out the JSON.stringify data dump of the data and then prints out each trip individually, converting the angle brackets of the triples first so that appending them to the page won't trigger an XHTML parsing error.

Example 19-4. Extracting RDFa from a page and embedding the data into the page

```
<!DOCTYPE html>
<html xmlns="http://www.w3.org/1999/xhtml"
      xmlns:rdf="http://www.w3.org/1999/02/22-rdf-syntax-ns#"
      xmlns:dc="http://purl.org/dc/elements/1.1/"
      xmlns:foaf="http://xmlns.com/foaf/0.1/" >
  <head profile="http://ns.inria.fr/grddl/rdfa/">
    <title>Biblio description</title>
<style type="text/css">
div { margin: 20px; }
</style>
  <script type="text/javascript" src="json2.js"></script>
  <script type="text/javascript" src="jquery.js"></script>
  <script type="text/javascript"
src="jquery.rdfquery.rdfa.min-1.0.js"></script>
  <script type="text/javascript">
  //<![CDATA[

    window.onload = function() {

      var j =  $('#biblio').rdf()
```

```
            .base('http://burningbird.net')
            .prefix('rdf','http://www.w3.org/1999/02/22-rdf-synax-ns#')
            .prefix('dc','http://purl.org/dc/elements/1.1/')
            .prefix('foaf','http://xmlns.com/foaf/0.1/');

        var d = j.databank.dump();
        var str = JSON.stringify(d);
        document.getElementById("result1").innerHTML = str;

        var t = j.databank.triples();
        var str2 = "";
        for (var i = 0; i < t.length; i++) {
          str2 =
str2 + t[i].toString().replace(/</g,"&lt;").replace(/>/g,"&gt;")
+ "<br />";
        }
        document.getElementById("result2").innerHTML = str2;
    }
  //]]>
  </script>
  </head>
  <body>
    <h1>Biblio description</h1>
    <dl about="http://www.w3.org/TR/2004/REC-rdf-mt-20040210/"
id="biblio">
      <dt>Title</dt>
        <dd property="dc:title">
RDF Semantics - W3C Recommendation 10 February 2004</dd>
      <dt>Author</dt>
        <dd rel="dc:creator" href="#a1">
         <span id="a1">
           <link rel="rdf:type" href="[foaf:Person]" />
           <span property="foaf:name">Patrick Hayes</span>
           see <a rel="foaf:homepage"
href="http://www.ihmc.us/users/user.php?UserID=42">homepage</a>
         </span>
       </dd>
    </dl>
    <div id="result1"></div>
    <div id="result2"></div>
  </body>
</html>
```

Figure 19-3 shows the page after the JavaScript has finished. The application uses the *json2.js* library for browsers that haven't implemented the JSON object yet.

You can also do a host of other things with rdfQuery, such as add triples directly, query across the triples, make inferences, and anything else you would like to do with RDF.

See Also

rdfQuery was created by Jeni Tennison. You can download it and read more documentation on its use at *http://code.google.com/p/rdfquery/*. When I used the library for writing this section, I used it with jQuery 1.42. Another RDFa library is the RDFa Parsing Module for the Backplane library (*http://code.google.com/p/backplanejs/*).

For more information on RDF, see the RDF Primer (*http://www.w3.org/TR/rdf-primer/*). The RDFa Primer can be found at *http://www.w3.org/TR/xhtml-rdfa-primer/*. There is a new effort to create an RDFa-in-HTML specification, specifically for HTML5.

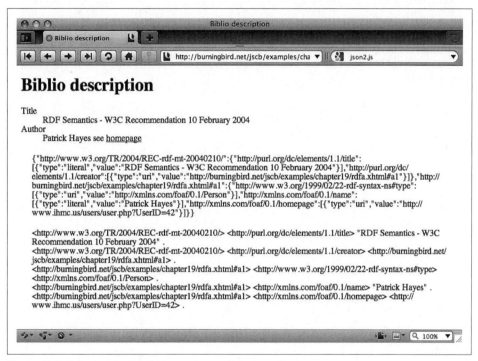

Figure 19-3. Running the RDFa extraction application in Opera

CHAPTER 20

Persistence

20.0 Introduction

In the early years of web development, to keep a value around as users moved from page to page, you'd have to make use of session persistence functionality built into the environment, attach the data to the web page URL, or provide it in a hidden form field. Of course, this persisted the data from page to page, but once you closed the browser, the data was lost.

JavaScript added a third approach, a cookie, which could not only persist from page to page, but cause the data to persist beyond the current session. With cookies, you could not only access data such as login information throughout a website, but you could close the browser and reopen it another day and still have access to the same data.

These techniques still exist, but now, because of the needs of more complex web applications, including applications that support offline functionality, browsers support a variety of sophisticated data storage and persistence techniques.

No area of JavaScript has gone through more upheaval recently than persistence. Whether it's storing data between sessions or enabling access to information while offline, complex new ideas have been spawned, supported by web pages and implementations, only to quietly fade away when something new and shiny appeared.

Probably one of the more famous examples of an idea that came and went is Google Gears—an offline storage mechanism that generated considerable excitement in 2007 when it debuted, only to die a fairly quick and unexpected death when Google announced in November 2009 that it was dropping support for Gears in favor of the new Web Applications/HTML5 persistence initiatives.

Fun new technology aside, the old approaches, such as using data encoding on an URL or a cookie, still exist and still provide a service that some of the newer techniques don't provide: simplicity. This chapter touches on all of the techniques, from the old time to the new, the simple to the complex.

Some of the methods explored in this chapter are cutting edge, based on specifications that are still being developed. Use with caution.

See Also

For more on Google's Gears decision, see the blog post at *http://gearsblog.blogspot.com/2010/02/hello-html5.html*.

20.1 Attaching Persistent Information to URLs

Problem

You want to store a small fragment of information so that the information is available to anyone accessing the page.

Solution

Persisting a fragment of information in a web page for general access by everyone is dependent on the old school capability of attaching information to a URL. The information can be passed as a page fragment:

```
http://somecompany.com/firstpage.html#infoasfragment
```

Discussion

JavaScript can be used to add a page fragment, though this is more of a way to store a simple state than anything more complex:

```
http://somecompany.com/test.html#one
```

The data can also be encoded as parameters in a query string, which starts with a question mark, followed by the parameters passed as key/value pairs separated by equal signs, and separated from each other by ampersands:

```
http://somecompany.com?test=one&test=two
```

There are limits to lengths of URLs, and probably for numbers of GET pairs, but I would hope we wouldn't ever approach these limits. This also isn't an approach you would use in place of a cookie. For instance, if you want to capture user input into a form, in case the users have to leave before finishing the form entries (or they accidentally close their browser tab page), you should put this data into a cookie, which is more secure, and more specific to the person.

Data encoding in the URL is more of a way to capture page state so that a person can send a link to the page in that state to another person, or link it within a web page. Example 20-1 demonstrates how something like data persistence via URL can work.

In the web page, there are three buttons and one `div` element controlled by the action of the buttons. One button moves the `div` element to the right, one button increases the size of the element, and one button changes its color. As each button is clicked, the `div` element is adjusted, and the newly applied CSS value is stored with the appropriate button.

When the state of the page is changed, a link within the page is updated to reflect the state of the page. Note that the actual `window.location` property and even the `window.location.search` property is not changed. The reason is that the page reloads as a security precaution when you update any component of `window.location` except the `hash` value.

 Allowing a person to change the URL in the location bar, which isn't reflected in the actual page, introduces the threat of spoofing—one page masquerading as another in order to scam passwords and other confidential information.

Now you can reload the page and have the script restore the page to the state in the URL when it reloads—but that's a lot of moving parts. In the example, we'll just create a static state link, and leave it at that.

Example 20-1. Using the URL and the query string to preserve state

```
<!DOCTYPE html>
<head>
<title>Remember me?</title>
<style>
#square
{
  position: absolute;
  left: 0;
  top: 100px;
  width: 100px;
  height: 100px;
  border: 1px solid #333;
  background-color: #ffff00;
}
div p
{
  margin: 10px;
}
</style>
<script>

  // found at http://www.netlobo.com/url_query_string_javascript.html
  function getQueryParam( name ) {
        name = name.replace(/[\[]/,"\\\[").replace(/[\]]/,"\\\]");
        var regexS = "[\\?&]"+name+"=([^&#]*)";
        var regex = new RegExp( regexS );
        var results = regex.exec( window.location.href );
```

```
        if( results == null )
          return null;
        else
          return results[1];
    }

    window.onload=function() {

      // set up button
      document.getElementById("move").onclick=moveSquare;
      document.getElementById("size").onclick=resizeSquare;
      document.getElementById("color").onclick=changeColor;

      var move = getQueryParam("move");
      if (!move) return;

      var size = getQueryParam("size");
      var color = getQueryParam("color");

      // update element
      var square = document.getElementById("square");
      square.style.left=move + "px";
      square.style.height=size + "px";
      square.style.width=size + "px";
      square.style.backgroundColor="#" + color;

      // update data-state values
      document.getElementById("move").setAttribute("data-state",move);
      document.getElementById("size").setAttribute("data-state",size);
      document.getElementById("color").setAttribute("data-state",color);
    }

    function updateURL () {
      var move = document.getElementById("move").getAttribute("data-state");
      var color = document.getElementById("color").getAttribute("data-state");
      var size = document.getElementById("size").getAttribute("data-state");

      var link = document.getElementById("link");
      var path = location.protocol + "//" + location.hostname + location.pathname +
            "?move=" + move + "&size=" + size + "&color=" + color;
      link.innerHTML="<p><a href='" + path + "'>static state link</a></p>";

    }

    function moveSquare() {
      var move = parseInt(document.getElementById("move").getAttribute("data-
state"));
      move+=100;
      document.getElementById("square").style.left=move + "px";
      document.getElementById("move").setAttribute("data-state", move);
      updateURL();
    }

    function resizeSquare() {
      var size = parseInt(document.getElementById("size").getAttribute("data-
```

```
state"));
        size+=50;
        var square = document.getElementById("square");
        square.style.width=size + "px";
        square.style.height=size + "px";
        document.getElementById("size").setAttribute("data-state",size);
        updateURL();
    }

    function changeColor() {
        var color = document.getElementById("color").getAttribute("data-state");
        var hexcolor;
        if (color == "0000ff") {
            hexcolor="ffff00";
        } else {
            hexcolor = "0000ff";
        }
        document.getElementById("square").style.backgroundColor="#" +
hexcolor;
        document.getElementById("color").setAttribute("data-state",hexcolor);
        updateURL();
    }

</script>
</head>
<body>
    <button id="move" data-state="0">Move Square</button>
    <button id="size" data-state="100">Increase Square Size</button>
    <button id="color" data-state="#ffff00">Change Color</button>
    <div id="link"></div>
    <div id="square">
        <p>This is the object</p>
    </div>
</body>
```

Figure 20-1 shows the web page after several changes to the square element, and after the page is reloaded using the link.

See Also

Recipes 8.7 and 8.8 demonstrate how to use the `location.hash` property to store state in the URL and return to that state when the page is reloaded. The query string routine in the example is described at *http://www.netlobo.com/url_query_string_javascript .html*.

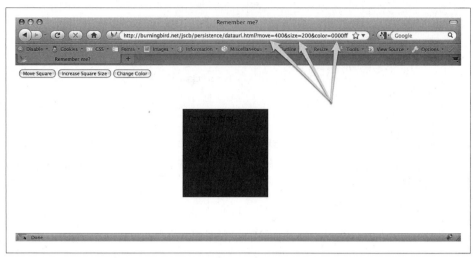

Figure 20-1. Page after reloading and using persistence through URL

20.2 Creating a Cookie to Persist Information Across Pages

Problem

You want to persist some information about or for the user within the existing browser session.

Solution

If the amount of data is less than 4k in size, use a browser cookie. A cookie is a patterned line of text that you assign to the `document.cookie` property:

```
document.cookie="cookiename=cookievalue; expires=date; path=path";
```

Discussion

Cookies are still one of the easiest, simplest, and most widely used persistent storage technique for web pages today. They're easy to set, safe, well understood by most people who browse web pages, and require little overhead.

People can also turn cookie support off in their browsers, which means your application has to work, regardless. In addition, the amount of data stored is small—less than 4k—and doesn't support complex data structures. There's also the security restrictions associated with cookies: they're domain-specific. Despite the restriction, though, cookies are also insecure, as any data stored is done so in plain text. You don't want to use cookies to store passwords.

Read the article "Improving Persistent Login Cookie Best Practice" (*http://jaspan.com/improved_persistent_login_cookie_best_practice*) if you're interested in implementing "Remember Me" using cookies on your site.

Cookies are created by assigning the cookie to the `document.cookie` property. The cookie consists of a name/value pair, separated by an equal sign:

```
document.cookie="cookiename=cookievalue";
```

There are parameters that can follow the cookie/value pair, all separated by semi-colons (`;`). The parameters are:

`path=`*path (such as* `/` *or* `/subdir`*)*
> Defaults to the current location.

`domain=`*domain (such as* `burningbird.net`, *for all subdomains, or a given subdomain,* `missourigreen.burningbird.net`*)*
> Defaults to current host.

`max-age=`*maximum age in seconds*
> Meant more for session-based short restrictions.

`expires=`*date in GMTString-format*
> Defaults to expiring at end of session.

`secure`
> Can only be transmitted via HTTPS.

Here's an example. This cookie keyword is `Language`, with a value of `JavaScript`, set to expire at a given time with `expires`, and with `path` set to the top-level domain:

```
Language=JavaScript; expires=Mon, 22 Feb 2010 01:00:59 GMT; path=/
```

If we wanted the cookie to expire when the browser closes, all we need do is leave off the `expires`.

To retrieve the cookie, we have to retrieve the entire `document.cookie` property, which returns all cookies set on the domain. The application needs to find all of the cookies, and then look for a specific one. To erase the cookie, all we need do is set it with a past date.

To demonstrate, Example 20-2 contains a web page that has two input fields, one for the cookie name and one for the value. Clicking the Set Cookie button creates the cookie; clicking the Get Cookie retrieves the value for the given cookie; clicking the Erase Cookie button erases the cookie.

Example 20-2. Demonstrating cookies

```
<!DOCTYPE html>
<html dir="ltr" lang="en-US">
<head>
<title>Persisting via Cookies</title>
<style>
div
{
  margin: 5px;
}
</style>
<script>


// if cookie enabled
window.onload=function() {

  if (navigator.cookieEnabled) {
    document.getElementById("set").onclick=setCookie;
    document.getElementById("get").onclick=readCookie;
    document.getElementById("erase").onclick=eraseCookie;
  }

}


// set cookie expiration date in year 2010
function setCookie() {

    var cookie = document.getElementById("cookie").value;
    var value = document.getElementById("value").value;

    var futureDate = new Date();
    futureDate.setDate(futureDate.getDate() + 10);

    var tmp=cookie + "=" + encodeURI(value) + "; expires=" +
                   futureDate.toGMTString() + "; path=/";
    document.cookie=tmp;
}

// each cookie separated by semicolon;
function readCookie() {

  var key = document.getElementById("cookie").value;

  var cookie = document.cookie;
  var first = cookie.indexOf(key+"=");

  // cookie exists
  if (first >= 0) {
    var str = cookie.substring(first,cookie.length);
    var last = str.indexOf(";");

    // if last cookie
    if (last < 0) last = str.length;
```

```
    // get cookie value
    str = str.substring(0,last).split("=");
    alert(decodeURI(str[1]));
  } else {
    alert("none found");
  }
}


// set cookie date to the past to erase
function eraseCookie () {

    var key = document.getElementById("cookie").value;

    var cookieDate = new Date();
    cookieDate.setDate(cookieDate.getDate() - 10);

    document.cookie=key + "= ; expires="+cookieDate.toGMTString()+"; path=/";
}
</script>
</head>
<body>
<form>
<label for="cookie"> Enter cookie:</label> <input type="text" id="cookie" /> <br />
<label for="value">Cookie Value:</label> <input type="text" id="value" /><br />
</form>
<div>
<button id="set">Set Cookie</button>
<button id="get">Get Cookie</button>
<button id="erase">Erase Cookie</button>
</div>
</body>
```

See Also

See Recipe 3.6 for how to access a future date.

20.3 Persisting Information Using the History.pushState Method and window.onpopevent

Problem

You've looked at all the ways of handling the back button and controlling page state for an Ajax application, and you're saying to yourself, "There has to be a better way."

Solution

There is a better way, a much better way...but it's going to be some time before you'll be able to incorporate the technique into your applications: using HTML5's new history.pushState and history.replaceState methods to persist a state object, and the window.onpopevent:

```
window.history.pushState({ page : page}, "Page " + page, "?page=" + page);
 ...

window.onpopstate = function(event) {
      // check for event.state, if found, reload state
      if (!event.state) return;
      var page = event.state.page;
}
```

Discussion

Addressing the significant problems Ajax developers have had with trying to persist state through back button events or page reloads, HTML5 has new history object methods, pushState and replaceState, to persist state information, and then an associated window.onpopevent that can be used to restore the page state.

In the past, we had the ability to persist information regarding the page state, though we've had to be conservative in how much data we persist. A popular approach, and one demonstrated in Recipe 20.1, is to store the data in the page URL hash, which updates the page history and can be pulled via JavaScript.

The problem with this approach is that updating the hash may update the history. If you hit the back button, the URL with the hash shows in the location bar, but no event is triggered so you can grab the data and restore the page. The workaround was to use a timer to check for the new hash and then restore the page if a new hash was found. Not an attractive solution, and one most of us decided just wasn't worth trying.

Now, you can easily store any object that can be passed to JSON.stringify. Since the data is stored locally, the early implementor, Firefox, limits the size of the JSON representation to 640k. However, unless you're recording the state of every pixel in the page, 640k should be more than sufficient.

To see how the new event and methods work, Example 20-3 is a recreation of Example 8-2, from Recipe 8.8. The changes to the application include the removal of the use of the hash location fragment, which is replaced by history.pushState, and the window.onpopstate event handler, both of which are highlighted in the code. There's one other minor change—in the functionOne function, also highlighted—and I'll get into the reason why after the example.

Example 20-3. Shows Example 8-2 from Recipe 8.8 converted to using the new history.pushState and window.onpopstate event handler

```
<!DOCTYPE html>
<head>
<title>Remember me--new, and improved!</title>
<meta http-equiv="Content-Type" content="text/html;charset=utf-8" />
<script>
   window.onload=function() {
```

```
      document.getElementById("next").onclick=nextPanel;
}

window.onpopstate = function(event) {
  // check for event.state, if found, reload state
  if (!event.state) return;
  var page = event.state.page;
  switch (page) {
    case "one" :
      functionOne();
      break;
    case "two" :
      functionOne();
      functionTwo();
      break;
    case "three" :
      functionOne();
      functionTwo();
      functionThree();
  }
}

// display next panel, based on button's class
function nextPanel() {
  var page = document.getElementById("next").getAttribute("data-page");
  switch(page) {
    case "zero" :
      functionOne();
      break;
    case "one" :
      functionTwo();
      break;
    case "two" :
      functionThree();
  }
}
// set both the button class, and create the state link, add to page
function setPage(page) {
  document.getElementById("next").setAttribute("data-page",page);
  window.history.pushState({ page : page}, "Page " + page, "?page=" + page);
}

// function one, two, three - change div, set button and link
function functionOne() {
  var square = document.getElementById("square");
  square.style.position="relative";
  square.style.left="0";
  square.style.backgroundColor="#ff0000";
  square.style.width="200px";
  square.style.height="200px";
  square.style.padding="10px";
  square.style.margin="20px";
  setPage("one");
}
```

```
        function functionTwo() {
            var square = document.getElementById("square");
            square.style.backgroundColor="#ffff00";
            square.style.position="absolute";
            square.style.left="200px";
            setPage("two");
        }

        function functionThree() {
            var square = document.getElementById("square");
            square.style.width="400px";
            square.style.height="400px";
            square.style.backgroundColor="#00ff00";
            square.style.left="400px";
            setPage("three");
        }
</script>
</head>
<body>
<button id="next" data-page="zero">Next Action</button>
<div id="square" class="zero">
<p>This is the object</p>
</div>
</body>
```

In this example, the state object that is stored is extremely simple: a page property and its associated value. The `history.pushState` also takes a `title` parameter, which is used for the session history entry, and a URL. For the example, I appended a query string representing the page. What is displayed in the location bar is:

```
http://somecom.com/pushstate.html?page=three
```

The `history.replaceState` method takes the same parameters, but modifies the current history entry instead of creating a new one.

When using the browser back button to traverse through the created history entries, or when hitting the page reload, a `window.onpopstate` event is fired. This is really the truly important component in this new functionality, and is the event we've needed for years. To restore the web page to the stored state, we create a `window.onpopstate` event handler function, accessing the state object from the event passed to the window handler function:

```
window.onpopstate = function(event) {
    // check for event.state, if found, reload state
    if (!event.state) return;
    var page = event.state.page;
    ...
}
```

In the example, when you click the button three times to get to the third "page," reload the page, or hit the back button, the `window.onpopstate` event handlers fires. Perfect timing to get the state data, and repair the page. Works beautifully, too. In the Firefox Minefield edition, that is.

One other change that had to be made to the older example, is that `functionOne` had to be modified and the following style settings added:

```
square.style.position = "relative";
square.style.left = "0";
```

The reason is that unlike Example 8-2, which goes through a complete page reload, the new state methods and event handler actually do preserve the state *in-page*. This means the changes going from step one to step two (setting position to `absolute` and moving the `div` element) have to be canceled out in the first function in order to truly restore the page state. It's a small price to pay for this lovely new functionality.

Again, the example only worked with the Firefox nightly. However, the back button did seem to work with the WebKit nightly.

20.4 Using sessionStorage for Client-Side Storage

Problem

You want to easily store session information without running into the size and cross-page contamination problems associated with cookies, and prevent loss of information if the browser is refreshed.

Solution

Use the new DOM Storage `sessionStorage` functionality:

```
sessionStorage.setItem("name", "Shelley");
sessionStorage.city="St. Louis";
...
var name = sessionStorage,getItem("name");
var city = sessionStorage.city;
...
sessionStorage.removeItem("name");
sessionStorage.clear();
```

Discussion

One of the constraints with cookies is they are domain/subdomain-specific, not page-specific. Most of the time, this isn't a problem. However, there are times when such domain specificity isn't sufficient.

For instance, a person has two browser tabs open to the same shopping site and adds a few items to the shopping cart in one tab. In the tab, the shopper clicks a button to add an item because of the admonishment to add the item to the cart in order to see the price. The shopper decides against the item and closes the tab page, thinking that action is enough to ensure the item isn't in the cart. The shopper then clicks the checkout option in the other opened tag, assuming that the only items currently in the cart are the ones that were added in that browser page.

If the users aren't paying attention, they may not notice that the cookie-based shopping cart has been updated from both pages, and they'll end up buying something they didn't want.

While it is true that many web users are savvy enough to not make this mistake, there are many who aren't; they assume that persistence is browser-page-specific, not necessarily domain-specific. With sessionStorage (to paraphrase the famous quote about Las Vegas), what happens in the page, stays in the page.

As an example of the differences between the cookies and the new storage option, Example 20-4 stores information from a form in both a cookie and sessionStorage. Clicking the button to get the data gets whatever is stored for the key in both, and displays it in the page: the sessionStorage data in the first block, the cookie data in the second. The remove button erases whatever exists in both.

Example 20-4. Comparing sessionStorage and cookies

```
<!DOCTYPE html>
<html dir="ltr" lang="en-US">
<head>
<title>Comparing Cookies and sessionStorage</title>
<meta http-equiv="Content-Type" content="text/html;charset=utf-8" >
<style>
div
{
  background-color: #ffff00;
  margin: 5px;
  width: 100px;
  padding: 1px;
}
</style>
<script>
  window.onload=function() {

      document.getElementById("set").onclick=setData;
      document.getElementById("get").onclick=getData;
      document.getElementById("erase").onclick=removeData;
  }

  // set data for both session and cookie
  function setData() {
    var key = document.getElementById("key").value;
    var value = document.getElementById("value").value;

    // set sessionStorage
    var current = sessionStorage.getItem(key);
    if (current) {
      current+=value;
    } else {
      current=value;
    }
    sessionStorage.setItem(key,current);
```

```
      // set cookie
      current = getCookie(key);
      if (current) {
        current+=value;
      } else {
        current=value;
      }
      setCookie(key,current);
    }

    function getData() {
      try {
        var key = document.getElementById("key").value;

        // sessionStorage
        var value = sessionStorage.getItem(key);
        if (!value) value ="";
          document.getElementById("sessionstr").innerHTML="<p>" +
value + "</p>";

        // cookie
        value = getCookie(key);
        if (!value) value="";
          document.getElementById("cookiestr").innerHTML="<p>" +
value + "</p>";

      } catch(e) {
        alert(e);
      }
    }

    function removeData() {
      var key = document.getElementById("key").value;

      // sessionStorage
      sessionStorage.removeItem(key);

      // cookie
      eraseCookie(key);
    }
    // set session cookie
    function setCookie(cookie,value) {

      var tmp=cookie + "=" + encodeURI(value) + ";path=/";
      document.cookie=tmp;
    }

    // each cookie separated by semicolon;
    function getCookie(key) {

      var cookie = document.cookie;
      var first = cookie.indexOf(key+"=");

      // cookie exists
      if (first >= 0) {
```

```
                var str = cookie.substring(first,cookie.length);
                var last = str.indexOf(";");

                // if last cookie
                if (last < 0) last = str.length;

                // get cookie value
                str = str.substring(0,last).split("=");
                return decodeURI(str[1]);
            } else {
                return null;
            }
        }

    // set cookie date to the past to erase
    function eraseCookie (key) {
        var cookieDate = new Date();
        cookieDate.setDate(cookieDate.getDate() - 10);
        var tmp=key +
"= ; expires="+cookieDate.toGMTString()+"; path=/";
        document.cookie=tmp;
    }
</script>
</head>
<body>
    <form>
        <label for="key"> Enter key:</label>
<input type="text" id="key" /> <br /> <br />
        <label for="value">Enter value:</label>
 <input type="text" id="value" /><br /><br />
    </form>
    <button id="set">Set data</button>
    <button id="get">Get data</button>
    <button id="erase">Erase data</button>
    <div id="sessionstr"><p></p></div>
    <div id="cookiestr"><p></p></div>
</body>
```

Load the example page (it's in the book examples) in Firefox 3.5 and up. Add one or more items to the same key value, and then click the button labeled "Get data", as shown in Figure 20-2.

Now, open the same page in a new tab window, and click the "Get data" button. The activity results in a page like that shown in Figure 20-3.

In the new tab window, the cookie value persists because the cookie is session-specific, which means it lasts until you close the browser. The cookie lives beyond the first tab window, but the sessionStorage, which is specific to the tab window, does not.

Now, in the new tab window, add a couple more items to the key value, and click "Get data" again, as shown in Figure 20-4.

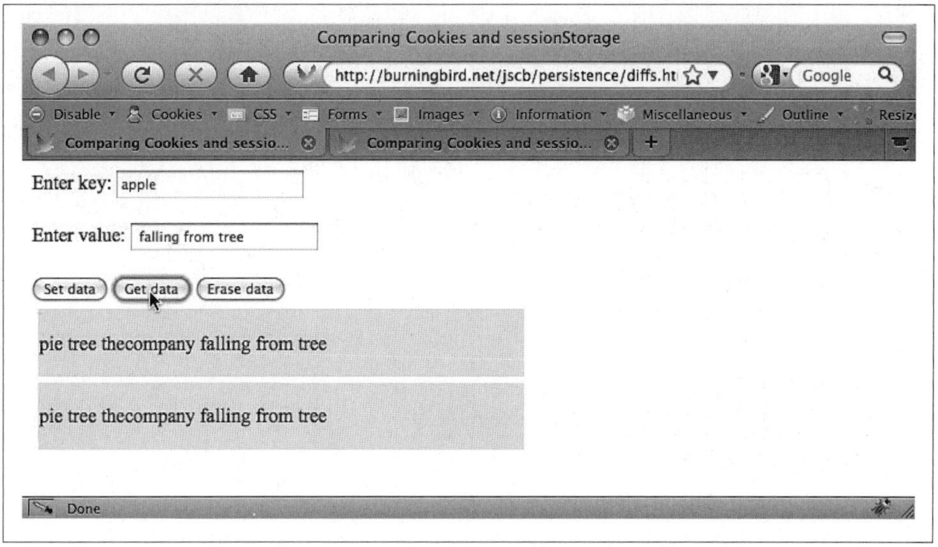

Figure 20-2. Showing current value for "apple" in sessionStorage and Cookie

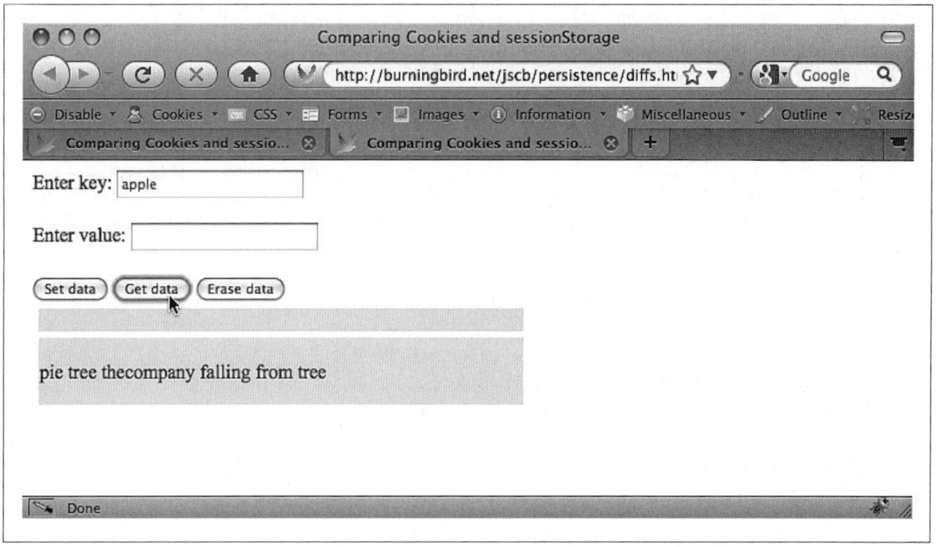

Figure 20-3. Again, showing current value for "apple" in sessionStorage and Cookie, but in a new tab window

Return to the original tab window, and click "Get data". As you can see in Figure 20-5, the items added in the second tab are showing with the cookie, but not the sessionStorage item.

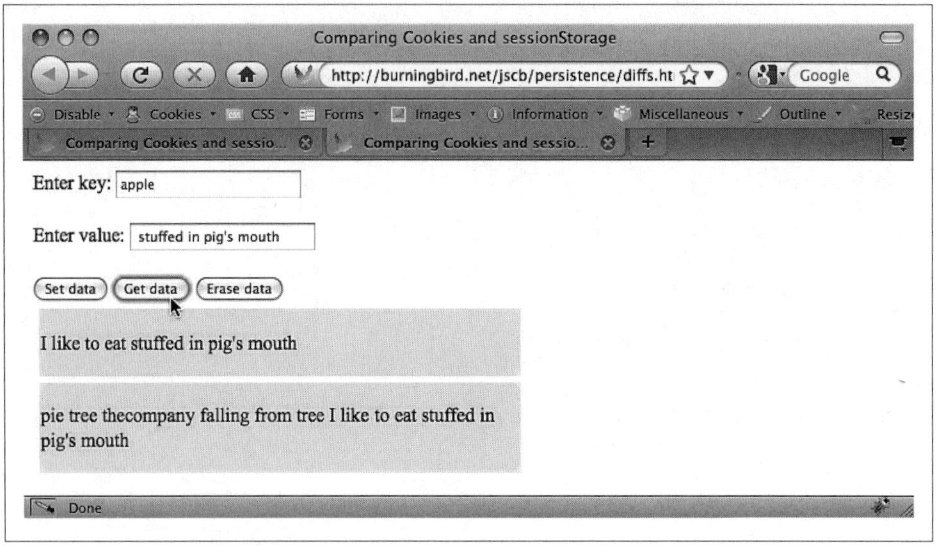

Figure 20-4. Adding more values to "apple" in new tab window

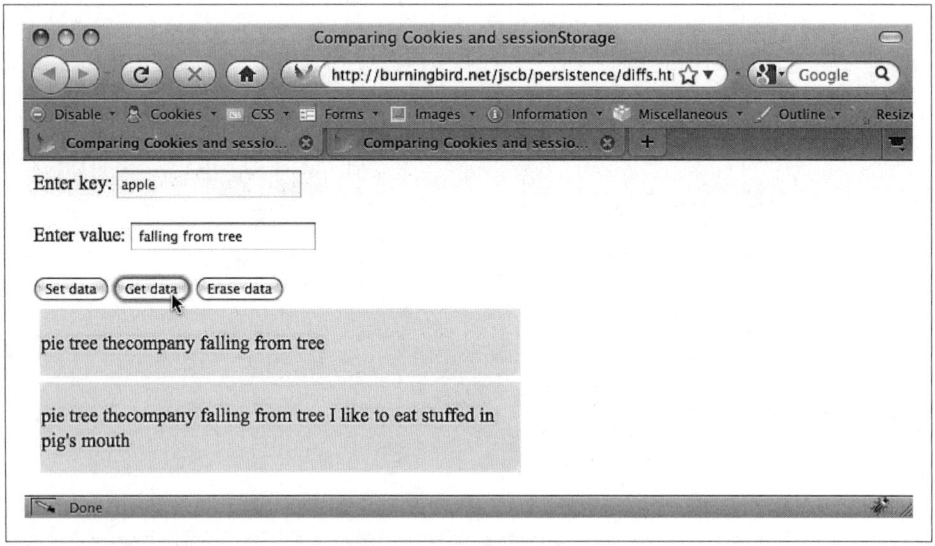

Figure 20-5. Returning to the original tab window and clicking "Get data" with "apple"

Lastly, in the original tab window, click the "Erase data" button. Figure 20-6 shows the results of clicking "Get data" on the original window, while Figure 20-7 shows the results when clicking "Get data" in the second tab window. Again, note the disparities between the cookie and sessionStorage.

The reason for all of these images is to demonstrate the significant differences between sessionStorage and cookies, aside from how they're set and accessed in JavaScript.

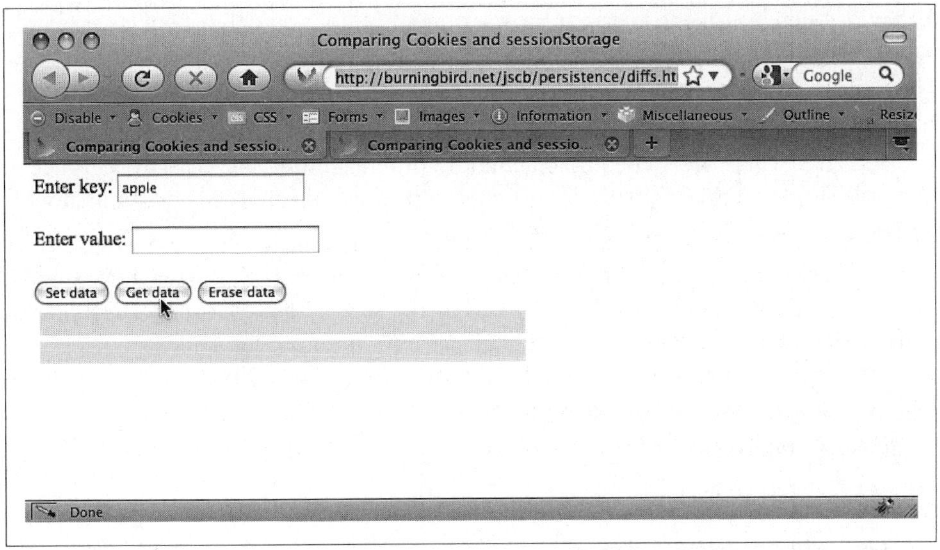

Figure 20-6. After clicking the "Erase data" button in the original tab window, and then clicking "Get data"

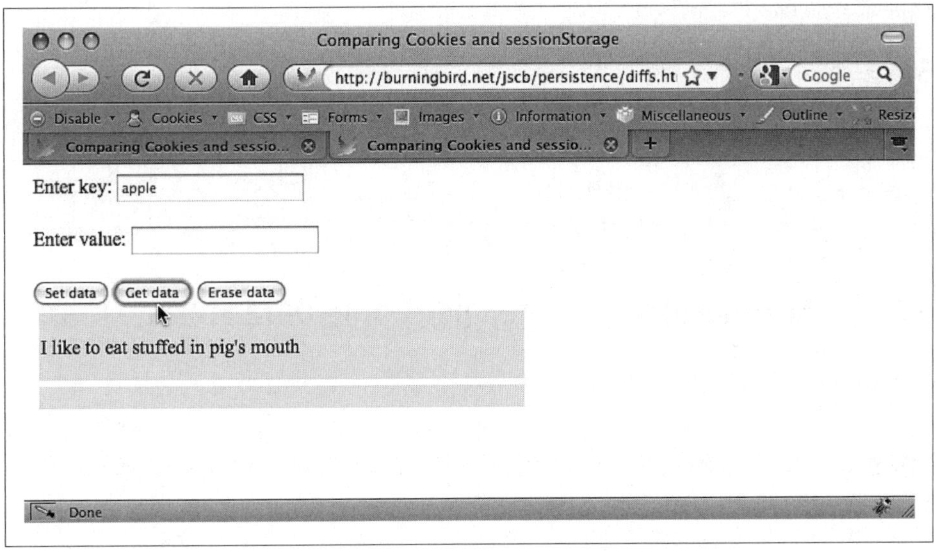

Figure 20-7. Clicking "Get data" in the second window, after erasing data in first

Hopefully, the images and the example also demonstrate the potential hazards involved when using `sessionStorage`, especially in circumstances where cookies have normally been used.

If your website or application users are familiar with the `cookie` persistence across tab-bed windows, `sessionStorage` can be an unpleasant surprise. Along with the different behavior, there's also the fact that browser menu options to delete cookies probably won't have an impact on sessionStorage, which could also be an unwelcome surprise for your users. Use sessionStorage with caution.

The sessionStorage object is currently supported in Firefox 3.5 and up, Safari 4.x and up, and IE 8. There are some implementation differences for sessionStorage, but the example shown in this recipe is consistently implemented across all environments.

One last note on sessionStorage, as it relates to its implementation. Both sessionStorage and localStorage, covered in the next recipe, are part of the new DOM Storage specification, currently under development by the W3C. Both are window object properties, which means they can be accessed globally. Both are implementations of the Storage object, and changes to the prototype for Storage result in changes to both the sessionStorage and localStorage objects:

```
Storage.prototype.someMethod = function (param) { ...};
...
localStorage.someMethod(param);
...
sessionStorage.someMethod(param);
```

Aside from the differences, covered in this recipe and the next, another major difference is that the Storage objects don't make a round trip to the server—they're purely client-side storage techniques.

See Also

For more information on the Storage object, sessionStorage, localStorage, or the Storage DOM, consult the specification (*http://dev.w3.org/html5/webstorage/*). See Recipe 20.5 for a different look at how sessionStorage and localStorage can be set and retrieved, and other supported properties on both.

20.5 Creating a localStorage Client-Side Data Storage Item

Problem

You want to shadow form element entries (or any data) in such a way that if the browser crashes, the user accidentally closes the browser, or the Internet connection is lost, the user can continue.

Solution

You could use cookies if the data is small enough, but that strategy doesn't work in an offline situation. Another, better approach, especially when you're persisting larger amounts of data or if you have to support functionality when no Internet connection is present, is to use the new localStorage:

```
var value = document.getElementById("formelem").value;
If (value) {
    localStorage.formelem = value;
}
...
// recover
var value = localStorage.formelem;
document.getElementById("formelem").value = value;
```

Discussion

Recipe 20.4 covered sessionStorage, one of the new DOM Storage techniques. The localStorage object interface is the same, with the same approaches to setting the data:

```
// use item methods
sessionStorage.setItem("key","value");
localStorage.setItem("key","value");

// use property names directly
sessionStorage.keyName = "value:
localStorage.keyName = "value";

// use the key method
sessionStorage.key(0) = "value";
localStorage.key(0) = "value:
```

and for getting the data:

```
// use item methods
value = sessionStorage.getItem("key");
value = localStorage.getItem("key");

// use property names directly
value = sessionStorage.keyName:
value = localStorage.keyName;

// use the key method
value = sessionStorage.key(0);
value = localStorage.key(0):
```

Both also support the length property, which provides a count of stored item pairs, and the clear method (no parameters), which clears out all Storage (but Firefox only supports clearing storage for localStorage). In addition, both are scoped to the HTML5 origin, which means that the data storage is shared across all pages in a domain, but not across protocols (e.g., http is not the same as https) or ports.

The difference between the two is how long data is stored. The sessionStorage object only stores data for the session, but the localStorage object stores data on the client forever, or until specifically removed.

The sessionStorage and localStorage objects also support one event: the storage event. This is an interesting event, in that it fires on all pages when changes are made to a localStorage item. It is also an area of low-compatibility among browsers: you can capture the event on the **body** or **document** elements for Firefox, on the **body** for IE, or on the **document** for Safari.

Example 20-5 demonstrates a more comprehensive implementation than the use case covered in the solution for this recipe. In the example, all elements of a small form have their **onchange** event handler method assigned to a function that captures the change element name and value, and stores the values in the local storage via `localStorage`. When the form is submitted, all of the stored form data is cleared.

When the page is loaded, the form elements **onchange** event handler is assigned to the function to store the values, and if the value is already stored, it is restored to the form element. To test the application, enter data into a couple of the form fields—but, before clicking the submit button, refresh the page. Without the use of `localStorage`, you'd lose the data. Now, when you reload the page, the form is restored to the state it was in before the page was reloaded.

Example 20-5. Using localStorage to back up form entries in case of page reload or browser crash

```
<!DOCTYPE html>
<html dir="ltr" lang="en-US">
<head>
<title>localstore</title>
<meta http-equiv="Content-Type" content="text/html;charset=utf-8" >
<style>
</style>
<script>
    window.onload=function() {
      try {
        var elems = document.getElementsByTagName("input");

        // capture submit to clear storage
        document.getElementById("inputform").onsubmit=clearStored;

        for (var i = 0; i < elems.length; i++) {

          if (elems[i].type == "text") {

            // restore
            var value = localStorage.getItem(elems[i].id);
            if (value) elems[i].value = value;

            // change event
            elems[i].onchange=processField;
          }
        } catch (e) {
          alert(e);
        }
      }
    }

    // store field values
    function processField() {
      localStorage.setItem(window.location.href,"true");
      localStorage.setItem(this.id, this.value);
```

```
    }

    // clear individual fields
    function clearStored() {
      var elems = document.getElementsByTagName("input");
      for (var i = 0; i < elems.length; i++) {

        if (elems[i].type == "text") {
          localStorage.removeItem(elems[i].id);
        }
      }
    }

</script>
</head>
<body>
  <form id="inputform">
    <label for="field1">Enter field1:</label> <input type="text" id="field1" />
<br /> <br />
    <label for="field2">Enter field2:</label> <input type="text" id="field2"
/><br /><br />
    <label for="field3">Enter field1:</label> <input type="text" id="field3" />
<br /> <br />
    <label for="field4">Enter field1:</label> <input type="text" id="field4" />
<br /> <br />
    <input type="submit" value="Save" />
</body>
```

The size alloted for localStorage varies by browser, and some browsers, such as Firefox, allow users to extend the Storage object limits.

The localStorage object can be used for offline work. For the form example, you can store the data in the localStorage and provide a button to click when connected to the Internet, in order to sync the data from localStorage to server-side storage.

See Also

See Recipe 20.4 for more on the Storage object, and on sessionStorage and localStorage.

20.6 Persisting Data Using a Relational Data Store

Problem

You want a more sophisticated data store on the client than what's provided with other persistent storage methods, such as localStorage. You'd also like to use your mad SQL skills.

Solution

You can use SQL in client applications, with some significant limitations. There is a W3C Web SQL Database Working Draft for using a relational database such as SQLite on the client, but support for the specification is provided only in WebKit browsers (Safari and Chrome) and the latest Opera (10.5):

You can create a database:

```
var db = openDatabase("dbname","1.0", "Bird Database", 1024 * 1024);
```

and you can create tables, within a transaction:

```
db.transaction(function(tx)) {
    tx.executeSQL('CREATE TABLE birdTable(birdid INTEGER NOT NULL PRIMARY KEY
AUTOINCREMENT, birdname VARCHAR(20) NOT NULL)');
```

Then query on the tables:

```
db.transation(function(tx)) {
    tx.executeSQL('SELECT * birdTable', [], sqlFunction, sqlError);

var sqlFunction = function(tx,recs) {
    var rows = recs.rows;
    for (var i = 0; i < rows.length; i++) {
        alert(recs.rows.item(i).text);
}
```

Discussion

I hesitated to cover the Web SQL Database specification because the implementation is limited, and the specification is currently blocked at the W3C. Only WebKit (and Chrome and Safari) and Opera have made any progress with this implementation, and there's no guarantee that Mozilla or Microsoft will pick up on it, especially since the specification is blocked.

It is an interesting concept, but it has significant problems. One is security, naturally.

In our current applications, the client part of the applications handles one form of security, and the server component handles the other, including database security and protection against SQL injection: attaching text on to a data field value that actually triggers a SQL command—such as drop all tables, or expose private data. Now, with client-side relational database support, we're introducing a new set of security concerns on the client.

Another concern is the increasing burden we put on client-side storage. Each new innovation exposes new vulnerabilities, increases the size and complexity of our browsers, and embeds all sorts of data on our machines. Yet the vast majority of JavaScript applications don't need to create their own version of Gmail, or a Photoshop-like paint program.

Then there's the separation of a skill set. While it's true that in small-to-medium shops, the same people who develop the frontend application probably participate in the server-side development, it's not unusual in many shops to have the tasks handled by different groups. So people who may not be terribly experienced at relational database management might be tossing around SQL transactions (and believe me, relational database application development is a dedicated skill).

From an implementation point of view, only SQLite is currently supported. One difference in implementations, if you have worked with server-side SQL applications, is that client-side SQL is asynchronous by default. This means your application is not blocked until the transaction completes, which provides its own challenge.

However, there's nothing wrong with playing around with something new. If you're interested, pick up a browser that supports the functionality and give it a shot. However, I would avoid production use until we're sure this technology is going to have a life beyond 2010.

See Also

The Web SQL Database specification can be found at *http://dev.w3.org/html5/webda tabase/*.

CHAPTER 21

JavaScript Outside the Box

21.0 Introduction

I believe JavaScript is the most important programming language a web developer should learn. Sure, you can learn Java or PHP, Python, Ruby, ASP.NET, or any other programming environment or language, but one thing all these options share is that eventually, one way or another, you'll probably need to use JavaScript.

JavaScript is fun, too. You have to spend a considerable amount of time working on architecture issues and setup issues in many of the other environments, but all you need with JavaScript is a browser and a text-editing tool. When I say you can go from opening your text editor to your first real JavaScript application in five minutes, I'm not exaggerating. Take the following file:

```
<!DOCTYPE html>
<head>
<title>Blank</title>
<meta http-equiv="Content-Type" content="text/html;charset=utf-8" >
</head>
<body>
</body>
```

Add the following script after the `title` element:

```
<script>
alert("Wow, that was easy!");
</script>
```

Open the page in any browser, and you're done. The only thing simpler in application development would be direct thought transference.

In the first 20 chapters of this book, I covered how to use JavaScript primarily to build standard web applications, but that's only part of the JavaScript story. JavaScript is an important component of major frameworks such as Microsoft's Silverlight, as well as desktop development environments, such as Adobe AIR. JavaScript and JSON are the baseline functionality for Apache's new CouchDB, which features a JSON-enabled database and query engine.

JavaScript is also used in many different applications and development environments, some of which are only indirectly related to typical web page functionality.

In this chapter, I'm going to provide a sampling of out-of-the-box JavaScript uses that exist today, touching on some of the more popular. By the time you're done with the chapter, you'll understand why every developer needs to know JavaScript.

 Wikipedia's page on JavaScript (*http://en.wikipedia.org/wiki/Java Script*) includes one section titled "Uses outside web pages," which can be a good resource for seeing how JavaScript can be used for something other than web applications.

21.1 Creating a Browser Add-On, Plug-in, or Extension

Problem

You have an idea that would make a good browser add-on, plug-in, or extension, but you want to leverage your JavaScript skills to make the application.

Solution

Use the browser's plug-in SDK, Extension API, or other packaged functionality that lets you use JavaScript to create the application.

Discussion

Not all browsers provide a relatively simple way to create browser add-ons, plug-ins, or extensions. Opera doesn't provide this functionality at all, and WebKit's plug-in architecture isn't trivial. However, if you're motivated, you should be able to use your JavaScript skills to create any number of useful browser tools.

Creating Google Chrome extensions

A Google Chrome extension is the simplest development environment of all the browsers. Your extension can consist of a manifest file, created in JSON, a download icon, and then the extension web page and JavaScript. It's uncomplicated, and it's the environment I recommend you try first, before developing an extension for other browsers. You can run through the beginning tutorial and have your first Chrome extension finished in an hour.

If, I should add, you can run Chrome in your environment at all, as Google also provides limited platform support for its browser. Currently, the Google Chrome extension environment only seems to work in Windows, though you can see about getting into an early release program for Mac and Linux. Note that Chrome's Mac support is for Intel-based machines only.

If you can work with Chrome, your extension begins with a manifest file that uses JSON and looks like:

```
{
  "name": "Hello World",
  "version": "1.0",
  "description": "Giving this a try",
  "browser_action": {
    "default_icon": "icon.png",
  "popup" : "popup.html"
  }
}
```

You'll provide an extension name and description, provide the environments in which you'll work ("permissions"), such as Google or Flickr, and provide browser actions to load pages or add icons.

The *popup.html* file for my first extension has a **style** section and a **script** section:

```
<style>
body {
  min-width:357px;
  overflow-x:hidden;
  background-color:  #ff0000;
  color: #ffff00;
  font-weight: bold;
  font-size: 48px;
}

</style>

<script>
window.onload=function(){
  var txt = document.createTextNode("Hello World!");
  var div = document.createElement("div");
  div.appendChild(txt);
  document.body.appendChild(div);
}
</script>
```

After you create the manifest and application page, you'll load the extension in Chrome via the Tools menu, choosing Extensions. Make sure the Developer Tools are exposed, and click the "Load unpacked extension..." button for the extension folder, as shown in Figure 21-1. If all goes well, the icon shows in the toolbar.

If you click the icon, the extension pop-up should open, as shown in Figure 21-2.

 Access the Google Chrome Extension Lab at *http://code.google.com/ chrome/extensions/overview.html.*

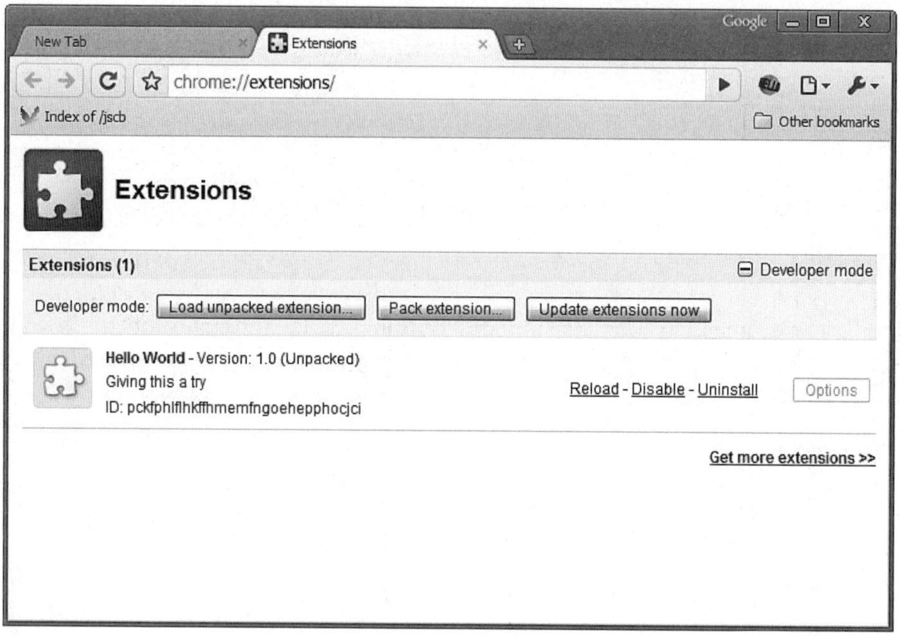

Figure 21-1. Loading a Chrome extension

Mozilla extensions

The Mozilla extensions for the organization's applications, including Firefox and Thunderbird, are reasonably uncomplicated to create, but even then, the number of files you need in order to implement an add-on is a little awe-inspiring.

To assist the new extension developer, Mozilla provides a section on extensions, including how to set up a development environment, what all of the files mean, and what you need to bring your application together. There is also an Extension Wizard, which can simplify your work.

The functionality for your Firefox add-on is going to be based, in part, on JavaScript, though the environment may not be one you recognize. For instance, your extension could consist of an XPCOM component, which has to be compiled using the Gecko SDK.

Robert Nyman provided probably one of the cleanest tutorials on creating a Firefox extension, including a no-nonsense description of what files are needed, and where they are located. Once you plow through all of the files, you'll find a JavaScript code listing. Though the objects in the code are unfamiliar, the coding is not.

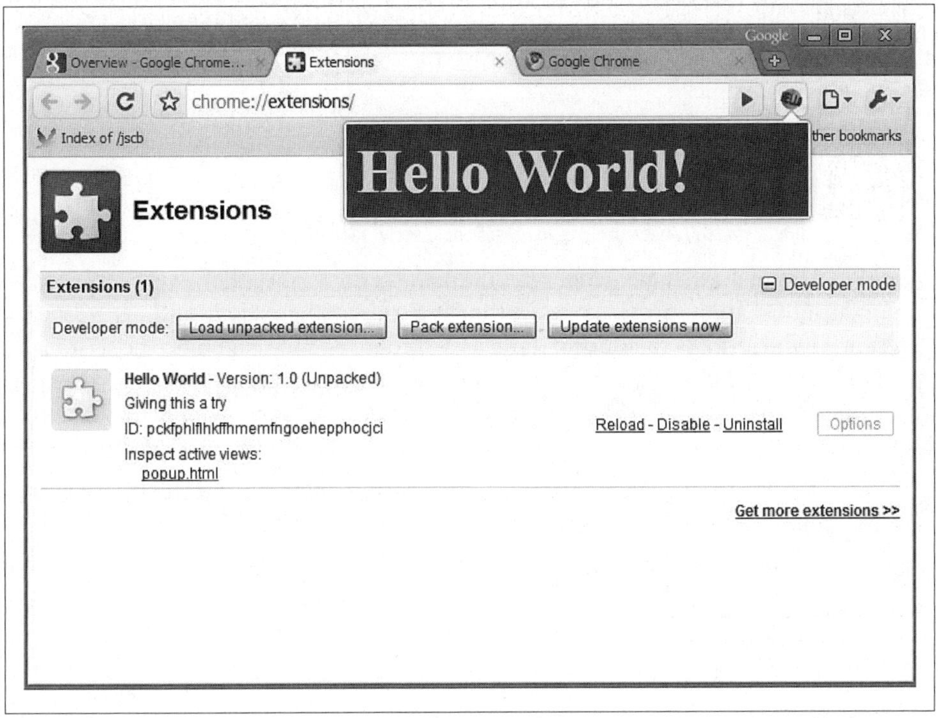

Figure 21-2. Trying out my first Chrome extension

The Mozilla Extensions site is at *https://developer.mozilla.org/en/Exten sions*. The Extension Wizard can be found at *http://ted.mielczarek.org/ code/mozilla/extensionwiz/*. A tutorial on how to build XPCOM components using JavaScript can be found at *http://ted.mielczarek.org/code/ mozilla/extensionwiz/*. Robert Nyman's Extension tutorial can be found at *http://robertnyman.com/2009/01/24/how-to-develop-a-firefox-exten sion/*.

Creating a Greasemonkey script

Greasemonkey is a popular Firefox extension that simplifies the process of building new functionality for the browser. Rather than going through the entire extension-building process, you can create a Greasemonkey script using JavaScript, and not have to worry about XUL, XPCOM, or intimidating file structures.

Mozilla recently released the first milestone release of the Jetpack SDK, providing a simpler environment for creating Firefox extensions. Read more about it and download the SDK at *http://mozillalabs.com/jetpack/ 2010/03/09/announcing-the-jetpack-sdk/*.

A Greasemonkey script has a metadata section, which provides information about the script. Following the metadata section is the application functionality. Here's an example of the beginning of a Greasemonkey script, from the popular YouTube Enhancer Greasemonkey script:

```
// @name      YouTube Enhancer
// @author    GIJoe
// @license   (CC) by-nc-sa
// @include   http://*.youtube.*/*
// @include   http://userscripts.org/scripts/show/33402*
```

This partial list of the metadata describes the name of the script and the author, provides copyright information, and also several include rules. The *include* and *exclude* rules determine if the script is run or not. If the include dependency isn't met, the script isn't run; similarly, if what's listed in the exclude rule is met, the script isn't run. This prevents running of script where it does no good, or may conflict with other applications.

The code, though, is very familiar. The following is a snippet from the UnShortEmAll Greasemonkey script, which unshortens the shortened URLs in Twitter:

```
var as = document.getElementsByTagName('a');
for (var i = 0; i < as.length; i++) {
   var a = as[i];
   if (isshort(a)) {
      unshorten(a);
   }
}
...
function unshorten(short_link) {
   GM_xmlHttpRequest( {
      method: "HEAD",
      url: short_link, href,
      headers: {"User-Agent": "Mozilla/5.0", "Accept": "text/xml"},
      onload: function(response) {
                  short_link.href=response.finalUrl;
      }
   });
}
```

The code looks familiar. What's different is the objects, and how the objects are used. However, we've used libraries before, and the objects are intuitive.

 Download Greasemonkey from Greasespot (*http://www.greasespot .net/*). Get Greasemonkey scripts at *http://userscripts.org*, and the YouTube Enhancer script at *http://userscripts.org/scripts/show/33042*. The Greasemonkey Manual can be found online at *http://wiki.greasespot.net/ Greasemonkey_Manual*.

21.2 Creating Desktop and Mobile Widgets

Problem

You want to create a widget that can be run in a browser, on the desktop, or in a mobile device.

Solution

Use a widget development toolset.

Discussion

The world is widget-crazy, and rightfully so. Rather than large cumbersome multipurpose applications, a widget is a small, friendly little bit of single-purpose functionality that is easy on our eyes, wallets, and computer resources.

Widgets are especially attuned to the mobile environment, requiring little space and providing simple or no required interaction—they just work, as the saying goes. More importantly, widgets make use of existing technology, including HTML and JavaScript, and minimize the esoteric file structures endemic to browser extensions and full-blown phone applications.

Widgets can be defined for a specific environment, such as the desktop, or can easily migrate from desktop to mobile. The difference is the toolset used.

 Microsoft also supports HTML-based widgets in Vista and Windows 7 (*http://www.microsoft.com/windows/windows-vista/features/sidebar -gadgets.aspx*). Yahoo! has a nice summary of desktop widgets at *http: //widgets.yahoo.net/blog/?p=16*.

Developing Mac Dashboard widgets

Widgets came into their own when Apple released the Mac Dashboard, an environment conducive to embedding small, single-purpose applications. Currently on my Mac's Dashboard, I have a weather widget, a clock, a calendar, and a countdown timer. Some I downloaded, some I made.

The best environment for building Dashboard widgets is to use Apple's Dashcode, which comes bundled with Xcode 3.0 and up. Dashboard comes prebuilt with templates you can select from in order to short-cut the widget development effort. As Figure 21-3 shows, there are a lot of different widget templates.

Once you've picked a template, you'll get a project interface where you can change the widget attributes, mark off completed workflow items, modify the graphics, include a widget icon, and package the whole thing. You can also add in JavaScript and see the existing script by clicking the View→Source Code menu option.

Figure 21-3. Choosing a Dashboard widget template

At any time in the development process, you can run the widget to see how it looks, as shown in Figure 21-4 with a little book draft countdown widget I created. Notice the JavaScript in the window in the background.

You can also use Dashcode to create a mobile Safari application.

> Dashcode is installed with the XCode tool set, which you can either install from your Mac discs or access from *http://developer.apple.com*.

The Opera Widgets development environment

Opera doesn't have an add-on or extension API/SDK, but it does have a very nice widget development environment. This isn't surprising when you consider Opera's focus on its very popular mobile browser. However, you can also run Opera widgets as stand-alone desktop applications, as long as Opera 10.2 or higher is installed somewhere on your computer. Beginning with Opera 10.5, the widgets install as first-class citizens (like a regular application).

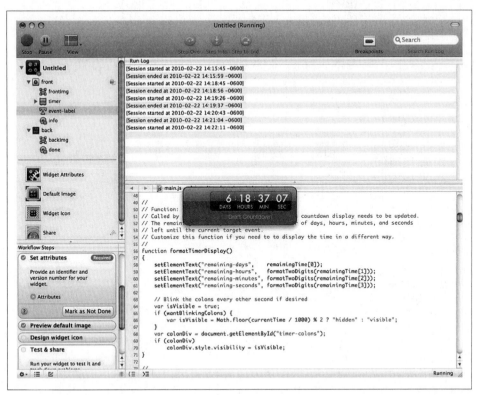

Figure 21-4. A snapshot of an in-progress Dashboard widget project

Building an Opera widget is little different than building any other widget: you create an HTML file for the widget, add script, a CSS stylesheet, and a configuration file (in XML) to manage the packaging of the widget. Opera widgets can be downloaded and installed and given chrome—more like an application than a widget.

I created a simple Opera widget, but instead of the traditional Hello World, decided to print the date and time. I also added widget-like behavior to flip the widget when the front is clicked, in order to show the back, and to return.

The HTML file is simple, and includes `stylesheet` and `script` inline:

```
<!DOCTYPE html>
<html>
  <head>
    <title>Date/Time</title>
    <style>
      body
      {
          background-color: #006600;
          color: #ffff00;
          font-weight: bold;
          font-size: 24px;
```

```
        }
        span
        {
            padding: 10px;
        }
        p a
        {
          color: #fff;
        }
    </style>
    <script type="text/javascript">
      window.addEventListener("load", function () {
            // print out date
            var dt = new Date();
            var dtStr = dt.toDateString();
            document.getElementById("date").innerHTML=dtStr;

            // time
            var timeStr = dt.toTimeString();
            document.getElementById("time").innerHTML=timeStr;

        }, false);
    </script>
  </head>
  <body>
      <div id="datetime"><span id="date"></span><br /><span id="time"></span></div>
  </body>
</html>
```

One very nice thing about developing for a specific browser and environment, is you don't have to worry about cross-browser support, and can use something like addEventListener for the window load event without worrying about IE. I could have also split the style into a stylesheet and the script into a script file—separate or inline, makes no difference.

The *config.xml* file is also simple, just providing some basic information about the widget and the widget author:

```
<?xml version='1.0' encoding='UTF-8'?>
<widget>
  <widgetname>Date and Time</widgetname>
  <description>Prints out current date and time</description>
  <width>440</width>
  <height>200</height>
  <author>
    <name>Shelley Powers</name>
    <email>shelleyp@burningbird.net</email>
    <link>http://burningbird.net</link>
    <organization>Burningbird</organization>
  </author>
  <id>
    <host>burningbid.net</host>
    <name>DateTime</name>
    <revised>2010-03</revised>
```

```
    </id>
  </widget>
```

To package the widget, all we need do is zip it up and change the file extension to *.wgt*. When downloaded and double-clicked, the widget is installed and run, as shown in Figure 21-5.

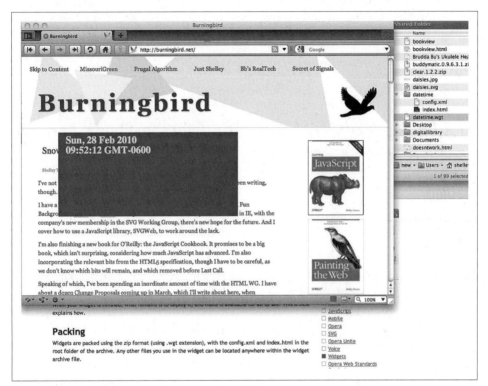

Figure 21-5. My little Opera widget on my Mac desktop

Of course, this is a simple widget, without chrome (which can be added), or controls (ditto), and it doesn't update the time with a timer. But it does demonstrate how simple it can be to create a working widget.

There are any number of widget SDKs and instructions for making both desktop and mobile widgets. Among those I thought most interesting are the following:

- The Opera Widget Developer Community (*http://dev.opera.com/articles/widgets*).
- The W3C's Widget Packaging and Configuration specification (*http://www.w3 .org/TR/widgets/*) is in Candidate Recommendation state.
- The Yahoo! Konfabulator SDK (*http://widgets.yahoo.com/tools/*). The site also provides a widget converter.

- Microsoft has provided a how-to on creating widgets for Windows Mobile 6.5 (*http://msdn.microsoft.com/en-us/library/dd721906.aspx*). Windows Mobile 7 should be released towards the end of 2010.

- The Mobile Safari Web Application Tutorial at Apple (*http://developer.apple.com/safari/library/documentation/AppleApplications/Conceptual/Dashcode_UserGuide/Contents/Resources/en.lproj/MakingaWebApp/MakingaWebApp.html*).

- Widgetbox (*http://www.widgetbox.com/*) is a commercial site that provides tools and hosting for widgets. You can use the site's free services, or sign up for a Pro account.

- Create Google Gadgets (widgets) for Google Desktop (*http://code.google.com/apis/desktop/*).

21.3 Creating JavaScript Applications for the iPhone, Android, and BlackBerry with PhoneGap

Problem

You want to develop a smart phone application using JavaScript.

Solution

For many different platforms, including the iPhone, Android, and BlackBerry, use PhoneGap to create the application with HTML and JavaScript,.

Discussion

Smart phone development requires a commitment of both time and money. No matter how clever the tools you use, you'll need to test your application in a real device, and therein lies the cost. In addition, setting up the development environment and becoming familiar with the SDKs and plug-ins, as well as with PhoneGap, is not a trivial undertaking. However, smart phone applications are a hot commodity now, as well as an interesting environment, and can be worth both the time and the cost.

PhoneGap provides a way to develop an application once in HTML and JavaScript, and port that application to the three smart phone environments: iPhone, Android, and BlackBerry (and Windows Mobile, Palm, and so on). What it doesn't provide is a way to work around any environment restrictions, such as having to have a Mac Intel machine in order to develop for the iPhone.

If you don't have a Mac Intel machine, though, you can still try out the tool for other phones, even if at first you don't have the phones for testing. PhoneGap provides an emulator, as does Android and BlackBerry. BlackBerry provides a variety of simulators for every type of device.

You'll need to install the Eclipse development environment, but this application is freely available for most environments. You'll also need to download either the BlackBerry or Android SDKs, and/or Eclipse plug-ins. It does take a nontrivial amount of time getting to know the environments, the files, and how everything holds together.

Once you've met these background requirements, you're back on familiar ground: using HTML, CSS, and JavaScript. For instance, the following code snippet (from the book *Building iPhone Apps with HTML, CSS, and JavaScript (http://oreilly.com/catalog/9780596805791/)*, by Jonathan Stark, published by O'Reilly) demonstrates using jQuery for building an iPhone application:

```
if (window.innerWidth && window.innerWidth <= 480) {

    $(document).ready(function(){
        $('#header ul').addClass('hide');
        $('#header').append('<div class="leftButton"
            onclick="toggleMenu()">Menu</div>');
    });
    function toggleMenu() {
        $('#header ul').toggleClass('hide');
        $('#header .leftButton').toggleClass('pressed');
    }
}
```

As you can see, once you get past all of the framework issues, the JavaScript is little different than what you use for your web applications.

See Also

Download PhoneGap and find the help wiki at *http://phonegap.com/*. You can also separately download the PhoneGap emulator, which runs on Adobe AIR. I found the emulator to be helpful when it came to debugging how my many websites look on various mobile devices.

Another helpful tool for jQuery development for the iPhone is jQTouch, a jQuery plug-in developed by David Kaneda to simplify converting HTML pages into iPhone applications. The plug-in comes with prebuilt animations, as well as event handling specific to iPhones, such as swipe detection. You can download the plug-in and see documentation at *http://www.jqtouch.com/*. Jonathan Stark provides a how-to tutorial on using jQTouch on YouTube at *http://www.youtube.com/watch?v=6X4K2MQsSeI*.

Eclipse can be downloaded from *http://www.eclipse.org*. The Android development environment can be found at *http://developer.android.com/sdk/index.html*, and the BlackBerry at *http://na.blackberry.com/eng/developers/*.

If you have the bucks to ensure you have the development machine, the iPhone development center is at *http://developer.apple.com/iphone/*. If you are interested in iPhone development, I recommend *Building iPhone Apps with HTML, CSS, and JavaScript (http://oreilly.com/catalog/9780596805791/)* by Jonathan Stark (O'Reilly). Jonathan provides a chapter on using PhoneGap for iPhone development.

21.4 Enhancing Tools with JavaScript

Problem

You have a favorite tool, such as Photoshop or Adobe Bridge, or a favorite application, such as OpenOffice. You want to add an extension or macro that takes a set of behaviors written in JavaScript and integrates it into the product.

Solution

A quick search online is going to show if you can extend your favorite tools, utilities, and applications with JavaScript. In most cases, you already have the tools you need.

Discussion

When we hear *JavaScript*, we think *web*, and forget that JavaScript is a compact, easy-to-learn language being incorporated as the basic scripting language for many applications.

In this section, we'll look at how JavaScript can be used to extend, enhance, or package reusable functionality, and then be integrated into two different applications.

Working with the Adobe Bridge SDK and the ExtendScript Toolkit

JavaScript can be used with the Adobe Creative Suite (CS) products, using the Adobe Bridge SDK and the ExtendScript Toolkit (ESTK) that's installed with the Suite. There are SDKs currently available for CS3 and CS4. You can use any editor for the JavaScript, but the ESTK allows you to build and test within the environment in which the scripts run.

The easiest way to get started with writing scripts for the Creative Suite products is to open it and take a close look at the samples provided with the SDK and Creative Suite installations, most likely under a subdirectory labeled Scripting Guide. Both the SDK and the CS come with extensive documentation.

For the Adobe Bridge SDK, the JavaScript samples are located in the *sdksamples/javascript* subdirectory. I picked one called *ColorPicker.jsx*, and double-clicked the file to open it within the ESTK, as shown in Figure 21-6.

The Photoshop script files have a specialized ESTK file extension, *.jsx*, but they contain regular JavaScript. The sample code is well documented and easy to follow. Utilizing the advice in the CS3 Scripting Guide, I created a PhotoShop version of Hello World with the following JavaScript:

```
// Remember current unit settings and then set units to
// the value expected by this script
var originalUnit = preferences.rulerUnits
preferences.rulerUnits = Units.INCHES
```

```
// Create a new 2x4 inch document and assign it to a variable
var docRef = app.documents.add( 8, 8 )

// Create a new art layer containing text
var artLayerRef = docRef.artLayers.add()
artLayerRef.kind = LayerKind.TEXT

// Set the contents of the text layer.
var textItemRef = artLayerRef.textItem
textItemRef.contents = "Hello, World from Shelley!"

// Release references
docRef = null
artLayerRef = null
textItemRef = null

// Restore original ruler unit setting
app.preferences.rulerUnits = originalUnit
```

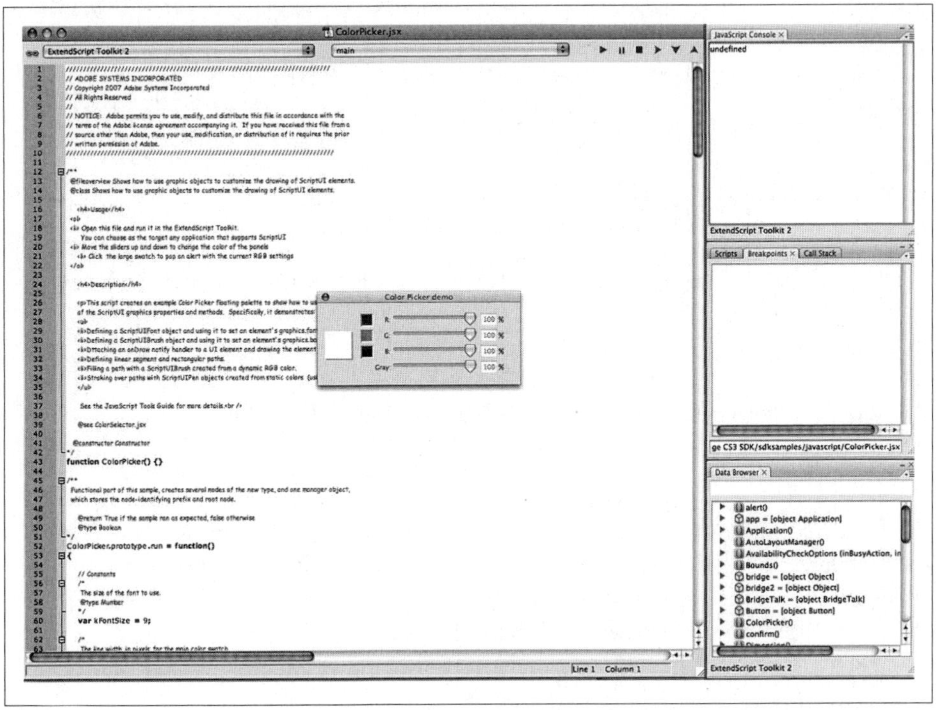

Figure 21-6. Opening the ColorPicker JavaScript file in the ExtendScript Toolkit

I saved the file as *helloworld.jsx* in the CS3 Photoshop→Presets→Scripts subdirectory, and when I started Photoshop and selected File→Scripts, my `helloworld` script was displayed in the menu that opened. Clicking it opened a very plain document with my simple message.

As you can see, the JavaScript is simple, but you do have to spend a significant amount of time becoming familiar with the Adobe CS environment and objects.

 You can download the Adobe Bridge SDK from the Photoshop Developer Center (*http://www.adobe.com/devnet/photoshop/sdk/*).

Creating an OpenOffice macro

Most office-like tools provide some form of extensibility, though not all applications allow JavaScript. OpenOffice, which is the tool I'm using to write this book, allows us to write macros using JavaScript within the ScriptingFramework architecture.

A JavaScript macro is created in its own subdirectory, with a *parcel-descriptor.xml* file providing a descriptor for the macro. A very simple example is my own modified version of the Hello World JavaScript macro that is installed with Open Office. The descriptor looks as follows:

```
?xml version="1.0" encoding="UTF-8"?>

<parcel language="JavaScript" xmlns:parcel="scripting.dtd">

    <script language="JavaScript">
        <locale lang="en">
            <displayname value="Shelley's Hello World"/>
            <description>
                Adds the the string "Hello World, from Shelley!"
into the current text doc.
            </description>
        </locale>
        <functionname value="helloworldfromshelley.js"/>
        <logicalname value="ShelleyHelloWorld.JavaScript"/>
    </script>

</parcel>
```

Pretty simple and intuitive: a display name, a description, the function name (which is the filename), and a logical name. The JavaScript is almost as simple:

```
/ Hello World in JavaScript
importClass(Packages.com.sun.star.uno.UnoRuntime);
importClass(Packages.com.sun.star.text.XTextDocument);
importClass(Packages.com.sun.star.text.XText);
importClass(Packages.com.sun.star.text.XTextRange);

//get the document from the scripting context
oDoc = XSCRIPTCONTEXT.getDocument();

//get the XTextDocument interface
xTextDoc = UnoRuntime.queryInterface(XTextDocument,oDoc);

//get the XText interface
```

```
xText = xTextDoc.getText();

//get an (empty) XTextRange interface at the end of the text
xTextRange = xText.getEnd();

//set the text in the XTextRange
xTextRange.setString( "Hello World, from Shelley!" );
```

All macros have access to the OpenOffice API through the **XScriptContext** object, shown highlighted in the code snippet, which provides an interface between the macro and the OpenOffice documents.

Once both of the files were created, I uploaded my macro subdirectory to the Open-Office macro subdirectory, and when I clicked on Tools→Macros→Organize Macros→JavaScript, the dialog opened, showing my newly installed Macro, as in Figure 21-7.

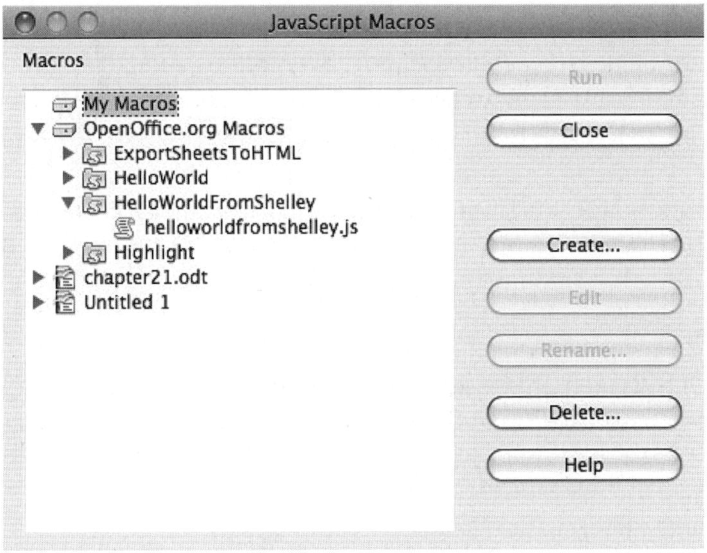

Figure 21-7. OpenOffice dialog showing my newly created JavaScript macro

Running the macro creates a line of text in the top of the document that says, "Hello World from Shelley!"

Simple, true, but the line could have easily contained the typical header for all of your letters, preformatted and ready to insert into the page by clicking a key that is bound to the macro.

The OpenOffice Writing Macros page can be found at *http://wiki.serv ices.openoffice.org/wiki/Documentation/DevGuide/Scripting/Writing _Macros*.

21.5 Creating Efficient Desktop Applications with Web Workers and the File API

Problem

You're interested in adding the necessary functionality so that your browser-based on-line application can function as a full-featured desktop application.

Solution

In addition to using many of the other technologies covered earlier in the book, add four new capabilities to your JavaScript/CSS/HTML-based application: application cache, so your site can function offline; geolocation, if your application is mobile-based; direct file access through the File API; and Web Workers, for efficient concurrent processing.

Application cache isn't JavaScript-specific, and the geolocation API requires specialized equipment for testing, so I'm going to focus on the File API and Web Workers in this recipe.

Discussion

The File API bolts on to the existing input element `file` type, used for file uploading. In addition to the capability of uploading the file to the server via a form upload, you can now access the file directly in JavaScript, and either work with it locally or upload the file using the `XMLHttpRequest` object.

There are three objects in the File API:

`FileList`
 A list of files to upload via `input type="file"`.

`File`
 Information about a specific file.

`FileReader`
 Object to asynchronously upload the file for client-side access.

Each of the objects has associated properties and events, including being able to track the progress of a file upload (and provide a custom progress bar), as well as signaling when the upload is finished. The `File` object can provide information about the file, including file size and MIME type. The `FileList` object provides a list of `File` objects, because more than one file can be specified if the input element has the `multiple` attribute set. The `FileReader` is the object that does the actual file upload.

Example 21-1 is an application that uses all three objects in order to upload a file as text, and embed the text into the web page. In the example, I'm using it to access uncompressed ePub book chapters. Since ePub chapter files are valid XHTML, I can use the built-in XML Parser object, `DOMParser`, to process the file.

Example 21-1. Uploading an ePub chapter into a web page

```
<!DOCTYPE html>
<head>
<title>ePub Reader</title>
<meta charset="utf-8" />
<style>
#result
{
  width: 500px;
  margin: 30px;
}
</style>
<script>

window.onload=function() {

  var inputElement = document.getElementById("file");
  inputElement.addEventListener("change", handleFiles, false);
}

function handleFiles() {
  var fileList = this.files;
  var reader = new FileReader();
  reader.onload = loadFile;
  reader.readAsText(fileList[0]);
}

function loadFile() {

  // look for the body section of the document
  var parser = new DOMParser();
  var xml = parser.parseFromString(this.result,"text/xml");
  var content = xml.getElementsByTagName("body");

  // if found, extract the body element's innerHTML
  if (content.length > 0) {
    var ct = content[0].innerHTML;
    var title = document.getElementById("bookTitle").value;
    title = "<h2>" + title + "</title>";
    document.getElementById("result").innerHTML = title + ct;
  }
}
</script>
</head>
<body>
```

```
<form>
<label for="title">Title:</label>
<input type="text" id="bookTitle" /></br ><br />
<label for="file">File:</label> <input type="file" id="file" /><br />
</form>
<div id="result"></div>
</body>
```

Figure 21-8 shows the page with a chapter of one of my books loaded.

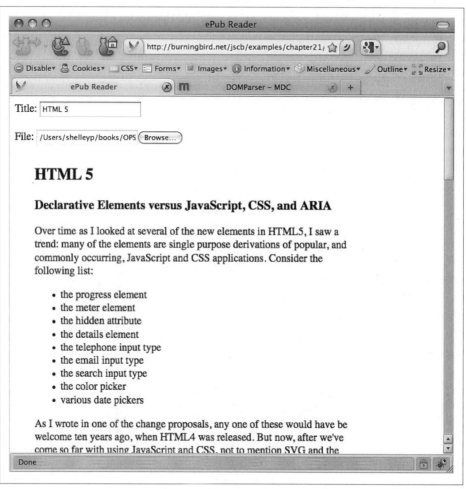

Figure 21-8. Using the File API to read a chapter of an ePub book

The File API is still a work in progress, and only Firefox 3.6 and up support it. However, it's an intriguing functionality that's also necessary for an application to be considered a "desktop" application—if you want to be able to upload and work with files when your application is currently offline. It's also pretty handy for other uses.

The File API is a W3C effort. You can read the latest draft at *http://www .w3.org/TR/FileAPI/*. Read Mozilla's coverage at *https://developer.mozil la.org/en/Using_files_from_web_applications*.

The last new technology I'm going to cover in this book is Web Workers. Before I get into the new functionality, though, I want to provide a brief introduction to multi-threaded development.

In a language such as Java, you can create multiple threads of execution, which can operate concurrently. Computers and operating systems have long had the ability to support multiple threads, switching the necessary resources among the threads as needed, demonstrated in Figure 21-9. Handled correctly, threads can make your application run faster and more efficiently. Multithreaded development also provides the functionality necessary to ensure the threads are synced, so the applications are accurate, too.

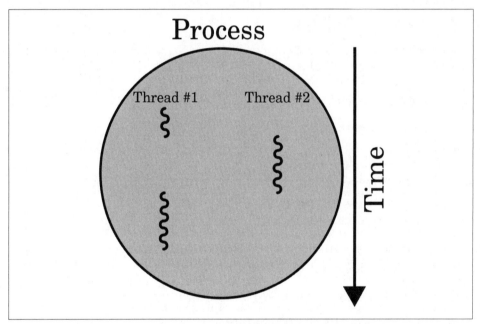

Figure 21-9. Example of concurrent threads, from the Thread Wikipedia entry

In the past, a major difference between JavaScript and these multithreaded programming languages is that JavaScript runs within a single thread of execution. Even when a timer fires, the associated event falls into the same queue as other pending events. This single-execution-thread queue is why you can't absolutely depend on the preciseness of a JavaScript timer. With Web Workers, introduced as one of the W3C WebApps 1.0 specifications, for better or worse, this all changes.

I say "for better or worse" because thread-based development has always been a two-edged sword in most development environments. If they're not properly managed, multithreaded applications can crash and burn rather spectacularly. Of course, with most of the other multithreaded environments, you also have more control over the creation and destruction of threads. Web Workers provides threaded development, but at a higher, hopefully safer level.

To create a web worker, all you need do is call the Worker object constructor, passing in the URI for a script file to run:

```
var theWorker = new Worker("background.js");
```

You can also assign a function to the web worker's onmessage event handler, and onerror event handler:

```
theWorker.onmessage = handleMessage;
theWorker.onerror = handleError;
```

To communicate with the web worker, use the postMessage method, providing any data it needs:

```
theWorker.postMessage(dataObject);
```

In the web worker, an onmessage event handler receives this message, and can extract the data from the event object:

```
onmessage(event) {
    var data = event.data;
    ...
}
```

If the web worker needs to pass data back, it also calls postMessage. The function to receive the message in the main application is the event handler function assigned to the web worker's onmessage event handler:

```
theWorker.onmessage= handleMessage;
```

The function can extract any data it's expecting from the event object.

Normally the script you'd run would be a computationally intensive script, with results that aren't immediately needed. Mozilla's example for web workers demonstrates a script that computes a Fibonacci sequence. It reminded me of the recursive function I demonstrated in Chapter 6, the one that reversed arrays.

In Example 21-2, I converted the reversed array function into a web worker JavaScript routine. In the JavaScript library, an onmessage event handler function accesses the data from the event object—the array to reverse—and passes it to the reversed array function. Once the function finishes, the web worker routine calls postMessage, sending the resulting string back to the main application.

Example 21-2. Using web worker JavaScript to reverse an array and return the resulting string

```
// web worker thread - reverses array
onmessage = function(event) {

    var reverseArray = function(x,indx,str) {
        return indx == 0 ? str :
reverseArray(x,--indx,(str+= " " + x[indx]));;
    }

    // reverse array
    var str = reverseArray(event.data, event.data.length, "");

    // return resulting string to main application
    postMessage(str);
};
```

I copied and modified the application in Example 21-1 to Example 21-3. When the application retrieves the uploaded file and extracts the **body** element, it splits the content into an array based on the space character. The application sends the array through to the reversed array web worker. Once the web worker finishes, the data is retrieved and output to the page.

Example 21-3. The ePub reader in Example 21-1, using a web worker to reverse the content

```
<!DOCTYPE html>
<head>
<title>ePub Reader</title>
<meta charset="utf-8" />
<style>
#result
{
  width: 500px;
  margin: 30px;
}
</style>
<script>

window.onload=function() {

  var inputElement = document.getElementById("file");
  inputElement.addEventListener("change", handleFiles, false);
}

function handleFiles() {
  var fileList = this.files;
  var reader = new FileReader();
  reader.onload = loadFile;
  reader.readAsText(fileList[0]);
}

function loadFile() {

  // look for the body section of the document
  var parser = new DOMParser();
```

```
    var xml = parser.parseFromString(this.result,"text/xml");
    var content = xml.getElementsByTagName("body");

    // if found, extract the body element's innerHTML
    if (content.length > 0) {
        var ct = content[0].innerHTML;
        var ctarray = ct.split(" ");
        var worker = new Worker("reverse.js");
        worker.onmessage=receiveResult;
        worker.postMessage(ctarray);
    }
}

function receiveResult(event) {
    document.getElementById("result").innerHTML = event.data;
}
</script>
</head>
<body>
<form>
<label for="file">File:</label> <input type="file" id="file" /><br />
</form>
<div id="result"></div>
</body>
```

As you can see in Figure 21-10, the results are interesting. Not very useful—except they demonstrate that the web worker performs as expected, and quickly, too.

Firefox 3.6 is the only browser that supports both File API and Web Workers at the time this was written. WebKit, and WebKit-based browsers, Safari and Chrome, support Web Workers. To test the result in the WebKit browsers, I converted the main application to work on a statically created array, rather than an uploaded file:

```
window.onload=function() {

    var ctarray = ["apple","bear","cherries","movie"];
    var worker = new Worker("reverse.js");
    worker.onmessage=receiveResult;
    worker.postMessage(ctarray);
}

function receiveResult(event) {
    document.getElementById("result").innerHTML = event.data;
}
```

I ran the application in Firefox and then in Safari, and ended up with unexpected results, as shown in Figure 21-11.

The Firefox results are what I would expect: the array entries are reversed, and the entries converted to a string. The result from Safari, though, is unexpected: every character within the string is reversed, including the commas between the array elements.

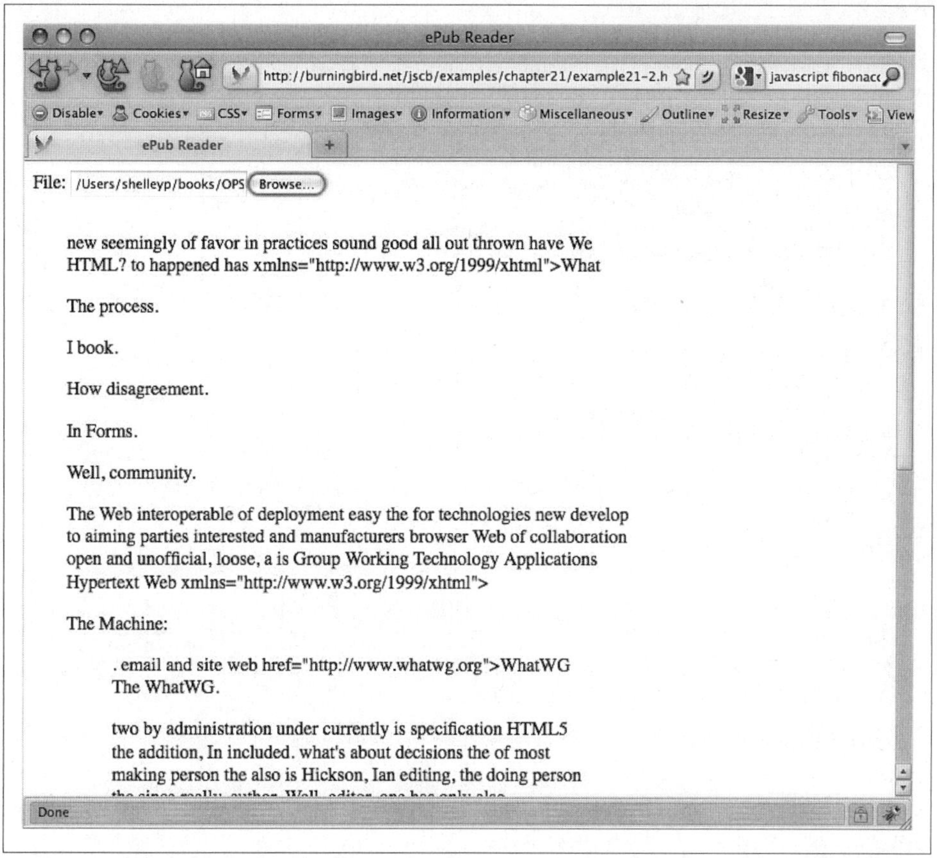

Figure 21-10. Reversed array from uploaded file displayed in page

Running the application again, but this time in the newest WebKit nightly build, the results match the Firefox result. What happened with Safari 4 is that `postMessage` didn't serialize the object correctly when it transmitted the object to the web worker routine. The newer WebKit nightly shows that this bug was fixed, and the object is now serialized correctly.

However, to ensure that objects are passed correctly, regardless of browser version, we can use `JSON.stringify` on any object before we send it, and `JSON.parse` on any data that we receive, in order to ensure the object is handled correctly regardless of browser and browser version:

```
window.onload=function() {

   var ctarray = ["apple","bear","cherries","movie"];
   var worker = new Worker("reverse2.js");
   worker.onmessage=receiveResult;
   worker.postMessage(JSON.stringify(ctarray));
}
```

```
function receiveResult(event) {
    document.getElementById("result").innerHTML = event.data;
}
```

In the web worker, we use JSON.parse to restore the serialized version of the object:

```
// web worker thread - reverses array
onmessage = function(event) {

    var reverseArray = function(x,indx,str) {
        return indx == 0 ? str :
reverseArray(x,--indx,(str+= " " + x[indx]));;
    }

    // reverse array
    var obj = JSON.parse(event.data);
    var str = reverseArray(obj, obj.length, "");

    // return resulting string to main application
    postMessage(str);
};
```

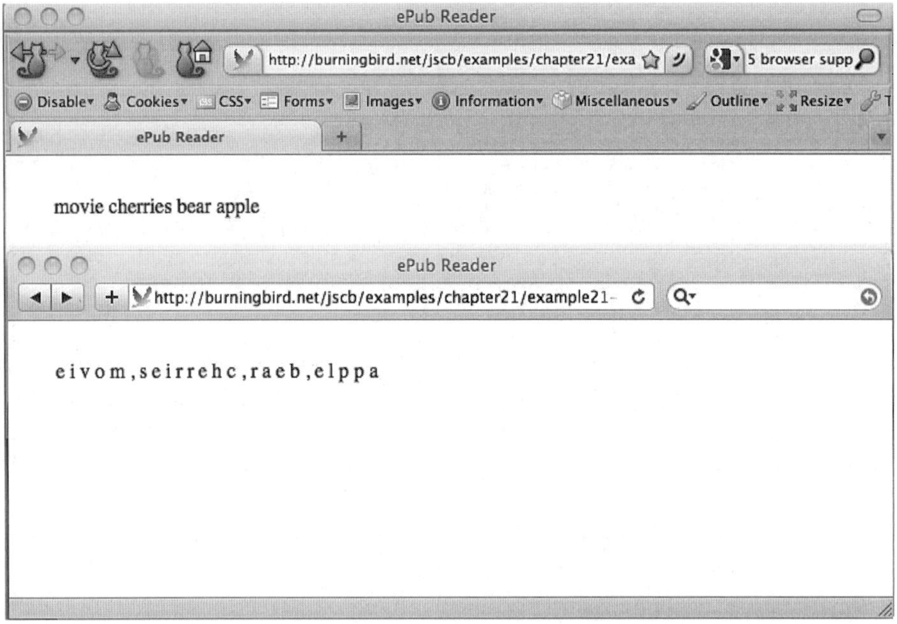

Figure 21-11. Interesting—and differing—results when running application in Firefox and Safari

Now the application works the same in Firefox 3.6 and Safari 4. The application should also work with Chrome. Web workers don't work with Opera 10.5, or IE8. However, both browsers should support web workers, and hopefully the File API, in an upcoming version.

See Also

See Recipe 6.6 for a description of the array reversal recursive function. The `postMessage` method is introduced in Recipe 18.10, and JSON is covered in Recipes 19.4 and 19.5.

Index

We'd like to hear your suggestions for improving our indexes. Send email to *index@oreilly.com*.

cancelPropagation method, 128
canPlayType method (media elements), 355
canvas elements, 325, 326–328
 converting hCalendar Microformat
  annotations into, 447–450
 dynamic line charts, 330–333
 implementing in IE, 328–330
 integrating with SVG in HTML, 347–350
capitalization (see case)
^ (caret) in regular expressions, 23
case (capitalization)
 comparing strings and, 5
 converting, 5
 ignoring in pattern matching, 26
 uppercase greater than lowercase, 7
catch statements, for exception handling, 183
ceil method (Math), 57
chaining constructors, 366
chaining methods, 236, 385–387, 402
change events, 116
characters, 14
 (see also strings)
 breaking strings into individual, 14
 capitalization of (see case)
 escape sequences for, 15
 matching in regular expressions, 23
 pattern matching (see regular expressions)
 special, in regular expressions, 23
checkbox elements, 162
 finding all checked, 233–234
checked options, finding all, 233–234
:checked pseudoclass, 233
childNodes collection, 215, 256, 440
Chrome extensions, building, 484–485
Chrome (Google), debugging in, 208–209
circles that fit page elements, 65–67
circular arcs, calculating length of, 67–68
class name, collecting elements by, 231–232
className property (HTMLElement), 244
clearRect method (canvas), 327
click events, 116
 with form elements, 162
click location (mouse), capturing, 119–122
client-side storage
 cookies (see cookies)
 localStorage objects, 476–479
 relational data stores, 479–481
 sessionStorage objects, 469–476
ClientRect objects, 272

clientWidth property, 271
cloneNode method, 257
closePath method (canvas), 331
closures, 105
 (see also currying)
CMS templates, breadcrumbs in, 150–152
code, packaging into files, 390–392
code compression with minify, 397
collapsible form sections, 277–280, 312–316
colorDepth property (Screen), 147
colors
 changing stylesheets based on support of,
  147–149
 flashing, to signal action, 316–320
 generating randomly, 60–61
columns, table, summing all elements in, 234–
  236
Comet concept (Ajax communication), 428
comma-delimited strings, breaking apart, 13–
  14
communication APIs (see Ajax; postMessage
  functionality)
comparing strings, 5–8
comparison operators, 6
compressing code with minify, 397
concat method (Array), 80
concatenating strings, 3–4
 with other data types, 4
concurrent form submissions, preventing, 169–
  171
|| (conditional OR) operator, 120
configurable attribute (objects), 370
confirm pop up boxes, 144
confirming user actions, 144
Console panel (Firebug), 191
constructor chaining, 366–369
constructors, 360
controls attribute (audio element), 352
cookie collection (document element), 212
cookie property (document), 462, 463
cookieEnabled property (Navigator), 146
cookies, 457, 462–465
CORS (Cross Origin Resource Sharing) API,
  413
cos method (Math), 57, 346
createAttribute method, 251–252
createElement method, 64
 adding elements before other elements,
  242–246

converting objects to strings, 445–446
converting RDFa into, 450–455
generating JavaScript objects with, 442–443
parsing JSON-formatted strings, 444–445
JSONP (JSON with Padding), 423
JsUnit, testing code with, 392–396

K

keyboard events, 116, 129–132
  with textarea elements, 163
keyboard listening, page overlays with, 308–312
keydown events, 130
keypress events, 130
  with form elements, 162
keys method (Object), 375, 376
keyup events, 130
-khtml-user-drag CSS setting, 135

L

language property (Navigator), 146
lastIndex property (RegExp), 31
lastIndexOf method (Array), 78
lastIndexOf method (String), 9
left-padding strings, 19–20
left property (bounding rectangle), 272, 273
length property (NodeList), 216
length property (String), 11
< (less than) operator, 7
<= (less than or equal) operator, 7
libraries, 389–411
  combining several, 408–411
  converting to jQuery plug-ins, 404–407
  external, using, 400–402
  hosting as open source, 397–399
  JsUnit, testing code with, 392–396
  minify, to compress code, 397
  packaging code into files, 390–392
  using existing jQuery plug-ins, 402–404
LIFO (last-in, first-out), 76–77
line charts (canvas), 330–333
line feed (\n), 16
  matching in regular expressions, 23
lineNumber property (Error), 183
lines in textareas, processing, 16–17
links, replacing links with, 254–257
links collection (document element), 212

listeners (see event listeners)
listener/sender functionality, 431
literals, 1
live regions, accessibility of, 323–324
LN10 property (Math), 56
LN2 property (Math), 56
load events, 115
load method (media elements), 355
localeCompare method (String), 8
localStorage objects, 476–479
location data for elements, 273–276
location elements, 143, 150
  bookmarking dynamic pages, 153
log method (Math), 57
LOG10E property (Math), 56
LOG2E property (Math), 56
&& (logical AND) operator, 11
long polling, 429
loops through array elements, 71
lowercase (see case)

M

\m flag (regular expressions), 26
Mac Dashboard widgets, 489–490
map method (Array), 83
match method (String), 26
matching (see regular expressions)
math, 55
  (see also numbers)
  calculating arc lengths, 67–68
  converting degrees and radians, 64–65
  finding circles that fit page elements, 65–67
  summing column of numbers, 62–64
Math objects, 56–57
  building clock with, 345–346
max-age= parameter (cookies), 463
max method (Math), 57
media (see rich media)
media attribute, 148
@media rule, 149
memoization (caching calculations), 109–112
message property (Error), 183
meta elements, 211
method chaining, 236, 385–387, 402
methods, object
  creating, 362–364
  keeping private, 361–362
  preventing any changes to, 380–381

R

radians, converting with degrees, 64–65
  calculating arc lengths, 67–68
radio buttons clicks, acting on, 164–166
radiobutton elements, 162
  performing actions after events, 164–166
radix parameter, parseInt function, 61
random color generation, 60–61
random method (Math), 57, 60
random number generation, 59–60
RangeError errors, 184
RangeException exceptions, 185
RDF plug-in, 450–455
RDF (Relational Data Framework), about, 452
RDFa, converting into JSON, 450–455
rdfQuery, 450–455
ready event, 401
readyState property (XMLHttpRequest), 420,
  428
readyState property (XMLHttpRequest), 415
recurring timers, 50–51
recursion, 101
recursive algorithms, 101–103
refactoring code, 392
ReferenceError errors, 185
Refresh button, preserving state for, 156–157
RegExp literals, 22
RegExp objects, 24
regular expressions, 21–38
  finding all instances of pattern, 28–31
  replacing certain substrings, 31–32
  replacing HTML with named entities, 36–
    37
  searching for special characters, 37–38
  with String.split method, 14
  swapping order of strings, 32–35
  testing for contained substrings
    case-insensitive matching, 25–26
    case-sensitive matching, 24–25
  trimming strings of whitespace, 35–36
  validating social security numbers, 26–28
relational data stores, 479–481
reload events, 116
removals value (aria-relevant attribute), 324
removeAttribute method, 253
removeAttributeNS method, 254
removeChild method, 260, 262
removeEventListener method, 125
removing (see deleting (removing))

replace method (String), 32
  special patterns for, 33
replacer functions, 444
replaceState method (history), 466
replacing
  array elements, 80–82
  substrings with other substrings, 31–32
requests, Ajax (see XMLHttpRequest objects)
resource window (Safari), 205
responseText property (XMLHttpRequest),
  415
responseXML property (XMLHttpRequest),
  415, 436
REST guidelines, 417
return statements, 95
return values, functions, 95–96
RGB values, random, 60
rich media, 325–357
  accessing SVG from page scripts, 335–338
  adding JavaScript to SVG, 333–335
  building analog clock, 345–346
  controlling video from JavaScript, 353–357
  embedding SVG into HTML pages, 339–
    345
  emulating SVG in IE, 338–339
  integrating SVG and canvas, 347–350
  running routine with audio file, 351–353
  using canvas (see canvas elements)
  WebGL support, 350–351
right-padding strings, 19–20
right property (bounding rectangle), 272
role attribute (ARIA), 301
round method (Math), 57
rows, table
  adding, 257–260
  deleting, 262–264
  summing all elements in, 234–236

S

\s in regular expressions, 23
\S in regular expressions, 24
Safari, WebGL support in, 350–351
Safari orientation events, 140–142
Safari's development tools, 201–205
  using breakpoints, 207–208
same-origin security restriction, 415
saving (see storing (saving))
scheduling future dates, 48
scope, function, 104, 383–385

About the Author

Shelley Powers has been working with and writing about web technologies—from the first release of JavaScript to the latest graphics and design tools—for more than 15 years. Her recent O'Reilly books have covered the semantic web, Ajax, JavaScript, and web graphics. She's an avid amateur photographer and web development aficionado.

Colophon

The animal on the cover of *JavaScript Cookbook* is a little (or lesser) egret (*Egretta garzetta*). A small white heron, it is the old world counterpart to the very similar new world snowy egret. It is the smallest and most common egret in Singapore, and its original breeding distribution included the large inland and coastal wetlands in warm temperate parts of Europe, Asia, Africa, Taiwan, and Australia. In warmer locations, most birds are permanent residents; northern populations, including many European birds, migrate to Africa and southern Asia. They may also wander north after the breeding season, which presumably has led to this egret's range expansion.

The adult Little Egret is 55–65 cm long with an 88–106 cm wingspan. It weighs 350–550 grams. Its plumage is all white. It has long black legs with yellow feet and a slim black bill. In the breeding season, the adult has two long nape plumes and gauzy plumes on the back and breast, and the bare skin between its bill and eyes becomes red or blue. Juvenile egrets are similar to nonbreeding adults but have duller legs and feet. Little egrets are the liveliest hunters among herons and egrets, with a wide variety of techniques: they may patiently stalk prey in shallow waters; stand on one leg and stir the mud with the other to scare up prey; or, better yet, stand on one leg and wave the other bright yellow foot over the water's surface to lure aquatic prey into range. The birds are mostly silent, but make various croaking and bubbling calls at their breeding colonies and produce a harsh alarm call when disturbed.

The little egret nests in colonies, often with other wading birds, usually on platforms of sticks in trees or shrubs, in reed beds, or in bamboo groves. In some locations, such as the Cape Verde Islands, the species nests on cliffs. In pairs they will defend a small breeding territory. Both parents will incubate their 3–5 eggs for 21–25 days until hatching. The eggs are oval in shape and have a pale, nonglossy, blue-green color. The young birds are covered in white down feathers, are cared for by both parents, and fledge after 40 to 45 days. During this stage, the young egret stalks its prey in shallow water, often running with raised wings or shuffling its feet. It may also stand still and wait to ambush prey. It eats fish, insects, amphibians, crustaceans, and reptiles.

The cover image is from *Cassell's Natural History*. The cover font is Adobe ITC Garamond. The text font is Linotype Birka; the heading font is Adobe Myriad Condensed; and the code font is LucasFont's TheSansMonoCondensed.

Web Programming

ActionScript 3.0 Cookbook

ActionScript 3.0 Design Patterns

ActionScript for Flash MX: The Definitive Guide,
 2nd Edition

Adobe AIR 1.5 Cookbook

Adobe AIR for JavaScript Developer's Pocket Guide

Advanced Rails

Ajax Design Patterns

Ajax Hacks

Ajax on Rails

Ajax: The Definitive Guide

Apache 2 Pocket Reference

Apache Cookbook, *2nd Edition*

Building Scalable Web Sites

Designing Web Navigation

Dojo: The Definitive Guide

Dynamic HTML: The Definitive Reference, *3rd Edition*

Essential ActionScript 3.0

Essential PHP Security

Ferret

Flash CS4: The Missing Manual

Flash Hacks

Head First HTML with CSS & XHTML

Head First JavaScript

Head First PHP & MySQL

High Performance Web Sites

HTTP: The Definitive Guide

JavaScript & DHTML Cookbook, *2nd Edition*

JavaScript Pocket Reference, *2nd Edition*

JavaScript: The Definitive Guide, *5th Edition*

JavaScript: The Good Parts

JavaScript: The Missing Manual

Learning ActionScript 3.0

Learning PHP and MySQL, *2nd Edition*

PHP Cookbook, *2nd Edition*

PHP Hacks

PHP in a Nutshell

PHP Pocket Reference, *2nd Edition*

Programming ColdFusion MX, *2nd Edition*

Programming Flex 2

Programming PHP, *2nd Edition*

Programming Amazon Web Services

Rails Cookbook

The ActionScript 3.0 Quick Reference Guide

Twitter API: Up and Running

Universal Design for Web Applications

Upgrading to PHP 5

Web Database Applications with PHP and MySQL,
 2nd Edition

Website Optimization

Web Site Cookbook

Webmaster in a Nutshell, *3rd Edition*